The Dickens Myth

The Dickens Myth

Its Genesis and Structure

GEOFFREY
THURLEY

University of
Queensland Press

© University of Queensland Press
St. Lucia, Queensland, 1976

Printed and bound by Silex Enterprise & Printing Co.
Hong Kong

Distributed in the United Kingdom, Europe, the Middle
East, Africa and the Caribbean by Prentice-Hall
International, International Book Distributors Ltd., 66
Wood Lane End, Hemel Hempstead, Herts., England.

National Library of Australia
Cataloguing-in-Publication Data
Thurley, Geoffrey John
    The Dickens myth.

    Index.
    Bibliography.
    ISBN 0 7022 1144 3.

    1. Dickens, Charles, 1812—1870 — Criticism
and interpretation. I. Title.

823.8

12 968

To my Father,
whose love of Dickens first inspired me

An imaginary universe, apparently completely removed from any specific experience — that of a fairy tale, for instance — may, in its structure, be strictly homologous with the experience of a particular social group or, at the very least, linked in a significant manner, with that experience.

Lucien Goldmann, "The Sociology of Literature: Status and Problem of Method", *International Sociological Journal* 19 (1967) no. 4.

Contents

Acknowledgments

My thanks go to Susan and Reginald Hicklin for a roof during the early stages; to the entire secretariat of the English Department of the University of Adelaide for endless typing patience; and to Robin Eaden for excellent work on the index.

1 Introduction: In Search of Charles Dickens

Dickens has been revived, but the ceremony has been somewhat morbid, and the kiss of life seemed often a kiss of death. Unable to shake off preconceptions about the nature of good fiction often irrelevant to Dickens, many of his critics have tried to show that he was really doing the same sort of thing as respectable realists like Henry James, and succeeded too often in making him appear laboured and simple-minded. However important it is to establish Dickens's greatness again, it will not be done by casting him as a cut-price Henry James, a plucky vulgarian strutting in the borrowed garments of his betters. Much of the new criticism in fact betrays a radical ambivalence beneath the whole re-valuation: under the feeling that there is something to respect runs the old dogged resistance to the great entertainer foot-noted in *The Great Tradition* — the family man and humorist George Eliot and other liberal intellectuals have always found it impossible to take seriously. The Gross-Pearson anthology of 1960, *Dickens and the Twentieth Century*,[1] for instance, is riddled with doubts: Gabriel Pearson thinks Dickens never quite "got there"[2] (there being realization of "mature human relationship" — that phrase gives the game away); John Jones thinks "Dickens has nothing of interest to say on the subject of death";[3] John Holloway thinks that "the hint of theatricality . . . is never quite absent in Dickens";[4] John Gross thinks that *A Tale of Two Cities* is "thin . . . a melodrama",[5] it fails to "present society in depth", and the theory of history which Dickens — poor idiot — was compelled to grasp was "primitive". And so on. It is not a question of the odd sentence, but of a general tone of deep inward resistance and reservation underlying the whole volume. For these critics, plainly, a "serious" novel is still the sort of thing Henry James produced, or George Eliot, or Tolstoy. Now Dickens is simply not to be understood in those terms. The revaluation of Dickens — assuming that to be the aim — is not to be achieved by blackballing his nomination for membership of the realist club, and finding an alternative basis for his inclusion — as a hired entertainer, perhaps, allowed to use the bar. It can only be achieved by disbanding the club altogether: the critical preconceptions behind most of the reformist criticism, deriving as they do from the doctrine and practice of novelists like James, simply do not satisfy the demands made on us by Dickens's quite different art. And when I say quite different I do not mean, as some readers might understand, somehow inferior, not to be taken seriously. I mean of another creative type. Dickens's art, with its rich verbal harmonies, its powers of natural symbolism, its organic structuring, its insistence on total relevance within its imaginative field, is in many respects qualitatively superior to the psychological realism of Tolstoy and George Eliot. Any mooted revision of critical judgment on Dickens must begin, therefore, not with an attempt to align his novels with others quite different in purpose and style, but with a radical re-thinking of the bases of his novels. Before we decide how good a writer is, that is, we must ask ourselves what kind of writer he is.

It seems necessary to establish the nature of his vision itself — the mode of perception by which his meanings were conveyed — before we attempt the larger task of describing the nature of his development. To do this we must rid ourselves of the heresies of the realist hegemony. Dickens not only saw and felt in a manner quite different from realists like Flaubert and James, he actually felt and saw different things. For the vision — the mode of perception — naturally determines the contents of perception. The question of

Dickens's creative type therefore assumes a certain importance. The right answer will help us correct many critical misconceptions by showing them to have been based upon a faulty notion of what Dickens was trying to achieve. Several recent critics have given accounts of the nature of Dickens's vision. Mr. Taylor Stoehr for instance has assumed the primacy of "the dreamer's stance", that Dickens's novels are constructed after the fashion of dreams.[6] This seemed to help explain some things in the novels which earlier critics had either set aside as blemishes, or used as evidence against the acceptance of Dickens as a serious artist. The wild coincidences, the elaborate matching of internal volition and external event, the patterns of revenge and retribution, all these ingredients (common to so much inferior fiction) were now seen to come right — our conception of the enterprise once enlightened — as elements in a dream-logic which enabled Dickens to say things which his "realist" contemporaries were incapable of saying. In my view this basic assumption has much to recommend it: there are certain resemblances between Dickens's novels and the dream-consciousness, and we should adjust our notion of what a good novel is not to excuse Dickens's improbabilities and coincidences, but to explain why they do not worry us. In reading Dickens as straight realism, earlier critics were simply not seeing him, and in suggesting a different model for his novels Mr. Stoehr made it possible for many critics and readers baffled and offended by things they would not accept in a novel by James or Flaubert to see them as logical and meaningful in the Dickens world. Yet there is something disturbing in Stoehr's consistent assumption that Dickens "dreamed" passively and unintelligently from first to last: Mr. Stoehr treats the Dickens of *Great Expectations* and *A Tale of Two Cities* in the same sort of way as I should be inclined to treat *Oliver Twist* and *The Old Curiosity Shop*.

Mr. Stoehr in fact creates his own Dickens monster — a basically inhuman creature possessed of a brilliant faculty for telling his dreams, or dreaming aloud. Mr. Stoehr admits, in the process, that Dickens said a lot about Victorian prejudice and preoccupations, but he shows no sign of believing that Dickens thought seriously about himself and his fellow Englishmen while he was awake; or that he matured enough to subject his own fantasies and nightmares to critical analysis. Now there are in fact several Dickens monsters in currency, and it is my great fear that I shall appear to have created another in the following pages. So this catalogue of other critics' mistakes (as I see them) is far from being gloating or complacent: the dangers are manifold, and Dickens lends himself to this kind of speculation just because he was, in certain ways, a monster-ous writer. He was a *monstre,* in the sense in which Lope de Vega and Mozart were — *un monstre sacré* — in his incomprehensible fluency and fecundity. But we must learn to look past the brilliance and see the human being behind it.

Another Dickens monster is the creation of Mr. Robert Garis.[7] Now the real actor-manager of *The Dickens Theatre* is Mr. Garis himself, and a very clever one he is. From Mr. Garis's creation, too, great art could not seriously be expected: this heartless gesticulating mime with no knowledge of himself or of others, devoid of the "inner life" and of the "sympathetic imagination" needed to divine its existence, this cheap entrepreneur with vulgar taste and indifferent judgement, this Crummles among novelists — how could he possibly have won the admiration of Tolstoy and Dostoievsky? Few critics seriously maintain now the old snobbish mandarin thesis that Dickens won an easy popularity by pandering to the low taste of an ignorant public. Many who once expressed these views have long since forgotten they ever held them. Yet here is Mr. Garis putting forward for our acceptance a cardboard entertainer who could no more create a serious work of art than fly in the air. Mr. Garis indeed doesn't think Dickens *is* a serious artist: serious art is what we have in *Madame Bovary, The Portrait of a Lady,* and *Middlemarch.* This is to my mind a sufficient reason for rejecting Mr. Garis's thesis, along with his theatre, out of hand without further consideration. His basic mistake is akin to Mr. Stoehr's: like Mr. Stoehr, he treats Dickens as capable of only one function. Mr. Stoehr's Dickens dreams, Mr. Garis's mimes. Now Dickens in fact did a good deal of both activities; but he was also a mature and profound human being, capable of growing and reflecting and changing and feeling. Mr. Stoehr treats Dickens as incapable of waking thought, Mr. Garis treats him as incapable of the slightest human reflection or maturation. The truth is so much more complex than their extrapolations: they conceive mechanical monsters incapable of transcending or understanding their own limitations, monsters who in fact end up by devouring their own original. Charles Dickens is nowhere to be seen in *The Dickens Theatre* or *The Dreamer's Stance.*

A later consideration of Dickens's creative processes and the nature of his "vision" has in fact been offered by Mr. Harvey Sucksmith in his book *The Narrative Art of Charles Dickens.*[8] If Taylor Stoehr sees Dickens as a professional dreamer, Mr. Sucksmith sees him quite simply as a Jungian introvert. Now methodologically this seems the most problematic of the three attempts to describe Dickens's imaginative equipment so far considered. What we should be concerned with is the work, and the understanding of the work is not to be furthered by speculations on the artist's personality. It will be objected that Mr. Sucksmith's act of pigeon-holing was done on the strength of the evidence offered in the work. Precisely; he is allotting the artist his psychological type-label on the evidence of the work, which he then proceeds to interpret in the light of the label he has allotted him. This is a tiresome circularity. But it is more than tiresome, it is misleading. What if we are wrong in our diagnoses? Jung himself, Mr. Sucksmith's mentor in this psychologizing, was all too aware of the dangers; at the end of a lengthy discussion of the introverted characteristics of Plato's writings, he says: "A really careful and minute examination of Plato's authentic writings considered as his 'documents humains' might possibly allow one to conclude to which type he personally belonged. For my own part, I would not venture to pronounce any positive judgement. If someone were to furnish evidence that Plato belonged to the extroverted type, it would not surprise me."[9] This is a cautionary spirit Mr. Sucksmith himself would have done well to mark before rushing in. There is much to admire in Mr. Sucksmith's book; it is much closer to the spirit of Dickens than either *The Dreamer's Stance* or *The Dickens Theatre*. His attempt, moreover, to establish the transcendentally religious nature of Dickens's *Weltanschauung*, though not original (Trilling had spoken of his imagination as being "under the domination of a great articulated idea, a moral idea which tends to find its full development in religious experience"),[10] is wholly welcome. He states his case like this:

> The rhetoric of sympathy enables Dickens to explore the common bond between all things and to involve the reader in this process of viewing the world as a vital experience to make him feel his identity with all creation ... Not only is animism characteristic of the introverted vision but so also is the awareness of a force which permeates all things, a primitive identity.[11]

The passage upon which Mr. Sucksmith bases his postulation of Dickens's introversion is as follows:

> They ... are often preoccupied with images from the collective unconscious. Even precise observation of reality does not stop the subjective factor from working — such people cannot see buses or trams without thinking of fiery dragons, trees have faces, and inanimate objects spring to life; they think they see people who are not really there, and have curious experiences with "ghosts" ... If ... he remains faithful to his irrationality ... the objective world will appear a mere make-belief and a comedy.[12]

(He is quoting from Mrs. Fordham incidentally; Jung does not read quite like this.) Now this might well seem to end the matter: such a capacity for animistic metaphor and the more or less habitual interpretation of the inanimate world — houses have faces, a paddle-steamer moves like a prehistoric monster — is one of the most striking and important aspects of Dickens's style. It is what, presumably, in part prompted the post-Jamesian reaction against Dickens: it was all "larger-than-life", exaggerated, not done with the correct Flaubertian restraint and impersonality. It is also the sort of consideration which must have prompted Mr. Stoehr and Mr. Garis to make their own particular adjustments to the prevalent views of Dickens. (Mr. Garis consistently objects to the "animism" of Dickens's style, or at least to the vocal "presence" of the author that necessarily accompanies it.)[13]

But in fact the faculty of vision Jung is describing at the point of *Psychological Types* upon which the Fordham quotation is based is not wholly characteristic of "the introverted type", and to cite it in isolation, as Mr. Sucksmith does, certainly gives a false impression of the whole notion of introversion, especially as it might relate to Dickens. The most important distinguishing feature of introversion in general — according to Jung — is to value the subject above the object, or the subjective over the objective, to lay more emphasis upon the inner vision than on the outer fact. The introverted consciousness, as it were, continually seeks an image which "has no existence in reality", and "from objects that never fit in with its aim it seems to glide unheedingly away . . . " "It strives after an inner intensity, to which at the most, objects contribute only as accessory stimulus".[14]

Now there is no doubt in my mind that the general type of consciousness Jung is describing here is emphatically not that of Charles Dickens. Dickens was driven primarily by an intense interest in the external world: his metaphoric and analogical procedures are designed to increase our perception of the actual, to render more faithfully the appearance of the world, and thereby to make clear its "inner" reality. How often in reading Dickens do we feel, yes, that's exactly what it looks like, how it smells? Dickens, in short, is dominated by the extrovert's object-consciousness, not by the introvert's subjectivity.

It is the great strength of what we can, I think, justifiably call the Cambridge school that it has held fast to a conception of a human Dickens. One understands why the Leavises, irritated by the "transatlantic thesis-writers",[15] refuse to countenance any "Dickens problem", and simply concentrate their attention on elucidating and indicating the strengths as they appear. In most cases one must surely applaud the intention and the work done: Mrs. Leavis's "Tolstoyan" *David Copperfield* is much the sanest and wisest critique of the novel that has appeared, and I should myself put just such a sanity about *David Copperfield* high on the list of critical requirements. The same goes of course for the essays on *Hard Times* and *Dombey and Son* with which F. R. Leavis long ago set about redirecting the current of Dickens criticism. The Leavises have (or should have) made it impossible to wonder aloud any longer whether Dickens was *really* a great novelist. They suggest that there is no need for any case to be made out, that the best of his writing is self-evidently great by any standards. Yet they still leave a great deal to be done. It is not so much F. R. Leavis's over-emphasis upon Toodle that causes concern, as the postulation of *Dombey and Son* as "the first major novel", and the consequent ignoring of so much that seems crucially important in Dickens. The Leavises seem still to identify the earlier Dickens with Tiny Tim and Little Nell, and to fear that to countenance novels like *The Old Curiosity Shop* and *Martin Chuzzlewit* at all will be to open the flood-gates of Chestertonian enthusiasm. In point of fact, it seems to me essential to redeem the early writing, not merely because so much of it is very good indeed – some of Dickens's finest work appears there – but because we still need an account of Dickens's *oeuvre* as a whole, an account which will show the profound connexions between the very first novels and the last, and also incidentally suggest the significance of the two historical novels.

Now the real core to the old "realist" resistance to Dickens had a great deal to do with a certain conception, or related group of conceptions, of what "normal" behaviour was and, therefore, of how "real" characters were to be created in novels. Even today we tend to take for granted that we know what is real and normal in art: the novelist is probably a liberal-minded bourgeois like ourselves, he only knows other liberal-minded bourgeois, and does not care to speculate on the extremes of social or psychological behaviour. So we get the tidy, rather grey world of the naturalist and post-naturalist novel, in which evil plays no part; action has been replaced by the sequential following-out of a limited range of human predicaments; and symbolism, if it exists at all, is confined to certain simple association-patterns exploited for the purposes of mild emotional scoring. Now the case that (still) needs to be argued is that in all these respects — in respect of the understanding of evil, the functional use of action, and the genuinely poetic (as opposed to the merely prettifying) use of symbolism — Dickens was incomparably superior to the novelists who have so often been used to demonstrate by contrast the nature of his weaknesses. And this includes not merely modest writers like E. M. Forster, but great masters like Tolstoy. In no matter has this systematic misapplication of criteria been more unjust to Dickens than in that of characterization. First revered as the creator of Great Characters (Pecksniff, Gamp, Micawber), Dickens was then reviled as a lightning sketcher of caricatures. Recent criticism, I began by noting, has attempted to make up for this deficiency by trying to show that Dickens was much closer than earlier critics had supposed to realists like Tolstoy and James. Rather than try to force Dickens's characterization into the moulds of realism in this way, we should ask ourselves why it is, for instance, that Dickens is such a preternaturally exact observer of the human organism, and Tolstoy so vague and conventional about Anna Karenin's "sparkling eyes".[16] It is no use pretending that Tolstoy's impoverished perceptual equipment is part of some sort of super-aesthetic. He simply did not "see" people as Dickens did, and we have here an important difference in creative type. We could add to a list of Tolstoy's "deficiencies" the facts that he had no sense of evil, little sense of humour, and a fairly rudimentary vision of society. This would be an unjust distribution of emphases, but no more so than Dickens has been subjected to for the past fifty years. The question of rankings does not matter; what does matter is the accuracy of our image of Dickens, and the relevancy of our judgmental criteria to his complex works. In point of fact, Dickens's extraordinary knack of picking on the right behavioural detail to "get" a character amounts to very much more than a developed sense of caricature. For Dickens knew that what we see is in important respects identical with what a thing *is*: it would be a mistake to try and reduce his characterization to behaviourism, in which there is an essentially inhuman reduction of humanity and a denial of consciousness. But behaviourism accepts what Dickens knew: the fallaciousness of the Ghost in the Machine myth. Or, to borrow a notion from the Gestalt school, Dickens understood that the gestures people make, the grimaces they practise, the behaviour routines in which they are trapped, are *isomorphic* with "themselves":[17] more, we are the sum of what we do, and there is no gap between our states of mind and our bodily behaviour. This is not to suggest that what George Eliot does when she follows out a pattern of motivation in a man like Edward Casaubon is somehow invalid. But critics had mistaken the *image* of consciousness George Eliot offers in those great analyses for the portrayal of the actual substance of consciousness itself. In point of fact, the "substance" of consciousness is, as James Joyce shows in *Ulysses,* an intermittent, patchwork, shoddy sort of stuff, a raggedly hummed and forgotten tune, something very much closer, in fact, to what Dickens had suggested with such astounding accuracy in his observations of the way people moved, spoke, and acted. There is in fact much in common between Dickens and Joyce: they were both probably what Jung would have called extroverted, though of different functional type — Joyce thinking, Dickens intuitive. Robert Garis shows a general tendency to lump together novelists of many different orders when he aligns Joyce with George Eliot (as serious) as opposed to the non-serious Dickens: he associates George Eliot's great description of the "equivalent centre of self" in *Middlemarch* with "what Joyce achieves in his characterization of Leopold Bloom".[18] But Bloom is in fact pure Dickens: he has no "centre of self"; he *is* his talk, his idioms, his *clichés,* his obsessions, exactly as Mr. Jingle is his. Bloom's so-called stream of consciousness is nothing but banality, nothing but words. And this is Joyce's intention, for Bloom is, like Jingle and Mrs. Gamp, a great comic character.

It is a grave error in fact, to suppose that Dickens's method of characterization — with its swift brilliance of effect and its endlessly inventive mastery of mannerism and gesture — is concerned with appearances or superficies: on the contrary, it is the reverse of impressionistic. It is not the appearance of people Dickens is really interested in, nor yet what the appearance tells us of what is going on inside; these are related fallacies. What we have in Dickens's unforgettable portrayals is not what people *look* like, but what they *are* like: he grasps essences, identities, configurations of qualities that utter the personality and constitute it. Of all nineteenth century novelists, Dickens shows the greatest insight into what psychologists call psychogenic illness — psychosomatic disorders, such as Mrs. Clennam's guilt-promoted paralysis, and Dr. Manette's pathetic dependence on the boot-making which held his personality together through the years in the Bastille.

The neurologist Russell Brain has paid a professional scientist's homage to Dickens's extraordinary understanding of amnesia, for instance, or febrile states. To praise Dickens for such things is not merely to point to his extraordinary anticipations of medical science and psychiatry: it is to indicate the nature of his intuitive powers, powers that express themselves not only in his characterization, but in the animistic textures that have drawn so much attention from his recent critics.

Dorothy Van Ghent is surely close to the truth about the relations between the characterization and the metaphoric vitality of the writing when she observes that "the principle of reciprocal change between the human and the non-human bears on the characteristic lack of complex 'inner life' on the part of Dickens' people — their lack of a personally complex psychology. It is inconceivable that the fungoid Miss Havisham should have a complex inner life, in the moral sense. But in the *art* of Dickens . . . there is a great deal of 'inner life', transposed to other forms than that of human character . . . Without benefit of Freud or Jung, Dickens saw the human soul reduced literally to the images occupying its 'inner life' ".[19] At first sight, Freud and Jung — plumbers of the "deep mind" — would seem extraneous to this context; but Mrs. Van Ghent is right to invoke them. For psychoanalysis understands consciousness generally in terms of symbols and imagery, just as it interprets physical behaviour often in psychosomatic terms. When we consider that Dickens's novels characteristically form patterns of imagery and gesture in which nothing is irrelevant, we begin to understand the force of Mrs. Van Ghent's remark that in Dickens's art there is a great deal of "inner life", though we may find good reason to question the lack of a "personally complex psychology". We must, I think, acknowledge the existence of a dichotomy among creative artists similar to, though not identical with, the classic dichotomies of Schiller, Nietzsche, Worringer and others. The terms to hand are expressionist and impressionist, and we must align Dickens with the art of the expressionist type: a class that includes Dostoievsky but not Tolstoy, Balzac but not Flaubert, Emily Brontë but not Jane Austen, D. H. Lawrence but not James Joyce, Faulkner but not Hemingway, El Greco but not Velasquez, Turner but not Constable; and so on. Art of this type is not of a uniform or consistent texture; it is not predominantly neurotic or hysterical, but it does, let us admit it, have a characteristic tendency to heighten in the direction of hysteria: if intensity is its defining strength, hysteria is its defining weakness. The art of expressionism is typically affective rather than dispassionate, inflected rather than impersonalist, continuously under duress, and incapable of detaching itself from experience which is nevertheless experienced intensely as *outside* itself. Once we grant the primacy of such creative laws in the art of Dickens, the freakishness of much of the earlier writing ceases to appear as merely grotesque distortion.

The vision which has shown the tendency to animate objects so that nothing is without its meaningfulness, effects also the inward structure and organization of the books. Characteristically, Dickens's novels are organized about the consciousness of a central character. Thus, the world he creates is one in which, after the expressionist model, every particle of energy diffuses from the node which is the consciousness of the whole work. Now, the heroes and heroines of Dickens's novels are supposed to be uninteresting —

especially if we consider them in separation from the novel, or in comparison with the great "Dickens characters" around them. We could express this simply by saying that Dickens's heroes arc not Dickensian, and this would have its point. But we must remember in fact that this curious non-egocentric mode (what we might have predicted from a Jungian view of Dickens's character) is deceptive: there is all the difference in the world between the experience of reading one of Dickens's novels whole and attending an Emlyn Williams performance at which only the rogues and comic monsters are represented. There is an extraordinary disparity between the absorption with which we follow the adventures of Dickens's heroes and heroines and the relative uninterestingness of their actual personalities. I say relative, because they are really no less interesting than we are ourselves, as can be proved by contrast with Dickens's own failures: to work, the Dickens novel must compel our belief and interest in the life of the central character. Critics have been misled because the heroes themselves — Oliver Twist, Little Nell, David Copperfield, Pip, Florence Dombey — pale beside the magnificent monsters around them. But Dickens's heroes and heroines are only the nodes of the novels in which they appear. The Dickens novel is an imaginative project in which Dickens must persuade us, his readers, to undergo the vicissitudes, tensions, and resolutions which it is the purpose of the whole novel to create. Characteristically, the filings in the magnetic field of the book are arranged about the consciousness of the central character, the hero or heroine whose fortunes the fable follows. If I may be allowed a bad pun, these heroes and heroines are "eyes", in that we must be able to experience what they see free of the distortion of a quirky vision; but they are also "I's", in that we must be able to live with and through them.

To explain the Dickens hero, then, is not to excuse him: he need not be other than he is. More, he should not be, and E. M. Forster's often quoted observations about the flatness of Dickens's characters in *Aspects of the Novel* show a complete misunderstanding not only of Dickens, but of the art of the characterization in general. Forster makes an exception for David Copperfield and Pip, who "attempt roundness but so diffidently that they seem more like bubbles than solids".[20] This is a complete misapprehension. In the first place, the art of characterization is being conceived in terms more appropriate to cookery: "for a pleasantly rounded character, take one positive and two negative characteristics, mix well, and simmer for three hundred pages" — something of this kind. Then, Forster mistakes the whole purpose of the hero in Dickens, who is in reality a character whom we experience *only as we experience ourselves,* not so much by recollecting our own qualities as by interaction with the forces and things outside us. The enveloping frame of our own consciousness has the form of a narrative, a fiction, in which we ourselves are curiously inactive participants. The force and power of Dickens's novels (which so many critics of the earlier twentieth century have striven against) testify to the skill with which he persuades us to identify with his central eye/I, and experience his world. The point of the exercise is less to communicate certain societal and psychological facts, than to compel us to experience certain mental states and patterns of experience. This could perhaps be rationalized by saying that in Dickens the self is experienced not as an objective fact, but as a subjectivity, and the key to the process which makes this experiencing possible is identification.

Identification is a word now freely used in relation to books and films. It is in fact the key concept in the development of the novel as a form, and no one understood its nature better than Freud: "It has struck me", Freud wrote in one of his most important papers, "that in many of what are known as 'psychological novels' only one person — once again his hero — is described from within. The author sits inside his mind, as it were, and looks at the other characters from outside."[21] An apparently simple observation, yet it takes us far towards a complete understanding of the novel as a genre. It enables us to discriminate for instance between characters like Isabel Archer, David Copperfield, and

Gwendolen Harleth, and the people around them: not all characters are treated in the same way, in other words, though much criticism of the novel seems to assume that they are. More than this, it opens up a new avenue of analysis. For if the novelist is, as Freud suggested, sitting inside the head of one character and observing what goes on around him, it follows that the reader will do the same. The reader will also take up the novelist's position: and for this process we use the word identification. What distinguishes the nineteenth century novel from the eighteenth century novel is precisely that in the novels of Fielding and Smollett no such identification takes place: we watch Tom Jones and Roderick Random as Fielding and Smollet watch them — from above, and from the outside. The novel grew and matured by acquiring self-consciousness, and the index of this growth is the new structural relation between reader, writer, and central character. It would not be accurate to say that the hero *is* the writer, nor quite that he is a projection of him. Such external relations — relations between what happens inside the covers of the book and the biographical facts of his life — are rarely helpful. We can confine ourselves to internal relations quite easily. A novel is never an "autobiography" no matter how "autobiographical" the scholar's researches show it to have been. Let us say simply that the hero of a novel plays a uniquely privileged role and that there is a special relationship between him, his creator, and his reader — a relationship which is the key to the novel's peculiar function, and which is associated with the process of identification. Certainly, the whole *oeuvre* of George Eliot or Jane Austen or Dickens can only be made full sense of when we pay due attention to the nature of the evolution that takes place in the hero/heroine structure. In the case of Dickens this is of crucial significance. But before we go on to describe the nature of this evolution, there is another factor to be taken into account, and once again it is to Freud we must turn for guidance.

Freud was quite matter-of-fact about the nature of fiction: the modern novel he regarded as a permitted day-dream, a half-way house between fantasy and reality. He was prepared to admit that only "the less pretentious authors of novels, romances and short stories, who nevertheless have the widest and most eager circle of readers of both sexes,"[22] could with any confidence be aligned with the day-dreaming of the poor errand-boy or the frustrated spinster. But he hinted that in fact all fiction, no matter how sophisticated, "could be linked with naive day-dreaming through an uninterrupted series of transitional cases."[23] Now Freud was no aesthetician and had no real understanding of what might distinguish a "serious" novel from a pulp novelette. He went so far as to confess that the "art" made no sense to him except as a bribe, an "incentive bonus" to make us accept the more readily the grossly indulgent fantasies of "His Majesty the Ego".[24] But just this myopia of Freud's, his basically philistine indifference to Culture, made it possible for him to stare through reputation and the preconceptions of the art-establishment and see what it was that Shakespeare might have in common with the pantomime, and to posit a chain connecting pulp-fiction with high art. And this perception I think is a valid one: fiction is based initially upon wish-fulfilment.

Most eminent novelists are indeed related to those popular romancers Freud saw as the prototypes of the fictional artist. Dickens, in particular, has always been too close to the popular imagination for the comfort of many mandarins, who have tended to regard him as the hired entertainer of a culturally illiterate mass-readership. Just how close Dickens's early novels are to popular wish-fulfilment fantasy can be shown by turning again to Freud. Freud gives us the example of a "poor orphan-boy" who has been given "the address of some employer where he may perhaps find a job."[25] The boy, Freud suggests, imagines that "he is given a job, finds favour with his new employer, makes himself indispensable in the business, is taken into his employer's family, marries the charming young daughter of the house, and then himself becomes a director of the business, first as his employer's partner, and then as his successor."[26]

Freud is referring to popular fiction and films, of course, and it is just this conscious intention of describing the most naive form of popular wish-fulfilment, that makes it so extraordinarily impressive that he has given us the synopsis of almost all Dickens's early fiction. In essence (and often in fact) what Freud's orphan errand-boy dreams is what happens to Dickens's early heroes — Kit Nubbles, Oliver Twist, Abel Garland, Nicholas Nickleby, and Martin Chuzzlewit, even Walter Gay. Looked at from the Freudian angle, books like *Oliver Twist* and *The Old Curiosity Shop* are pure wish-fulfilment fantasy. It is probably awareness of this fact that has stood in the way of a mature recognition of these books: how can one take seriously this blatant exercise in economic wish-fulfilment, which does not apparently even try to disguise its motivation from the reader, so that the penniless orphan is miraculously rescued by magically empowered old gentlemen, and evil gets its deserts? Yet the effort to understand these books must be made unless we are prepared to sacrifice any organic account of the whole Dickens canon. The later books themselves can really only be partially understood in terms of their "criticisms" of Victorian commercialism — unless their provenance out of the earlier is spelled out. And the central position Dickens holds in the history of the novel as a whole stems largely from experience and attitudes crystallized in a recurrent plot-structure initially expressed in the first books and then criticized.

For at this stage I have to remark on an important deficiency in Freud's theory of fiction. That is, Freud's patent inability to allow for mature criticism and the growth of self-awareness in the artist. Freud treats the novelist as a patient: it never occurs to him that a writer might actually become aware of the drives and fantasies that inform his own earlier writing, and, indeed, make them the subject of his art. This of course is what we see at work in the development of the Jane Austen heroine from Elizabeth Bennett to Emma Woodhouse, and the George Eliot heroine from Maggie Tulliver to Gwendolen Harleth. In no novelist is the process so complete as in Dickens: the evolution from Oliver Twist to Edwin Drood is unbroken.

We shall be in need of a technical term to facilitate reference to this evolutionary process, and I propose to use the word myth to designate the narrative pattern which underlies Dickens's work. A myth, says Denis de Rougemont, is "a bold and simple design, a kind of archetype of our most complex feelings of unrest".[27] The purpose of Dickens's development is, we can say, to bring this unrest, this hidden content, to light. More specifically, a myth also refers to the conception a man has of himself: Dickens is at the centre of all his own work. We can describe his entire *oeuvre* in terms of a primal wish-fulfilment fantasy, at first simply enacted with extraordinary power and richness, then raised to awareness, and finally subjected to criticism. The elements of this myth can be summarized as follows. The child abandoned by feckless or unfortunate parents climbs out of the abyss of poverty and darkness towards security, peace, and light. In the early books the hero is helped by the patronage of benevolent retired uncles, or by the revelation of concealed kinship with them; he is hindered by fearsome ogres, powerfully attractive demons from whose clutches he cannot escape until they are ritualistically slain. This is the most naive stage of the myth. The development of Dickens's art in part takes the form of a critique of the evil that looms so large in these early books. The ogres and demons wither into neutrality (the "devourers" of *Bleak House* and *Little Dorrit* have lost nearly all the malignancy of Quilp, Fagin, and Squeers). When malignancy does appear in the later books, in Rigaud of *Little Dorrit* for instance, it is only to prove that the dynamic relations between good and evil have altered beyond recognition: evil no longer hypnotizes good; is no longer, in the same way, held responsible. The responsibility of course has shifted onto the hero's shoulders. In Dickens's development the two processes continue step by step. As one changes, the other changes in the same degree: as Oliver Twist becomes David Copperfield and David Copperfield becomes Pip, so Fagin becomes Uriah Heep, and Uriah Heep becomes — no one in particular. It is important to get this straight: there is an important structural relation between *Oliver Twist* and *Great Expectations*: Pip is to Compeyson as Oliver is to Monks. But there is no Fagin in the later book, and in *Oliver Twist,* Fagin is evil. Thus what we might, with pardonable over-simplification, call Dickens's progress towards self-knowledge, proceeds hand in hand with the diminution of the ogres, the neutralization, in a sense, of evil itself. This does not indicate a tendency to "explain" evil in the later books, much less to deny its existence. On the contrary, an irritated hatred informs his treatment of evil in books like *Little Dorrit* and *Great Expectations.* But Dickens shows an increasing awareness both of his own complicity in the formation of the early devils, and of his own sheer ambivalence towards them: Fagin and Quilp have a glamour which aspires to the charismatic, and this is entirely absent from the devouring predators of the later novels.

In these later novels, the deliverance of the hero from darkness and obscurity becomes highly ambiguous: it is effected by means of a legacy which materializes, as it were, out of the wish-fulfilment fantasies of the hero. Now the legacy is practically a *leit-motif* of nineteenth century fiction. It figures in works which would appear on the surface quite detached from the economic struggle for survival: James's *Portrait of a Lady* turns upon the money left to Isabel Archer, and the efforts of Gilbert Osmond to get his hands on it. It provides Thackeray with his fundamental plots: *Vanity Fair,* for instance, rests upon two bequests — the money Rawdon and Becky hope Rawdon's aunt will make over to them, and the fortune George and Amelia hope George's father will leave to them. In both novels, the actual plot-dynamism derives from the legacy and its significance in people's lives. Isabel, who is supposed to be launched on the Touchett bequest, is in fact imprisoned by it; the *Vanity Fair* characters spend their lives simply hanging around. Waiting, we might say, is Thackeray's fictive rhythm. Again and again, the notion of the legacy or the bequest appears in nineteenth century fiction. It is obsessively present in Balzac, of course.

But even in an intellectual masterpiece like *Middlemarch* it crops up: in the codicil of his will, Casaubon tries to reach Dorothea in death as he never could in life.

Dickens investigated the moral and psychological — and through symbolism, the philosophical — implications of the legacy as none of his contemporaries did, and his artistic development cannot be understood without an appreciation of its significance. In the first novels it is taken for granted: the hero/heroine confidently awaits the materialization of the worldly goods, the golden fruit that underlies the whole folk-tale tradition with which the Dickens novels have so much in common. Gradually, this assumption is raised to the surface. In *David Copperfield* (mid-way in Dickens's career) it is treated for the first time as a property of the conscious universe, and counteracted by the work-ethic: in the middle Dickens, work is authenticity, and it is contrasted with the bad faith of Mr. Micawber's "waiting for something to turn up". Mr. Gabriel Pearson has suggested an earlier appearance of the satire on the "expectations": Grandfather Trent's "illegitimate dreams of wealth", he says, sound "however mutedly, the first criticism of the Great Expectations theme so complacently approved in *Oliver Twist.*"[28] In *David Copperfield,* the criticism is not at all muted, and in the later novels the theme — the expectations, the legacy, the windfall, the golden fruit — provides Dickens with all his major narrative and symbolic structures. *Bleak House, Little Dorrit, Great Expectations,* and *Our Mutual Friend* examine different aspects of the idea. *Great Expectations* clearly has a special place in Dickens's work in the light of these considerations: it represents the moment of full conscious emergence, but it also combines theme and action in a very special way. If we can argue that *Oedipus Rex* has as its actual plot the implicit substance of all tragedy (the sex-guilt, the mother-love, the father-enmity, the generation-conflict), so we can argue that *Great Expectations* has as its plot the substance of all novels.

All novels? *Anna Karenina? Madame Bovary? Crime and Punishment?* In what sense is *Great Expectations* the para-

digm novel? In the sense that it takes for its narrative action
the social and psychological conflict which generated the
novel as a genre. The novel is the great art-form of bourgeois
man, of the capitalist world. It is historically delimited,
beginning around the middle of the first half of the eighteenth century in England and expiring — everywhere — in
the first quarter of the twentieth century.[29] The necessary
prerequisites for the existence of the novel are social
mobility, technological and economic expansionism, and
political libertarianism. The modern novel, like the industrial
revolution and modern political democracy, was initially an
English development, as we can see by turning to the fiction
of other cultures. It is doubtful if proper comparisons can be
made between the novels produced in advanced capitalist
democracies and those produced in a semi-feudal state like
nineteenth century Russia. What we can do is point to the
significant differences between the narrative nuclei of
Russian and English novels, and observe that the world of the
Russian novel is an arrested world, in which social apathy and
political repressiveness produce a stasis. On one level, the
characters of Tolstoy and Turgenev talk about social problems; on another, they act, and what they act is the romance
drama of the Tristan myth. Turgenev's novels consist of con-
frontations between enlightened landowners who fear change
and nihilists who want to tear everything down; on top of
this is grafted the "love story" — Bersenev and Elena,
Barazov and Anna. (The structures of *Anna Karenina* and *War
and Peace* provide confirmation.) This is because the romance
was the great literary form of feudal society. In the English
novel, the romance has much less currency. In hardly any of
the great English novels does the romance provide the core of
the narrative. What takes its place is the mechanism of the
social climb: the novel reflects the need of man in a new
situation for some form of certitude and self-definition. And
if the mechanism of the novel is the social climb, its spiritual
condition is alienation: the novel becomes the mode of exploration for man in a new and difficult situation. Man is
now uncertain of his basis and his identity, and bereft of the

sense of perpetuity and solidity imparted by the traditional social and spiritual establishment. It did not happen overnight: it had begun several centuries back, in the age of Shakespeare. But the conditions became especially accentuated in the eighteenth century, and the novel arose in answer to the need.

Dickensian man is undermined by certain fears. One of the most disagreeable symptoms of bourgeois man's disorder is snobbishness. *Great Expectations* is the greatest study of snobbishness, because it probes the deeper purposes served by the strategy of snobbishness. But snobbishness is pervasively present in all Dickens's work. In Dickens to be a snob is not, as it largely is in Thackeray, for instance, to be a cad, guilty of certain offences against good form. It is to be guilty of far worse offences against oneself. Man, as Marx observed, is more fundamental than the citizen. More fundamental, too, than the gentleman. In Thackeray the bourgeois snob is the man who does not play the game according to the rules, who looks down on his inferiors; he is ridiculous because he thinks that this is how the aristocrat behaves. The rules of the game, we note from *The Book of Snobs,* remain inflexible about who is considered a gentleman; only, the gentleman is "nice" to and about his inferiors, treating them as equals while knowing they are not. Dickens wasn't a gentleman at all. His social inferiority in fact was of the most vulnerable kind, and made him a snob as Thackeray never was. But, we might almost argue, it was necessary that Dickens should be a snob: it was precisely this representativeness of position that afforded Dickens his great insight into the nature of snobbishness: he knew that it was not merely not "nice", or "bad form" (he didn't know what good form was), but that it *alienated the snob from himself.* It was Dickens — supremely in *Great Expectations,* but in all the novels, in fact — who understood that, far from being a faintly ridiculous and ephemeral property of Manners, snobbishness was a paradigm of the social consciousness of bourgeois man: that snobbishness is simply the most characteristic disease in modern society.

It is undoubtedly the failure to appreciate the nature of this fact that vitiates so much modern American criticism of Dickens. Americans have a tendency to identify class with money, and such an identification is fatal to an understanding of Dickens, or indeed of the English novel in general. A failure to understand the English novel's dependence on class-feeling rather than on money-values vitiates Mr. Stoehr's whole thesis.[30] In Mr. Garis's case the fallacy is overlaid by the more obvious fallacies of his basic view of Dickens in terms of mechanicalization, system, and theatricality, fallacies in which he has been tutored, it seems to me, by Mrs. Van Ghent. There is no better example in *The Dickens Theatre* than the author's attitude towards the Meagles family. "But why," Mr. Garis asks, "is no point made of the meaning of Pet's choice of Gowan over Clennam?"[31] Gowan is good-looking, charming, "artistic", presentable, and blue-blooded; Clennam dull, middle-aged, commercial, grey, and bourgeois: Pet makes her choice and gets what she deserves. What on earth is Dickens supposed to add? It is the sort of choice Gweldolen Harleth made in *Daniel Deronda*, and Dickens's whole handling of the matter is on the whole more sensitive and sympathetic (compare, for instance, Grandcourt's cold-blooded sadism — all too much the bourgeois view of the aristocrat — with Gowan's intermittent but genuine affection for Pet). This whole strand of the novel turns upon class-feeling, and the critic who does not see this can hardly claim to have got to grips with the book in general. Predictably, Mr. Garis is as insensitive in his treatment of Meagles himself; Meagles is, we are informed, "someone about whose good heart we are to approve quite unequivocally."[32] Unequivocally? There is nothing unequivocal about Mr. Meagles — that good-hearted snob, who patronizes his intellectual superiors in true English fashion, despises France and all it stands for, and is so abject in his abasement towards his "betters" that he can derive genuine consolation at the presence of real aristocrats at his only daughter's wedding. It would be much easier to put such a man down just as a snob, but Dickens doesn't, and this is really the point. It is Mr. Garis who wants unequivocal pointers, who wants to be told how to think, and so feels more comfortable in the world of George Eliot, in which the pattern may be complicated but is usually unambiguous. Mr. Garis is so insistent upon Dickens's insistence that he cannot see or understand Dickens's genius for creating characters whose behaviour is complex and self-contradictory, both approved and wrong-headed, lovable yet self-deluding, generous and snobbish, all at once.

At any rate, there is no doubting Mr. Garis's general insensitivity not just to the nuances but to the very modality of the class-feeling in Dickens. The same charge must be levelled at American criticism of Dickens in general. American critics have been encouraged in these essentially facile views of the matter by English critics like Humphry House, to whom snobbishness is simply beastly, and so to be put out of mind. No one was more aware of the peculiar nastiness of snobbishness than Dickens; but taking a superior view of the phenomenon will not help us understand the centrality of snobbishness and class-consciousness in our kind of society, nor the subtlety and finality of Dickens's treatment of it. Humphry House's proper but limiting distaste for snobbishness — the ultimate crime in the gentleman's calendar — is something the American critic, with his cruder sense of caste, can understand easily enough, especially as it can so easily be equated with a more obviously nasty money-consciousness. We know from the example of Scott Fitzgerald that there is a deep malaise about money and caste in American society, exacerbated by the deeply embedded schism between Wasp and immigrant. Americans too have much to learn from Dickens hereabouts, and much to benefit from a more analytic view of class-consciousness and snobbishness.

No critic in my opinion has ever got closer to the true nature of the class-problem in Dickens than G. K. Chesterton. *Appreciation and Criticism of Charles Dickens' Works*[33] seems now not only one of the finest books ever written about Dickens (in the poise of so many of its judgments, in its wit, in the intellectual precision required to crystallize the wit), but one of the few which have concerned themselves to any effect with the social aspect of Dickens, not from the point of view of reform and the local problems, but in its deepest meaning. Ironically — in view of the kind of reception likely to be accorded this suggestion in Cambridge — only the Leavises' book seems to display a comparable grasp of the issue. F. R. Leavis's *Hard Times* thesis puts its emphasis on two major foci — Life, and the fundamental mechanics of society upon which the Life so importantly depends. Chesterton's *Appreciation and Criticism* is distinguished not only by its intelligent reverence for the *life* of Dickens (no critic in my view has ever got closer to describing the indescribable vitality of Dickens's writing), but also by its acute sense of the class-realities underlying this life. This emerges nowhere better than in his account of Trabb's boy in *Great Expectations:* "This quality is the quality which has always given its continuous power and poetry to the common people everywhere. It is life; it is the joy of life felt by those having nothing else but life. It is the thing that all aristocrats have always hated and dreaded in the people. And it is the thing which poor Pip really hates and dreads in Trabb's boy."[34] Chesterton was of course close enough to Dickens's England to be aware of its class-relations as we can hardly be today. We are inclined to remember Chesterton for saying that all Dickens' books are Christmas books,[35] and to dismiss him therefore as a sentimental enthusiast rather than an acute critic, forgetting that he also said that all Dickens's novels could be called *Great Expectations,*[36] putting his finger on the real pulse of Dickens's art — its hypersensitive consciousness of modern man's peculiar uncertainties, his fears, his debilitating hopes, and his absence of identity.

Dickens knew that the desire for wealth, for position, for affluence, is strictly neurotic: it represents a need to make oneself distinct, to prevent oneself being absorbed by the mass, by darkness. The ambition to be rich, secure, is a product of fear. This explains the great universality of Dickens's work. For in whom does not exist the fear of the disintegration of that social order in which he lives? We are all bourgeois under the skin. This fear controls — in England especially — even our sense of accent. No accent is really more agreeable than another, though we often seek quasi-phonetic reasons for justifying our preference for the accents of the well-to-do. It is something like a fear of anarchy that bids us prefer the speech of the educated. This fear also explains that climbing of the social ladder which provides the dynamism of Dickens's novels. Nor is it simply money that explains the need to rise. People sometimes make financial sacrifices to guarantee themselves a certain degree of gentility. Thus, the reasons for the social climb and the neurosis of the social climb are no longer purely economic. The higher up the ladder we go, the farther the abyss recedes beneath us, and the greater grow the fear of falling and the pull of the depths. Civilized man has a mania for keeping up standards that refers to a need to resist sliding back into the abyss. In a highly elaborate, richly encrusted society like England's, this relates to financial or property values often only in an indirect way.

Dickens's cycle of novels is the great exposure of the nature of these tensions and internal contradictions of ours. Dickens's radical admirers felt let down by such presentations of the Capitalist as Bounderby.[37] Dickens did not know at close range the workings of industrialism: his know-how is not of the modern blockbuster novelist's order, a familiarity with procedures and facts. He possessed a far more central knowledge of the pressures and strains placed upon people by the requirements of history (economic and material) in his time.

Dickens was in fact all too well-qualified to analyze the bad faith of which snobbishness is merely a symptomatic strategy. He understood how snobbishness derived from anxiety, and, in consequence, how both the enlightened philanthropic concern and the snobbishness so characteristic of the Victorians reflected the fact that the bourgeoisie had become estranged from its lower self. Dickens's greatness is vitally connected with his own participation in the dynamic growth of Victorian capitalism: he could present it with complete authority because he was part of it, a living proof of its greatness and its squalor. The conclusion that he reached was that this colossal empire of brick and soot had been acquired at a crippling cost. This expressed itself in two ways. More obviously in the vast social injustice: the physical ugliness, the maiming and distortion, not only of human tissue, but of nature and the environment. Less obvious perhaps, and more relevant to us today, the social injustices largely having been redressed, is Dickens's increasingly subtle analysis of the effect of the capitalist dynamic upon the moral and psychological being of those participating in its upward thrust. Man in the bourgeois world — which is to say, simply the western world after the industrial revolution — exists in a state of extreme discomfort: he does not know who he is (his teleologies and ontologies having been uprooted and routed in the process of modern scepticism and secularization); neither does he know "his place". With the disintegration of the social order, and the accession of social mobility which characterizes bourgeois democracy, every man can either rise or fall: he is in danger of rising as much as of falling. He could "better" himself, or he could slip back — back into the new poverty and urban squalor yawning under the new affluence. Thus, the discomfort of modern man is of two sorts, compounded equally of the fear of falling (of oblivion, of being lost, of darkness), and the gnawing possibility of rising, which imposes an obligation reinforced by the fear of falling: not to lift himself is to risk being bypassed by others, and thus left to fall.

The persistent primal fantasy of the Dickens novels (what I have called their myth) directly reflects the striving upward movement of modern society, and the spiritual discomforts it brings with it. Dickens did not treat the decline of the *haute bourgeoisie* as Thomas Mann did in *Buddenbrooks,* and Bennett in *The Old Wives Tale,* nor had he the experience to do so. Yet his own particpation in the drama of his time — his at times almost neurotic dread of darkness and contamination, and his restlessly energetic determination to fight his way towards a permanent security and peace — made him more eligible than either Mann or Bennett to analyze the societal dynamic of the modern world. Dickens is an active participant in his novels. Hence, his nightmare is a social nightmare, and the "Freudian" aspect of his work cannot be made full sense of without the "Marxian". Unfortunately, it has always been fashionable in Anglo-Saxon circles to regard "social" writing as some inferior activity indulged by reflectors of "Manners", like Galsworthy and Shaw. Socially orientated criticism in English has been left to stolidly "sociological" writers like Williams and Hoggart, or to "Marxists" like Kettle, who on the whole lack the intellectual tradition and equipment of their great continental counterparts. Other critics, like Humphry House, simply equate social significance with social reform, and debunk Dickens as a failed reformer. Dickens's reforming zeal is important, of course, but his significance as a social analyst goes far beyond this limited campaigning, and has relatively little to do with the isolated and ephemeral evils associated with Dotheboys Hall and Chancery. In point of fact, Dickens's famous social compassion is of less significance than his snobbishness. His "heartlessness" towards Mealy Potatoes and Bob Fagin and the other boys he knew to be condemned to the Blacking Factory for life is far more interesting to the student of Dickens's fiction than his famous compassion. It was the drive to escape the dungeon of poverty and the contaminating association with the working class which gave Dickens his dynamism, not his sympathy with the underdog. It was the intensity of this drive and the overmastering need to comprehend it that gave rise to the compassionate vision of his later novels. It cannot be stressed too strongly that the stringent analysis to which Dickens subjects his myth in his last novels is indistinguishable from his investigations into contemporary commercialism. And to understand the continuity of this preoccupation, we cannot afford to regard *Dombey and Son* as the "first major novel". We must go back to the beginning of it all, where the anxieties and the hopes are strongest.

In Dickens, as in Balzac, the Transvaluation of all Values means the corrosion of the human spirit by capitalism. It is pointless of course to abstract from this process an evil entity — Capitalism — as though it were a virus injected into the otherwise healthy system by evil profiteers. "Capitalism" is simply the label we apply collectively to the human community at this stage of its technological and political development, just as "bourgeois" is the label we apply to man himself in these conditions. Today, it is true, we have absorbed the fact of money to a large extent, so that it no longer affords the novelist the leverage it afforded artists like Dickens and Dostoievsky. (Beneath the "soul-consciousness" of the Russian master is the Dickensian obsession with money — it is a money-lender Raskolnikov murders, and gold for which Father Karamazov is killed). But the passing of feudalism and mercantilism has not dated Dante or Shakespeare; and the passing of Victorian capitalism with its nightmare slump-boom rhythm has not made Dickens any less relevant to an age in which Keynesian economics has largely neutralized the violent transformations of fortune which Dickens dramatized so magnificently. On the contrary: we are as obsessed today with the idea of "success" as Dickens's contemporaries were. The desire for wealth and affluence is fundamentally a need to make oneself distinct, to prevent oneself being absorbed. There is nothing intrinsically "evil" in the desire to raise oneself above the others, or even to "keep up with" them. It is akin to the glory-lust of the statesman or the artist, and stems from the drive that took man above the animals in the first place. But it should not be disguised as something nobler than it is.[38] Universal affluence would mean universal peace. But the trouble is that we have only partial affluence — our rat-race is a competition for limited gains, we lack absolute and inexhaustible wealth, superabundance of all things for all men. The ambition to be rich, secure, powerful, a "success", is a product of fear and sickness: it is, as I have said, a neurosis. But it must also be acknowledged as a "natural drive", and nothing has contributed more to the misunderstanding of Dickens, and his American equivalent, Scott Fitzgerald, than the well-meaning moralism of those critics who would have us accept that the object of *Great Expectations* and *The Great Gatsby* is to teach us that snobbishness is nasty, or materialism evil. There is something ineradicably beautiful about success, and we are just as obsessed with it, with our television quiz shows and our national lotteries, as Dickens's contemporaries were. It is Dickens's great distinction to have first laid bare the heart of the neuroses and preoccupations that are endemic to capitalist societies: his work has lost none of its relevance. Confronted by darkness and violence, the Oliver Twist rouses up in all of us, and few of us, set to choose between decayed gentility and hard labour, would avoid the "mistakes" made by the hero of Dickens's greatest novel.

This representativeness is what is mainly overlooked by the Continental school of Marxist and structuralist critics, whose general conception of Dickens runs roughly parallel to that of the liberal mandarins whose errors I attempted to expose at the beginning of this chapter. "The reason why Dickens' novels — so marvellously rich in comic characters — seem in the end so flat and moralistic," wrote Georg Lukacs in 1916, is that "he had to make his heroes come to terms, without conflict, with the bourgeois society of his time, and, for the sake of poetic effect, to surround the qualities needed for this purpose with a false or anyway inadequate, poetic glow."[39] Lukacs had not yet turned Hegel on his head at this stage of his life, but the judgment remains typical of the Marxist view of Dickens as a facile popular entertainer. Lukacs's view of the novel is purely critical: the function of literature is seen as the revelation of the evils and delusions of "society". The hero of the novel must, in Lukacs's view, be "problematic because the society he lives in is evil, and he must be at odds with it, or forfeit our respect." But not only is that society *not* wholly evil, it is positively delusory for us to imagine that we can effectively divorce ourselves from it. The political economist can regard it "objectively" because his own participation in it does not affect his findings. But the artist cannot: the "analysis" of the artist, like his criticism, is of a more complex order. The artist celebrates and analyzes at the same time, and what he celebrates and analyzes is not "society" or "man", but himself-in-society and society-in-himself. When we make this sort of adjustment of our conception of things, the real greatness of Dickens begins to emerge.

The inadequacy of the Marxist conception of the subject is directly related, of course, to the poverty of the German novelistic tradition: in failing to produce an adequate realistic fiction, a realistic drama, and a critical philosophy, Germany failed ever to mirror itself and to see itself mirrored, and hence remained politically immature and unstable. The realism I refer to is one of the more inward variety. Germany has an abundance of naturalist novels and plays, slavishly copying the exteriors of things, which parallels its abundance of lofty music and disembodied speculative philosophy. But between the two runs man himself, "Man alive", as D. H. Lawrence called him. Art is the most central human activity, because it is more like consciousness than any other of man's abstract pursuits. Consciousness is at once objective and subjective, analytic and synthetic, cognitive and experiencing: man observes and participates in society, as in his own mental world, and we cannot hope to improve or understand our society if we adopt towards it a spuriously critical attitude, as though its evils were not ours also. In Germany, it is the critic who "knows", not the artist, and this is simply to have things the wrong way about.

What I have done here is to replace the essentially critical conception of the novel with a model based upon the facts of identification and participation. It has also been necessary to abandon the Goldmannesque notion of the "vision du monde"[40] which reduces the artist to the role of manifester of a social sub-group's symptoms, its ambitions and frustrations. We need a more complex notion of the artist as the leading point of society's coming-to-consciousness of itself. There is an important apperceptive element in all artistic creation, and the novel in its great period takes over this role from poetry and drama. Dickens is treated, of course, as being importantly "typical" of a class, though I prefer the word representative. But it has not seemed possible to accept

Goldmann's notion of the social sub-group whose limited slant on things gives rise to the "vision du monde". The neat social groups Goldmann liked to isolate ("Noblesse de robe", for example) vanish in the capitalist world: we cannot isolate the "lower middle class" with any degree of precision, and I prefer to replace the idea with a vaguer but ultimately perhaps more precise notion of a social centre of gravity, which could be defined in terms of aspirations and ambitions themselves brought into being by the modes of production, social relations, and historical circumstances of the given age. Thus, although it may seem vague and metaphysical to speak of "capitalist man", as I have, it is really more honest and accurate to do so: for all the air of scientific precision about Goldmann's controlled experimental situations, there is something curiously a-historical about his findings. He does not, for instance, account for the fact that situations ostensibly similar to those obtaining in Racine's France fail, in other centuries and other countries, to produce the same kind of "tragic" philosophy. The answer is that history dictates the range of ambitions and expectations in any given period, so that we are on safer ground speaking of "capitalist man" or "feudal man" — once we accept the need to specify the specific class-colouring of particular cases, — than attempting to treat isolated social sub-groups as if their ambitions and exasperations can be "explained" in terms of their specific class-situation. The spirit of the age, the social centre of gravity, the range of conscious expectations — these notions are less precise on the face of it, but more adequate to the truth, I believe. It means restoring an important historical objectivity to things, an objectivity negated, I think, in Goldmann's relativism. The nature of the historical situation remains the same, whatever our particular class-angle on it may be. There is a feudal age, and a capitalist age: an age in which the highest aspiration of man was expressed in the court, and one in which the court does not exist. Outside us, yet also within us, is the historical fact-world, and it determines what we can think and feel from within our limited class-situation. In our time, this fact-world is that of capitalism and democracy, and the scramble for limited gains is what we have to get on with.

2 *Oliver Twist*

Any account of its action makes it perfectly clear that *Oliver Twist* is a novel to which the word fantasy in its technical Freudian sense applies with almost embarrassing completeness: Dickens takes his hero from the workhouse to unending security by means of outrageous coincidence and smiling chance. If this implies a limiting criticism of the novel it also indicates the nature of its virtues. For although it is probably the most mechanical of all Dickens's novels from the point of view of the dependence of the action upon sheer accident, there is throughout an intense clarity of vision which not only heightens the characterization with a strange super-reality, but unites the apparently random event-sequence with a strange spendthrift economy. What we have here is not a realistic novel creaking at the joints with absurd coincidences and long-lost relationships, but a novel governed from within by a different logic. More than any other of Dickens's early books, *Oliver Twist* reveals the tendency towards order and design that underlies the profligacy of the invention and the wealth of characterization. G. K. Chesterton observed that the plot of the novel is "preposterous".[1] The truth is surely that the action of *Oliver Twist* is not an affront to decent realism — something to be stomached for the other excellences offered — but integral to the vision behind it, and essential to the meanings proffered by that vision.

It is to its moral vision that we must attribute the enduring grip of a novel which, considered from many points of view, must seem absurd. In point of fact, the oscillations of the hero's fortunes are neither the arbitrary seesawings of bad picaresque, nor the rational moral-pointing of Goldsmithian fable: the pattern they make is of the very essence of the book's meaning. Briefly summarized, the skeleton of the plot is as follows: Oliver, born in the workhouse, leaves his master (the undertaker Sowerberry) to "seek his fortune" in London; he falls in with the Artful Dodger, who takes him to Fagin's den; he is arrested for pickpocketing, then instated not in prison but in the middle-class paradise of his unknowing godfather; he is snatched back for Fagin by the prostitute Nancy; once more restored to safety and family through the failure of a housebreaking job he is forced to take part in by Bill Sikes; is threatened one last time by Fagin and his own half-brother, Monks, but remains secure, while Fagin, Monks, and Sikes are all destroyed. That is more or less all. So presented it seems identical with innumerable cautionary tales penned by mid-Victorian do-gooders: at first sight, at least. When we take a closer look, even the skeleton reveals certain more interesting features.

First, Oliver is rescued or captured in every case while he is engaged on someone else's project: the pickpocketing expedition with the Dodger and Charley Bates, the errand to the bookseller's for Mr. Brownlow, the Chertsey job for Sikes and Fagin. Every time Oliver changes worlds, in other words, it is through a misfiring of a plan. Moreover, the plans which misfire have consequences morally opposite to those intended: Mr. Brownlow stumbles across his long-lost nephew by having him arrested for thieving. Then, it is precisely Mr. Brownlow's trust and faith in Oliver that leads to his being snatched back by Nancy and Sikes: the five pound note and the parcel of books symbolize Mr. Brownlow's faith in Oliver. He is saved a second time by the failure of a criminal venture: the Chertsey crib is the means by which Oliver is restored to middle-class order and serenity. The evil is consistently a means of arriving at the good, and vice versa. The pattern runs right through the book. The sweep Gamfield's brutality is in part at least the cause of Oliver's falling under the kinder influence of Mr. Sowerberry; whose own kindness towards Oliver is again at least in part a cause of Noah Claypole's and Mrs. Sowerberry's hostility. When Oliver first arrives in London, the Artful Dodger — who picks him up in Barnet — shares his food with him; later, when Oliver is introduced into Fagin's den, the "Merry Old Gentleman" makes him laugh, feeds him, and gives him a roof and a bed. The purpose of all this hospitality is, ultimately, to corrupt him, but the immediate impression is of a spontaneous camaraderie[2] which contrasts ironically with the coldness and inhumanity Oliver has known earlier in life.

The pattern of the book — a remarkably pure and beautiful one — is then more intricate and purposeful than might at first appear likely. But this is only half the story. The pattern constitutes the most naked and indeed flagrant version of the Dickens myth we could imagine: this is a "success" story of the kind every Victorian *petit bourgeois* or proletarian longed to live out in reality. It is indeed just because Dickens so obviously wanted to write a happily-ever-after fairy-story with a few social pungencies on the side that the actual nightmarish plunges into the abyss and dreamlike emergences into light and cleanliness have such a powerful grip on the imagination. In writing *Oliver Twist* Dickens was possessed of deeper fears than he was consciously acquainted with: Oliver's swings into and out of the clutches of Fagin reveal, surely, a fascination with evil, sordidity, and degradation that exerts a frightening drawing-power on the mind. Like Dostoievsky, Dickens invests evil with a profound ambivalence, and this ambivalence is what is reflected in the rhythmic pattern of the narrative.

When, for instance, Oliver is rescued by Mr. Brownlow and installed in "the neat house in a quiet shady street near Pentonville", the psychic contrast with the Saffron Hill jungle is at once blissful and ominous. When he later comes across Sikes and Nancy on the way to the bookseller the effect is not at all of arbitrary plot-making (as by realistic rights it should be), but of sickening inevitability. In one's faith in Oliver's purity, one was not seriously concerned when he initially fell in with the Dodger and Fagin; nor even when he was implicated in the theft outside the booksellers. But after the blissful awakening in Pentonville, and the serene existence amid china and chintz, with the promise of a life of quiet study, the lunge back into the labyrinth of Saffron Hill and the clutches of the ogre Fagin, has a natural horror which engages our susceptibility to nightmare and regressive fear as few incidents in fiction do. It is commonplace nowadays to refer to *Oliver Twist* in terms of its dreamlike logic.[3] The idea is a good deal older than recent criticism would have us believe. G. K. Chesterton – in some of the finest pages that have ever been written about Dickens – observed some fifty years ago that "There is a sort of lurid conviviality that accompanies the panic; as if the nightmare could accompany, not follow the heavy meal."[4] *Oliver Twist* is, he later observes, "the first of [Dickens's] nightmare novels". As sensible critic, Chesterton felt obliged to observe that the plot is "preposterous"; but there is no doubt that he felt the power of the novel's "dream" logic. We cannot, in point of fact, cut the book up into acceptable and preposterous elements (based upon some criterion of realistic verisimilitude) without destroying it altogether. For the power of the fable is expressed specifically in terms of dreamlike eventualities. Mario Praz has sarcastically observed that Oliver seems magnetically drawn to the houses of his relatives.[5] So he is and this is the point. The magnet is in our own secret dreads and desires, not concealed in the cloak of an incompetent conjuror.

When, some weeks after the return to Fagin's den, Oliver is taken out on the burgling expedition at Chertsey, the sequence we have just remarked upon – from light to darkness – is once again reversed: after the heightened nightmarishness of the robbery and the wounding – the blinding pain, the bewildering faces staring down at Oliver, Sikes from one side, the servants from the other – comes the dreamlike awakening again, accompanied by the well-remembered pleasant exhaustion: "The boy stirred and smiled in his sleep . . . " And this idyll is in its turn smashed by the sudden apparition of Fagin and Monks at Oliver's window. Considered in terms of probability, this casement scene is absurd: in its own dream terms, it is frighteningly effective. Fagin is in his true diabolical element suddenly appearing at a window; to imagine him — as we then have to — haring across fields and ducking behind hedges is quite impossible. Sensing this, Dickens cuts the chapter off at Oliver's shout in the room, thus giving the chase — in which there is no quarry, only hunters — the chance of a new plane of reality. The terror aroused by these scenes is of the very essence of the book's inner logic: the "unlikeliness" of these incidents does not threaten the tension, it creates it.

The source of the nightmare is, on one level, the dread of poverty and degradation underlying the myth of which this novel is, I have argued, the most naked enactment in all Dickens. But this polarity of darkness and light, poverty and affluence, violence and tranquillity, possesses a spiritual counterpart. In articulating so brilliantly the Victorian fear of poverty and lost-ness, Dickens at the same time enunciated a religious parable of great beauty and purity: it is the human soul which is threatened in the person of Oliver Twist, that soul which modern man has so much feared to lose in his new urban, technological, and commercial environment. *Oliver Twist* is about the soul of man under capitalism, but it is also about the soul of man under the constant and perennial pressure of evil. It is not so much that we can see the sequence of events making up the narrative "in two ways", or on two planes, as that we cannot fully understand them unless both the social and the spiritual aspects are taken into account together. Now Dickens is remarkably free with words and images which dictate a quasi-religious interpretation. In no other Dickens novel is evil more powerfully evil, or good more radiantly and unequivocally good. The action makes up, in fact, an astonishingly natural and unadorned morality.

The devil is of course more "interesting", and Fagin is without question one of the most powerful and pregnant embodiments of evil in nineteenth century fiction. In Fagin

we are brought into direct contact with evil. The apprehension is instinctive and simple, but what is apprehended is
compound, a rich amalgam of attraction and revulsion. Fagin
possessed an innate charisma, a charm, almost, which fascinates Oliver. It is curious in fact that at no point does
Dickens say that Fagin repels Oliver or show Oliver recoiling
from him. Certainly this is in keeping with the general treatment of Oliver and of the whole narrative: we register things
through his eyes, but what is registered, horrible as it often is,
is not coloured by the child's eye. We know of his dread of
Fagin and of the life he stands for through his protestations
of gratitude to Mr. Brownlow and the Maylies, and his pleas
not to be returned. But when the vile ethos is actually
described the narrative is sober, the child impassive. Fagin
starts to beat Oliver in one scene, but the action is uncharac-
teristic and is soon interrupted by Nancy. Otherwise, the
merry old gentleman treats Oliver with a courtly gaiety. "The
Prince of darkness is a gentleman", and so in a sense is the
red-haired fence we first meet like this: "In a frying pan,
which was on the fire, and which was secured to the mantel-
shelf by a string, some sausages were cooking; and standing
over them, with a toasting-fork in his hand, was a very old
shrivelled Jew, whose villainous looking repulsive face was
obscured by a quantity of matted red hair." (Chapter 8, p.
56)* The toasting-fork is a characteristically subtle invention,
giving an ironically theological tone to the whole portrait: this
is the devil, and Oliver is fascinated. The narrator, of course,
is not. And we have here an instance of a phenomenon which
has been treated by other critics,[6] and which is prevalent
throughout *Oliver Twist*. Dickens maintains — with a dexterity extraordinary in a man of twenty-four — a cool distance between the "public" tone of his official record (this is
Charles Dickens, an angry observer, reporting facts to Her
Majesty's Government and to Her subjects), and the inner
narrative, which is, as it were, experienced by Oliver himself
— though also at other times by Nancy. The effect of the
whole novel is undoubtedly compounded of the enveloping
rhetoric of the public narrator and of the raw experiences

rendered powerfully and subtly within the rhetoric. It would be a mistake to assert that we could dispense with the outer rhetoric (the comedy of the workhouse, for instance, would be lost with it), but there is no doubt that the peculiar ambivalence with which Oliver regards Fagin, and which Dickens himself consistently associates with evil in the early novels, derives solely from the dispassionate susceptibility of the "experienced" narrative.

Now this narrative — it can be seen from the sketch of it given above — really has only one subject: the safety of Oliver Twist. It is a remarkable achievement to sustain so intense an interest upon such a fragile basis. Apart from the skilfully balanced marriage situations (the hateful, calculating Bumbles exactly invert the graceful though conventionally self-effacing Harry and Rose), the novel is without a second subject. Yet this sparseness of narrative material, far from being a weakness, is precisely the secret of its excellence. The narrative flickers with apprehension whenever Oliver's security is threatened; a large number of the secondary characters in the novel exist only to menace Oliver — Noah Claypole, Mrs. Sowerberry, Bumble himself, Mr. Fang the magistrate, Gamfield. In no other Dickens novel are there so many overheard conversations or eavesdroppings; people are tailed and watched — and if they are not actually, they imagine they are.

This is all spectacularly true of Fagin's aide, Monks, Oliver's half-brother, whose machinations against him provide the novel's major action. Monks is in fact a minor study of a major nineteenth century preoccupation — the satanic personality.[7] Physically, he bears a marked resemblance to Ahab, Heathcliff, and Michael Henchard: he is, we learn, "tall and dark"; his eye is keen and bright, but shadowed by a scowl of distrust and suspicion . . . most repulsive to behold". (Chapter 38, p.286.) During a conversation with Bumble Monks refers to himself as a friend of the devil; and when Bumble tells him that the midwife who brought his half-brother into the world is dead, his reaction is noted with a significant attentiveness by Dickens: "The man looked fixedly at him when he had given this information, and although he did not withdraw his eyes for some time afterwards, his gaze gradually became vacant and abstracted, and he seemed lost in thought." (Chapter 38, pp.288–89.) Such a melange of restlessness, abstractedness, and inward doubt is thoroughly characteristic of the satanic personality in nineteenth century fiction: it is of the essence of the character never to be inwardly at peace. When Bumble, scenting profit, tells him that the midwife spoke to a woman before she died — it was his own wife, of course — Monks is immediately thrown into agitation: "thrown off his guard and plainly showing that all his fears (whatever they were) were aroused afresh by this intelligence" (p.289). "Whatever they were" — that is an important parenthesis. For this Dostoievskian epileptic has his own hallucinatory obsessions, which counterbalance the fears and terrors of Oliver himself. Oliver in fact causes Monks an irrational horror which transcends the financial threat he represents. Oliver pops up to wreck Monks's peace of mind (such as it could be) as inevitably as Fagin shatters Oliver's:

> "Hah!" cried the man, fixing his eyes on Oliver, and suddenly recoiling. "What's this?"
> "I beg your pardon, sir," said Oliver; "I was in a great hurry to get home, and didn't see you were coming."
> "Death!" muttered the man to himself, glaring at the boy with his large dark eyes. "Who would have thought it!"
> "Grind him to ashes! He'd start up from a stone coffin, to come in my way!" (Chapter 33, p.244.)

After more provoking innocence from Oliver, Monk falls to the ground in the throes of a fit. The reaction seems disproportionate to the facts: in part, indeed, it is, and Dickens displays considerable skill in holding the neurotic obsessions before us for long periods before finally divulging their factual basis. When, at the end of the book, the story behind Oliver's parentage is finally revealed, partly by Mr. Brownlow and partly by Monks himself in an enforced confession, this impression is intensified: Monks was the legitimate son of Edwin Leeford, Oliver the illegitimate son of Leeford and Agnes Fleming (the book should by rights be called Oliver

Leeford, but Mr. Bumble's invention holds its place even after the revelations of chapter 51). By a late will, Leeford had left all his money to Oliver and his mother. Monks's mother burned this will, but she was obsessed with the idea that a son had been born: Monks had sworn to "hunt it down; never to let it rest; to pursue it with the bitterest and most unrelenting animosity; to vent upon it the hatred that I deeply felt and to spit upon the empty vaunt of that insulting will by dragging it, if I could, to the very gallows-foot." (Chapter 51, p.415.) It is hardly possible to reconcile the nebulous threat Oliver might possibly have posed (could the will have been remembered or revived) with the morbid ferocity of Monks's hatred: once again, it seems impossible to understand the novel without a religious or theological inter-pretation. We note that the will is "insulting" to Monks: he takes up his dead mother's cause with a puritanic zeal, a zeal engendered half by wounded pride, half by an innate hostility towards what is felt to be a more pure relationship. Monks cannot tolerate the very existence of the "natural" child: he wants to rid the world of its goodness.

Now the scene at the inn in chapter 51 in which these explanations are given was a dangerous one for Dickens to have undertaken: in giving us "explanations" of the events of the story in terms of inheritance and long-lost relationships, he ran the risk of compromising the integrity and force of the foregoing narrative, which was based, as we have seen, precisely on the skillful exploitation of irrational feelings we the readers showed ourselves only too willing to indulge. In one or two cases, I think, this does happen: it was tidy but mistaken of Dickens to explain, for instance, why it was that Monks and Fagin appeared at the casement in chapter 33. But on the whole, Dickens redeems the scene brilliantly. Monks puts on a tremendous display of satanic malice; he remains totally unrepentant, and his contempt for Mr. Brownlow, like his hatred of Oliver, emerges even more strongly from these explanations as being of an absolute and indissoluble kind. Like Ahab's obsession with the White Whale, Monks's fixation on destroying Oliver transcends all rational motivation: he loathes his half-brother as evil loathes good.

It is unquestionably the theological dimension in which Monks has his being that saves the character from unreality, even in scenes when Dickens overplays his hand. This is true for instance of chapter 38 where Monks keeps his rendezvous with the Bumbles: it is a "dark and stormy night", the surroundings are evilly sordid, beneath their feet flows a "turbid" stream. Monks is in his element, and all but gnashes his teeth — " 'Hear it!' he cries, when the thunder rolls, " 'hear it! Rolling and crashing on as if it echoed through a thousand caverns where the devils were hiding from it. I hate the sound!' " (p. 293). The stagily diabolic tone of Monks's speech here all but vitiates the fine work of the previous chapter, which has established so well his inward restlessness and unease. But the diabolism is offset by the comedy of the Bumbles (Dickens never handled the *comédie noire* of marriage better), as well as by certain authentic touches in the handling of Monks himself: his preoccupation, for instance, with "last things" (" 'If the sea ever gives up its dead, as books say it will, it will keep its gold and silver to itself, and that trash among it.' " p.299). "That trash" is the gold locket he had just purchased from Mrs. Bumble/Corney, incidentally: it will hardly be an exaggeration to note that Monks's concern for getting rid of this gold anticipates John Jasper's behaviour in *Edwin Drood*: Jasper — the traditional villain's name of course — forgets to remove Edwin's gold ring, and gold being impervious to fire, the omission was perhaps to have trapped Jasper at the end of the book. At any rate, Monks shares Jasper's restlessness of mind: in this scene he has a very minor fit — the second in the novel, and evinces an "invincible repugnance to being left alone".

A peculiarly disturbing feature of Monks's satanism is that he does not want Oliver killed, but corrupted. True, he gives as his reason for not wanting the boy murdered that the blood will haunt him, and this dread suits his morbid temperament. But it is not difficult to understand why having Oliver murdered (easily done, and far more rational

from the point of view of Monks's threatened inheritance)
would not satisfy him: it would confirm Oliver in his
innocence, and what Monks needs is to defile this innocence,
and prove Oliver no better than himself. Monks expresses this
desire to have Oliver corrupted most vehemently in the conversation with Fagin in chapter 26. Sikes and Oliver have not
been heard of since the failure of the Chertsey job; Fagin has
just visited the drunken Nancy at the Three Cripples. The
narrative sequence hereabouts is superbly strategic: for
Monks's desire to have Oliver corrupted — overheard by
Nancy in the event — counterpoints Nancy's own growing
remorse at having been instrumental in bringing Oliver back
to Fagin's den and the life of crime. Nancy had already inter-
vened on Oliver's behalf immediately on restoring him to
Fagin: it is now that the old Jew starts beating Oliver and the
action precipitates her own inward change. When Nancy
springs to his defence, the process of regret that is to end in
her death commences. It is, as I have said, her having been
instrumental in bringing Oliver to the threshold of corruption
that first awakens her own sense of what she herself has
become. Certainly, her tirade against Fagin in this scene
testified to a long-standing hatred of the fence; but it is one
thing to know that you are damned, another to be able to
articulate this awareness, as Nancy now does. It is herself she
sees in Oliver, and upon being reminded by Fagin that the
thieving and prostitution he introduced her to has been a
living, she retorts: " 'It is my living; and the cold, wet, dirty
streets are my home; and you're the wretch that drove me to
them long ago, and that'll keep me there, day and night, day
and night till I die!' " (Chapter 16, p.116.)

Nancy is caught here at a crucial stage of her own life; a
few years more, and the remorse would be beyond her, she
would be hardened beyond humanity. Oliver's innocence and
purity not only arouse her pity, but force her into an awareness of what she herself is. This awareness is still more poignantly aroused by the sight of Rose Maylie in the west end
hotel. Nancy has been bitterly insulted by the servants of the
hotel, and when she hears Rose's footsteps at last, she falls

into a panic of shame:

> there was something of the woman's original nature left in her still; and when she heard a light step approaching the door opposite to that by which she had entered, and thought of the wide contrast which the small room would in another moment contain, she felt burdened with the sense of her own deep shame, and shrunk as though she could scarcely bear the presence of her with whom she had sought this interview. (Chapter 40, p.301.)

But — "struggling with these better feelings was pride": Nancy puts on an act of brassy carelessness, because she cannot bear the contrast she makes with the "slight and beautiful girl" who stands before her: " 'It's a hard matter to get to see you, lady.' " The whole scene is beautifully managed, a superb confrontation of the soiled and the pure, in which each party watches its own anti-self in the other. It is significant, I think, that the scene actually serves no positive purpose: Nancy has nothing to tell Rose and Mr. Brownlow, and even obstructs Rose's desire to have Fagin's affairs investigated. What Dickens wants to do here is simply to give us the confrontation, and by so doing clarify the moral basis of the whole novel: Rose is what Nancy was before her "wasting life had obliterated so many, many traces when a very child." (p. 301). When Dostoievsky, in a well-known phrase, called Dickens "that great Christian", he must surely have been thinking of the radiant conception of humanity skilfully conjured in such scenes as this: without Nancy, Rose Maylie is a china doll; without Rose, Nancy an incomplete "fallen woman". Bringing the two images together Dickens poignantly evokes a full image of moral decline, through no personal weakness, but through the action of a "wasting life". "Wasting life" is a superb phrase, incidentally — one of several in the scene ("wide contrast", "deep shame") which help to define the situation in all its bitter pathos. Turning — as it is natural to want to — from this scene to the confrontation Dostoievsky engineers between Grushenka and Katerina Ivanovna in *The Brothers Karamazov*, we can hardly help being struck by the fact that with the greater psychological complexity he has acquired, Dostoievsky has lost the pristine force of the spiritual

confrontation Dickens presents between Nancy and Rose
Maylie. The purpose of each of the two scenes is ultimately
quite different of course, but there is an underlying affinity
between them. Dostoievsky's symbol of purity — Alyosha,
the equivalent of Oliver — arranges the interview between the
two women: although Dostoievsky's purpose is to suggest a
kind of eventual parity between the women, his scene lacks
that profound sense of moral polarity that distinguishes the
scene in *Oliver Twist*. He has lost that vision of human
radiance that was so important to him. Alyosha is unable to
sustain the tension himself — morally he is really outside it
(*above* it) — and the scene disintegrates into the merely nasty
antagonism so common in Dostoievsky.

The scene in the west end hotel leads directly to Nancy's
death. Her end is in the event brought about through the
agency of Noah Claypole. Claypole's reappearance late in the
novel seems a mistake, until we realize that he makes a
strange parody of the basic Dick Whittington role that Oliver
has already played. Like Oliver, Noah arrives in London by
the Great North Road; he is first observed pausing beneath
the archway at Highgate, which is traditionally associated, as
Dickens later ironically observes *à propos* of Sikes, with Dick
Whittington. Noah's intention is the same as Oliver's — to
seek his fortune in London; and he fits the part of the
country bumpkin — with his "long-limbed, knock-kneed,
shambling, bony" look, the dust on his boots, the guileless
arrogance and the vaguely Midland accent — much better
than Oliver. This is no doubt his function: to provide the
kind of focussing opposite for Oliver which Nancy, in
different ways, had provided for Rose Maylie. But for
circumstances, Nancy might have been Rose Maylie; but for
character, Oliver might have been Noah Claypole. Fagin soon
picks him up, as he had picked up Oliver, and Noah tumbles
over himself in his haste to be "corrupted". But when Fagin
sets him to watch Nancy, he begins to take on a more sinister
air, an air oddly familiar from another context. When Nancy
first meets Mr. Brownlow and Rose on London Bridge, "they
halted with an exclamation of surprise, but suppressed it

immediately; for a man in the garments of a countryman came close up — brushed against them, indeed — at that precise moment." (Chapter 46, p. 348.) A few moments later, "the countryman looked round, and roughly asking what they took up the whole pavement for, passed on." This ill-tempered, rough-tongued country spy, who slinks along "in the deepest shadow he could find", must inevitably remind the reader familiar with *Great Expectations* of Orlick, Pip's old antagonist, and Magwitch's betrayer. It is one of several parallels between the two novels. Another is that Orlick is in the pay of Compcyson, and Compeyson is a late counterpart of Monks. Claypole is not actually working for Monks, but in spying for Fagin on Oliver's relations he is of course furthering Monks's interest. More, Orlick at one time worked for Miss Havisham whom Compeyson jilted, so that there is a sort of distorted relationship between Miss Havisham and Fagin — the dirty, hirsute demon figures of the two books.

With the eavesdropping scene on London Bridge, the powers of evil start working out their own destruction. Noah Claypole's report to Fagin leads directly to the murder of Nancy, the flight and death of Sikes, and Fagin's own arrest and execution. Nancy's refusal to betray Sikes and the others is an important part of her nature. It is neither love, as ordinarily understood, that makes her stand by Sikes, nor loyalty; but something compounded of both — a composite sentiment that, simply, "you don't do that". At any rate, her standing by Sikes sheds a kind of humanity on Sikes himself. He is a brute, of course — brut*alized.* But there is an interesting contrast between Dickens's treatment of Sikes after the murder and Zola's handling of Laurent and Thérèse after the murder of Camille in *Thérèse Raquin.* Zola's lovers (bestial enough, admittedly, to begin with) are totally de-humanized by the crime, discounting the quite spurious *tendresse* which Zola melodramatically invokes at their double suicide. Sikes is, paradoxically, brought closer to humanity by his crime, and this is far more interesting. The pressure of the extreme experience forces him into an awareness of his need for human society and companionship — a need which of course Nancy had satisfied before without his knowing it. He becomes, as Jonas Chuzzlewit is to become in a later novel, more interesting to us after the act, almost at times sympathetic. Dickens's public voice assures us that "Of all the bad deeds that, under cover of darkness, had been committeed . . . that was the worst." (p.363) And his careful preparation of the scene fully justifies the tone adopted. But Sikes haunted by Nancy's eyes is a man being reached by remorse. He finds that he cannot drag himself away from London; he is haunted by shadows, everything he sees is interpreted in terms of his own dread. Most remarkably, he comes across a scene of fire-fighting in a farmyard: "There were people there — men and women — light, bustle. It was like new life to him." (p.369) A complete brute may fear death and capture, and even experience an inchoate discomfort that may appear a primitive remorse. But a man who distinguishes himself, as Sikes does in the fire, by acts of heroism and self-forgetfulness, is responding to more highly evolved and human drives. These are the first and last socially constructive and selfless acts Sikes ever commits. It is himself he is fleeing in committing them, but that in itself is a distinctly human requirement.

Sikes's end is sharply contrasted with that of Fagin:

> He cowered down upon his stone bed, and thought of the past. He had been wounded with some missiles from the crowd on the day of his capture, and his head was bandaged with a linen cloth. His red hair hung down upon his bloodless face; his beard was torn, and twisted into knots; his eyes shone with a terrible light; his unwashed flesh crackled with the fever that burnt him up. (Chapter 52, p. 408.)

Dickens devoted a great deal of care to Fagin's death. He clearly conceived of it not as the just punishment of a criminal, but as a ritual of exorcism and purification. The scene is built up symphonically, with noises off from the carpenters constructing the scaffold, the clock tolling the hours away, and the cheerful bustle of morning carried on as if the day were not out of the ordinary. At the centre of the whole, Fagin, in a terrible loneliness, is gradually disintegrating under the pressure. Finally, Oliver comes and sees him "seated on his bed, rocking himself from side to side, with a countenance more like that of a snared beast than the face of a man. His mind was evidently wandering to his old life, for he continued to mutter, without appearing conscious of their presence otherwise than as a part of his vision." (Chapter 52, p. 409.)

The dialogue that follows, or at least Fagin's wanderings sprinkled with comments from Oliver and the turnkey, is a magnificent achievement. Time and time again, in bringing his favourite villains to a crisis, Dickens produces his finest sustained writing; the speech of the villains in particular is sharpened beyond what it has been before, penetrating to a vein of significance that had not seemed possible earlier. Fagin's last lucid incoherencies carry Dickens's plan to its logical conclusion. Ambivalent as his attitude towards the Jew had been, there is no uncertainty in his final treatment of him. Dickens is attracted by his villains, and registers the attraction; but he is not taken in by them. Fagin acquired his magic power at the expense of his humanity; he was left with nothing inside. Dickens captures to perfection the nervous trembling of his speech, with its sudden darts of hope and flashes of recollection:

> "Good boy, Charley — well done," he mumbled. "Oliver, too, ha! ha! ha! Oliver too — quite the gentleman now — quite the — take that boy away to bed!"

And later:

> "He has been the — the — somehow the cause of all this. It's worth the money to bring him up to it — Bolter's throat, Bill; never mind the girl — Bolter's throat as deep as you can cut. Saw his head off!" (P. 410.)

With this final confrontation of Oliver and Fagin in the condemned cell, the novel reaches its real conclusion. For it is this confrontation that is at the centre of everything, like the melodic phrase or harmonic idea at the heart of a string quartet.

I have dwelt at length upon the dream logic of *Oliver Twist* and upon the nature of the evil in it, because these qualities determine each other, and indicate the way Dickens uses the basic myth at this stage. At the beginning of this chapter, it was suggested that this novel illustrates more than any other Freud's account of the nature of fiction. The story of Oliver's rescue from destitution and contamination with evil fulfills a deep-seated need in Dickens (and in many of his contemporaries) to re-enact, and thereby reaffirm, his emergence from the abyss of penury and degradation. To some extent we can see the thieves' kitchen in Saffron Hill and the Workhouse in the unnamed provincial town as heightened images of the blacking warehouse in the Strand. Whether we choose to do this or not, the fact remains that Dickens is going through a dreamlike performance here, that expresses a universal Victorian fear of falling from one class to the one beneath, and on a broader scale, the universal human fear of darkness or simply of being lost and corrupted. The true significance of the performance lies in the nature of the confrontation between good and evil.

The two novels that follow *Oliver Twist* — *Nicholas Nickleby* and *The Old Curiosity Shop* — share its basic pattern: in both, the hero/heroine is left destitute early in the story, either wholly or half-orphaned, and is harassed by a demon who is eventually exorcised, as Fagin was in *Oliver Twist*. At first sight, indeed, there is little to distinguish the three books from each other, or from the fantasy of Freud's "poor orphan-boy", except that in *The Old Curiosity Shop* failure and not success ends the enterprise. In each case, the worth of the hero or heroine is unquestioned, and the eventual materialization of the expectations confidently awaited. The parents, as is usual in Dickens, are either careless or dead or both. In *Nicholas Nickleby,* the blame is visited upon the fecklessness of the deceased father and the fluttery ineffectuality of the mother; in *The Old Curiosity Shop* upon the weakness of Nell's self-indulgent grandfather. Thus, in all three novels Dickens treats the myth at much the same stage of awareness. There is a common movement from destitution to prosperity, the agents of the rescue being magically empowered personages independent of the social structure, who defeat the ogres and their aides. Yet in fact the two later novels have different inner structures and explore different facets of the myth. Formally, *Oliver Twist* is the most rigorous and shapely of the three; it also presents the dream-technique at its purest with little or no encumbrance. By contrast, *The Old Curiosity Shop* seems, at first sight, indeed chaotic and disorganized. But in fact it is still driven by the dream-motor that sustained the momentum of *Oliver Twist* and its organization is far more coherent than is usually recognized.

The nucleus of the book is really the Quilp-Nell relationship. The charm of Fagin and the fascination of Oliver have been heightened into unambiguous sexuality. The fair young boy has become a pretty, cherry-lipped girl, and the long-haired devil a sexual sadist, who repels and fascinates in about equal measure. The sexual element that adheres perhaps to all our ideas of evil has thrust itself towards the surface, and in a disturbingly modern way.[1] The action of *The Old Curiosity Shop* really begins with the penetration of Quilp, the sexual aggressor, into the fragile womb of the Shop in search of Nell, whom he at once frightens out into the wide world. The rest of the novel, after the flight of Nell and her grandfather from the Shop, turns upon Quilp's attempts to find them and have them brought back to London. Now the truly extraordinary thing about the book is that right up to the moment of Nell's death it is pervaded with her dread of Quilp, yet, apart from one typically nightmarish occasion in a Midland town when she spots the dwarf in time to remain unseen by him, the two characters are never brought together after the flight from the Shop in chapter 12 — which is to say hardly one fifth of the way through. Yet Quilp haunts her constantly: she sees him everywhere, his agents are continually discovering her and wrecking the fragile peace she starts to build up in remote country villages. The mechanism is familiar from *Oliver Twist*. What is so extraordinary about *The Old Curiosity Shop* is the fragility of the nightmare's factual basis. Fagin after all is a thief, his household rife with murderers. We know what Oliver is afraid of. What are Nell and her Grandfather afraid of? Their flight is desperate in the extreme. Yet the most they need have feared was Quilp's patronage; the dwarf has no hold over them, and if Nell had been forced into a life of hard labour it could have been no more exhausting than the vagabond life the flight committed her to. If we

look at the story soberly, disregarding the power and magnetism of the writing, we are forced to conclude that Dickens
has simply failed to provide adequate motivation for the
action: the "objective correlative" is not objective enough,
nor does it correlate objects and emotions of equal weight. In
other words, the novel's network of galleries is unsupported
by adequate pitprops.

This is probably the most common verdict passed on the
book, and to some extent it must be accepted. Dickens's
dream art depends on a delicate balance of social and psychic
forces: its power to move us usually derives from our
accepting its mythic content as it were unwittingly, on the
strength of the overt social and moral designata. Thus, his
legacies, wills, long-lost relatives, and concealed identities
dovetail with the psychic pressures that in one sense provide
the content of his novels. The force of his art derives from
the completeness with which he persuades us to identify with
his central figures, and comparison with the essentially
inhuman world of the Kafka novel, in which the waking
correlatives have been dispensed with altogether, is sufficient
to make clear how important the manifest content of
Dickens's intentions is. Thus, the weakness of *The Old
Curiosity Shop* cannot be denied: Dickens never quite
succeeds in giving the nightmare a valid cause. Yet in a way
this makes it all the more extraordinary an achievement: the
very weaknesses of the narrative machinery bring it closer to
the pure dream-statement than any other Dickens book, even
Oliver Twist; the incidents of the action become so far
separated from probability that it is easy for us to fail to see
that the things Dickens is seeking to articulate — fear,
anxiety, tension — are strengthened precisely by the absence
of any really plausible motivation in social reality. Dickens's
hold upon our rational credulity was never weaker than in
this novel, his hold upon our imagination rarely stronger.
Thus, the actual incidents of the flight — the superficially
clumsy contrivances by which Dickens gets Nell and her
Grandfather into their difficulties: overheard conversations,
chance meetings, sudden apparitions, rumours of strange

characters — all serve the purposes of the inner action: they are removed to a different plane and, ceasing to be the resources of desperate realism, appear as the fortuitous relevances of dream. The basis of the dream is Quilp's haunting of Nell.

But as Nell's flight with her Grandfather develops, a second nightmare begins to usurp the first: Quilp is replaced by the kindly old Grandfather. On a suitably dark and stormy night, the fugitives shelter at an inn; Grandfather plays cards, loses, and, while Nell is asleep, he robs her. She is woken by an intruder (she has previously been scared by a dark figure in the corridor); paralyzed with fear, she follows the marauder — to the door of Grandfather Trent's room; fearing for his life, she enters to find that the intruder is Grandfather Trent himself, and that he has stolen from her.

Now the nucleus here is centrally Dickensian: a parent/ guardian steals from his own child; the child is not only paralyzed with psychological insecurity but physically afraid. The elder becomes a kind of ape — gliding along sinisterly, silently — like something out of Poe's *Rue Morgue*. Now the mastery reveals itself first in the sureness and consistency of touch:

> The child was returning to the room where they had passed the evening, when she fancied she saw a figure just gliding in at the door. There was nothing but a long dark passage between this door and the place where she had changed the money, and, being very certain that no person had passed in or out while she stood there, the thought struck her that she had been watched. (Chapter 29, p. 227.)

The glissando is felt at once: we shudder at the sinister, casual eventuality with Nell; and it is not the gliding figure that causes the fear, so much as that final mental realization, the thought striking her. What follows is hair-raising certainly, beyond all but the best of Poe, and far beyond Collins and Lefanu, even where Dickens carries the game into their territory. And how delicately maintained is the inner psychological integrity. Not only is the angle of narration maintained rigorously, but every suspension device in the thriller-writer's armory is exploited to conjure and place exactly the quality of Nell's fear. We have the serving-girl's casual chatter about her unsatisfactory position, Nell's anxious ramblings before sleep, the fitful sleep itself ("troubled by dreams of falling from high towers, and waking with a start and in great terror", p. 228), then again, the gliding figure, in the room this time . . . "there, between the foot of the bed and the dark casement, it crouched and slunk along, groping its way with noiseless hands, and stealing round the bed." Dickens has prepared the way for the realization well: every detail about the intruder suddenly remembers itself as being supremely applicable to the Grandfather himself. Dickens *has* been describing him all the time: like Nell we didn't know, and yet subliminally suspected. In retrospect the whole episode becomes a presentation of the old man's anti-self. Freed of the daytime persona, the Victorian gentleman plays out an under-life of crime and release. When the "figure" turns towards Nell, the old man achieves his greatest moment of demonic dignity:

> Back again it stole to the window — then turned its head towards her.
> The dark form was a mere blot upon the lighter darkness of the room, but she saw the turning of the head, and felt and knew how the eyes looked and the ears listened. (Chapter 29, p. 228.)

This is at once Dickens's subtlest insurance policy — we see (although we don't, quite) the intruder face to face, and therefore can hardly guess at his real identity, since Dickens isn't trying to conceal it — and the old man's own greatest piece of daring. He appears here divested of his grandpaternal robes, his doddering role; he is free to glide sinisterly. No detail in the episode suggests age: Grandfather Trent has slipped his identity — as he is trying to all the while in his gambling mania — and is correspondingly rejuvenated.[2]

Just before this scene, another of Dickens's deceptive simplicities has emerged in its subtler, underlying sombreness. Like the well-loved face of a doll or a mask distorted in dream, the droll grotesqueries of Mrs. Jarley's Waxworks have become identified in Nell's mind with the ogre of Quilp:

> Quilp indeed was a perpetual nightmare to the child, who was constantly haunted by a vision of his ugly face and stunted figure. She slept, for their better security, in the room where the wax-work figures were, and she never retired to this place at night but tortured herself — she could not help it — with imagining a resemblance, in some one or other of their death-like faces, to the dwarf, and this fancy would sometimes so gain on her that she would almost believe he had removed the figure and stood within the clothes. (Chapter 29, p. 217.)

Mrs. Jarley's Waxworks is one of Dickens's most lovable yet sinister inventions. There is something morbid about a wax-works at the best of times, with which Mrs. Jarley's cosy indefatigability strangely consorts. The list of her blithe transformations makes weird reading: Pitt in a nightgown becomes the hermaphrodite poet, Cowper; and Mary Queen of Scots in drag becomes — Byron. There are odd undertones here — no wonder Miss Monflathers's young ladies screamed! So that just as Grandfather Trent appears in the guise of a thief — and a sinister one, at that — the innocent waxworks reveal nasty ambiguities.

A hundred pages further on from the nocturnal episode at the inn, Grandfather Trent takes on a yet more sinister shade: Nell overhears him agreeing to rob Mrs. Jarley in order to pay his gambling debts to Isaac List and Jowl. The randomness of the actual narrative again does nothing to mar the effect of the writing. By this time the nightmare-mechanism is familiar to us. The systematic distortion of the friendly and the accepted into the alien and the threatening has so far pervaded the atmosphere of the book that Nell herself is transfigured:

> Half undressed, and with her hair in wild disorder, she flew to the old man's bedside, clasped him by the wrist, and roused him from his sleep.
>
> "What's this?" he cried, starting up in bed, and fixing his eyes upon her spectral face.
>
> "I have had a dreadful dream," said the child, with an energy that nothing but such horrors could have inspired. "A dreadful, horrible dream. I have had it once before. It is a dream of grey-haired men like you, in darkened rooms by night, robbing sleepers of their gold. Up, up!" (Chapter 42, p. 318.)

When they fly, again, as in the earlier episode, the two selves of the old man meet, and frighten the child: "As they passed the door of the room he had proposed to rob, she shuddered and looked up into his face. What a white face was that, and with what a look did he meet hers!" (Chapter 42, p. 318.) And with what a shock we read that! What *is* the old man, at that moment?

The chapter concludes with a paragraph of the utmost beauty — a marvel not of virtuosity or Gothic intensity but of tender serenity, formally won from the foregoing fear:

> But as they drew nearer the ruined walls, the moon rose in all her gentle glory, and, from their venerable age, garlanded with ivy, moss, and waving grass, the child looked back upon the sleeping town, deep in the valley's shade: and on the far-off river with its winding track of light: and on the distant hills; and as she did so, she clasped the hand she held, less firmly, and bursting into tears, fell upon the old man's neck. (Chapter 42, p. 319.)

(Dickens's use of the word "track" is of some interest, incidentally. It is a point I shall return to.) This is directly followed by the awful barge trip (beautifully managed, the bargees both brutal and indifferent); then comes the Black Country writing, magnificent in its spontaneous life and accuracy. The sequence is important: nowhere, probably, does *The Old Curiosity Shop* sustain its inner development to such purpose as here. By sinuously drawn paths Dickens has wound us into the heart of England — geographically and spiritually (these *are* Blake's mills) — and into the centre of Nell's nightmare. The descriptions are too familiar to need quotation: they exemplify the most characteristic features of Dickens's art — energy, local finesse and accuracy, and above all hallucinatory vision. To see the chapters in the Black Country as mere graphic brilliance is to place them with the best of *Sketches by Boz;* in fact, they are imaginatively and organically related to the real core of the novel, and in particular to the soberly rendered terrors of the two incidents I have dealt with above. Dickens has actualized that inferno Nell's mind has been hovering over in sleep since Quilp's insinuation into the womb-world of the Shop in the opening chapters. Dickens's triumph is to have reached this climax of intensity so naturally. As in the best of Dickens's later symbolism, the greatness of the achievement is the ease and convincing nature of its realism. Nothing of the realistic atmosphere is lost in acquiring symbolic dimensions: the Black Country is both inner and outer.

At this point in the novel, however, Dickens momentarily loses his grip on the inner reality of the story. And here one approaches the distinction between inner and outer actions. The actual incidents and contrivances by which Dickens manages to get Grandfather Trent into his scrapes — the overheard conversations, the chance meetings — all belong to the Gothic novel, and to the picaresque tradition proper. The inner purpose served by these superficially clumsy devices not only justifies but actually necessitates their employment. In the context of the evolving fable of the old man's double self, and Nell's flight from Quilp — and *then* from Grandfather himself — the wayside gypsies and even Mrs. Jarley's waxworks assume dreamlike significance. But the decline of the novel at this stage cannot be justified in this way: it is not the outer events that distress one, but the inner fable itself.

For Grandfather Trent's redemption now has to be engineered.

> It was a slight incident, and might have been design or accident, or the child's unconscious sympathy with youth. But it seemed to strike upon her grandfather, though he had not noticed it before. (Chapter 54, p. 408.)

After this, it comes as no surprise when the next chapter begins:

> From that time, there sprung up in the old man's mind, a solicitude about the child which never slept or left him. (P. 409.)

It is a tone familiar to readers of Dickens: it signals that an emotional change is being engineered. In the present case, the contrast with the delicacy of the best of the previous writing is painful. One remembers the balance of tone attained, the poise, in a mode that is as significant an element of Dickens's art as the blood and thunder: "It is a dream of grey-haired men like you, in darkened rooms by night, robbing sleepers of their gold." (P. 318.) Dickens's great achievement here is soberly to have registered the horrors of fear and uncertainty.

The quiet elegance of the movement of his prose at these moments stands in direct ratio to the intensity of the subject-matter. So that when one speaks of his expressionism it is this also one intends.

The decline becomes a rout downhill, of course, culminating in Nell's death, by which stage Dickens is totally absolved from imaginative participation in the true life of the story. The universal scorn for the famous episode is fair judgment on a major failure of Dickens's: only when she passes out of Dickens's hands into those of his public persona (into Quilp's, as it sometimes seems!) does Nell acquire the odious nimbus through which generations of readers have seen her. "She was dead. Dear, gentle, patient, noble Nell was dead." etc. It is his own childhood that Dickens is sobbing over here: but he is also pandering to the base sense of guilt with which he has harried his heroine throughout the book. Grandfather Dickens is flagellating himself to compensate for the demonic release of the double life.

The gruesomeness of the death scene itself has been often enough stressed. Yet the real tragedy is less that the ghost of Richardson should have triumphed over the ghost of Fielding, than that the genuine excellence of the earlier stages of Nell's dying should so totally be disremembered because of the final bathos. For here — very interestingly contrasted with Kit Nubbles's waking up to life under Barbara's coaxing — Dickens has been exploring a region to which he is the only guide in our literature: that is, the fading of youth into an awareness of the presence of death. (Interestingly, for a parallel to the achievement one must, I think, go to the expressionist painter, Edvard Munch, whose *Krankes Kind* seems possessed of the same kind of lambent awareness as Nell achieves.) We are made aware of this first by a new tone in the writing. After the fear of Grandfather's schizoid escapades, after the inferno of the satanic Midlands (so much closer to the spiritual agony of the Industrial Revolution than the carefully set up model of Coketown in *Hard Times*), Nell reaches the weird ante-world of the schoolmaster's house, with its church and ghostly sexton. The juxtaposition of virginal innocence, with all its immured hope and expectancy, and gentle age is familiar to the Dickens reader. In *Dombey and Son* the strange clairvoyance of little Paul brings to his aged companion, Mrs. Pipchin, an awareness that lifts her out of the comic caricature of her original conception. In *The Old Curiosity Shop* the outer growth seems on the whole to be more significantly responsive to the development of the inner story. Little Paul's death is a superb piece of writing, and his colloquies with Mrs. Pipchin are uncannily penetrating. But Nell's progress towards her death more richly fulfils the initial symbolic nucleus of the story. Nell has to die: yes, but this is not sadism or sentimentality on Dickens's part, it is the whole meaning of the novel that is concerned.

Nell is at this stage of the story surrounded by old people: first, there is the schoolmaster — one of those sad good men Dickens presents (Mr. Mell of *Copperfield* is another) as too passively kind to engage effectively in the social enterprise. His role here is to observe Nell's growing luminosity. ("The poor schoolmaster made her no answer, but bent over her in silence; for his heart was full." Chapter 54, p. 407.) This he does in such a way as to stand perfect interpreter between Dickens and the reader. There are then the Shakespearean elders — the sexton, and old David the gravedigger — with their vanity about their age which so materially assists Nell in arriving at her grasp of Time. Lastly, there is Grandfather Trent himself, symbolizing guilty age and repentence.

Now the church in which Nell begins to spend so much of her time is a religious version of the Curiosity Shop itself. We remember the superb historic atmospherics of the initial description, with its "echoes and gentle clangings". Dickens explores further the implications of that image of Time in the fantasies of the bachelor schoolmaster, which are at the same time acts of wishfulfilment and of moral discrimination: in repressing the unpleasant and exalting the noble aspects of the past, the bachelor instructs Nell in the lessons offered by History. "It was from the lips of such a tutor that the child learnt her easy task." (Chapter 54, p. 401.) The bachelor invests the past with value, he imparts to her a wisdom of truth beyond the ignorance of Quilp's lively malice, the ambiguous folly of Mrs. Jarley's Waxworks — likewise an absurd image of the past — and the simpering weakness of her Grandfather. (Grandfather Trent causes Nell unhappiness and misfortune precisely by his attempts to help her: his gambling and the release of his lower self proceed directly from the desire to get money to keep Nell. It is a typically Dickensian ambivalence.) The act of investiture itself revels in the sense of past we find in Keats's "Eve of St. Agnes" and Coleridge's "Christabel":

> When the bachelor had given her in connection with almost every tomb and flat gravestone some history of its own, he took her down into the old vault, now a mere dull vault, and showed her how it had been lighted up in the time of the monks and how, amid lamps depending from the roof, and swinging censers exhaling scented odours, and habits glittering with gold and silver, and pictures, and precious stuffs, and jewels all flashing and glittering through the low arches, the chaunt of aged voices had been many a time heard there, at midnight, in old days, while hooded figures knelt and prayed around, and told the rosaries of their beads. (Chapter 54, p. 401.)

It is significant that the heraldic wealth of this passage follows Nell's first conversations with the old sexton. Dickens returns here to an image he has used earlier in the novel, the well. (Chapter 15, p. 116.) It is perhaps the key-symbol of the novel. The sexton treats Nell to a chilling description of a well inside the Church (they are outside at the time): once it was full, he says, then progressively, as generation follows generation, less and less full, until you had to lower the bucket until your arm was tired and you had let out nearly all the cord, "you'll hear it of a sudden, clanking and rattling on the ground below; with a sound of being so far down, that your heart leaps into your mouth, and you start away as if you were falling in." (Chapter 53, p. 396.) Casually, Dickens has touched the deepest springs of the book; the well stands for the fear that underlies Nell's flight, and its slow emptying for the span of life. (Earlier the well image had stood for the dungeon of city life.) " 'A dreadful place to come on in the dark!' exclaimed the child who had followed the old man's words and looks until she seemed to stand upon its brink." (P. 396.) Not only Nell, but the reader, too, for Dickens has beautifully exploited the narrative-within-the-narrative to bring us the more surely to the brink of the realization. The sexton's next comment seems to place him as the graveyard sage who knows about the cycle of life and death: " 'What is it but a grave? What else! And which of our old folks, knowing all this, thought, as the spring subsided, of their own failing strength, and lessening life. Not one!' " (Chapter 53, p. 396.) We are impressed: *he* knows. But a little later he himself is surpassed by the current of his own thought: " 'I haven't many by me at this time of year, but these shelves will be full — next summer.' " (P. 397.) " 'How strange that this old man, drawing from his pursuits and everything around him one stern moral never comtemplated its application to himself; and while he dwelt upon the uncertainty of human life seemed both in word and deed to deem himself immortal.' " (P. 397.) At one stroke Dickens goes beyond the tempting profundity and catches the reader out. This, precisely, is the error the sexton sees others daily caught up in. Nell is involved, like the sexton, in the teachings of the dark grave-ridden place but in seeing the irony of the sexton's obliviousness to his own role in the comedy, she places herself in relationship to death. It is a withering wisdom to learn so young. Her own musings are tinged with melancholy: "She took a Bible from the shelf, and read: then, laying it down, thought of the summer days and the bright springtime that would come — of the rays of the sun that would fall in aslant, upon the sleeping forms — of the leaves that would flutter at the window, and play in glistening shadows on the pavement — of the songs of birds, and growth of buds and blossoms out of doors — of the sweet air that would steal in, and gently wave the tattered banners overhead. What if the spot awakened thoughts of death! Die who would, it would still remain the same: these sights and sounds would still go on, as happily as ever." (Chapter 52, p. 398.)

When the old men are niggling about each other's age, and snatching at wisps of hope, Nell cannot understand them, because she knows her day will come, and it makes no difference whether you are very old or very young, much less whether you are seventy-one or seventy-two. One's suspicion — that Nell is getting morbid — is again anticipated by Dickens. The schoolmaster reproaches her for being so sad (significantly, he is "sitting on a green grave in the sun" at the time). When he presses her to explain the reason for her despondency, she admits to having been depressed by the sexton's stories of how quickly people forget the graves they so earnestly tend in the green days of memory. The bachelor now completes his instruction and at the same time brings the entire fable to its true ending and beginning: " 'And do you think that an unvisited grave, a withered tree, a faded flower or two, are tokens of forgetfulness or cold neglect? Do you think there are no deeds, far away from here, in which these dead may be remembered? Nell, Nell, there may be people busy in the world, at this instant, in whose good thoughts these very graves — neglected as they look to us — are the chief instruments.' " (Chapter 54, p. 406.) She grasps the point with a readiness that betokens prior unarticulated awareness. " 'Tell me no more', said the child quickly. 'Tell me no more; I feel I know it. How could I be unmindful of it, when I thought of you?' " (P. 406.) He presses the point — " 'how much charity, mercy, and purified affection, would be seen to have their growth in dusty graves!' 'Yes,' said the child, 'it is the truth; I know it is.' " (P. 406.)

There remains but one unforgettable incident to complete the fable. Dickens returns again to the well image. In the earlier passage, it will be remembered, Nell was only told about the well — so vividly, that it is easy, in recollection, to think that she was actually shown it. It is almost as if Dickens forgot about it in the rhapsodizing over the beauties of the ruins. Now, at last the sexton shows her the well itself.

> They descended into the narrow steps which led into the crypt and paused among the gloomy arches, in a dim and murky spot.
> "This is the place," said the old man. "Give me your hand while you throw back the cover, lest you should stumble and fall in . . . "
> "A black and dreadful place!" exclaimed the child.

The masterstroke comes in the final paragraph, separated from the preceding passage by a space on the page:

> "The birds sing again in spring," thought the child, as she leaned at her casement window, and gazed at the declining sun. "Spring! a beautiful and happy time!" (Chapter 55, p. 413.)

The episode contains the essence of the tale, yet subtly varies the imagery. The well perhaps was made " 'to make the old place more gloomy, and the old monks more religious' " (chapter 55, p. 412) — a clear symbolic variant of the basic idea of the novel, the sacrifice of goodness to engender goodness. That the theme, thus stated, is Christian should not cause surprise. Dickens's Christianity, like Dostoievsky's, is radically allied to his artistic purposes, his entire message of purity, radiance, and charity. Fertility, though, suggests an equally pagan, anthropological interpretation. Such an interpretation really underlies the more specifically Christian emphasis on personal virtue and sanctity much as the older gods and rituals underlay Christianity. Dickens's work as a whole continually alternates between more conscious assertions of morality, and deeper, less easily expressible movements of the mind. In the present instance, the subtly simple detail of the "green grave" the schoolmaster sits on, and Nell's acclamation of spring, form part of a fable of sacrifice and regeneration, death and re-birth, which can be read, or rather felt, both as Christian and as pagan. (Pagan in this context will have to be taken as referring to a sense of rhythm and process that subtends the more ethical consciousness formed by Christianity.)

Nell dies so that others may be better through awareness of her life and death (the parallel with the graves which the schoolmaster tells her are the "instruments" of virtue in others), but also so that Kit Nubbles can be released to Barbara and the life of the body. When Nell is dead, Kit's deadly enemy Quilp is drowned and Kit wakes out of his dream of her to "see" Barbara for the first time.

Parallel with this process runs the redemption of Dick Swiveller, whose name alone suggests that he is the pivotal character of the novel. Swiveller's redemption by the

Marchioness reminds one strongly of Eugene Wrayburn's redemption by Lizzie Hexam in *Our Mutual Friend,* a novel which is also profoundly concerned with regeneration. What is most extraordinary about Dickens, perhaps, is the persistency of concern that runs through all the profligacy of invention: the pristine mythic fables of these first stories are later to be handled mythologically.

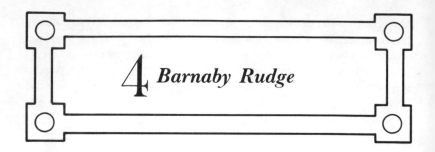

The two histories occur at interesting moments in Dickens's career, conferring a strange equilibrium on his total *oeuvre. Barnaby Rudge* comes at roughly the same stage in relation to the earlier work, as A *Tale of Two Cities* does to the later. In both books Dickens extends, deepens, and gives historical perspective to the vision of society elaborated in the other novels. They differ from the other novels in trying to present an analysis of that almost deterministic conception of the human condition that informs the concreta of his contemporary books and decides their sweep. Being histories, they concern themselves with what history itself presents us with — the movement of men, the spirit of time. As such, they are the most purely political novels he wrote: paradoxically, they are more directly concerned with society than the novels which actually mirror contemporary society. As such, moreover, they differ from most so-called historical novels; for they are not period pieces, where routine situations and stories are tricked out in fancy-dress and vaguely romanticized, like George Eliot's *Romola,* and Thackeray's *Esmond.*[1] They are genuine historical meditations, which lay bare the springs of the Dickens myth itself, and grasp the spirit, the very essence of political change and the class-struggle.

At first sight, the histories appear to step outside the slowly evolving continuum of the myth proper: neither *Barnaby* nor the *Tale* offers any direct parallel to the skeletal myth with its aspiring orphan, promised reward, sickeningly reversed fortune, and ultimate triumph, which we have observed to lie at the heart of his *oeuvre*. Yet it is more than the obsession with imprisonment that unites these two novels with the rest of Dickens's work. They not only continue the investigation into the foundations of the myth, they supply it with a political and historical rationale. For what is the Dickens myth but an implement by which Dickens seeks to lever himself out of darkness, poverty, and menace, and what is the subject of *Barnaby Rudge* but the irruption of this menace into the order and stability of civilized life? In *Barnaby Rudge* Dickens portrays the proletariat attempting to take over the bourgeois world. He is horrified at the thought, and tries to allay the dread by enacting the defeat of the revolt, and the restoration of order and the *status quo*. As we shall see this conscious intention is at many points frustrated and confuted by Dickens's own ambivalence towards the working class and towards the conservative order itself. He, too, wants to tear down the prisons. He sees, moreover, that inflexibility invites destruction. He is aware that society is a restlessly developing organism, and to this awareness he owes his central place in the tradition of European realism.

In *Barnaby Rudge* Dickens dramatizes and makes visible the intangible force of a crowd's will. In doing so, he realizes the abstract concept of historical change. He succeeds in relating the historical process to the quirks and intentions of private individuals, revealing the notion of historical change itself to be the action of a highly charged general will made by individuals, each with his own history, but collectively generating a vortex of force that sweeps everything up into itself to become something qualitatively different.

The structure of the book mirrors the way it was actually written. Other commitments forced Dickens to put the project aside for five years — fortunately, in the event: for the time-lapse enabled him to compose in the pre-conscious strata of the mind a relaxed polyphonic structure, whose serpentine involutions powerfully assist the inexorability of the basic theme. In the narrative itself, there is also a time-gap of five years, between the thirty-second and thirty-third chapters. In the first part of the story, the characters are involved together; time is allowed for them to fuse and mature. Psychologically the trick works, whether one reads the book slowly or at one sitting: the *fact* of the five-year lapse causes in the mind some digestive process such as Dickens requires for the development of his tale. The bridge, interestingly, is the Maypole Inn, symbol of stasis, of *l'ancien régime,* with its Hardyesque locals and its landlord John Willett, the stalwart representative of the Tory past. The inn is an important part of the novel's meaning; its homely warmth and solid old-world splendour are celebrated with deep affection:

> Blessings on the old house, how sturdily it stood! How did the vexed wind chafe and roar about its stalwart roof; how did it pant and strive with its wide chimneys, which still poured forth from their hospitable throats, great clouds of smoke, and puffed defiance in its face; how, above all, did it drive and rattle at the casement, emulous to extinguish that cheerful glow, which would not be put down and seemed the brighter for the conflict! (Chapter 33, p. 248.)

Houses often function in Dickens as symbols of beneficence or malignancy, as social or psychological symbols. The Maypole Inn receives the full treatment: even for Dickens the splendours of its bar (metaphorized as a grove in homage to its lemons) arouse an unusually powerful nostalgia for the past:

> The profusion too, the rich and lavish bounty, of that goodly tavern! It was not enough that one fire roared and sparkled on its spacious hearth; in the tiles which paved and compassed it, five hundred flickering fires burnt brightly also. It was not enough that one red curtain shut the wild night out, and shed its cheerful influence on the room. In every saucepan lid, and candlestick, and vessel of copper, brass, or tin that hung upon the walls, were countless, ruddy hangings, flashing and gleaming with every motion of the blaze, and offering, let the eye wander where it might, interminable vistas of the same rich colour. The old oak wainscoting, the beams, the chairs, the seats, reflected it in a deep dull glimmer. There were fires and red curtains in the very eyes of the drinkers, in their buttons, in their liquor, in the pipes they smoked. (Chapter 33, p. 248.)

And yet the wind is at it, ravaging and harrying, hungering to get in and have its way: "above the rumbling in the chimney, and the fast pattering on the glass, was heard a wailing, rushing sound, which shook the walls as though a giant's hand were on them; then a hoarse roar as if the sea had risen; then such a whirl and tumult that the air seemed mad . . . " (p. 247). The sea image dominates the crowd scenes in *A Tale of Two Cities*, where the handling of metaphor and personification is in general far bolder than in *Barnaby Rudge*. Here, almost unconsciously, the future violence is heard far off, as it is also ironically invoked in the emphasis upon the time-honoured peacefulness of the scene.

The Maypole is to be totally wrecked, its landlord, John Willett, driven half-witted. But the landlord's own crass stupidity seems, like the peace and complacency of his inn and the way of life it serves, to invite the nemesis. With heavy condescension, he drives his own son Joe out into the world, and tyrannically harbours the rebel gypsy Hugh. Thus, the Maypole idyll is not harped upon for merely dramatic reasons. Old John Willett's antiquated paternalism begs to be shaken out of itself. Dickens loved the prelapsarian world of eighteenth century England. It is the more interesting, therefore, that in stressing its lovable old ways, he suggests that things cannot continue like this forever: life does not allow it. Life is a process, and that which resists the most firmly, the most surely forces time or history to exert upon it pressure equal to its own recalcitrance, and destroy it. If the very solidity of the Maypole invites destruction, so does old John's high-handed treatment of his son, and his stupid blindness to the true nature of Hugh, the gypsy.

Dickens is careful from the start to juxtapose and contrast the old man's surly stolidity with the gypsy's wild abandon, his ramblings through the fields in company with the lunatic Barnaby and a pack of dogs. Barnaby's affection for Hugh endows the gypsy with a redeeming grace, in fact. If Barnaby stands for intuitive spontaneity, his fresh affectionate nature responds to something fine in Hugh's roughness. The gypsy's natural sexual vigour compels our admiration, in spite of his brutality. Thus, he takes on the libidinous energy usually reserved in the early Dickens for loyal retainers like Mark Tapley. In this book, in fact, the loyal servant, Hugh's fellow-sufferer Joe Willett, so completely identifies himself with his (freely chosen) master, Edward Chester, as to lose his proletarian manner completely, leaving Hugh to symbolize procreative energy alone. Unable to bear his father's treatment any longer, and (significantly enough) rejected by the flighty Dolly Varden, Joe runs away for a soldier, to return later in the story with his right arm missing, an appropriate symbolic castration. Thus far the fable is fairly clear: just as Rochester must be maimed and blinded before Jane Eyre can accept him, so Joe Willett has to be purged of his native sexual wholeness before Dolly Varden can offer herself to him, *com*passion conveniently taking over from passion.

If Joe sacrifices his virility in the process of becoming socially respectable, Hugh the gypsy in retaining his potency (and even increasing it) is pushed farther and farther out of decent society. Hugh's reaction to old John's high-handedness was always different from Joe's: his dumb insolence masked an uncrushable scorn. The landlord fears him but thinks he can control him, like a useful but treacherous dog that needs to be watched. But Hugh is also shown off to the visitors: to demonstrate his agility he is made to run up the maypole and stick the old man's hat on the top of it. If we see in the relationship between old John and Hugh a paradigm of the social structure — the landlord being to the established property-owning class what Hugh is to the (potentially lawless) working class — we observe once again the equation between energy, virility, and lawlessness that obtains throughout the early Dickens. Hugh's prank up the maypole reveals naturally and easily the phallic origin of the inn's name, and old John acts for his class in delegating sexual vigour to the repressed and outlawed element of society. Thus it is significant that Willett treats Hugh as "a animal" and that Hugh never loses his air of physical grace:

The light that fell upon this slumbering form, showed it in all its
muscular and handsome proportions. It was that of a young man,
of a hale athletic figure, and a giant's strength, whose sunburnt
face and swarthy throat, overgrown with jet black hair, might
have served a painter for a model. (Chapter 11, pp. 85—86.)

It is clear that Dickens too felt the attraction in Hugh. It is
this attractive satyr, bursting with life and sensuality, and the
idiot Barnaby, a saintly fool, all folk wisdom and true
naivety, who are to lead the rioters in their bid to overthrow
the established order — the order that is in part symbolized in
the doltishness of John Willett. Thus, the riots release
suppressed energy and imagination: ironically, Old John
regards Barnaby as lacking imagination. The book consistently aligns sexual energy with imagination in a most interesting way. G. K. Chesterton long ago noted Dickens's
ambivalence towards the riots,[2] especially as concentrated in
the Quilp-like figure of Dennis the Hangman, a ring-leader
among the rioters, who nevertheless retains a devout and
sincere faith in doing things in a "constitoosh'nal" way. Yet
the ambiguities comprehended in the figure of Barnaby and
Hugh are much more profound and interesting. Dennis after
all is a brilliant farce-figure, who, though lively, entirely lacks
Quilp's magnetism. Hugh's grace and Barnaby's intuitive
imagination, on the other hand, are so strongly rendered and
approved, that it seems especially important to find them on
the side of the rioters.

In point of fact, the lines of loyalty and legality are
crossed throughout the novel. Hugh, the bastard gypsy, turns
out to be the son of Sir John Chester, the viciously effete
Protestant gentleman, whose exquisite malice sets him against
his own son, the "good" Edward, and his rival, the sober
worthy Catholic, Geoffrey Haredale. (Dickens reverses the
traditional Puritan—Cavalier roles: the Protestant Chester is
vain, brilliant, callous; the Catholic Haredale, dour, puritanic,
dull.) The hatred between Haredale and Chester follows the
Catholic—Protestant schism at the heart of the riots themselves, and provides Dickens with his means of severing the
star-crossed lovers, Emma Haredale and Edward Chester. The

lovers are neither interesting nor memorable: they supply a quite routine source of narrative identification. It is their fortunes — threatened by the mutual hatred of their parents and by the irrational no-Popery of the rioters — we are absorbed in following. But Romantic situations of this kind are rarely more than functional in Dickens: even so early, he had outgrown the Romantic formula that stood Scott in such good stead, and continued to serve later novelists like Turgenev and Conrad. What is more interesting is the involvement in the riots of Mrs Varden, the hypochondriac Protestant wife of Gabriel, the locksmith once intended to be the novel's eponymous hero. Gabriel Varden is another of the book's powerful social archetypes, the sturdy artisan, compact of tolerance, good humour, and good sense, an old oak with strong roots neither to be torn up nor blown down. He stands in direct contrast to John Willett, with his inflexible paternalism. Like Willett, Varden is a pillar of the community, and *Barnaby Rudge* is, ultimately, a deeply, reverently conservative novel. It is this conservatism which gives all ambiguities and ambivalences their tension.

The fundamental conservatism emerges nowhere more acidly than in the treatment of Simon Tappertit, Varden's absurd upstart apprentice, and Miss Miggs, Mrs. Varden's conspiratorial maid. Tappertit — the "noble captain", luminary of the Secret Society of Prentice Knights — is a brilliantly comic study in petty ambition, in love with his own lower limbs. " 'His precious limbs!' cried Staff, clasping one of his ankles. 'Shall a Miggs aspire to these proportions!' " (Chapter 18, p. 140.) No, and neither shall Tappertit aspire above *his* station: he is mercilessly pilloried by his creator for daring to think romantically of his master's daughter:[3] " 'Something will come of this. I hope it mayn't be human gore' " Tappertit growls as he grinds Varden's tools — burlesque, yet real, precisely as the riots themselves are. Tappertit's story is carried through consistently in the same comic-cruel vein, from the fierce contemptuous imprecations that follow the blind man's mocking adulation of the "precious limbs", to the final glimpse we have of him after the riots — the precious limbs long since replaced by wooden legs — punished by his wife "by taking off his legs, and leaving him exposed to the derision of those urchins who delight in mischief." (P. 631.)

Something of this violent grotesque comedy attends all the characters who are implicated in the riots, from the active participants, like Simon himself and Dennis the Hangman, to those who, like Mrs. Varden, Miggs, and John Chester, are held responsible through some mean or vengeful spite. The riots may release repressed energy; they also express the narrow intolerance that has always historically attached to the Protestant religion. Miggs's vinegary malice, Mrs. Varden's hypochondria, Tappertit's envy, Sir John Chester's vindictive dislike of his Catholic school-friend, Haredale, all these elements fuse with the violent untapped energy of Hugh, the weird incorruptibility of Barnaby, and the sadism of Dennis into the collective unease that is to be channelled by Lord George Gordon, and his aide Gashford.

Dickens's treatment of Gordon is unimpeachably fair — an important moment for him to have suspended his customary rhetoric of persuasion. If Gordon had been treated like Gashford, the objectivity that gives the whole movement its head would be missing. Gashford caricatures an easily recognizable type forced to the surface in violent social upheaval — the evil lieutenant, eager for blood and destruction, tireless in his service of the Leader, yet ultimately treacherous, and ready to drop the Cause for the next that comes along. Gashford has this strange melange of fawning affection and ultimate treachery convincingly enough to make him a good foil for Gordon. But Dickens's handling of the leader is of a different order. Gashford is presented as a plain double-dealer, blatantly working on his master's vanities, and speaking villanies aloud when he has the stage alone — " '—Dreamed he was a Jew', he said thoughtfully, as he closed the bedroom door. 'He may come to that before he dies. It's like enough. Well! After a time, and provided I lost nothing by it, I don't see why that religion shouldn't suit me as well as any other. There are rich men among the Jews;

shaving is very troublesome; — yes it would suit me well
enough. For the present, though, we must be Christian to the
core . . ' ". (Chapter 37, p. 280.) If Gordon were presented
like this, there could be no dramatic force behind the riots at
all; they would be reduced to farce. But Dickens is scrupu-
lously careful in his handling of the Leader. The dream
Gashford is referring to here in itself strikes just the right
note of tortured paranoia: " 'I dreamed that we were Jews,
Gashford. You and I — both of us — Jews with long
beards.' " (Chapter 37, p. 279.) And the initial description of
Gordon sets a standard of psychological veracity from which
Dickens never deviates. The most important insight in the
portrait is the restlessness beneath the studious melancholy.
Gordon is, like Milton's Satan, "disfigured, more than could
befall Spirit of happy sort":

> As he stood musing in the red glow of the fire, it was striking to
> observe his very bright large eye, which betrayed a restlessness of
> thought and purpose, singularly at variance with the studied
> composure and sobriety of his mien, and with his quaint and sad
> apparel. It had nothing harsh or cruel in its expression; neither
> had his face, which was thin and mild, and wore an air of melan-
> choly; but it was suggestive of an air of indefinable uneasiness,
> which infected those who looked upon him, and filled them with
> a kind of pity for the man: though why it did so, they would
> have had some trouble to explain. (Chapter 35, pp. 266–67.)

Thereafter, the details of his deportment follow the pattern
laid down here. One remembers his horrible nail-biting, and
the ugliness of his oratory: he speaks "in a loud voice, and
with great abundance of ungainly gesture." (Chapter 43, p.
328.) It is a subtle portrait of a humourless innocent, com-
pensating for a deficiency in sympathy and sensibility with
an excess of rigorous righteousness.

Out of these elements the rebellion grows with steadily
mounting momentum: in the end we have the phenomenon
of history and social change concretely before us on the page.
The task made demands on Dickens's linguistic virtuosity
such as were, perhaps, never made again. All the force of his
animistic expressionism for once received an object equal to
its own nature. That excess (as it sometimes seems) of energy

that drove him into distortion and exaggeration of the "ordinary" here revels legitimately in external fury. German Expressionism was later to discover that the extremes of horror can be compassed only in two things: insanity and murder. Whatever our attitude towards penal measures may become, it is unlikely that murder and madness will ever lose the metaphysical horror they held for Poe, Dostoievsky, and Dickens. Ultimately, it seems, real evil can only be satisfactorily expressed in terms of physical violence.

In the Gordon riots, then, Dickens found the perfect correlative for his own inner turbulence. Paradoxically, the style strikes by its sobriety. It is, of course, a rhetorical sobriety: the air of factually recording what happened represents artificed achievement as much as the more obvious brilliance of his animism. The details of the violent action absorb the energy of his imagination: the result is a magnificent piece of "historical" reportage that contrasts interestingly with the excesses of Carlyle. Any excess of emphasis, Dickens seems to have felt, would reduce belief or blur the effect of objectively recorded violence he wanted.

The whole episode, from its beginning in the first assemblage at Westminster in chapter 48 to its exhaustion at the end of chapter 73, extends over two hundred pages. Never afterwards did Dickens surpass the sustained energy and brilliance of this achievement. It stands as the finest thing of its kind not only in Dickens, but in the entire canon of the European novel. The packed energy of the description, the surge and counter-surge of the action, the sinuous, unflagging momentum and vitality of the narrative line, make it a highpoint in the history of Western literature. Dickens's competitors here — Hugo, Sienkiewicz, Scott, Manzoni — simply fall by the way. In this, as in so many other modes, Dickens is without equal.

Quotation, clearly, cannot possibly suggest what is perhaps its greatest single quality — the controlled crescendo, rising from the initial restless stirrings at Westminster to the tearing down of the prison. Or the way in which Dickens times the pauses, the muttering of the citizens' counter-measures, the slow hesitant assertion of the Law, the lulls in the rioters' depredations:

> When the sun rose, it shone into handsome apartments filled with armed men; the furniture hastily heaped away in corners, and made of little or no account, in the terror of the time — on arms glittering in city chambers, among desks and stools, and dusty books — into little smoky churchyards in odd lanes and by-ways, with soldiers lying down among the tombs, or lounging under the shade of the one old tree, and their pile of muskets sparkling in the light — on solitary sentries pacing up and down in courtyards, silent now, but yesterday resounding with the din and hum of business — everywhere on guardrooms, garrisons, and threatening preparations. (Chapter 67, p. 513.)

And there it is, a city under siege, or during revolution, its ordinary business suspended. And suddenly, without pre-arrangement or premeditation, the mob reassambles and starts tearing things down again:

> ... in half an hour, or less, as though the setting in of night had been their preconcerted signal, the rioters having previously, in small parties, prevented the lighting of the street lamps, rose like a great sea; and that in so many places at once, and with such inconceivable fury, that those who had the direction of the troops knew not, at first, where to turn or what to do. (Chapter 67, p. 516.)

Here as everywhere in these astonishing two hundred pages, we find the historian at work, not the rhetorician. And no historian better understood the pulsations of time. Just as the whole movement appeared to be bred inexorably out of the tiny resentments, grudges, ambitions, and pettinesses of insignificant individuals, so, when the madness dies out, these same individuals meet appropriately savage fates. Hugh dies, heroically, on the scaffold; Tappertit, the vengeful little up-start, has his beautiful legs smashed for him; John Willett remains in the state of semi-idiocy to which the shock of the rioters' attack on his inn had reduced him; Mrs. Varden, spared but devastated, at last purges herself not only of her bigotry but of the vinegary Miggs, who, driven out of the Varden household, becomes a bitterly frustrated turnkey at a women's prison.

The ugly frustrated spinster, eaten away with envy of

pretty girls, is a common figure of fun in the early Dickens. On the whole this is not something the admirer of Dickens has much reason to be satisfied with. But Miggs's final leave-taking from the Vardens assumes a greater significance than such a scene would seem intrinsically to possess. For her last torrential outburst of malice and envy against Mrs. Varden and Dolly — whom ludicrously she had always assumed to be her rival for Tappertit's affections — in fact becomes a final warning to them: distorted as they are, Miggs's vicious taunts strike painfully at Dolly's silly flirtatiousness and Mrs. Varden's dreary hypochondria. So they can make no reply, and Miggs, "her vexation and chagrin being of that internally bitter sort which finds no relief in words, and is aggravated to madness by want of contradiction" (p. 618), at last collapses in tears, to reveal a degree of frustration which deprives the scene of the music-hall humour Dickens seems initially to have intended. The final vision of Miggs, deserted at last by her outraged nephew, and left to manage her box alone, is wretched and chastening by any standards: "Miss Miggs, all blowzed with the exertion of getting there, and with her sobs and tears, sat down upon her property to rest and grieve, until she could ensnare some other youth to help her home." (P. 618.) Dickens was in many ways a strikingly immature man at twenty-nine, when he wrote these words; yet his genius for inhabiting and enduring existences not his own has already carried him beyond his waking assumptions. So that although Gabriel Varden at once calls upon his wife to laugh at the incident, the sensible generosity of Varden himself robs the adjuration of any callowness. We remember again that the original title of the work was to be *Gabriel Varden, the Locksmith of London,* and Varden remained the book's centre of gravity, a reactionary figure, like Pickwick, yet, like him also, broad-minded, fond of his pint, and in every way opposed to the fanaticism of the sort of Protestantism that had made his wife so hard to live with. Thus, as in *Pickwick,* a Chaucerian Catholicity of outlook is set against a kill-joy bigotry, just as respect for order and tradition is set against counter-jumping and "absurd" pretension. At this stage at least, the workers are to know their place, and their over-weening ambition is punished.

Yet Dickens's attitude towards these matters was, as I have argued above, crucially ambivalent. Varden is admired for his flexibility as much as for the traditional solidity he shares with John Willett. It is as we have seen a savage book in the thoroughness of its vengeances. For that well-loved stage-coach world is, in effect, itself smashed by the emotional energy that wrecked Newgate. Contrasted with those earlier loving descriptions of the Maypole Inn in its prime is this grim evocation of its historical nemesis:

> The night, without, looked black and cold through the dreary gaps in the casement; the precious liquids, now nearly leaked away, dripped with a hollow sound upon the floor; the Maypole peered ruefully in through the broken window, like the bowsprit of a wrecked ship; the ground might have been the bottom of the sea, it was so strewn with precious fragments. (Chapter 55, p. 417.)

The powerful thrust of the sea-metaphor consummating itself here emphasizes yet again how profoundly poetic is Dickens's use of symbol, image, and figure. This is no added grace to the texture, no fortuitous recurrence of image, but the con-summation of meaning: Dickens's prose has seen to it that we too have experienced the process of the sea.

This is no impartial process: it reflects also Dickens's own fundamental self-division. It is more than that Dickens is both with and against the rioters. At one level, *Barnaby Rudge* is a horrified warning against political and industrial violence, stiffened by memories of the Poor Law and Chartist riots of the 1830s. At another, it is an attack on repressive institutions. And at the same time as it celebrates, nostal-gically, the virtues of stability and order, it ridicules the stupidity of ossified elitism. Thus the novel presents an image of historical inevitability that, against Dickens's own will as it were, transcends the individual ingredients. The image of the vortex which recurs several times in the description of the rioting is, perhaps, still more sharply focussed than that of the sea, and still more significant.

In the final analysis, too, the novel suggests the deepest scepticism as to the concept of Law. Dickens was always an enemy of the Law. Usually this emerges in contempt for legal chicanery. But *Barnaby Rudge* makes it clear that his misgivings go deeper than this contempt for the workings of the legal system: "The crowd was the law," he writes, "and never was the law held in greater dread, or more implicitly obeyed." (Chapter 63, p. 480.) The Law, in other words, emerges for the hollow abstraction it really is: when the greater Will takes over, the tacit agreement we call Law stands revealed as an assumption made upon the negative evidence of a general apathy. Only when the spirit of the mob has passed its zenith can the Law retaliate. This profound insight into the nature of the social contract and of legality is one, I fancy, Dickens would rather not have reached: it is stumbled upon, in the course of the imaginative exploration he was called upon to make in evoking the historical incidents.

Thus, *Barnaby Rudge* — the first contemplated of all Dickens novels, and therefore the closest to the traumatic incidents of his own early life — expresses more violently than any other Dickens work the abhorrence in which he held the "vengeful" proletarians. The working class appears here as not only potentially but actually destructive, lawless, violent. Yet he too is one of them; Newgate is torn down for his own gratification.[4] The peculiar nightmare dynamism of the early Dickens stems from this conflicting sense he had of being one with the working classes yet of needing to get away from contact with them.

5 *Martin Chuzzlewit*

It is surprising that the critics who have been so eager to interpret *Bleak House* in terms of the fog that pervades the first chapter of the book, have not yet seized upon the wind at the opening of *Martin Chuzzlewit,* and seen in it a comparable key-signature. Dickens does not, admittedly, interpret the phenomenon for us as he does when he associates the fog with the "groping and floundering" of the Court of Chancery; but it is in keeping with the general trend of his development to harness to deliberate symbolic purpose what had once been left to the reader's powers of imaginative synthesis. But, arguably, the wind that wakes up on the second page of the opening chapter of *Martin Chuzzlewit* (nominally chapter 2, of course — the first chapter is simply irrelevant) is no less the master-"symbol" of the ensuing narrative. The fog occupies only the first two pages of *Bleak House:* there is a reference to it on the fifth page, and the whole short first chapter takes place *within* the fog of that November afternoon. But only the first two pages actually *describe* the fog, and the impression that so many of us have that *Bleak House* is a novel enveloped in fog is a tribute to Dickens's descriptive powers. The wind rises on page two of *Martin Chuzzlewit,* after a loving evocation of the Wiltshire village which ranks as one of finest things in the earlier Dickens; the wind then teases the village, rowdies about uncontrollably, introduces us to Mr. Pecksniff (by knocking the great hypocrite over) and finally hurries away "rejoicing, roaring over moor and meadow, hill and flat, until it got out to sea, where it met with other winds similarly disposed, and made a night of it." (P. 10.) There is a primeval pagan energy in this wind, something that sends us back to Faust's *Walpurgisnacht* and Peer Gynt's tall stories for adequate comparison: Dickens is serving us notice here of a certain power of fantasy, of action, of coercion, which is to hurtle through the following eight hundred pages — a mischievous, malicious power, often, that makes free with conventions and norms of moral practice. No other Dickens novel has quite such tempestuous energy, quite such unpredictable gusto. In an *oeuvre* shot through by the excitement of travel, this is the novel whose narrative patterns most crucially depend upon the curious thrill and tension of setting off, and putting one's life in the balance. The action sweeps us from Wiltshire to London, from London to New York, from New York to Eden (the longest trip, in more ways than one), back again to London, in time for the young hero to witness Pecksniff's most bare-faced act, from there to Salisbury, and from Salisbury back finally to London, a showdown, and a peace of delighted exhaustion. The "problem" for the critic who wants to do more than merely gape and applaud the brilliance and panache of the writing is considerable: there seems to be no conscious design ordaining these reckless dashes and retrievals, yet our experience of art tells us that there is no such thing as the purely "intuitive" work; no work just gets itself written. What, then, is the "secret" of *Martin Chuzzlewit,* if we are to attempt the finer definition of these vague plaudits, and to establish respectably what ought, I think, to be accepted, that it is one of Dickens's most extraordinary and impressive achievements?

The wind-symbol, which might be offered as a kind of binding element, clearly won't do as an "explanation" of the novel's structure. The wind isn't labelled by Dickens or related by him to anything that happens later. This doesn't mean that it does not play the sort of role (semi-symbolic, semi-functional) I have attributed to it. On the contrary much of the structural work in a novel (which is a form innately hostile to self-identifying symbolisms) must be carried out in this way: the objects and events in the narrative themselves constitute the artistic significance of the work. It is a mistake to try to elaborate these significances in other terms than those in which they are embodied: one-to-one symbol structures are alien to the novel, yet symbolism which isn't dyadic is not really symbolism at all. Enough to say, then, that the wind has a peculiar appropriateness in the early pages of *Martin Chuzzlewit,* unleashing the events in a violent gusty way that succeeds in directing our attention and expectations as Dickens requires. The twists and turns the story takes will be, we may presume, *wind-like* — or Dickens has wasted his effort.

But there is of course another "device" in *Martin Chuzzlewit,* a more obvious form of structuring, one which many of my readers will have raised in their minds when I stated above that there is no apparent structural principle in the book. In one important respect, at least, *Martin Chuzzlewit* differs radically from its predecessors. For the grandfather of the novel's eponymous hero throughout the narrative is pretending to be what he is not: the events in the action are guaranteed from first to last by a concealed stratagem of old Martin Chuzzlewit. Everything in the book stems from this device. The element of sheer chance which time after time upsets and re-rights *Oliver Twist* has been eliminated, the whole basis of security upon which the young Martin Chuzzlewit stands (without knowing it for most of the book) is correspondingly stronger. Oliver was protected by the lucky charm of Dickens's wish-fulfilment; Martin is guaranteed by a moral ingredient of the book itself. The logic which works out the fall of the villains also works out the hero's salvation. The novel stands upon its own values. Thus old Martin's stratagem is more than a formal device (though it is also this): it is an integral part of the moral design of the novel. The plot is determined from within, since everything springs from the old man's decision in the early chapters. The fact that this is concealed from us, and revealed only at the end, in throwing our minds back retrospectively over what was experienced as uncertainty, only serves to increase the strength and solidity of the overall design.

This development, from the "chance" mechanism of *Oliver Twist* to the morally controlled structure of *Martin Chuzzlewit,* is not a matter of the replacement of less by more credible eventualities. We are not, in other words, concerned simply with Dickens's elimination of chance in the interest of a more "realistic" idiom. The use of chance and coincidence in *Oliver Twist* not only effectively serves the meaning and emotion the novel expresses, it *is* the meaning and emotion, in part at least. In *Oliver Twist* chance is used in response to unconscious demands. The kind of advance *Martin Chuzzlewit* represents is to be understood not in terms of any move towards "realism" or any improvement in technique (none was needed), but in the elimination of the element of chance itself: instead of relying on chance — trusting in it — to rescue his hero from impossible situations, Dickens now depends upon the conscious decision taken by the old man. By the same token, the mixture of nervy doubt (suppose Oliver *hadn't* ended up at the Maylies'?) and careless trust reflected in the *Oliver Twist* schema of helpless waif, nasty ogre, and fairy godfather, has been transformed into a greater moral confidence, which can afford to question itself and the world much more rigorously. On examination of *Martin Chuzzlewit,* we shall find that all the mythic elements have been either transfigured or eliminated. The apparent paradox that underlies this development is that the more tightly Dickens governs the moral logic of his novels, the freer he is to subject his materials to doubt and analysis. In this evolution, perhaps, Dickens's career presents in microcosm the development of the novel itself from its picaresque to its high Victorian stage.

The most important single development is the elimination of the fairy godfather figure of the Brownlow-Cheeryble-Garland type. The role played by these unreal gentlemen is taken over by old Martin Chuzzlewit. Now the old man's intention is to find out his relations by submitting them to the only satisfying sort of test: by appearing to be what he is not, he will bring out the real motives of those around him, confirm his suspicion of those he distrusts, and prove the quality of those he really loves. But to some extent one always retains the impression one first had of him in the country inn at the beginning of the novel — a tortured patriarch, surrounded by his hypocritical tribe, and driven to near-insanity by doubt. At first sight, he seems just the sort to fall for Pecksniff's cant and his nephew Jonas's cult of hard business-sense. Jonas Chuzzlewit in fact is like an evil shadow of the old man: they share a common rasping dryness, a familiar concern with money and property which has — apparently — destroyed every other emotion in them. This likeness (enhanced by Phiz's illustrations), serves to make the old man's stratagem credible enough. But there is more than this to be said of the old man's ambiguities: he has a lot to answer for. The plain source of the novel's structural principle, he is — like the Duke in *Measure for Measure* — responsible himself for the confusion of his subjects. He has more than a lot to answer for, in fact: he has everything to answer for. All the strands of the plot issue from him. Pecksniff's regency and his coercion of Mary Graham, young Martin's proving in America, the fraudulent schemes of Montague Tigg and the murder of Tigg by Jonas, even the later actions of the ungovernable Mrs. Gamp — everything can be related back to the old man's manoeuvres.

The old man's apparent abdication is neither godlike nor unambiguous, in point of fact: his experiment is groping and uncertain, and even undertaken for ambiguous reasons. He does not know what is going to happen, and the genuinely pragmatic movement of the narrative — volatile and unstable as it is — reflects this. This much is confessed in the great unmasking scene at the end of the book. This second family gathering echoes the first: once again the principals of the action are called together; Pecksniff seems to be in control, young Martin thinks he is still out of favour. It is the thrashing of Pecksniff we want to witness, of course, and Dickens doesn't disappoint us. But the scene is impressive most of all for the handling of the old man's role: the gathering is the occasion not for the triumphant revelation of purpose vindicated, but for confessions:

> "There is a kind of selfishness," said Martin: "I have learned it in my own experience of my own breast: which is constantly upon the watch for selfishness in others; and holding others at a distance by suspicions and distrusts, wonders why they don't approach, and don't confide, and calls that selfishness in them. Thus I once doubted those about me — not without reasons in the beginning — and thus I once doubted you, Martin." (Chapter 52, p. 804.)

Dickens's consistent use of the words self and selfishness is important: but it would be a mistake to allow the ultimate goal of this morality to blind us to the many subtleties and profundities of the means by which it is enunciated. If we just regard the book as a diatribe against selfishness we shall distort much of its actual content, and miss some of its most important findings. This will emerge as significant especially when we come to consider young Martin's experiences in Eden. Here, such an approach would confuse the issue of the old man's confessed implication in the action: it wasn't just selfishness that lay at the root of his own conduct, but suspicion, doubt, an inward duplicity bred by years of materialism and business. He does not know whom to trust because he knows of no certain source of illumination in himself: he has become consumed by the code of systematic scepticism and suspicion by which he has lived. Moreover, it was not a desire for Martin's moral maturation that prompted the experimental testing that drove him out of England, but pride and possessiveness: " 'I hoped to bring you back, Martin, penitent and humbled. I hoped to distress you into coming back to me. Much as I loved you, I had that to acknowledge which I could not reconcile it to myself to avow, then, unless you made submission to me first. Thus it was I lost you.' " (Chapter 52, p. 804.) This admission is followed immediately by old Martin's expression of regret as to the fate of Montague Tigg; he had paid Tigg to follow young Martin in London, and find out where he lived so that he could be sent money. From this small payment, perhaps, grew the little capital Tigg needed to set himself up in fraudulent business: " 'If I have had, indirectly, any act or part in the fate of that unhappy man, by putting means however small, within his reach; Heaven forgive me!' " (Pp. 806–7.) The old man's confession continues with an interesting reflection on his role-playing: his feigned "infirmity" not only teaches him what it would be like to be in misery, but it informs him that he would have brought it upon himself. (The young Martin Chuzzlewit is to find out something important about himself by a comparable switch of roles later.) It concludes with the admission that he had always known the young people — Mary Graham and Martin — to be right for each other, but that he could not bear their having found this out for themselves; "because the grace of his design was lost" (p. 808). But it was more than the jealous pride that enraged him. His compulsive suspicion of human motive had so far corrupted his judgment and feeling that he could take their love to be cynically adventuristic: they were "already like the world, and bent on their own selfish, stealthy ends". This is a far more damaging and a far more precisely formulated admission than any the old man has yet made; and it is typical of a kind of feeling or rather perversion of feeling that runs through the whole of *Martin Chuzzlewit*.

The Chuzzlewits are a great nineteenth century clan — a dynasty which, Dickens's actual first chapter (a disastrous relapse to the facetiousness of *Pickwick*) warns us, is going to be dealt with in predominantly comic terms. *Martin Chuzzlewit* is, we may as well state it directly, the great comic epic in the the English language. It is epic in its scale — its swiftness of movement, its impression of a society at work, its disregard, ultimately, for the private perspective; it is comic in the final ordering of its values and attitudes. But the comic vein in which it is handled shouldn't blur the relations its commerical dynasty holds with other nineteenth century families: one thinks of the Karamazovs, for instance; those later commercial dynasties of Gorky's — the Artamonovs and the Kashirins; and Galsworthy's Forsytes. Closer to hand, and less obviously related, is George Eliot's

Middlemarch, in many ways a "realistic" version of Dickens's book. Old Martin Chuzzlewit, paranoiacally at bay, reappears as Peter Featherstone, whose tribe also surround his bed, trying to steer the bequests their way; Mary Graham appears as Mary Garth (the old man's honest handmaid); there is a young man to be tried (Fred Vincy), and a master-hypocrite, Bulstrode, and so on. I cite the influence not in order to suggest rankings, but on the contrary to indicate the close relations that may run under surface disparity: George Eliot's characters may appear either dried out, in comparison with Dickens's, or simply more "real" — free of the grotesquerie. But it would be as sensible to disqualify Brueghel's peasants on account of an admiration for Van Eyck's burghers or to deny the pungency of Rabelais out of deference to Cervantes, as to value George Eliot's rational "normality" more highly than Dickens's Gothic expressionism.

There is some commonly limiting pride, hauteur, and suspicion running through Peter Featherstone and old Martin Chuzzlewit: it is the pride and the headstrong resentment of other people's claims to consideration that cause the rift between grandfather and grandson. The old man, I have noted, is a considerable advance on the benevolent capitalists of the earlier Dickens. So too is young Martin an advance on the early heroes and heroines: the fantasy-vehicle of the first books in fact has been abandoned. There is no Nell, Oliver, or Smike, and no need to re-enact the emergence from nightmare that held the early books together. The Freudian "explanation" is wearing thin, the imaginative vision changing fundamentally. Dickens's new hero resembles Nicholas Nickleby in his finely chiselled good looks. But his lounging indolence is from the first contrasted with his friend Tom Pinch's honest industriousness (which never quite becomes abject). Martin is arrogant, conceited, full of a sense of having been marked out by fate for a higher station than an architect's. In the first condescending conversation he holds with Tom (who is immensely impressed) it is made clear that he is riding for a fall. The solid virtue and charity of Tom Pinch imply the hollowness of Martin's conceit, which experience — we are to understand — will inevitably cave in. This is all a little too pointedly done, but it is still a considerable advance upon the unquestioned sanctity of Oliver Twist and even the unsullied decency of Nicholas Nickleby. Martin isn't quite the straightforward romantic lead he would have been earlier: he is to go through some kind of moral and experiential proving. Martin's come-uppance in America seems at first sight a fairly simple affair, the sort of thing one was accustomed to expect in Talbot Baines Reed: the flippant but basically decent swank is knocked off his high horse, and learns to respect the humble friend he has always scorned. The Lesson he learns is that of Self. Such an account — which is on the face of it by no means inadequate — doesn't seem too promising, especially if we have in mind — as Barbara Hardy clearly has in her essay on the book[1] — the various lessons learned by Isobel Archer, Gwendolen Harleth, and others. But it would, I think, be a mistake to take too loftily superior an attitude towards these episodes in *Martin Chuzzlewit*. For we have here an early instance of an imaginative model Dickens was to exploit (more thoroughly and searchingly) in many later books. This is the parabolic voyage through sickness to a new conception of the self and of that self's relations with the outside world. Accompanied by Mark Tapley, the loyal retainer of classical comedy, Martin embarks upon a harrowing journey down the Mississippi (a river Dickens grew to detest in his American tour). Now in the world of the novel, and in the entire canon of which it is a constituent part, the goal of this journey is significantly named: they are bound for a place called Eden, and the name simply but excellently satirizes the basic aspirations of all the early Dickens heroes. The difference between Martin and his predecessors is that Dickens now intimates his conviction that he expects too much from life: more than he should, or has the right to expect. He expects no less than Eden — an unsoiled paradise complete with endless material security and guilt-free sex. What we have here is the first really ironic view of the Dickens myth. In point of fact, the ironic parable is underwritten by the old man's stratagem:

there is a radical difference between Martin's come-uppance and Pip's experience in *Great Expectations*. But we do not know of the old man's plans at the time, and the Eden episode marks a significant stage in Dickens's development. Martin, like Pip, makes a decisive voyage down a river. Several significant mythological references signalize Dickens's intentions (it is always worth paying attention to Dickens's use of mythology). Here we have three main sources: the Genesis story, the Greek myth of Charon, and the mythology of English allegorists. The ironic tone is set by Mark who — on Martin's remarking satirically that he is growing "profoundly sagacious" — observes that it is because he is " 'a day's journey nearer Eden, and am brightening up before I die . . . Perhaps by the time I get there I shall have grown into a prophet.' " (Chapter 23, p. 374.) The gloom of the country that soon surrounds them suggests the Charon myth: "But that, at certain periods, they swallowed food altogether from a common trough, it might have been old Charon's boat, conveying melancholy shades to judgement" (p. 375). This isn't so far from the truth: it is certainly towards a familiarity with Death that Martin is travelling, and the allegoric nature of the journey is emphasized by the reference to Bunyan that follows:

> As they proceed further on their track, and came more and more towards their journey's end, the monotonous desolation of the scene increased to that degree, that for any redeeming feature it presented to their eyes, they might have entered, in the body, on the grim domains of Giant Despair. (Chapter 23, p. 377.)

The occurrence of the word *track* in the passage by the way has its own interest: it is a word Dickens always used superlatively well, and with a fatalistic-deterministic significance. *Way* or *journey* would have been more obvious words to use in the sentence quoted above. Dickens's use of *track* indicates the decisive nature of the journey Martin and Mark are embarked upon. Although the intentions of the parable Dickens is articulating are overt and straightforward — devoid, so it would seem, of any real interest — the complex power and concreteness of the writing make for an experience which is anything but simple. Dickens draws upon his own more or less paranoid reactions to the Mississippi swamp-land to give these paragraphs a particularized force that more than once anticipates the best of Hardy. It's hard, for instance, not to feel that the Hintock woods in *The Woodlanders* owe some of the mordant precision with which they are evoked to this eerie passage:

> The trees had grown so thick and close that they shouldered one another out of their places, and the weakest, forced into shapes of strange distortion, languished like cripples. The best were stunted, from the pressure and the want of room; and high above the stems of all grew long rank grass, dark weeds, and frowsy underwood: not divisible into their separate kinds, but tangled all together in a heap, a jungle deep and dark, with neither earth nor water at its roots, but putrid matter, formed of the pulpy offal of the two, and of their own corruption. (Chapter 23, p. 281.)

Much of Dickens's finest writing celebrates the physical world in an ecstasy of enthusiastic apprehension; but much also originates in near-paranoid revulsion of this sort. Horror and revulsion can relate the subject to the world just as surely as love and pleasure, and the expressionist art of Dickens owes much to this fact.

The experienced Dickens reader will, by this stage of the narrative, already be anticipating a symbolic dying: Mark's joke about being a day nearer Eden; the Charon reference; the frequent allusions to spectors, fatal maladies, decay and corruption; the statement, finally, that none of the men of the Eden settlement "were the men they had been" — the concern and drift are unmistakable. Martin soon wilts under the pressure, and declines into a fever. The experienced reader, again, will anticipate some deeper moral design beyond and within the fever: the self is to be melted down in sickness and re-born into a new awareness — and therefore, quite simply, into a new self altogether. The process has been anticipated in the hero's faintings and re-awakenings in *Oliver Twist*, where the sleep gives the narrative a kind of dream-validity. Oliver falls asleep in one reality, and wakes up in another. In later books — one thinks especially of *Bleak House, Little Dorrit, Great Expectations*, and *Our Mutual*

Friend — Dickens was to exploit the device with increasing profundity and subtlety. In *Martin Chuzzlewit,* we experience the evil swamp as an infernal landscape through which Martin must pass, but there is in fact no interior account of the sickness itself. Instead, we are shown the selfless devotion of his servant, Mark Tapley. Now this apparently should be all: Martin will recover, reflect upon his friend's unselfishness and the painful contrast it makes with his own past behaviour, and change for the better. But Dickens doesn't quite gratify the expectations he has aroused. The actual sickness doesn't of itself make any difference — so far as we know — to Martin's moral attitudes. On the contrary, Dickens is quick to note a characteristically self-preoccupied reaction soon after: "He was yet in a feeble and weak condition, when the misfortune he had so much dreaded fell upon them. Mark was taken ill." (Chapter 33, p. 523.) The noting of this (extremely understandable) fear of Martin's is the sign of a more dispassionate stance in Dickens than one would predict from a perusal of some critics on this episode. Dickens is onto something more interesting here than the simple didactic morality we had perhaps been anticipating.

For it is only now when Mark is ill and he himself at last is forced to swap roles with his loyal servant that Martin Chuzzlewit begins to wheel round to some kind of appraisal of himself. It isn't the moralist's didacticism that governs the narrative here, but the psychologist's curiosity: Martin starts finding out about himself through being forced into a different situation, into a role he has never played before, that of the helper or *servant*. And it is this exchange of roles that throws his own personality into focus — "he began to think, how was it that this man who had had so few advantages, was so much better than he who had had so many?" (P. 524.) In other words, the change that is worked in Martin involves very much more than the simple grateful perception that he had been helped in need, and should help others in turn, *etc.* His earlier reaction (dreading Mark's falling ill) was more than simple selfishness: it was the selfishness specifically of the gentleman *wholly dependent upon his servant.*

Mark had always performed the function he performs as nurse in Martin's sickness, and, initial gratitude once past, there is no reason to believe that the experience would have brought about any profound change in Martin. The real revolution that occurs in Martin Chuzzlewit is a revolution in attitudes towards his own personality, its limits and nature. The starting-point of this re-orientation is fairly straight-forwardly "moral". ("He began to think how it was that this man who had had so few advantages, was so much better than he who had had so many?") But even this moral question is couched in terms of the class-differences between the men ("advantages"), and the train of self-questioning that is prompted is concerned with realities, not duties: "he began to ask himself in what they differed". Now this is in fact a more promising question, because it reflects a newly engendered curiosity about the self, and is less likely to have its processes short-circuited (as Dickens's critics have so often had theirs) by moral attitudinizing. For the first time in his life, Martin is curious not about what he ought to be, but about what he is. To such curiosity, the overt moral aim is in a sense ancillary. Before he can change himself, he must know about himself.

In proof of Martin's new curiosity about himself is the complex reflection that occupies the next paragraph in the book:

> He was assisted in coming to a conclusion on this head by the frequent presence of Mark's friend, their fellow-passenger across the ocean: which suggested to him that in regard to having aided her, for example, they had differed very much. Somehow he coupled Tom Pinch with this train of reflection; and thinking that Tom would be very likely to have struck up the same sort of acquaintance under similar circumstances, began to think in what respects two people so extremely different were like each other, and were unlike him. At first sight there was nothing very distressing in these meditations, but they did undoubtedly distress him for all that. (Chapter 33, p. 524.)

Four personalities are now involved, pitched together in illuminating inter-relationship: Martin himself, Mark, Mark's friend, and Tom Pinch. He sees not merely that he is different from Mark and Tom, but that Mark and Tom are (*vis à vis* himself) more like each other than they are like him. Moreover, Tom *would have* treated the girl like that: that's the sort of person he is: the sort of person Martin, for instance, is not. Now this series of reflections involves a complicated set of adjustments and readjustments. It is the whole of his past life that is under revision, and the implicit assumption is that he acknowledges that this past life is *him*. You cannot see that another person is *such-and-such* without knowing at the same time that you yourself are not such-and-such. Significantly, Dickens says that the reflections seemed to have nothing distressing about them — but they distress Martin for all that. The relations between the understanding and the guilt could hardly be better expressed. They were not at first distressing because they were reached in a spirit of enquiry: only later do the implications come home in full force. This is the right way around for matters to proceed.

There follows an acute paragraph "explaining" Martin's selfishness. His grandfather is the villain as we shall come to see: "the meaner domestic vices," Dickens observes, "propagate themselves to be their own antagonists". (P. 524.) Martin's own rationale is given as follows: " 'My guardian takes so much thought of himself, that unless I do the like by *myself*, I shall be forgotten.' So he had grown selfish." (P. 524.) This rings true; it is neither an over-explanation (it still leaves Martin with a burden of responsibility — he needn't have let himself be determined in this way) nor special pleading.

But the most remarkable feature about the case history that is assembling — as we are to imagine it — in Martin's mind, is contained in the sentence that follows: "But he had never known it." This is the root of the trouble, this is what this kind of egotism is. Paradoxically, Dickens argues, the more wholly self-*ish* a man is, the less acquaintance with and awareness of that self he has. In other words, he is or has been unable to see himself as an object. Sartre has diagnosed *mauvaise foi* as the falsifying and estranging tendency to treat the self as if it were objective to the self: we cannot be, he argues, truly object-like in our own eyes, those eyes being the self towards which we are claiming to be objective.[2] When we say "*That* is my self", we lie, for we are what is saying "That is my self", and so on. But in point of fact growth and maturation of the personality require and depend on a dialectic of object- and subject-relations within the self. We do, as we grow, acquire a conception ourselves: I can know this Geoffrey Thurley as you can, though from a unique standpoint. The self that is the beholding consciousness must also, paradoxically, become aware of the collective bundles of memory-traces and behaviour-patterns that constitute, from an objective standpoint, personality. And we are required morally and legally to take responsibility for this self. Sartre's diagnosis assumes the inauthenticity of such a standpoint within the mind, and often enough he successfully shows up the *mauvaise foi* of our pretensions (to sincerity, for instance.) But experience, memory, and introspection tell us that it is possible, and essential to growth, to regard our selves in this light. Inauthenticity in fact often depends precisely on refusing to accept that this is so.

Now Dickens lays bare, with disarming simplicity, precisely the nature of this self-objectification: he shows that Martin's selfishness springs from an ignorance of the contours and nature of his personality bred by a headstrong egotism:

> If anyone had taxed him with a vice, he would have indignantly repelled the accusation, and conceived himself unworthily aspersed. He would never have known it, but that being newly risen from a bed of dangerous sickness, to watch by another couch, he felt how nearly Self had dropped into the grave, and what a poor dependent, miserable thing it was . . . Then the curtain slowly rose a very little way; and Self, Self, Self, was shown below. (Chapter 33, p. 524.)

It is easy to read that swiftly and facilely as moralistic remonstrance (as the repeated "Self", for instance, encourages us to). But in point of fact the really important thing in the sentence is less Martin's awareness of a despicable egotism that has always governed his behaviour, than the theatrical metaphor of a curtain. What is important is that something which has been concealed from awareness is now discovered: Martin beholds that hidden actor, his Self — not, be it noted, his selfishness — his Self. Paradoxically, we can say that it is in becoming aware of his selfishness that he comes to knowledge of his self. He has not, previously, really known that his self begins and ends, and is one of millions of others, as object-like to others as theirs to him. What follows confirms the general drift of my argument: Martin shows his new qualities not so much in being modest or nice to Mark, as in being objective about the past — " 'Mind! exclaimed Martin. 'I am to blame for coming here, and I would do anything to get away . . . If I had taken your opinion sooner, Mark, we never should have been here, I am certain.' " (P. 526.) It is notable, incidentally, that the process of maturation is materially assisted by the absence of Hope ("so far removed") and Ambition ("quenched"), and the presence of Death — the classic nineteenth century agent of self-awareness. Dickens was later to explore the peculiarly debilitating effects of Hope and Ambition more thoroughly. Here, meanwhile, Martin Chuzzlewit encounters himself in the swamps of the Mississippi, and the removal of the comforts and security that had kept him safe from perception of himself was an indispensable part of the process. It is, of course, an *askesis* which Dickens has touched in so economically, yet so convincingly.

It is, perhaps, an episode rather than a progression, but what of that? Not only the formal laws of this novel, but the actual nature of the content allow that this important theme be dealt with in this way. The proving of young Martin indicates the extent of the myth's inward development, but it is arguably a secondary product of the old man's stratagem. What concerns us more pressingly perhaps is the effect of this new conception of what was once the magically empowered godfather (old Martin) upon what was formerly the fascinatingly repulsive ogre. Jonas Chuzzlewit is Dickens's first significant essay in the portraiture of Victorian commercialism. It is hard to agree with Edmund Wilson in bracketing him with Arthur Gride (of *Nicholas Nickleby*) as a "conventional curmudgeon".[3] Jonas has a horrible life of his own and a vein of mocking humour. He is dry and arid, with none of the superabundance that made Quilp and Fagin attractive in their way. But this very barrenness is oddly impressive: Jonas consumes everything into nothing. In moving from Quilp and Fagin to such characters as Jonas Chuzzlewit, Dickens penetrates deeper into the nature of evil, and of the role it plays in society. A characteristic touch in the treatment of Jonas is the comic wooing of Mercy Pecksniff. He is more than a grasping fist; he has a sadist's lust inside him that is gratified by getting control of the pretty little girl who once taunted him.

Moreover, Dickens sees fit to retail some of the most powerful scenes in the novel through Jonas's eyes. The murder of Montague Tigg is on the face of it a simple enough act of violence with uncomplicated motivation. Yet after the crime, a deadly loneliness and desolation make the arrest of even so arid and loveless a man as Jonas Chuzzlewit an act of mercy:

> In his secret dread of meeting the household for the first time, after what he had done, he lingered at the door on slight pretexts, that they might see him without looking into his face; and left it ajar while he dressed; and called out to have the windows opened, and the pavements watered, that they might become accustomed to his voice. (Chapter 47, p. 729.)

The imaginative re-constitution of everyday experience — we have all endured the sensation of alienation from our acquaintance after absence from work or school, or through some shameful thing done — is possibly Dickens's greatest gift as a novelist. What, incidentally, could the "inner life" be, if it is not what Dickens is showing us in the tortured loneliness of Jonas Chuzzlewit? We do not expect from Dickens the same kind of *résumé* of motivation as we witness in George Eliot, for instance; but Dickens is plainly *inside* Jonas here, in precisely the same way as Dostoievsky is inside Raskolnikov. What he sees from that vantage-point he reports with superlative tact and precision, to build up an image of consciousness in many ways superior to the reports of George Eliot. This is, I have argued, the strength of what we might for purposes of argument call his extroversion. Mrs.

Van Ghent presents something like this position in a paragraph already cited: consciousness, to put it in Husserl's terms, is always consciousness of something, and we experience the "inner lives" of many Dickens characters as we largely experience our own mental worlds — by the evidence of the objects we behold. What George Eliot presents as introspection or self-awareness is in fact character-geology: we do not really experience ourselves in that way at all. If Mrs. Van Ghent had thought as much about the nature of consciousness as about the literary constructs before her, her insight could have been even more valuable. As it is, she allows her insight to become distorted into something mechanical. Her error — as I see it — originates, like Mr. Sucksmith's, in a mistaken view of Dickens's "animism" — or what she calls his "fairly constant use of the pathetic fallacy".[4] Now in point of fact the whole notion of the so-called pathetic fallacy is one that has undergone some rigorous criticism recently. Rudolf Arnheim points out that the "analogies" made or pointed out in the literary figures often described (and denigrated) in terms of the pathetic fallacy are in fact often objectively real: there is for instance an actual structural and expressive relation between feeling sad and weary and the sorts of curve we see in "weeping willows".[5] This confirms my own view that the aim of Dickens's animistic devices is nothing but objective clarification — the establishing of truths about the way things are. This itself presupposes that things are how they appear, or behave. This — I have argued — disposes of Mr. Sucksmith's postulation of a systematic introverted distortion of reality in Dickens. It also, I think, undermines Mrs. Van Ghent's suggestion of a sort of systematic transposition of human and non-human attributes: "people are described by non-human attributes, or by such an exaggeration of or emphasis on one part of their appearance that they seem to be reduced wholly to that part, with an effect of having become 'thinged' into one of their own bodily members or into an article of their clothing or into some inanimate object of which they have made a fetish."[6] I can find no evidence of this fetishism myself. This bears especially upon the treatment of Jonas Chuzzlewit at this point of *Martin Chuzzlewit*. But now seems as good a context as any for contesting the whole theory — yet another contribution, as it appears to me, towards the dehumanization of Dickens. The general wrongness of Mrs. Van Ghent's case appears evident from a perusal of her examples and then from a consideration of the transposition of attributes she postulates in Dickens's acknowledged successes. We observe, quite simply, that at its best Dickens's characterization is so subtle and indefinable — conveyed by so many subtly observed behaviour patterns — that the rigidifying effect of imposing the kind of comparison Mrs. Van Ghent postulates would shatter the illusion. The comparison that is made, for instance, between the rent-collector Pancks and a tug-boat in *Little Dorrit* signalizes an inherent uncertainty in Dickens: the character is not really grasped, and Dickens resorts to his figurative analogues — steaming, coaly, hard, bitty, etc. — in order to hold some sort of image fast before our eyes. Now the example could fit well into Mrs. Van Ghent's theory: the rent-collector might be dehumanized by his soul-destroying function. But the truth surely is that Dickens resorts to the image not to point up the inhumanity of Pancks — on the contrary, he turns out to be warm and spontaneous inside, and it's only the energetic, endearing aspects of the tug that are stressed — but because he doesn't feel confident about the character. Where he does feel confident of his characterization, he will sometimes use a similar device to fix some mannerism or physical effect: an instance is Wemmick's "post-box" mouth in *Great Expectations*. The image is "just right" for the occasion: we know instantly what *kind of face* Wemmick has, and the posting of sandwiches, far from being a sign of dehumanization ("Wemmick's job has mechanized him into a grinning slot"),[7] contributes to a rather endearing image of the man. Just as we (in general) tend to associate small close-set eyes with cunning and meanness, so we tend to see in a loose square mouth a kind of naive good-humour. The sandwich-posting is an instantly effective comic stroke that has nothing to do with the rather admirable business code which makes him one man in Walworth and another in Little Britain. The kind of "universality" Dickens achieves here — a brilliant poetic percipience into types of personality and behaviour — needs no other justification than its own success, and the tendency of Mrs. Van Ghent's rationalization — for this reader at least — is to diminish the interest of the achievement.

In the case of Jonas Chuzzlewit, we have a character already — we could argue — dehumanized. But even here the formulation cuts across the lines of the characterization: nobody is *quite* dehumanized, and it's difficult to escape the feeling that Mrs. Van Ghent is short-circuiting her own investigations by making "dehumanized" an approximate equivalent of "evil". Jonas might moralistically be described as "dehumanized", but in fact isn't he *human-all-too-human*? One's discomfort with Mrs. Van Ghent's panacea becomes acute when she comes to interpret those knockings in the water pipes at the inn where Jonas is spending the night before he is to murder Montague Tigg: "Not only do the pipes serve to interpret Jonas's fears", says Mrs. Van Ghent, "but they appear to have been released by the act which dehumanizes Jonas into a busy life of their own".[8] (Mrs. Van Ghent's phrasing is misleading to the reader without fresh acquaintance with the text: Jonas hasn't at this point committed the murder, though he has decided on it.) What does Dickens actually say? This: "It was a blotched, stained, mouldering room, like a vault; and there were water-pipes running through it, which at unexpected times in the night, when other things were quiet, clicked and gurgled suddenly, as if they were choking." (Chapter 46, p. 718.) A characteristically brilliant evocation of a common enough phenomenon: the sudden, alarming waking up of water pipes the other side of the wall in an otherwise dead house with which we are not familiar. It would be misleading to call this "scoring", nor is it yet "description": it's fully functional all right, and goes well beyond the suspense-building of the skilled thriller-writer. But how Mrs. Van Ghent draws her conclusion from these lines I do not know: de-humanized? Isn't the whole point of this superbly incisive writing lost if we don't feel with and through Jonas at this point? This is not to say quite that we "sympathize" with him. But the strained awareness of tiny physical events, experienced almost as though they are within our own consciousness, must surely in part explain the deep impression the scene made upon Dostoievsky,[9] and the total experience an intelligent reading of the passage offers is surely marred beyond recognition by Mrs. Van Ghent's suggestion that Jonas is here "dehumanized" (whatever that ultimately means). It would be worth the paradox to assert that murdering — or meaning to murder — Tigg makes Jonas more human: like Sikes earlier, he is heightened in these terrible experiences. The room like "a vault", the "choking" pipes, above all the "sense of fever in the mouth, a taste of rust, and dust, and earth, and rotting wood" — the notation of these things, and the heightened sensitivity they attest, almost make a hero of Jonas, and we wouldn't be far out, I fancy, to find here the conceiving place of Raskolnikov. For although Jonas's is a stupid murder (a mere commercial necessity), and Raskolnikov's an "intellectual", we know that Dostoievsky found it difficult to "find" a reason for the crime,[10] and may well conclude that it wasn't the rationale of murder that Dostoievsky found so intensely absorbing but the kind of mental ordeal it offered. In this Dickens is unquestionably his mentor. We notice, moreover, that the angle of narration has shifted from chapters 42 and 44, in which the "evil journey" culminating in the actual murder is begun and continued, to chapters 46 and 47, in which it ends. In the two earlier chapters the reader is compelled to experience Tigg's fears and suspicions, with the appalling dream of the door nailed with twigs and worms which ends with his waking to find Jonas at his bedside. In the later chapters the narrative centre is Jonas: his is the dread and anxiety we now experience, his the dreams (pure Dostoievsky, these, with their strangely public confessions) we have to endure. His, too, is the loneliness afterwards, bringing something dangerously close to sympathy into play.

Many readers will undoubtedly rebel against being asked to accept that the central interest of *Martin Chuzzlewit* lies in Jonas Chuzzlewit and Montague Tigg, and not in Pecksniff and Mrs. Gamp, and the young hero. Certainly, the Anglo-Bengalee Disinterested Loan and Life Assurance Company has no great claim on our attention. Yet the power of the writing in the passages dealing with the murder suggests that it represents a kind of psychical climax in the novel. Dickens devotes too much time and patient energy to building up the storm and the protracted journey to Salisbury (interrupted as it is, or simply suspended, by other matters) for it to be a minor episode. Just as the storm later in *David Copperfield* serves to bring the whole novel to a crisis, so here the nervously gorgeous atmospherics on the coach-trip to Salisbury prepare us for the blood-letting which strangely consummates the various themes Dickens has interwoven with deceptively casual brilliance. The intensity of these pages is a sufficient index of their significance. But it is worth observing that although *Martin Chuzzlewit* manifests many of the extravagant intensities of Gothic expressionism, its intensity never results in loss of clarity: it is the psychological penetrativeness of the best Dostoievsky that it recalls, not the morbid hysteria of Poe.

Another significant characteristic of the Jonas-Tigg experiences is that when, at moments of maximum intensity, Dickens moves inside Jonas or Tigg, *it ceases really to matter whose personality we are inhabiting*. We are not aware of Tigg, the pathetic swindler, or Jonas, the mordant miser: we are not indeed aware of any personality at all. In the same way, Claudio in *Measure for Measure* ceases to be a weak-willed rather nondescriptly selfish young man — *l'homme moyen sensuel* — and becomes, with his "Ay, but to die and go we know not where", Man under immediate threat of death, so that his great speech — a gaze into oblivion — bears none of the psychological hallmarks of the character "Claudio". There is something curiously de-personalizing (not de-humanising) about extreme or ultimate experience. This reflection might help us place still more precisely the nature of the relations between Dickens's central characters and the "Dickens characters" around them. I have touched on this already, and shall do so again. Here, in the most unlikely way — Jonas Chuzzlewit is about as far from the modest self-effacingness we associate with the Dickens hero as we could imagine — we find further support for the idea that the purpose of the identification-process in Dickens is to make us endure certain experiences, not to apprise us of certain moral truths, although there is of course no absolute disjunction between the two things. At any rate there is no doubting the imaginative integrity of the murder scenes in *Martin Chuzzlewit:* we see through Jonas's and Tigg's eyes, their dreads and fears are ours, and we are no more aware of their personalities at these moments than of our own in similar circumstances in real life. And with this reflection, I think, we can leave for good the question of the "inner life", or at least Dickens's handling of it: the "inner life" was never more intensely yet clearly experienced in art.

The arrest of Jonas has a force quite different from the capture of Fagin, and the difference reflects the greater definition of evil in the later novel. Fagin was the centre of evil and had to be sought out and destroyed before Oliver could breathe freely. The real climax of *Martin Chuzzlewit* is not the apprehension of Jonas, but the murder of Montague Tigg. Certainly Fagin's capture was part of a causal chain, and attended by a measure of inevitability. But there was still an element of the fortuitous in the event, still a willed necessity about it. The causal chain of which Jonas's arrest forms a link, on the other hand, is one which was started by old Martin in the first chapters of the novel.

The *dénouement* involves not only the cleaning-up of the fraudulent company and the restoration of the young hero to his rights, but the "brain-washing" (or so it appears) of some of the most beloved of all Dickens's characters. I refer to the treatment of Pecksniff and Mrs. Gamp.

The scene of the arrest of Jonas is prepared for by one of Dickens most inspired comic scenes: the tea-party, the last as it was to be, between Betsey Prig and Sairey Gamp. Betsey is spoiling for a row from the first moment of her arrival, and the encounter reaches an irrevocable climax when Betsey Prig crosses her arms and says "Bother Mrs. Harris!" followed by "The tremendous and memorable words": "I don't believe ther's no sich a person!" That a scene between two gin-soaking old nurses can have the power to move, as this scene undoubtedly does, argues roots deeper than simple comedy. Both within *Martin Chuzzlewit* itself, and within Dickens's work as a whole, the cruel exorcism of Mrs. Harris is of considerable importance. For, with the laying of this beloved ghost[11] and the consequent normalizing of Mrs. Gamp — without Mrs. Harris, she shrinks to the disreputable old sot she really is — Dickens himself takes leave of the world of Fantasy, rather as Shakespeare does with the casting-off of Falstaff. Hereafter, his world is saner and harder; even Micawber, of all the characters to come the most "Dickensian", is placed with point and even acidity both in his social context and ethically. From now on, everyone has to justify his existence. In fact, Mrs. Gamp reappears in her new perspective as Mrs. Crupp, David Copperfield's landlady, an amusing but not at all magical old alcoholic.

The process is given definition in the actual arrest of Jonas, in which Mrs. Gamp performs her first — and last — socially constructive act: she helps to hold Jonas while old Martin, Nadgett and Lewsome arrive and unmask him. Appalled by the sacrilegious impropriety of this, one is touched as well by the final functional "appearance" of the now defunct Mrs. Harris: Sairey pretends that the other nurse — "Turn and turn about; one off, one on" — attending an old Chuffey upstairs is Mrs. Harris. The ghost is thus doubly laid; first by Betsey Prig's scepticism, then by Sairey's own exploitation of her. While the forces of responsibility march on triumphant-ly, Dickens himself lingers with Mrs. Gamp, who is through-out unable to show any real interest in what is going on: "'Her name,' said Mrs. Gamp, 'is Harris.' It was extra-ordinary how much effort it cost Mrs. Gamp to pronounce the name she was commonly so ready with." (Chapter 51, p.

778.) Not unreasonably, Jonas takes her laboured breathing to be the consequence of gin.

The *dénouement* of *Martin Chuzzlewit* is a watershed in Dickens's creative life. It marks his recognition of the seriousness of the task that confronted him. For, hilarious though she is, Mrs. Gamp is utterly callous in her treatment of her patients and must be severely — fatally — brought to heel. This of course sounds intolerably priggish and pompous; who would want Mrs. Gamp to be other than she is in any detail? *Martin Chuzzlewit* is, I have suggested, Dickens's great comic epic. As such it presents a world in which the comic spirit is given free play, without hindrance, law, or restriction. But after *Martin Chuzzlewit,* Dickens begins to phase out the comedy upon which so much of his reputation stands, and by which he made such a great contribution to the literature of the world. Mr. Micawber is to come, but he, I shall argue, only confirms the general drift of the tide. For the truth is that the essence of the comic spirit is its celebration of absolute and unbreachable egotism. In all comedy, the driving force is not sympathy, but its opposite — laughter, in which there is always an element of *Schadenfreude*: laughter is always *laughter-at*.[12] When we laugh at someone, we enjoy their discomfiture or their momentary absurdity. Now in fact we often associate Dickens's genius (with its "vitality", exuberance, fecundity) with his genius for laughter. We fabricate, often, a spurious picture of a comic muse, full of genial jollity, and overflowing with good humour. Milton commits this fault in *L'Allegro,* perhaps because he lacked a sense of humour, perhaps because he allowed a natural sense of humour (evident from the odd grim jest in *Paradise Lost*) to be overladen with — simply — more serious concerns. In point of fact, the laughter of true comedy does not come from this kind of geniality: there is something sinister about the habitual or professional laugher. The case of Dickens proves this, I think. We could gauge as much from one occasion, at least, when, accepting for a moment the publicly fostered image of himself as Father Christmas, he attempts the creation of a natural, spontaneous, good-humoured laugher — Tim Linkinwater in *Nicholas Nickleby*. Now there are few pages in literature quite so wearing and wearying as those in *Nicholas Nickleby*: the sheer strain of trying to keep up with this monstrous *bonhomie* would be daunting enough if it were based upon psychological truth. But it isn't: it is totally false, one of the very few instances of sincere but undoubted falsity in Dickens. We simply do not laugh in these situations or for these reasons, and Dickens — master-psychologist of the laughter mechanism — knew it quite well. As well, in fact, as he knew the real reasons for amusement and laughter — a sense of our own or, more often, someone else's discomfort or absurdity. Dickens possessed about as cruel and remorseless a sense of human absurdity as any man who ever lived. Only Swift and Jonson can equal him for it in our literature, I think.

Now of course it is important to stress that there is only an element of *Schadenfreude* in comedy and laughter. Perhaps it would be as well here to distinguish comedy from laughter: comedy — the art of laughter — comes into existence only when something more is brought to laughter than the simple physical response. Comedy cannot exist without laughter (properly speaking), but there is a great deal of laughter even in the confines of literature which does not rise to the level of comedy. A humorist who *just* exploits our readiness to enjoy discomfort and absurdity or inadequacy is either stonily unamusing (as witness the vast majority of so-called humorous writers), or self-congratulatory.

In Dickens's case, the superabundant comedy of the first period novels (we could call it his comic period) culminates in the figures of Mrs. Gamp and Mr. Pecksniff. What these great creations have in common with each other is a total indifference to the rest of the human race: they are monsters of egotism. Now in some way they perform an important service for Dickens and his readers. We enjoy, along with him, the absolutely unbridled play of their egotism at the same time as we laugh at them. In other words, we do not have the lurking, transcending sense of self-correction which comes into shadowy being when we laugh at characters like Miss

Miggs in *Barnaby Rudge*.

This egotism, it seems to me, lies at the heart of the comic character. W. H. Auden argued precisely the opposite view of Falstaff (the greatest example, I should have thought, of the comic character considered in this light): "He is never tired, never bored, and until he is rejected he radiates happiness as Hal radiates power, and this happiness without apparent cause, this untiring devotion to making others laugh becomes a comic image for a love which is absolutely self-giving."[13] Mr. Auden purchases his case at the expense of some of Shakespeare's most incisive points (the casting-off, which is barely mentioned, certainly could not move us as it does, were we to regard Falstaff as "love"), and by identifying — or very nearly — laughter with love: "Laughing and loving have certain properties in common."[14] Well, maybe: most things have something in common with most other things; but laughing and loving have much more that is mutually excluding. Laughter is prohibited for instance to lovers: it would destroy love, as much as if *he* realised that her breath smelt, or *she* that his ears stuck out. And Falstaff is, I submit, the very opposite of Mr. Auden's Christian image — a wholly self-absorbed man, who can draw people into his own world (as he draws Hal) only at the cost of their true interest. The whole point of course is that we would not have him or them otherwise, and thus find ourselves in a deep dilemma. As Mr. Auden says, Falstaff is a fountain of energy, we love to have him around, and "we cannot wish people or things we find amusing to be other than they are".[15] But in fact Falstaff does absolutely nothing that is not totally selfish — in the usual meaning of that word: his behaviour at the pricking is villainous, his behaviour on the battlefield monstrous,[16] he lets his confederates down at the Gad's Hill episode, and so on. There is a rueful edge to Bardolph's admission in *Henry V*:

> *Boy*: Do you not remember 'a saw a flea stick upon Bardolph's nose, and 'a said it was a black soul burning in hell?
> *Bardolph*: Well, the fuel is gone that maintain'd that fire: that's all the riches I·got in his service.

Yet Bardolph had already remarked in the same scene "Would I were with him, whersom'er he is, either in heaven or in hell." Dickens exploits the same sort of paradoxical collocation of feelings in making us relish Pecksniff's and Mrs. Gamp's company while wholly "disapproving" of them. Nor is it the point that we suspend or waive judgment: on the contrary, the quality of our enjoyment, like the quality of laughter itself, is compact of an irreconcilable amalgam of relish and disapproval. We laugh while knowing that we shouldn't; and the point of the comedy is lost if we don't think we shouldn't. I do not pretend to know what are the precise relations between laughter and sympathy; but I am fairly sure that the one ends where the other begins, and that although we can, like Tchekhov, love people whom we find amusing, or find those we love absurd, we cannot really sympathize with someone at the moment of laughing at him. I think the inverted example of Miss Miggs demonstrated this amply enough: the moment that he becomes aware of a pity for Miggs, Dickens ceases to find her amusing, or to make her funny.

But with Miss Miggs there was always something strained in the laughter: the target was too easy, she was being ridiculed simply for being ugly and frustrated, and our response to Dickens's nudges had something ill-bred and underhand in it, something dangerously close to the jeering of Mr. J. D. Salinger. The "problem" of comedy is to reconcile these irreconcilables: to reconcile the fact of our amusement with the claims of sympathy or charity. Great comedy does this by using the laughter first as an emetic — we take ourselves "too seriously" and in the wrong way — then as a lever upon our complacency: we too share this absurdity, and simply ought to be better than we are, or at least aware of our absurdity. Dickens, like Shakespeare, finally solves the problem by investing all our laughter in egotistical monsters in whom we can enjoy the full play of our own repressed egotism (laughter is destructive, and therefore anti-social) without feeling guilty. Cervantes took the self-enclosed nature of the comic character to its logical conclusion by making his great hero a lunatic; but he too suborned his own plan by finding his hero more and more pitiful and less and less amusing. The egotist, alone in his self-contained world, is the perfect target for comedy. It is not difficult to see how such a conception of comedy fits into the plan of *Martin Chuzzlewit,* or how Pecksniff and Gamp parallel Jonas and Tigg.

Pecksniff remains more gull than villain, in spite of Dickens's vituperation. Technically, he is perhaps the binding element of the whole. He is as much a fantasist as Mrs. Gamp, only it is himself he believes in — not a Mrs. Harris. Like Mrs. Gamp, he is broken at the end, but really believes his own cant. His breaking therefore takes a different form from hers. Implicated in the fraudulent company, he, who thinks himself so deep, is revealed as a babe in the cut-throat world of Tigg and Jonas. Pecksniff in fact is his own biggest dupe, and, though discredited in the final unmasking, remains unable to see himself from without. But he has lost the esteem of the world, so that his parting words have a comic hollowness:

> "I have been struck this day," said Mr. Pecksniff, "with a walking-stick (which I have every reason to believe has knobs upon it), on that delicate and exquisite portion of the human anatomy, the brain. Several blows have been inflicted, sir, without a walking-stick, upon that tenderer portion of my frame — my heart." (Chapter 52, p. 811.)

Pecksniff keeps his fantasy world, but it now stands revealed as a private world; Pecksniff no longer dominates in the real world. He shrinks to what he is, and one is reminded of certain public-house characters, living in an illusory world of personal grandeur. What Dickens has done is to show us Pecksniff from the inside, and then reduce him to life-size, shorn of the esteem of people like his daughters and Tom Pinch that kept him buoyed up. The last reports about him — he becomes a tavern braggart who cadges drink-money from Tom Pinch and abuses him as soon as he is drunk — are therefore perfectly judicious.

Pecksniff thus unites the fantasy world of the novel with the evil. He represents in exaggerated form the subtle comedy that attaches to evil, which was earlier foreshadowed in Quilp and Fagin, and which is here refined to an awareness of its essential gullibility. This, indeed, is the real import of the novel. The self-destructiveness of evil is ultimately a more damaging judgment on it than any the world of legitimacy can pass. Jonas Chuzzlewit not only brings the edifice down upon his head (as Tigg had before him); he creates for himself, with his most final act, a hell that is unendurable, even for him. The broadest implications of this aspect of crime, and, we may infer, of sin, are pursued by Dostoievsky in *Crime and Punishment*: Raskolnikov discovers that there are areas of experience where acts must be considered as absolute in themselves, irrespective of their consequences. Thus, though he kills the money-lender for motives of good, he finds that he has cut himself off from human society. He has, in fact, placed himself outside himself. Similarly, Jonas Chuzzlewit discovers that there is a world of difference between the "innocence" before the murder — in which he can bully and coerce everybody around him, and in so doing feel in contact with the world — and the terrible, irrevocable withdrawal of the rest of the human race after the act, when his threatening tone and overbearing manner, just because determined by a more savage necessity (his life being now at stake), somehow fail to connect him with the outside world. Whereas Mrs. Gamp and Pecksniff depended for their inner life on *not* having diplomatic relations with the world of reality, and were, in their different ways, broken when the world breached the walls of their debased fantastic fortresses, Jonas is destroyed when contact — such as it has been, a vulgar, brutal trafficking — is finally removed. He has no inner resources to sustain him.

Something of this ultimate inner emptiness was suggested in Fagin. But on the whole both he and Quilp relished their evil to such an extent as to make the people around them seem a little dull. Shakespeare himself never got closer to the gleeful autonomy of a certain kind of devil than Dickens did in these two monsters. Much of this quality adheres to Mrs. Gamp and Pecksniff. The difference, though — that they are largely ineffectual — is crucial. Evil has split into two elements, which are never really to be fused again. The grotesque abundance has gone into Pecksniff and Mrs. Gamp, and, really, dies with them. The effectual power and the malignancy have been narrowed down to characters like Jonas. Instead, therefore, of reacting to evil with a fascinated horror (in which there is certain ambivalence), and rushing to draw a magic circle around his good characters, Dickens is confident enough to place evil, not, certainly, so as to reduce it to cause and effect cycles, but to trace it to inner weaknesses.

6 Dombey and Son

Dombey and Son completes the process started in *Martin Chuzzlewit*. It is achieved with a new aesthetic calm and finish that impressed Dickens's contemporaries as a new maturity — almost, one fancies, a welcome respectability. "There is nothing in all his writings more perfect," Forster wrote, "for what it shows of his best qualities, than the life and death of Paul Dombey. The comedy is admirable; nothing strained, everything hearty and wholesome in the laughter and fun . . . "[1] At several places in his chapter on *Dombey* Forster makes use of an implicit dichotomy between "art" and "genius" reminiscent of eighteenth century Shakespeare criticism: " . . . it not seldom occurs that the genius and the art of the master have not pulled together at the close," he observes, and refers to a consciousness in Dickens himself "of the tendency of his humour to exuberance",[2] a consciousness which in turn produced the appropriate restraint. In other words, Dickens is growing out of the gothic vitality of his first period, with its tremendous grotesques and horrifying villains. "Restraint" has been suggested either by other friends or reviewers, or by Dickens's own growing awareness of the sources of his art.

It is usually critics who think and speak in terms of such simple-minded dichotomies as "exuberance" and "restraint"; "genius" and "art", reducing the creative process to the balancing of clear antinomies. This kind of account has its validity, because it is applied from the outside, as we have to experience the work itself. But it is really facile, and probably false. The real significance of the newly chastened surface of *Dombey* is the change it reflects in Dickens's own *Weltanschauung,* and this change had already taken place when he wrote *Martin Chuzzlewit.* We can regard *Martin Chuzzlewit* itself as the end of Dickens's "comic" period: it is the last novel in which the expressionist extravagance dominates both texture and characterization. But from another angle the novel can be seen as an emergence, initiating Dickens's second major period. From the point of view of texture, *Dombey and Son* and *Martin Chuzzlewit* belong to different periods. But as far as the organization of their material is concerned, *Martin Chuzzlewit* is distinct from *Oliver Twist, The Old Curiosity Shop,* and *Nicholas Nickleby,* and related to the more thoughtfully structured *Dombey and Son.* And this, in terms of Dickens's evolution, means that the underlying myth has altered, and with it Dickens's spiritual and moral orientation. This can be seen clearly in the treatment of young Paul Dombey.

Paul Dombey is, of course, the child of the early novels, brother to Oliver Twist, Smike, and little Nell. Nothing better suggests the development that takes place in the period separating *Dombey* from *Nicholas Nickleby* than the status of the child-hero. Formerly, the child's vision had substantially created and coloured the world of the novel, and the exorcism of his nightmare largely made up the structure. Now, the child — more luminously and precisely presented than ever — fades out of the novel at its halfway stage. In other words, the story of the novel no longer follows the fantasy of its central innocent eye. This means more than a change of camera angle: it means that the vein of fantasy-satisfaction that had generated such tension and energy in the early books had been worked out. Dickens no longer derived satisfaction from the re-enactment of his basic nightmare. The "wish-fulfilment" projection had to be replaced by some other form of structuring in answer to different underlying drives.

This could be expressed by saying that Dickens had started

to die, in spite of the fact that Micawber lay just ahead. The genius shares with many more routine neurotics the ability to preserve his childishness; and the gradual growth of Dickens's art must be measured against the decline of his fertility, reflected in the gradual freezing-up of his childhood vision. Can this be so, with his two most famous childhood books to come? The paradox can be maintained: indeed it must, since the relationship between Oliver Twist, David Copperfield, and Pip to a large extent explains Dickens's entire *oeuvre*.

The elimination of the chance-mechanism — easily perceptible from the most cursory comparison of *Oliver Twist* and *Dombey and Son* — is no mere improvement of technique or methodology, but the sign of a changing attitude to experience. It could hardly fail to be significant that a man ceased to believe in his luck, in chance, in good fortune: it means that he no longer regards the universe as being on his side. By the same token the evil forces also evaporate: Dickens is no longer ridden by his nightmare, just as he no longer believes in the power of the fantasy re-enactment to exorcise the malign forces that threatened him. Thus, the way Dickens observes the dying of Paul Dombey (however much pathos he extracts from the situation) is totally different from the unconscious identification he cannot help making with Oliver Twist and Little Nell. In fact, Paul yields the hero-role to Florence Dombey, his sister, and her lover, Walter Gay. Hence, there are three central figures — young Paul, Forence, Walter — none of them satisfactorily filling the role played by the child-heroes of the early books.

This uncertainty about the foundations of *Dombey and Son* at one stage fascinatingly foreshadowed the way Dickens was to develop after this second period: the revision of the original intention towards Walter Gay shows that at the time of writing *Dombey*, Dickens was himself in a state of transition from one phase to the next. As Dickens finally presents him, Walter Gay is a purely conventionalized Romantic lead, a cross between Joe Willett and Edward Chester of *Barnaby Rudge*. Originally, though, Dickens had intended to have him fade away into frustration and failure, as Richard Carstone does in *Bleak House*. He wrote to Forster, "About the boy who appears in the last chapter of the first number, I think it would be a good thing to disappoint all the expectations that chapter seems to raise of his happy connection with the story and the heroine, and to show him gradually and naturally trailing away from that love of adventure and boyish light-heartedness, into negligence, idleness, dissipation, dishonesty and ruin."[3] Later on, the plan was shelved, as Forster notes, "for reasons that need not be dwelt on here . . . and Walter was reserved for a happier future."[4] With a characteristically swift change of plan, Dickens held back the more serious possibility for a more suitable context. The original plan again confirms the new formal principles, related to the changing attitudes initiated in *Martin Chuzzlewit*. The new critical spirit of that novel, in which the good fortune that attends Martin is merely a formal endorsement of the basic optimism rather than a preconscious enactment of an inchoate fantasy, in *Dombey* dictates more calculated textures. Yet formally, *Dombey* is one of Dickens's less satisfactory books, in spite of (or because of) the conscious care taken with its narrative structure.

The book fails because Dickens attempted to combine one kind of story — the "realistic" portrayal of Dombey's pride, his bitter failure in personal relationship — with the mythic fantasy of the earlier novels: the quite inadequate depiction of the rise of Walter Gay. As we have seen, this mythic fantasy supports and vitalizes all the novels of the first phase of Dickens's creative life. As we have also seen, there is no reason to blush before the naivety of this fantasy: on the contrary, the strength, representativeness and centrality of novels like *Oliver Twist* and *The Old Curiosity Shop* derived precisely from the fullness with which Dickens re-enacted in them the emergence from darkness and squalor which obsessed the nineteenth century mind. But the very qualities (up to a point rightly) praised by Forster in *Dombey and Son* tell us that Dickens has left this phase behind. At first he is true to his new self: the aesthetic finish of the surface is matched by a poise in judgment and a calculated penetrativeness in perception which do seem new in his work. There is nothing in the early novels quite like the presentation of Dombey's pride or the relations holding between him and his daughter. The father's growing jealousy of the warmth that springs up between his son and his daughter, his bitterness against her and his dead wife, the tenderness of the boy's death, the awareness in simple folk like Richards of the girl's almost extravagant love for her father, this very emotion itself — all this is done with a delicacy and tact that leave nothing to be desired. This study of the love of a girl for her father is carried out with such a wealth of detailed, accurate observation, and with such poise of tone, that the critic is forced back upon the kind of talk about poetic abundance, about "life", that bedevils Dickens criticism. It is, within its limits, perfectly achieved.

Things go wrong only when, young Paul interred, Dickens seeks to replace his *ingénu*. He tries to do so by resurrecting the naive form of the myth: Walter Gay meets Florence, falls in love with her, is loved in turn, banished by Dombey, only to return successful, and finally marry his boss's daughter. This is the myth as Freud saw it — naive wish-fulfilment of the sort common in popular novels and films for over a hundred years. Certainly, Dickens needed Captain Cuttle and Sol Gills to set against Dombey and Mrs. Chick. But he should have avoided the tangle of unconvincing plot by which Carker first of all becomes suspicious of Walter, gets him sent away, and finally sets Rob the Grinder to spy on the Gills's shop during Walter's absence. This is narrative invention about as weak as Dickens ever devised. It is absurd to suppose that Walter could ever have seemed a serious threat to Carker. It is even more absurd for him to go to the lengths he does in following up his suspicion: " 'I want to know all about that old gentleman, and how he goes on from day to day — for I am anxious to be of service to him — and especially who comes there to see him. Do you understand?' " (Chapter 22, p. 28.) This is Rob's brief, and its urgency prepares us for something significant. In fact, nothing stems from it, and the peculiar involvement of

Carker in Rob's family life has, as I shall argue later, other purposes. Carker loses interest in Florence as soon as Edith comes on the scene, and the villainy towards Walter is so much wasted effort.

This is, I think, more than merely inadequate carpentry on a sub-plot. Dickens is nostalgically re-invoking the world of the early books here, and in doing so, cutting across the development of the rest of the book. The Ships Instruments Shop is a version of the Old Curiosity Shop, Gills a version of Grandfather Trent (failing Walter much as the old man fails Nell). Florence is like Nell, actually getting back to the shop. In *The Old Curiosity Shop,* Nell never returns to the shop after her flight from it at the beginning of the story, and the pathos and tension of the novel derive from this estrangement. In a strange dreamlike performance, Dickens returns to the womb in *Dombey and Son*: Florence rushes to the old waterfront shop in flight from the empty horror of her father's house.

But the dream has lost its compulsiveness, and with it its power over Dickens and over his readers. What was an inchoate, half-conscious act of exorcism and clarification here turns into indulgence. The final relenting of Dombey through suffering is reasonable. But the happy gathering in the old shop, with the broken old capitalist sitting at table with Captain Cuttle, is simply absurd:

> A bottle that has been long excluded from the light of day, and is hoary with dust and cobwebs, has been brought into the sunshine; and the golden wine within it sheds a lustre on the table.
> It is the last bottle of the old Madeira.
> "You are quite right, Mr Gills," says Mr Dombey. "This is a very rare and most delicious wine."
> The Captain, who is of the party, beams with joy. There is a very halo of delight round his glowing forehead. (Chapter 62, p. 873.)

This is a feeble recreation of the old convivialities; no imaginative effort of ours can get Dombey and Captain Cuttle together round the table. Dickens has confused his modes here, or rather distorted what had been objective, and blurred what had been clear. All of which means that he had been trying to wring still more pathos out of the mythic situation. The mechanism fails him, and we have to wait for *David Copperfield* for the next advance.

Much the same sort of criticism must be applied to the Carker-Ally entanglement, which is sheer melodrama. Dickens bores us with all this sexual remorse, just as he irritates us in insisting that a villain like Carker must have a dirty past to hide. The contrivance of a past for Carker is no more successful than George Eliot's introduction of Raffles to "explain" Bulstrode in *Middlemarch*. In both cases, the character is victimized and mechanicalized and the tone of the writing degenerates from fine realism to black-and-white melodrama.

Yet its treatment of evil, so much more cool and analytic than any earlier essay, and the masterly account of Dombey himself, together represent an impressive advance in Dickens's art. To define its significance, it seems necessary to direct attention away from its more effectively Dickensian aspects (the marvellous lambency of the young Paul Dombey episodes, for example) in favour of what is new in it, the delicate intelligence with which certain sexual ambiguities are revealed. This involves the rather unpalatable procedure of apparently ignoring Dickens's conscious explanations and going beyond them to a layer of significance hidden from him.[5] This method is, I think, justified by Dickens's habitual translation of sexual material into socio-economic terms.

In *Dombey and Son,* a whole series of episodes, characters, and situations seems to make consistent sense only on a sexual plane. This is especially true of Florence, who gradually assumes the key role in the narrative. She forms violent emotional attachments throughout the book, to her young brother, to Edith, to her father above all. She is really the "heroine" of the story. Although Walter Gay is the young man of the myth, it is Florence through whose eyes we endure the experience of nightmare and fear we have learned to associate with the Dickens hero-figure. Her meeting with Walter Gay in fact is brought about by means of one of the most frightening episodes in all Dickens.

Florence is taken by her nurse to a visit in Camden Town, unknown to her father. (The address is significant: Dickens's family spent one of its more wretched periods there, when Dickens himself gained his experience of pawnshops and street-wandering.) Quite suddenly they find themselves in the middle of a street-fight that flares up from nothing. In the confusion, Florence gets separated from Richards, and as suddenly as the fighting sprang up around her, it ends, and she finds herself alone in the middle of an unknown street that has emptied except for a leering crone approaching her from the other side of the way. The old women, who introduces herself as Mrs. Brown, takes Florence by the hand and leads her away through squalid streets to a small hut in the middle of desolate waste ground. In the hut she forces Florence to take off her clothes — and makes her put on some old rags instead of them. A hundred years later the scene would certainly have had a sexual climax. The Victorian taboo, indeed, enforcing obliquity, also builds up a compulsiveness that would probably have been dissipated in direct treatment. This is not the only place in Dickens where a fear that comes across as vaguely sexual is explained in other terms — usually of robbery and non-sexual violence. Think, for example, of David Copperfield's walk to Dover:

> The trampers were worse than ever that day, and inspired me with a dread that is yet quite fresh in my mind. Some of them were most ferocious-looking ruffians, who stared at me as I went by; and stopped, perhaps, and called after me to come back and speak to them, and when I took to my heels, stoned me. (*David Copperfield*, chapter 13, p. 186.)

We are continually being told throughout the book how nice-looking David is; Steerforth calls him "Daisy" and even asks him whether he has a sister, because he thinks " 'she would have been a pretty, timid, little, bright-eyed sort of girl.' " (*David Copperfield*, chapter 6, p. 87.)

It is inconceivable that such a child in such a desperate and unguarded situation as David found himself in on the road to Dover should not have been the object of sexual threats or overtures. As an unusually good-looking boy wandering loose in the darkest quarters of a city as notorious as London was for its depravity and child-vice, it is equally inconceivable that Dickens himself should have remained unaware of these dangers. This could explain perhaps the fierce compulsiveness of *Oliver Twist* and the ambivalent horror aroused by Quilp and Fagin. In fact, there is probably a strong connexion in Dickens between sexual and economic security. Certainly, the fear the abyss of poverty exercised over (or rather under) the Victorians was of an intensity which, to the post-Freudian mind, immediately suggests a sexual origin. However, even granting that, for a Victorian, an economic trauma might have functioned as a purely sexual one would today, it is certain that *we* cannot read these passages in Dickens without seeing them in terms which, if not definitely psychoanalytical, are at least vaguely tinged with Freudian thinking. About the abduction of Florence Dombey and the above excerpt from *David Copperfield* there seems to me no reasonable doubt; and seeing how often, and how obsessively, Dickens returns to the theme of the defenceless innocent loose in a world of threatening ogres, I feel that the conclusion is forced upon us that his early experience punched sexual and economic fear into the same coin. Biographical speculation on the subject would certainly yield little: "Was Dickens sexually intimidated as a child?" seems as barren a title as "Did Shakespeare visit Italy?" Some such possibility cannot be entirely discounted: Dickens found it hard enough to tell his best friend that he was once employed in a menial capacity, so his utter silence on an even more unmentionable matter could easily be explained. But we do not require this kind of evidence to be sure of the close and alarming connexions his imagination habitually promoted between darkness, poverty, crime — and an unquenchable vitality. This knot of associations lies at the heart of Dickens's work, and helps us to understand its extraordinary power and fascination, a power and fascination which have so easily outlived the overt social problems that gave occasion to its themes. As I have repeatedly stressed, Dickens's attitude towards the proletariat, as at once the seat of crime and yet the repository of an energy and good-heartedness often ironed out of their social betters, is absolutely crucial to our understanding of his development.

The actual boy-meets-girl thread is about the most perfunctory in the novel. Structurally it tightens the whole, and the ambience of the quaint old shop with its quaint old virtues is needed as a contrast to the Dombey deadness. Moreover, the class difference produces some characteristic discords in passing. For example, when Solomon Gills goes bankrupt, Captain Cuttle gets Walter to use the credit his rescuing of Florence gained him to borrow some money to set Gills on his feet again. Walter is acutely aware of the misconstruction Dombey is bound to put upon this actually generous act, but places his obligations to Gills above his own sensitivity. The scene with Dombey is so exquisitely done that we see Walter through his master's eyes, and understand how squalid a piece of fortune-hunting this must appear to him. Dombey's cold emphasis on form is played off, too, against Captain Cuttle's bluff salty good-heartedness — the Captain insists on accompanying Walter on the mission, and even, to Dombey's mortification, throws in his bundle of old spoons to make up such money as Dombey might propose to lend. The relations between Captain Cuttle and Dombey appear more truly in the incident of the spoons Cuttle dumps on Dombey's desk than in the essentially sentimental scene around the supper-table at the end of the novel. The situation is worsened by the much more acute class-consciousness of Carker, who feeds Dombey's suspicion, and, fearful of Walter's designs on Florence, whom the chief clerk has marked down for himself, sees to it that the young man is got out of the way. The idea recommends itself to Dombey, and Walter is despatched to the firm's branch in the West Indies. Since Walter's role in the novel is essentially technical — he is a balance for Florence rather than a character interesting in his own right — this is a shrewd move of Dickens's, especially as it starts a general exodus of the sympathetic characters which finally leaves Florence deserted in the middle of the Dombey antarctica. The low water-mark of Florence's fortunes is the desertion of Edith; Richards has been dismissed, so has Miss Nipper. Walter's sea-voyage is followed by Edith's elopement with Carker. Florence rushes out into the street sobbing.

After this her fortunes can only rise. The process starts with her being taken in by Captain Cuttle at the Ships Instrument Makers Shop (Gills himself meanwhile having gone off in search of Walter). The mechanism is similar to the process by which Mary Graham is abandoned and deserted in *Martin Chuzzlewit*. We may find a little too much design, a little too much self-consciousness in the handling of the theme in *Dombey*. Yet the significance of the opposition made between Captain Cuttle and Solomon Gills on the one hand, and Dombey and Carker on the other, cannot be exaggerated. Mary Graham is merely left at Pecksniff's mercy (or apparently so); Florence is removed from opulence and civilized decorum and placed in the midst of humble quaintness. The frigid civility of the *haute bourgeoisie* in other words is felt to have failed her: she finds warmth, protection, companionship first in the company of the nurse Richards, then among the obscure oddities of Solomon Gills's shop. To go further than this at this stage is to anticipate *Hard Times,* and we must be careful in hindsight not to project our own patterns onto material that only incompletely accepts them. Nevertheless, it is this tight nucleus of preoccupations that makes *Dombey and Son* so powerful a work. As so often in Dickens, we find that one incident or complex of incidents causes reaction and repercussion in quarters that may at first seem unconnected. Here, Florence's fear and flight are made to dovetail with her father's own emotional predicaments. The breaking of Dombey, paralleled by the breaking of Thomas Gradgrind in a later, and the deflation of Mrs. Gamp in an earlier novel, releases forces hitherto held sterilely in check. In all Dickens's novels, in fact, the *Höhepunkt* of the drama is the sacrifice or the cracking, or the breaking out, of some character. The whole of *Dombey and Son* turns on the eventual destruction of Dombey's pride, and no account of the book which misses the significance of the fact is worth anything.

The exorcism of Mrs. Harris, like the casting-off of Falstaff, revealed the profound truth that it is a terrible — if at times necessary — thing to break a person's identity, even if the prop that holds it up is fantasy or lechery; and that a person who is so broken simply becomes nothing. It is astonishing that so good a critic as Taine can have failed to perceive in this the meaning of *Dombey and Son*.[6] Perhaps because the profoundest moral and psychological truths are simple and apt to be taken in too easily without really being understood, perhaps because of the easy parallel with the conversion of Scrooge, the fall of Paul Dombey *père* and the significance of its centrality in Dickens's development have not, I feel, been accorded the attention they deserve. Taine's misunderstanding is not isolated. Edmund Wilson is willing to go along with him: "The most conspicuous example of this process is the reform of Mr. Dombey, who, as Taine says, 'turns into the best of fathers and spoils a fine novel.' But the reform of Scrooge . . . shows the phenomenon in its purest form".[7] Scrooge, as a matter of interest, is not so much unreal as deliberately contrary to fact. Dickens knew his readers knew that men like Scrooge are not converted overnight, and this is precisely the point of this exercise in the Christmas spirit. Scrooge and his conversion are as unreal — and in the same way — as the fantastic outburst of good will that signalizes the season.

The case of Dombey is totally different in kind, intention, and execution. Where *A Christmas Carol* is pure modern fairy-tale (though with the customary Dickensian relevance to contemporary commercialism), *Dombey and Son* is rigorously accurate, in nothing so much as in the breaking of its central character. To see the final crushing of Dombey as a "reform" at all, indeed, to see it as marring rather than rounding off and making complete sense of a fine novel, is to have misunderstood the whole enterprise. For what is concerned in the case of Paul Dombey Senior is not the magical replacement of one quality by another, but the sudden revelation of inner hollowness within the carefully preserved shell of a lifetime's self-ignorance. Dickens himself had to supply the clue in the preface he wrote for the edition published twelve years after the first:

> The two commonest mistakes in judgement ... are, the confounding of shyness with arrogance ... and the not understanding that an obstinate nature exists in a perpetual struggle with itself. Mr. Dombey undergoes no violent change, either in this book, or in real life. [8]

No indeed; and it should not have been necessary for him to underline a point made so well in the novel. Dickens here pays the penalty for artistic perfectionism — misunderstanding: George Eliot would have included the "explanation" quoted above (and a good many others to the same end) in the novel itself, so that there would be no possible ground for her being misunderstood.

"No violent change" — this is the crucial phrase. For Dombey remains untutored by experience: he acquires nothing in the way of wisdom or sympathy, until the shell of his pride is at last smashed in by a blow even he cannot ignore. He therefore breaks only under the most intense pressure and with the utmost finality. He is left not the best of fathers, but a basically pleasant, broken man. Again Dickens himself gives the hint: "Ground, long undermined, will often fall down in a moment ... " (Chapter 59, p. 842.) The metaphor is vitally important and leaves no room for debate. When Dombey finally does break there is a sense of relaxation, almost of relief, that this once-proud man can admit that things happened as they happened: "And now he felt that he had had two children born to him in that house, and that between him and the bare wide empty walls there was a tie, mournful, but hard to rend asunder, connected with a double childhood, and a double loss." (Chapter 59, p. 840.) Inevitably, one thinks of Lear. Yet, although we appreciate the inexorability of the fall, we do not, I submit, with deference to Kathleen Tillotson's analysis, respond as we do to Lear's. The process is unfailingly well-observed, as Mrs. Tillotson shows, and yet the climax lacks impact. Dickens's problem, as he himself recognized, was to dramatize "stiff-necked sullen arrogance": it is of the essence of Dombey's pride that it discloses little. Where Lear raves,

Dombey holds his peace. Thus, we assent, and even sympathize, but neither so readily, nor so deeply as to Lear. The two cases are different, of course, because the temperaments are different, so that the comparison, though inevitable, should not be urged too closely. The truth is that Dickens loved Dombey a good deal less than Shakespeare loved Lear; and this lukewarmness communicates itself to the reader. Dombey's coldness creates a chill at the heart of the book, which all Florence's warmth cannot thaw. This coldness is augmented by Edith: with two such marble figures at the centre, the novel never really takes hold. Yet Dombey and Edith, both in themselves and in their social predicaments, represent a strange interaction of sexual and economic factors. It is their frozen relations which drive Florence weeping into the streets, and these relations depend ultimately on the societalized character of Dombey himself. His is the infertility, the blockage, the impasse, which produces the diseased feeling pervading the entire novel.

Now his pride is based upon his great financial success: it is the House of Dombey that matters, not the people who live in it. It cuts him off from real emotional experience. Yet one cannot really say that his coldness and egotism derive from his commercialism; nor that his "fault" is to have put name and firm before life. In fact, his pride has a certain superbness which places it above mere sordid commerce; if he had been more simply commercial, indeed, he would not have crashed the way he did. It is true that his every act has the remoteness of a transaction, nowhere more painfully so than in the "buying" of his second wife. Yet Dombey has not, like Jonas Chuzzlewit, got a cash-box for a heart. There is something more icy than avarice about his pride, and a deeper block than money holds him. There is a distinctly sexual element in his frigidity — its frozen marble whiteness — which nevertheless finds its expression in commercial terms. The same quality which brings about his financial ruin wrecks his emotional life. His Olympian aloofness — the delegation of his menial business duties to his chief clerk, Carker — makes him out of touch with his own affairs, and thus puts him completely at the mercy of his social inferiors. (A similar point is made in Tcheckov's *Cherry Orchard,* in which the peasant, Lopakhin, ends up by buying out his former masters, who have incapacitated themselves from sordid business competence by over-refinement.) At the same time, Dombey's pride leads him so utterly to misread the emotions of Edith, his second wife, that she allows herself, more or less out of revenge, to fall in with the overtures of his chief clerk, Carker, a man she detests. Thus, Carker is able to cuckold his master and swindle him with the same blow — or very nearly.

This close interaction of sexual and economic elements is further seen in a series of ambiguities, affecting Edith Dombey, Florence, Carker, Rob the Grinder, old Mrs. Brown and her daughter Alice. Edith Dombey first appears with her mother in Leamington Spa, a snobbish resort where almost the only activity is opportunistic match-making. It is a hideous market where impoverished good breeding compounds with *nouveau riche* obscurity. The social portraiture here is rich and varied, embracing much that in sheer ugliness (Major Joe Bagstock, for example) surpasses anything in earlier Dickens, and much (as witness Miss Tox) that is delicately compassionate.

The relationship between Edith and her mother immediately suggests the more familiar one between Estella and Miss Havisham: Edith, like Estella, is cool and aloof, saying little, out of a mixture of boredom and disgust. Her contempt for her mother, and what her obsessive schemings have made of herself, transfers naturally to the men who complete the bargains in which she, Edith, is a chattel. For her dead husband Grainger she feels nothing at all, while towards Dombey she feels revulsion aroused not only by his utter disregard for her as a human being, but by his patent blindness to the indifference for him she makes no effort to disguise. It is surely Dombey's stupid inability to see this indifference, exemplified in his use of Carker as a go-between, that pushes her, our of scorn, into the chief clerk's arms.

Carker is certainly not a success. Dickens is at too great

pains to fix him with imagery — variously a cat, a shark, and a snake — for him to be really alive; but he is an integral part of the story. His agency in the plot resembles Heep's in *David Copperfield*. In fact, Carker partakes of the sexual ambiguity that pervades the whole novel. In the first place, Dickens describes, with exquisitely malicious touch, his house in the suburbs — a prissy imitation of Dombey's great mansion: "And yet amidst this opulence of comfort, there is something in the general air that is not well. Is it that the carpets and the cushions are too soft and noiseless, so that those who move or repose among them seem to act by stealth?" (Chapter 33, p. 471.)

The social nuances are subtle enough, but there are overtones which are not social, and which are taken up more fully in the treatment of Carker elsewhere. For throughout the book there is in his behaviour, in his cat-like walk, his elegance, and his affected speech, a strain which would place him in the Angus Wilson world. This emerges most pointedly in the scene in which Carker cows Rob the Grinder, a sullen young lout, spoiled rather than leavened by his little learning. Detached from its context, the whole episode would fit into a modern novel as a tendentiously homosexual relationship. This association of the waspish-tongued old "queen" and the surly Ted, the class differences adding frissons of their own, is a basic element of homosexual literature. In this particular scene, the way in which Carker, exploiting with great enjoyment his class superiority, establishes the desired domination over Rob calls to mind a scene from Sartre's *L'Age de Raison*. It is the relish of the cat and mouse manoeuvring that Sartre's Daniel and Dickens's Carker have most strikingly in common. The tone of the two passages is similar, suggesting that the parallel is no accidental correspondence of situation:

> The moment they were face to face alone, Mr. Carker, without a word of preparation, took him by the throat, and shook him until his head seemed loose upon his shoulders . . .
> "Come, Sir! You let me alone, will you!"
> "Let you alone!" said Mr. Carker. "What! I have got you, have I? . . . You dog . . . I'll strangle you!" . . .

"I haven't done nothing to you, Sir," said Biler, otherwise Rob, otherwise Grinder, and always Toodle.

"You young scoundrel!" replied Mr. Carker, slowly releasing him, and moving back a step into his favourite position. (*Dombey and Son*, chapter 22, p. 304.)

Here is the Sartre:

"So," said Daniel, "you aren't afraid of anyone, eh? Not of anyone?"

Ralph flushed. "The big chaps aren't the strongest," he said.

"And what about you? Let's see how strong you are," said Daniel, pushing him. "Just let's see."

Ralph stood for a moment with his mouth open, then his eyes glittered.

"As it's you — I don't mind. For fun, of course," he said in a sibilant voice. "And no dirty business. You won't get the best of it."

Daniel grabbed him by the belt: "I'll show you, my poppet." [10]

In both cases there is a sense of impropriety in the mere presence of the two men in the same room, a sense of something which should be explained. Why is this presentable, even elegant, middle-aged man closeted with this sullen young lout? The socio-economic factor definitely prompts embarrassment, well-rendered by Dickens not only here but in an oddly similar confrontation in *Our Mutual Friend,* between Mortimer Lightwood, an elegant lawyer, and Charley Hexam, the son of a "water-rat". There is nothing of the homosexual in Lightwood, nor for that matter in Charley. But structurally the scene has something important in common with the other scenes mentioned, and Dickens is subtle enough to communicate such shades of atmosphere. The critical difference is that while Sartre's Daniel wants to dominate his youth (he does it eventually by means of physical combat) for purely sexual reasons, Carker wants to get Rob to spy on the people at Solomon Gills's shop. Characteristically, Dickens gives his sexual conflicts an explanation in other terms. Whatever his explanation, the sexuality persists as a flavour: Rob's vigilance, as we have seen, bears no fruit.

If Edith is too much for Dombey — her superbness is never in danger of capitulating to his frozen masculinity — it is obvious that she will be too much for the ambiguous Carker. It is impossible to imagine him seducing her. And in fact it is really not Carker who displaces Dombey but Florence. Emotionally, this is the real climax of the novel. The situation has been so carefully prepared for that the attraction that springs into being seems natural and inevitable. Florence is probably the first really warm, affectionate human being Edith has ever met. One understands now the elaborate patience with which Dickens has followed Florence's emotional development. She emerges as one of those impulsive, outward-going women Dickens always cherished as a kind of sexual ideal. Astonishingly, he succeeds with the type more often than not: Florence is a much more real creation than Walter Gay, and manages to create a kind of heart at the centre of a book, of which the purpose, ultimately, is to locate the causes of various kinds of heartlessness.

So carefully has Dickens built up this world of flattery, sycophancy, vaingloriousness, and deceit, that the emotional confusions and blockages appear as the natural outcome of misplaced interest and false values. Correspondingly, the relationship between Edith and Florence emerges, at least as far as Edith is concerned, as the only conceivable one. Her mother has killed her capacity for responding to male domination, though one senses that it is still perhaps capable of revival in the presence of a masculinity whose authority is natural and based upon a power more deeply rooted than Dombey's distant pride. The imagery Dickens uses at the most intense moments of the relationship emphasizes the contempt which has made her cold to male sexuality. On the eve of the marriage to Dombey, she takes leave of her mother, who is at the root of the whole disorder: "Without a tremor in her voice, or frame, and passing onward with a foot that set itself upon the neck of every soft emotion, she bade her mother good night . . . " (Chapter 30, p. 434.) And later, when she kisses the sleeping Florence, "Its touch was like the prophet's rod of old upon the rock. Her tears sprung forth . . . " (Chapter 30, p. 435.) The thwarted phallicism that underlies the emotion, at least in its extreme forms, of an older, stronger woman for a younger, is the more power-fully suggested for its being so well concealed. In the first quotation, the snake image is not explicitly mentioned: but "the neck of every soft emotion" is ophidian; treading on the snake here means, surely, treading on the aspirations of the male. Edith remains very feminine: she is the Brunhilde type, a fortress unconquered, not the trousered male-substitute. Her love for Florence only releases the untapped affection in her.

The elopement that follows between Edith and Carker devolves from the situation in Dombey's house. The point is lost, of course, if Edith's motivation is misunderstood. She is perfectly aware how she is playing her cards, and her flight with her husband's clerk has a cold savagery that contrasts with the warmth she has displayed towards Florence. The blow is aimed at Carker as much as at Dombey. Dombey has been — apparently — cuckolded, but the humiliation of the presumptuous clerk is far more devastating. This even com-pensates in part for the patent staginess of the *never-darken-my-portals-again* scene, in which Edith finally disabuses Carker of his hopes. It is his inferior sexuality she is repudia-ting, not his lower-class origin, to which she, with her experience of Leamington Spa, must be pretty indifferent.

The whole theme, finally, is counterpointed by the story of old Mrs. Brown's daughter, Ally, who turns out to be Carker's long-lost mistress. Ally too, has been hardened out of femininity, and when she weeps, it is not like a woman, but "like a stern man". Her hair is compared to a "heap of serpents". Her response to Carker's sister, Harriet, faintly recalls Edith's to Florence. Carker, incidentally, has never really forgiven Harriet for choosing to live with their brother James, rather than himself. He expresses his jealousy of his brother by his domineering attitude towards him in the office.

Thus, the main conflicts of *Dombey and Son* are emotional and sexual, though they are examined in social and economic terms. The guilt of Dombey by far outweighs that of Carker, who simply exploits the weaknesses in his master's defences. Dombey's pride, moreover, is a result of a deep block of feeling in himself. In the same way, other characters — Florence, Edith, Carker, Ally — are full of emotional and sexual tensions. These tensions relate fundamentally to the class pride which in a way explains Dombey himself. The novel shows Dickens's growing awareness of the price the middle class has to pay for its gentility. In the early books, poverty was an abyss, a disaster the magnitude of which lent the enactment of the myth its force and compulsion. The proletarians were a rabble of beggars, thieves, and prisoners. Faithful retainers like Mark Tapley, Sam Weller, and Joe Willett only proved the rule to which they were the exceptions: it seems that Dickens's early proletarians only achieved humanity at the price of class treason.

In *Dombey and Son* a significant change has taken place: the pillorying of the aristocracy is something the reader of the early Dickens novel would have been accustomed to. But the suggestion that the solid commercial middle class, hitherto represented by lovable old uncles like the Cheerybles and Mr. Pickwick, had purchased its gentility at the sacrifice of its own humanity — a curious yet logically determined inversion of the class treason of the early proletarians — this was something new and startling in Dickens. I have already remarked on the significance of the genuinely picaresque episodes of *Nicholas Nickleby* and *The Old Curiosity Shop*. In *Dombey and Son,* the low-life characters — Captain Cuttle, Polly Toodle, and Richards — have a warmth Florence fails to find in her own father. At the same time as this new orientation towards the class situation is taking place, Dickens is beginning to explore new aspects of the relations between the sexes, especially as these are implicated in the economic set-up. What is wrong with Dombey? And Carker? Why does Edith hate men? What sort of blockage produces the reserve and distance characteristic of the English bourgeoisie? It would be absurd to suggest that *Dombey and Son* is peopled exclusively by lesbians and homosexuals. But there seems little doubt that Dickens was becoming in this book increasingly conscious of anomalies and abnormalities of behaviour and of the conditions and attitudes that tended to produce them. The book unquestionably demolishes the Victorian male's conception of his greatness.

7 *David Copperfield*

Oliver Twist, David Copperfield, and *Great Expectations* occur at decisive moments in Dickens's career. Allying to lucidity of vision a structural solidity which makes them in certain ways the most satisfying of Dickens's works, they represent the most clearly defined stages of the basic myth in its evolution from something close to wish-fulfilment to definitive critique: in them, we can see the history of his development in an almost diagrammatic way. Dickens's new hero stands halfway between Oliver Twist and Pip. Walter Gay was an offstage figure, principally important as a balance for Florence. In choosing to write (in however disguised a way) his autobiography, Dickens placed himself at the heart of things in *David Copperfield.* David is orphaned relatively late in the book — about one fifth of the way through — but his mother's death only completes a process begun a hundred and fifty pages earlier with her re-marriage to Mr. Murdstone. But instead of showing us the orphan cast out on the world and delivered from evil by chance and a fairy-godmother, Dickens presents us with a much more representative kind of predicament: Aunt Betsey shapes like the traditional fairy-godmother, but loses her ogreishness when David grows up, and becomes a fussy old maid who loses her fortune (or feigns to have). In other words, Dickens has withdrawn the lucky charm from his hero. The forces of evil alter accordingly, and at the same time questions of individual responsibility begin to arise here as they had not before: the book is as pervaded by moral as *Dombey and Son* is by sexual ambiguities.

All this suggests what is true: that Dickens has caught up with himself here, and reached a point of balance. As much is suggested in the story's even motion: the flanks keep pace with the centre, and the whole narrative progresses at an even trot. Far from being a holiday in Dickens's work, as Edmund Wilson claims,[1] *David Copperfield* is absolutely central to an understanding of his development.

Of the opening part of the book — up to David's seventeenth year, say, and his looking about him — it is difficult to make any comment that isn't both superfluous and inadequate. Yet the apparent effortlessness of the writing shouldn't blind us to the careful construction of a powerful and integrated design. Dickens's triumph, certainly, is to have given an impression of careless ease, but no novel was ever less casual than *David Copperfield*. Without doubt, we must reject any account of the book which sees it as falling away from the childhood experiences into something less worthy of our attention. It is common enough for an autobiography — however disguised — to fail to survive its childhood phase, and we needn't look far for the reason. Childhood is, in Shelley's phrase, "the longest journey", and therefore the best digested period of our lives. It is also pregnant with (now dead) possibilities, promise, and hope. Maxim Gorky's autobiographical trilogy is probably the best example in modern literature of the evaporation of "magic" and interest with youth. But more striking is the negative evidence of the innumerable reminiscences which never get beyond the childhood phase at all.

Certainly, Dickens is not writing this sort of loving memorial of childhood. The childhood scenes, though decisively influential in European writing, are not proffered for their magic, nor do they monopolize the artist's attention. To see the book as falling off from the opening material is to distort that material itself even more than what follows. The act of recollection sustained throughout the novel requires the knowledge of later revelations to have been assumed from the beginning; and we would destroy the peculiarly subtle balance Dickens in fact achieves of generalized conspectus and local experience, if we did not take account of the influence of the later view upon the understanding of the earliest memories. In no other novel of his, in fact, is Dickens more fruitfully preoccupied with the intricacies of attention and awareness, of perception of growth; these are all preoccupations which depend upon the sustaining of a single act of recollective concentration.

The intimate attentiveness to the motions of consciousness produces — *en passant* — a liberal supply of wittily precise notations of common experiences: young David's pretence of not having seen little Emily, the twice-noted sensation of having experienced this before and knowing the next thing that is going to be said, David's impression that only his hair is drunk, the nature of drunken self-alienation itself — such observations are of the essence of *David Copperfield,* and they amount to much more than the sum of them all added together: they are a kind of modality. Never was a writer more inwardly attentive to the nature of his own sensations, and to the disparity that sometimes subsists between our awareness of our own experiences and what seems to be going on "outside". But there is also throughout the book a preternatural alertness to the life of the past self (or selves) within the present self. Or, to put it in reverse, the presence of the recollecting consciousness among the scenes which it forces its past selves to recollect. How accurately, how sensitively, for instance, Dickens evokes the sense of loss in chapter 9, when David is told of his mother's death. The self — the real self, heart, soul, and organism — responds deeply and instinctively and produces the "mist" that rises to cover David's eyes. But something is there recording the scene so that the recollector can later recollect it. Note for instance that David says "I felt the burning tears run down my face" (p. 123), not "the burning tears ran down my face". The event is registered as though by someone distinct from the self that is hurt. Almost immediately after this, David remembers a still more real awareness of the difference between himself and — well, himself:

> If ever child were stricken with sincere grief, I was. But I remember that this importance was a kind of satisfaction to me, when I walked in the playground that afternoon while the boys were in school. When I saw them glancing at me out of the windows, as they went up to their classes, I felt distinguished and looked more melancholy, and walked slower. (Chapter 9, p. 124.)

David is *playing the role* of the bereaved here, and it is wholly characteristic of Dickens's refinement of feeling and precision of notation that he can so clearly and delicately articulate the separation between the "grief" on the one hand, and on the other the consciousness of grief that chooses to convert its natural physical symptoms (tears, slowness of movement, length of face) into a constant image of desolation, without invalidating the grief itself. A crude criticism might cite this as evidence of some callowness in David that Dickens has presented as needing to be knocked out of him. What we have in fact is a far more valuable penetration into the nature of consciousness, and once again Dickens has not only anticipated but (surely) helped direct the thinking of twentieth century psychologists. When Sartre in a famous passage describes his waiter as "playing at being a waiter in a café",[2] he treads a path long since trodden by Dickens (and other nineteenth century novelists).

Now throughout *David Copperfield,* Dickens takes a virtuoso's delight in such facts of self-separation. It is a stunning performance, and Dickens here, for the first time in his life, becomes fully aware of the nature and extent of his gifts. At several places in the childhood chapters Dickens shows off the prodigiousness of his observational faculties. After a characteristically "inimitable" description of Peggotty as first recalled by the infant David, Dickens remarks that "the memory of most of us can go farther back into such times than many of us suppose . . . most grown men who are remarkable in this respect may with greater propriety be said not to have lost the faculty than to have acquired it . . . " Such men moreover "retain a certain freshness, and gentleness, and capacity of being pleased, which are also an inheritance they have preserved from their childhood" (chapter 2, p. 13). A little later the author claims this sort of distinction explicitly for himself: "I undoubtedly lay claim to both of these characteristics . . . " (p. 13). We are accustomed to identify self-awareness in moments at which our deficiencies appear obvious to our consciousness, for the clear but inadequate reason that the unpleasant facts about ourselves are likely to be concealed from awareness by repression, and therefore to require more virtuous effort in the unmasking. Such an attitude may be morally beneficial, but intellectually it is at least as important that we should be "aware of" ourselves in moments of exultation, triumph, or in the exercise of our most distinguished skills. *David Copperfield* is a book by a very successful man indeed, and Dickens shows his distinction of mind in nothing so much as in his lucid awareness of the nature of his genius. The book is — as John Jones points out[3] — the portrait of an artist; but it is so less in that it concerns the maturing of a professional writer, than in its analytical presentation of the very rare and strange perceptual skills of a great artist. Joyce's *Portrait* could not — obviously — have come into being without Dickens's work. But Joyce's is an ideological novel: Dickens's simply is not, and to concentrate on the similarities rather than the dissimilarities between the two novels will probably lead us, as Mr. Jones is led,[4] to the conclusion that Dickens's portrait is a "worldly" one. In fact, we are not required to be interested in the *raison d'être* of David's writing, as we must be in Stephen Dedalus's: Joyce demands that we accept the spiritual superiority of Stephen and his way of life; Dickens is concerned with different relations obtaining between his writer and his world. Which is to say ultimately that his ideological position is different from Joyce's: for Joyce's work takes its place in the mainstream of the European romantic-symbolist *avant garde*; Dickens's within the imaginative life of a society from which Joyce was ideologically cut off. These differences are reflected in — as they reflect — the different recollective techniques of the two writers.

Joyce's *Portrait* began in the years of his full artistic

self-consciousness: it originated in *Stephen Hero,* which concerns only the author's late adolescence, and his emergence into artistic self-consciousness. It then proceeds — somewhat laboriously — to reconstruct the past back to Stephen/ Joyce's infancy. Because it is anchored in this way — nailed down to and by its concluding paragraphs (carefully, lovingly cherished diary entries from real life) — Joyce's portrait necessarily lacks exploratory surprise. Joyce does not need or wish to find out who he is, since this is already established; his recollection is to that extent bogus — a pretence of discovering a pattern which is in fact determined beforehand and dictated by the artist's self-conception. In fact, as we know from Stanislaus Joyce,[5] this same self-conception systematically distorted the "truth", by turning "sunny Jim", generally popular and good at games, into the shy Byronic introvert presented in the pages of the *Portrait.* The degree of the distortion doesn't vitiate Joyce's novel, of course: what matters is the stance taken, and the facts Stanislaus Joyce observed did after all have an inwardly experienced dimension, as well as an outwardly observed one. Joyce had the right to his ideology. What concerns us here is the effect of the governing rationale upon the actual writing of the book, especially in respect of its recollective mechanisms. Joyce's childhood recollections, clinically accurate as so many of them are (wetting the bed, for instance, or clapping one's hands over one's ears in the playground), have a stillness about them which reflects the inauthenticity of the writer's recollective act as much as the poet's consciousness of silence. Joyce's past is a museum in which he rearranges things at certain points in order to make up a particular desired tableau. Dickens, on the other hand, remembers with a vibrancy which wholly transforms the objects of memory into subjects: he moves back and forth, into and out of his story, now freezing the action in order to place himself as he was then in relation to the self he is manifesting now; now merging into past self, now withdrawing from himself as he writes of those earlier apparitions. Never, we may say, has the nature of the act of recollection been so convincingly exercised before us: in being so exercised, it becomes fully transparent and visible to itself. It is the interaction of several different modes of presentation that creates this impression, and this cannot be easily demonstrated in quotation. But attention may be drawn to the strategically small number of present-tense insertions in the first two hundred pages or so, insertions which not only facilitate the onward movement of the narrative by reminding us in fact of the distance in time at which the events took place, but also suggest the strange presence of unreality in life even when these events are experienced. It is this constant reference back to the act and moment of writing that creates the three-dimensionality of the whole book. Dickens never pretends, as Joyce in effect does with his solemn *distanciation,* that his narrative is an objectified record of events in which the will of the creator has no influence. On the contrary, the constant presence of his own voice never lets us forget that this is a *bona fide* act of reminiscence, with all the liability to distortion this involves.

At four points in the narrative, moreover, Dickens expands the present-tense insertions into what he calls "Retrospects". This is strange, seeing that the whole novel is a retrospect, and that we are constantly being reminded of the fact. At any rate some special significance attaches to these retrospects: they appear to be streams of time from which Dickens consciously stands aside:

> My schooldays! The silent gliding on of my existence – the unseen, unfelt progress of my life – from childhood up to youth! Let me think, as I look back upon that flowing water, now a dry channel overgrown with leaves, whether there are any marks along its course, by which I can remember how it ran. (Chapter 18, p. 265.)

It is by means of such retrospective withdrawals that the novel's supernal dimension is achieved: the retrospects make contact with a realm transcending the facts of the narrative, and – by implication – the fact of the narrator's recording them. There is a current running through the novel, or on which the novel floats, and the retrospects, in standing aside from facticity, disclose them: how else could the very fact of an "unseen, unfelt progress" of a life be made visible to our contemplation? To have conveyed not merely the results but the actuality of some process which cannot in fact be consciously known — that is the great achievement of Dickens's novel. And in this it surpasses, to my way of thinking, all other novels of recollection: in Joyce, the recollected "fact" is trophied in a museum; in Proust — much closer to Dickens — a prodigious faculty of recall feeds upon present *symbols* in order to re-invoke its early experiences. Neither Joyce nor Proust succeeds so well as Dickens in exploiting recollection in order to marshal the separate selves of which the present self is compacted.

The fine exploratory movement of the prose in the opening lines of chapter 18 makes it clear that the metaphor of the stream is no casual one. A slightly later passage confirms our sense of an important underlying dimension or modality, of which this metaphor is merely an instrumental analogue:

> — and what comes next? *I* am the head-boy, now! I look down on the line of boys below me, with a condescending interest in such of them as bring to mind the boy I was myself, when I first came there. That little fellow seems to be no part of me; I remember him as something left behind upon the road of life — as something I have passed, rather than have actually been — and almost think of him as some one else. (Chapter 18, p. 268.)

A double *distanciation* is experienced here: the whole frame of the retrospect suggests the mature David looking back on the young David, now head boy; but *that* David too is looking back, and not only looking back, but physically looking down at the younger boys, and in doing so seeing himself. (How true is the suggestion, by the way, that we feel special interest in the people who remind us of our younger selves.) The transition from the head boy David's physical looking to his mental remembering — "that boy" might have been an actual boy seen by David, but is David himself — forms a transition in the larger scale of the story. In recording a moment at which he became aware of having himself changed, David renders visible not merely the *fact* of change and growth, but the mechanism. The epochs at which we can look back on ourselves as "someone else" mark the larger stages of our growth and maturing.

The metaphor of the "road of life" goes along with that of the stream of time as an instrumental analogue of the novel's underlying dimension. (We shall see later that both the roads and the river in *David Copperfield* lead to the sea.) Both roads and rivers are likely to be called "tracks" in Dickens: the road under rain is like a stream, and the riverbed dried out becomes a way for walking. Both are highways used for traffic. In this way, Dickens's symbols reinforce each other. The metaphor of the "road of life" gives us the shape of the whole narrative: how commonplace a figure it is, yet how deep and real is its occurrence here. We think of David's walk to Dover, and thence of Oliver Twist's walk to London, which also took seven days; of Pip's journey down the Thames to self-discovery. Surely, we have here one of Dickens's key metaphors. He was always peculiarly sensitive to travel, as we have seen in *Martin Chuzzlewit,* and to the strange collapsing of space and time it involves: in travelling, one moves forward at once in space and in time. We experience the movement of time even if we sit in a closed room for a year; but when we travel, physically, it is as if time would have stood still had we not gone to meet it. Experience, we may say, is itself the synthesis of the dimensions of space and time. And all roads lead not to death, but to the self that *is* now. Yet in experiencing the strange shock of alienation from himself, in becoming aware of a past version of himself (one's self is all one's selves, and to be alienated from one is to be alienated from all), David/Dickens sets the entire narrative, including the act of writing it now, in a transcending perspective. This will become plain when we come to deal with the Steerforth-Emily theme.

For the moment let us consider another aspect of the childhood scenes of the novel: their more or less continuous unpleasantness, and their almost equally continuous effect of eclipsing or setting at nought the narrator's personality.

The idyllic phase of David's childhood — the life with the

mother and the faithful servant — is rudely disturbed by the
first appearance of Mr. Murdstone's "ill-omened black eyes"
on the nineteenth page of the book. From this moment,
David's peace is gone. Now Murdstone is unquestionably one
of the most unpleasant characters in the whole of Dickens.
He would seem to have taken over the burden of the powerfully attractive villainy of the early books, but his treatment
differs significantly. Soon after his first appearance in the
book, Murdstone takes David on a day-trip to the coast; this
is to please David's mother alone. David observes him at close
range and gives us a closer account of those black eyes: "He
had that kind of shallow black eye — I want to express an eye
that has no depth in it to be looked into — which, when it is
abstracted, seems, from some peculiarity of light, to be disfigured, for a moment at a time, by a cast." (Chapter 2, p.
22.) We have an excellent instance here of Dickens's method
of characterization: that cast in the eye, or the appearance of
a cast, that shallow depth that cannot be looked into, the
capacity for abstraction — these *are* Murdstone, and no other
artistic method could conceivably increase our subtle, disturbing knowledge of the man. Aestheticians since the
German Romantic philosophers have been at pains to
emphasize the capacity of art to give us a kind of knowledge
that cannot be obtained from science or any other source.
The art of Dickens is a case in point: no one could tell us
more than Dickens tells us in these uncanny physical observations. More is to be revealed of the Murdstones later: though
not "explained" by their awful religion (which is itself a
symptom), they are comprehended in it. But here in the
second chapter of the book we know the man and fear him,
as intimately as David in his childishness is pressed up against
him, bringing home to him the force of Murdstone's dark
masculinity:

> Several times when I glanced at him, I observed that appearance
> with a sort of awe, and wondered what he was thinking about so
> closely. His hair and whiskers were blacker and thicker, looked at
> so near, than even I had given them credit for being. A squareness
> about the lower part of his face, and the dotted indication of the
> strong black beard he shaved closely every day, reminded me of

the waxwork that had travelled into our neighbourhood some half-a-year before. This, his regular eyebrows, and the rich white, and black, of his complexion — confound his complexion, and his memory! — made me think him, in spite of my misgivings, a very handsome man. I have no doubt that my poor dear mother thought him so too. (Chapter 2, p. 22.)

There follows the sophisticated scene at the coast with Murdstone's associates, a curiously Joycean scene, dominated by the joke about Brooks of Sheffield, and the man called Quinion: Dickens captures exactly the right feeling of childhood incomprehension here. The Brooks of Sheffield joke is never explained, but it is taken in with a residual understanding that hindsight will later interpret aright. Whatever David understands, he knows enough to feel deep misgivings about his mother, just as he *knows* Murdstone, with the exact subtlety of which children are so often capable. It's safe to say that no other novelist could have given us Murdstone at all: no *explication* of that horrible mind could add an iota to our intimate knowledge of the man. Murdstone is given with the infiniteness of a real human being, whose own experience of himself has neither beginning nor end, but is simply timeless and ongoing. What *is* Mr. Murdstone thinking about on the road to the coast? Mrs. Copperfield? The coming marriage? Murdstone and Grinby's failing fortunes? God? Swift? All of these, perhaps, and none of them. Such explanations could be given of Mr. Murdstone. But Dickens has performed the far rarer and more valuable service of giving us the quality of a man's consciousness itself: Murdstone is simply within his "life" — being-Mr.-Murdstone. The "shallow black eye", the appearance of a cast, the care in shaving, the heavy masculinity, the air of abstraction — these things tell us so much more than a chapter of exegesis, teasing out the path of his ruminations, and explaining his "character". The "character" indeed could be explained; what can't be explained is the man inside it.

Two further points in Dickens's handling of Murdstone show an increasing delicacy in his attitude towards unsympathetic people. In the first place, he is described as having "beautiful hair". The physical appearance of his characters is one of Dickens's principal ways of expressing their inner nature, and the attribution of any kind of beauty to one so unpleasant as Murdstone reveals a subtler awareness of the nature of evil and of the ambivalence of his own reactions to it than Dickens had shown before. Evil often exerts a powerful attraction because it has force and self-determination, in contrast to the drift and dither of much that is morally neutral or good. The attraction Murdstone exerts over David's mother is very easy to understand, and Dickens has the delicacy not to adopt a piously reproving attitude towards her.

Secondly, on David's return to Blunderstone after hearing the news of her death, Murdstone is described as "sobbing quietly". There is no doubt about the genuineness of his grief, nor of his love. He finds David intolerable, indeed, precisely because he reminds him of his dead wife. One's final image of Murdstone is of a strangely impressive though horrible man, tortured by his own puritanical obsession with sex. In an earlier novel, Dickens would undoubtedly have seen him as wicked step-father pure and simple. The increasing control Dickens was able to exercise over the moral and technical structure of his novels is seen nowhere more impressively than in this new delicacy and sureness in handling what previously had haunted him. Murdstone's reality, drained of what heavy attractiveness it had in him, appears also in his sister, Jane, jangling with sadist symbols — keys, and cruel reticules and bunches of metallic fingers. It is many years later that we encounter her again, attached to the pretty, helpless Dora Spenlow. In choosing Dora, David chooses his mother; it is no real surprise, either to him, or to us, to find Jane Murdstone already ensconced at the virgin's side.

Helpless as she was, David's mother cannot be wholly exonerated from the blame of what happened to her son both after her marriage and after her death. She must have realized soon enough that David and Murdstone detested each other, but she did not let it influence her decision to re-marry. It is the shallowness of her fluttery femininity that really registers; and this is the first in a series of such criticisms made throughout the book. In varying degrees, most of the major characters are held partly responsible for what happens and are guilty of some form of moral myopia or inadequacy: yet these inadequacies are still held to be not only natural but inevitable. It is, perhaps, the purpose of the book, or at least the "moral" one can least help deducing from it, that out of such minor foibles and weaknesses, themselves hardly amounting to faults but becoming faults in combination with circumstances and with each other, grow the tragedies upon which hindsight later passes judgments that largely ignore the true causes.

After the implicit criticism of Mrs. Copperfield (and how priggishly this rings by comparison with the delicacy of the novel), the first hints of what is to come occur in the juxtaposed episodes of David's first visit to Yarmouth and his initiation into the squalid ways of Creakle's school. I refer to Emily's discontent, her yearning to be a lady — in which there is the germ of her downfall — and to David's immediate infatuation with Steerforth. The two themes are closely related, and the means of the relation is tne class-consciousness which is so radically a part of the ethos of *David Copperfield*. The novel stands, I have observed, at a crucially important stage in Dickens's development of the basic myth. It is Emily who most clearly forefigures the preoccupation behind the myth at this stage: the desire to emulate the superior classes.

We are introduced to this desire of Emily's at second-hand, through the distorting jealousy of Minnie Joram, the daughter of the Yarmouth undertaker who plays a significant choric role throughout the novel. On several occasions, David goes out of his way to step into the undertaker's shop, talk with the strangely wise proprietor, and to overhear the "tune" that runs through and behind the facts of the narrative itself, as steadily as the stream of time and the road of life: the tapping of hammers as coffins are made. In the front of the shop sit Joram's young ladies, sewing: it is a wholly characteristic contrivance, in fact, at once furnishing us with a detached yet sympathetic commentary on the events of the novel, and revealing to us the ceaseless reality of death that underlies them. It is here that Dickens first informs us of the alienating ambitions of little Emily: " 'You see,' " Mr. Joram says, in explanation of his daughter's attack on Emily, " 'she hasn't taken much to any companions here; she hasn't taken kindly to any particular acquaintances and friends, not to mention sweethearts. In consequence, an ill-natured story got about that Em'ly wanted to be a lady.' " (Chapter 21, p. 305.) A little later, Mr. Joram tells us of the "situation" Emily had acquired — " 'to keep a fractious old lady company' ", though " 'they didn't very well agree, and she didn't stop' " (p. 306). Emily, it is clear, is in much the same situation as Pip in *Great Expectations:* Dickens isn't, as it were, quite ready yet to put himself in this position, but the theme is significantly foreshadowed. There are no signs of this kind of class ambition in David himself, but there are many tell-tale details which reveal Dickens's awareness of the class-consciousness underlying his disguised autobiography. For David has had the experience of a proletarian, and he is aware of the need for keeping it quiet, though he is never touchy on the subject. Late in the novel, Uriah Heep is to refer to David's shameful working-class background: David is yoked together with Micawber by Heep's class-hatred, and the worst he can hurl at them is to suggest that they are no better than he is. To all this David (or Dickens) remains curiously impassive, as though keeping still were for the time being the best policy.

What brings out David/Dickens's acute sense of class most strongly in fact is the association with the Peggottys. Peggotty herself virtually becomes David's mother and Dan Peggotty plays something of the Magwitch role in *Great Expectations.* In a strange dreamlike way, David cannot escape the Peggottys; even though they help him feel closer to Steerforth's level (having servants proves him not a proletarian himself), David is later made uncomfortable by his acquaintance with them, and even more by his loyalty to them. This is particularly true in the case of Rosa Dartle, who lashes David for having contaminated the *bon bourgeois* household with his nasty working-class friends; and in the case of that terrifying character Littimer, the gentleman's gentleman, to whom I shall return later.

David's friendship with Steerforth comes about through the medium of Creakle's so-called Academy. Steerforth is throughout handled with the most exquisitely controlled delicacy. There is always a sense of the fallaciousness of the whole cult, a suspicion of this too eligible beauty, this too easy charm, but Dickens never surrenders to the tempting categorizations. The tone of voice in which David refers to him is throughout of great tenderness. It is Steerforth who dispenses the food at the dormitory feast, and also the magic, so strangely reminiscent of *Le Grand Meaulnes:*

> ... the moonlight falling a little way into the room, through the window, painting a pale window on the floor, and the greater part of us in shadow, except when Steerforth dipped a match into a phosphorus-box, when he wanted to look for anything on the board, and shed a blue glare over us that was gone directly! A certain mysterious feeling, consequent on the darkness, the secrecy of the revel, and the whisper in which everything was said, steals over me again, and I listen to all they tell me with a vague feeling of solemnity and awe ... (Chapter 6, p. 85.)

Only Alain Fournier, in my experience, has succeeded in treading ground so fraught with dangers of sentimentality and glamorization, with comparable certainty to achieve a comparable freshness. What is unique to Dickens is the ability to divest himself of so many later selves, to re-experience the enchantment, localized here in the superb present tense insertion, "I listen", so that he, the mature man looking back, is again there with them, dissolving across time the accumulated patina of experience. When Dickens changes the tense from past to present, we experience the whole process of nostalgia as a physical event.

David's hero-worship of Steerforth is love in its fullest Romantic sense, both pure and undemanding. It is a theme in itself, and this is the classic treatment of it in the language. But the suggestion that its absoluteness has its dangers is never far below the surface. There is something doomed about Steerforth from the very beginning, that is implicit pre-eminently in the deference everyone shows to him. In the chapters at Creakle's school, it is the scene in which he humiliates kind Mr. Mell that makes this most apparent. Yet Steerforth, careless to the point of callousness, never quite forfeits our sympathy, his beauty waives the usual strictures. Only Traddles, as a matter of fact, stands out against the general condemnation of Mr. Mell, to be beaten by Creakle, and scorned by Steerforth — a good instance of Dickens's careful planning: we never quite lose *this* Traddles, honest and pugnacious, beneath the Herbert Pocket geniality David condescendingly buries him in later, so that his final agency in the *dénouement* is appropriate.

After the hints given in the Yarmouth chapter, it is obvious that Emily will be helpless before Steerforth. His class superiority (he is at Oxford when they first meet) and personal charm are exactly calculated to catalyze her own uncertainties, just as David's middle-classness had stimulated them earlier. Emily could never have been really happy with Ham, who is always rather patronized by David. His oafishness, which grates even when he is being kind, never seems adequate to her, so that it seems a little priggish to blame Emily for being so rapidly and completely smitten by the glamorous Steerforth. Nor is this simply class, although the class differences naturally exacerbate. Ham's softness and mushiness do not exist in his Uncle Dan. Even Ham's speech mannerisms — especially the "Mas'r Davy Bor" — irritate in a way that Dan Peggotty's do not, so that one secretly agrees with Steerforth's careless dismissal of him as not good enough for Emily. Much of this is implied in David's first assessment of Ham, "a huge, strong fellow of six feet high, broad in proportion, and round-shouldered; but with a simpering boy's face and curly light hair that gave him quite a sheepish look." (Chapter 3, p. 29.) Adjectives like *round -shouldered, simpering,* and *sheepish* are quite unequivocal (most of us use "round-shouldered" depreciatively); the collocation of them all together gives a sharp impression of someone young David, with his quick eye for the soft and the absurd, never quite took to. It is not unreasonable to expect Emily to fall out of love with such a person, irrespective of class. In fact, the profound love Emily feels for Uncle Dan is a response to qualities Ham patently never had. David himself, though he joins in the general lamentations over the seduction when it comes, remains to the end neutral on the score of Emily's guilt. He genuinely laments her fall from grace, socially and morally, but sees no reason for blaming her. Ham drops out of the book, except in the reports of others, until the final resolution of the whole story in the great shipwreck, and his fatal attempt to save the last man alive on it — who turns out to be Steerforth. In spite of all the talk about fallen women, and the regrettable part played by Martha Endell, the inevitability of the whole tragedy overrides the arm-upraised Victorian horror. The interaction of these three personalities — the "chuckle-headed" Ham, Emily, and Steerforth — could only end in this kind of loss and waste.

Dickens had, in fact, cast a shadow over the future in the scene on the eve of Steerforth's and David's departure from Yarmouth at the end of that fatal visit on which all the mischief was done. David had returned to the boat-house to find Steerforth brooding in front of the fire:

> . . . even my entrance failed to rouse him. I was standing close to him, looking at him; and still, with a heavy brow, he was lost in his meditations.
> He gave such a start when I put my hand upon his shoulder, that he made me start too.
> "You come upon me," he said, almost angrily, "like a reproachful ghost!"
> "I was obliged to announce myself, somehow," I replied.
> "Have I called you down from the stars?"
> "No," he answered, "No." (Chapter 22, p. 321.)

The tenderness of the emotion David then feels for his hero is beautifully played off against his own evident naivety (imagining Steerforth to be up in the stars), a naivety which Steerforth's firmly repeated "No" makes it clear he himself is well aware of. Steerforth, indeed, though in part corrupted by the cult of himself, is never really taken in by it. The whole passage, with Steerforth's self-denunciations following, has a strongly valedictory air.

The ensuing narrative is a masterpiece of concealed guile. Several structurally necessary hints are dropped in the only way, ultimately, they should be: they are interesting in their own right, and therefore allay any suspicions the reader might otherwise have entertained of joinery. I refer to the arrival of Littimer, ostensibly to take care of the boat Steerforth has had built, but actually, as we learn later, to take charge of Emily. David is still intrigued and intimidated by Littimer and this adds a sinister note to the whole chapter. Finally, the randy Miss Mowcher arrives, suggesting Steerforth's familiarity with things David is still innocent of, so that the new image of him begins to form in the mind. By a characteristically brilliant exploitation of the limitations of the first person narrative, Dickens now takes David off to London, immediately immersing him in other concerns of the novel — his own future after Aunt Betsey's "crash", Agnes Wickfield's predicament with Uriah Heep, the meeting with Dora Spenlow, and the fortunes of the Micawbers. By the time David is called back to Yarmouth by Barkis's illness, the Emily-Steerforth affair has been simmering unnoticed for long enough for the revelation — immediately after the death of Barkis — to be both shattering and half-expected. Critics of *David Copperfield* have made a lot of its occasionally over-signalled logic[6] — Aunt Betsey's "blind, blind", the husband who haunts her, but (we feel sure) will die conveniently enough, and so on. We hear less of the narrative's general ease and brilliance, presumably because of the naturalness with which they are achieved. In the strategy with which the strands of the story are exposed, developed, dropped, re-introduced, varied, and finally completed, *David Copperfield* has no equal: we must call it polyphonic, I'm afraid, unsatisfactory as the musical metaphor is. The episodes and themes are placed easily before us, we are engrossed; without either break or artificial transition, they are submerged and others come to the surface, while the earlier themes work on us unconsciously: the former themes are then re-introduced — into a world altered by what has happened since we heard them last.

In the resolution of the three major themes in the novel — the Emily-Ham-Steerforth triangle, the David-Dora-Agnes triangle, and the fortunes of the Wickfield-Heep-Micawber alliance — Dickens set himself a problem of enormous difficulty: how was he to organize his novel so that it could achieve consummation without either repressing the import of the themes not represented in that climax or on the other hand toppling over into bathos with a succession of mini-climaxes, one piled on top of the other? In the present instance — the half-climax of the revelation of the elopement of Emily and Steerforth — much of the work is done by metaphor. Immediately before Steerforth reappears in the story, to be introduced to the Peggottys, David has visited Covent Garden for a production of *Julius Caesar*. His intoxication with the performance is the occasion of a recurrence of the road-of-life metaphor:

> I was so filled with the play, and with the past — for it was, in a manner, like a shining transparency, through which I saw my earlier life moving along — that I don't know when the figure of a handsome well-informed young man, dressed with a tasteful easy negligence which I have reason to remember very well, became a real presence to me. (Chapter 19, p. 286.)

Steerforth, of course, is always associated both with David's Romantic sense of himself and with the class-consciousness catalyzed on that long walk to Dover, during which David had stopped in the shelter of the old school wall, imagining his old friends on the other side. Soon after, when David introduces Steerforth at Yarmouth, a new note is added to the sombre tonality of the seascape against which *David Copperfield* is played out. Again, it is associated with the romantic feeling Steerforth inspires in David: "If any one had told me, then," David writes of Steerforth's brilliant success with the locals and yokels, "that all this was a brilliant game, played for the excitement of the moment, for the employment of high spirits, in the thoughtless love of superiority, in a mere wasteful careless course of winning what was worthless to him, and next minute thrown away: I say, if any one had told me such a lie that night, I wonder in what manner of

receiving it my indignation would have found a vent!"
(Chapter 21, pp. 310–11.) Is this dramatic irony? Is it, that
is to say, an exact description of what Steerforth is doing and
will do? Or a genuine denial of an unfair construction? We
can't quite say. Certainly, the words which follow these are a
startling indication of the sense of Romantic fatality that
underlies the whole novel: "Probably only in an increase, had
that been possible, of the romantic feelings of fidelity and
friendship with which I walked beside him, over the dark
wintry sands towards the old boat." (P. 311.) The last
phrases sound the sombre note I have mentioned, by the
way, and a significant note it is in the world of the whole
novel. From the very beginning of David's acquaintance with
the Yarmouth ethos, the boat on the sands had held some
strange significance — at once homely and doomed, warm
and isolated, secure and at the mercy of storms. The wind is
always howling out on the desolate desert of the Yarmouth
beach; on this occasion, Steerforth articulates its particular
message:

> "Dismal enough in the dark," he said; "and the sea roars as if
> it were hungry for us." (Chapter 21, p. 311.)

It is, and he appreciates his own position acutely:

> "Contented?" he answered merrily. "I am never contented,
> except with your freshness, my gentle Daisy. As to fitfulness, I
> have never learnt the art of binding myself to any of the wheels
> on which the Ixions of these days are turning round and round. I
> missed it somehow in a bad apprenticeship, and now don't care
> about it. You know I have bought a boat down here?" (Chapter
> 22, p. 324.)

It is impossible to read this without thinking of Byron, of
course, and it seems significant that the demotic and industrious Dickens alone of Victorian novelists should have
shown himself sensitive to the situation of the "bourgeoisified" Byronic personality in the nineteenth century.
Steerforth's destructiveness, the love of exciting sensation
that can be satisfied only in actual physical activities like
sailing, the indulgence of dangerous social behaviour — all
this goes back directly to Byron, and can be found paralleled

in numerous Continental poets and novelists: one thinks of Lermontov's unknown yachtsman, "hoping in storms to find peace", and of Stavrogin. It is, in a sense that could fairly be defined in social terms, an accursed, or at least a fated personality. In Steerforth's case, the quality of fatality is still more finely and powerfully expressed a little while after the conversation just cited has taken place. David and Steerforth are walking back to their lodgings after a visit to the Peggottys' boat-house. They pass Ham and Emily, and Emily withdraws her hand from Ham's: she is embarrassed. A moment after they have passed, they are followed by a "black shadow", the local prostitute, Martha Endell, proffered, clearly, as an image of what Emily might become (one thinks of Rose Maylie and Nancy). The whole passage is an excellent example of Dickens's way with the presentation of meaning through scene, image, and action: the chance conjunction of personalities — Steerforth, David, Ham, Emily, Martha — stands for a detailed exposition of the possibilities. More, it amounts to a kind of encapsulated plot: David introduces Steerforth to his childhood friends Ham and Emily, Steerforth seduces Emily, Emily ends up like Martha — perhaps. All this is evoked in our minds, and immediately punched home by a superb piece of imagery:

> As the dark distant level, absorbing their figures into itself, left but itself visible between us and the sea and clouds, her figure disappeared in like manner, still no nearer than before.
> "That is a black shadow to be following the girl," said Steerforth, standing still; "what does it mean?" (Chapter 22, p. 326.)

No critic, I imagine, is going to accuse Dickens of over-pointing his logic here: Steerforth feels a shudder of prescience, and Dickens transmits it surely and delicately. But "a dark distant level": somehow this image of the horizon that absorbs everything into itself compresses or conceals the strange drawing-power shaping the whole narrative. In *A Tale of Two Cities,* Dickens was to use the image of the horizon, the thread, the line, in various ways to articulate the notion of a complex fatality beyond and yet within human "destiny". All roads in *David Copperfield,* I have suggested, lead to the sea; and sea meets sky in this "dark distant level". The "sense", if you like, of the incidents in the novel lies outside them all: it is beyond the horizon, the horizon which reduces everything to a dark line, and which brews storms as yet out of sight.

Caught between Steerforth and the Peggottys, David in a sense sustains a heavier blow at the seduction than anyone else. It is worth bearing in mind that when Steerforth seduces Emily, David, although he tends to patronize the Peggottys, stands by them: there is too acute an awareness of Steerforth's own patronage of them (" 'Mr. Peggotty,' he said, 'you are a thoroughly good fellow, and deserve to be as happy as you are tonight.' " pp. 315–16), for David himself to be oblivious to the dangers. But David stands by Steerforth as well — in word and in spirit: the acuteness of his discomfort, indeed, derives precisely from his refusal to abandon either of his loyalties.

Once again the real quality of *David Copperfield* — the basis of the high claim one must make for the book — is seen to consist in its strange marriage of contraries. It is a wonderfully generous book: yet, in its undeceivableness, Dickens's vision creates many complex images and penetrates many facades. I have already noted the sombre anxiety that in fact informs the famous evocation of childhood at the beginning of the book. A similar ambiguity impregnates the entire narrative. This is the great difference between it and *Pickwick,* and indeed between Samuel Pickwick Esq. himself, and his surrogate, Mr. Micawber. One of the few respects in which G. K. Chesterton lets his reverence for Dickens's art simplify the image produced by that art, is the implication we cannot help taking from his study that Micawber is a kind of Pickwick.[7] There is of course a crucial relationship between the two characters, a relationship both clarified and obscured by their status as great "Dickens characters". They *are* great characters, and this greatness is what we must admire in Dickens. Chesterton is so near to the truth about Dickens when he observes that "All the critics of Dickens, when all is said and done, have only walked round Micawber wondering what they should say."[8] Yet this "all" that is said and done, can be said and done either well or badly. When Chesterton himself observes that "Micawber is not a man; Micawber is the superman",[9] the basis of the judgment is not unsound. Micawber discourages the critic: one might as well criticise the sun. Why not just enjoy it? But Micawber isn't the sun. Pickwick was, but Micawber isn't Pickwick, and Chesterton tends, I think, to conflate the two characters. Now even this error is an intelligent one. There is more than a generic Dickensian benignancy in common between the two men: there is the same firm rotundity, the gentility, the baldness, the smiling grace, an energy of charm that makes people who know them feel close to the centre of things. With Micawber, as with Pickwick, life is a feast, and it is as the presiding master of ceremonies at innumerable dinner parties that we best remember Mr. Micawber. But Micawber has none of that quality of innocence Dostoievsky noted in Pickwick, and Micawber is "slippery". His gentility is backed up by no private income, his tights are shabby, his whole demeanour is in some sense founded upon falsehood.

The greatest Micawber scene in the novel is the dinner party that occupies the whole of chapter 28; this is the dead centre of the narrative, in fact. The chapter is called "Mr. Micawber's gauntlet", referring to the challenge Mrs. Micawber throws down on her husband's behalf — a challenge for England to awake and recognize his qualities. But in fact we are more likely to think of the gauntlet of creditors Micawber runs every day of his life than of this strictly unreal challenge. The chapter in fact significantly reveals the extent of Mrs. Micawber's complicity in Micawber's own inability to take mature responsibility for his life. We cannot but feel that her "faith" in Mr. Micawber helps sustain him in his unreality. The whole chapter is remarkable, but especially so in its meticulous observation of Micawber. He is as much in his element here, improvising a tasty meal — "a Devil" — from Mrs. Crupp's ruins, as he is "playing a lively game of skittles" in the Kings Bench. Conferring an aura of sheer pleasure in being alive upon the despoiled and the mediocre

— that is Micawber, and in this he is not the superman but *menschlich, allzu menschlich.* I hope this doesn't seem like another petty diminution of the art. It seems to me, on the contrary, to enhance the nature of the art: there is something heart-breaking about Micawber, something piercingly poignant in the increasingly haggard pretence of gentility. Dickens catches it most beautifully perhaps in Steerforth's careless enquiry towards the end of the scene: "Who's our friend in the tights?" I say pretence, but again this must not be taken to cut Micawber down to size. He is an aristocrat of the spirit, for whom work, routine, "responsibility", are simply too low. That is precisely why the whole portrait is so remarkable. It is of the essence of *David Copperfield* that it can convey so superbly the nervous, debilitating conflict of the forces of life and gaiety with the constructions of our modern society. Energy is a source of discomfort in *David Copperfield,* unless, like that of David himself, it finds a wholly exceptional path through to wholly exceptional success.

If Micawber is poised uncertainly upon the class-divide, continually drawing upon reserves he does not possess, David himself and Traddles are also uneasily insecure members of the striving middle class. This is the key to the quite extraordinary impact upon the happy gathering of Littimer, the gentleman's gentleman:

> We were at the height of our enjoyment, and were all busily engaged, in our several departments, endeavouring to bring the last batch of slices to a state of perfection that should crown the feast, when I was aware of a strange presence in the room, and my eyes encountered those of the staid Lattimer, standing hat in hand before me. (Chapter 28, p. 414.)

David's immediate response is one of guilt: " 'What's the matter?' I involuntarily asked." But the guilt is more than personal: they have all been caught out, caught out in their abject *petit bourgeois* enthusiasm, doing the cooking, like the proletarians Littimer makes them all feel. "A devil", indeed! Steerforth, as David observes, would have been less dreadful an apparition: his easy patronage they could all tolerate, and he *is* their superior. But Littimer, the gentleman's gentleman, the proletarian who knows the upper classes, is truly terrifying: he comprehends the full scale of their ignominious *Burgerlicherheit* with a keen sense of every degree of pretension, and vulgar enthusiasm. He provokes a significant response from every one of them. Micawber affects unconcern: "humming a tune to show that he was quite at his ease, [he] subsided into his chair with the handle of a hastily concealed fork sticking out of the bosom of his coat, as if he had stabbed himself." (P. 414.) Mrs. Micawber needs to remind herself of her gentility: she "put on her brown gloves and assumed a genteel languor". Traddles, better bred than any of them, stares "in confusion at the table", while David, as usual, feels young — or does he? There is perhaps a shade of disingenuousness in Dickens's reiteration of this motif: doesn't Littimer really sense the old connexion between Micawber and David, apprehending with the English butler's preternatural alertness to these nuances, some stain of the old Murdstone and Grinby days? The entire passage, anyway, is an excellent instance of Dickens's mature manner: a situation of considerable complexity is given with maximum economy, through the delicate articulation of gesture and physical behaviour.

The scene includes too a significant hint of Micawber's unscrupulousness. His irresponsibility builds up a defensive callousness in him, which extends gradually to everyone about him. It is poor Traddles, warned too late by David, who falls foul of a criminal carelessness in Micawber, a carelessness which has in fact turned into a cunning anything but careless. The shiftiness which accompanies the Micawber panache is more uncomfortably evident in the later dinner scene of chapter 36, in which Micawber delivers his I.O.U. to Traddles with such bravado and conviction, that Traddles feels half-paid. It is at the end of this chapter that David describes Micawber as "slippery", but he concludes with a note that strongly favours him: " . . . I was probably indebted to some compassionate recollection he retained of me as his boy-lodger, for never having been asked by him for money. I certainly should not have had the moral courage to refuse it; and I have no doubt that he knew that (to his credit be it written) quite as well as I did." (Chapter 36, p. 536.)

Micawber, it is plain, is a satire on just that sanguineness as to the likelihood of something turning up which in fact underlies the basic myth of the early novels. This is perhaps the best way of indicating the advance made in *David Copperfield*.

If the old comic egotism receives a decisive transformation in Micawber, so does the fascinating demonism in Uriah Heep. In the first stages of their relationship, David quite frankly confesses an attraction towards Heep:

> But, seeing a light in the little round office, and immediately feeling myself attracted towards Uriah Heep, who had a sort of fascination for me, I went in there instead. I found Uriah reading a great fat book, with such demonstrative attentiveness, that his lank forefinger followed up every line as he read and made clammy tracks along the page (or so I fully believed) like a snail. (Chapter 16, p. 324.)

Heep is a snail, and later many other repulsive creatures, but he still fascinates David. These pages are pervaded by Heep's influence: he pops up in all sorts of odd places, and if he does not, David's imagination does the work for him: "Leaning out of window, and seeing one of the faces on the beam-ends looking at me sideways, I fancied it was Uriah Heep got up there somehow, and shut him out in a hurry." (Chapter 15, p. 225.) The portrait is indeed established by a handful of such glimpses — Uriah at his stool, peering unexpectedly out of the turret window, seen a long way off, through several doors, in another room. The red-haired leering devil haunts Dickens's readers as compulsively as it haunts his narrator. David fears to touch him, and no other Dickens portrait is quite so tackily physical as this. Yet this creature attracts Dickens in a strange way. David expresses his ambivalence quite frankly: "I really had not yet been able to make up my mind whether I liked Uriah or detested him," he observes (chapter 17, p. 253).

The ambivalence is resolved in the scene at Dr. Strong's Highgate home, at which Heep shows the full range of his coarseness by accusing Annie Strong of being a corrupting

influence for Agnes. The scene is in many respects an important one. It serves both to point up the degeneracy of
Wickfield, by now a mere pawn of Heep's, and to bring to a
crisis David's own relationship with Uriah himself. The
doctor and Mr. Wickfield having gone, Uriah and David are
finally left alone together.

> As we stood, front to front, I saw so plainly, in the stealthy
> exultation of his face, what I already so plainly knew; I mean that
> he forced his confidence upon me, expressly to make me
> miserable, and had set a deliberate trap for me in this very matter;
> that I couldn't bear it. The whole of his lank cheek was invitingly
> before me, and I struck it with my open hand with that force that
> my fingers tingled as if I had burnt them. (Chapter 42, p.
> 619–20.)

The whole relationship — its deep-seated, unarticulated
resentments and uncertainties — suddenly explodes in that
slap. How superbly Dickens. captures the electric atmosphere
of any physical violence, and holds it with the next lines:

> He caught the hand in his, and we stood in that connexion,
> looking at each other. We stood so a long time; long enough for
> me to see the white marks of my fingers die out of the deep red
> of his cheek, and leave it a deeper red.
> "Copperfield," he said at length, in a breathless voice, "have
> you taken leave of your senses?" (Chapter 41, p. 620.)

I doubt if Dickens — or anyone else — ever wrote more
exactly, to greater purpose, every phrase sustaining the
tension and adding some to it. The relaxation that follows,
full of inner trembling and misgiving for David, is no less
brilliantly done, as Heep forces forgiveness upon his adver-
sary. From this moment, the relationship takes a decisive
turn. The uncertainty is shocked into hatred. One must
believe Uriah when he says here "And yet I always liked you,
Copperfield", just as, after the showdown at the end, one
believes the hatred he professes. One thing is certain: that the
emotion that went into that slap by far transcended the cause
Heep had given David in the Dr. Strong affair — for that,
rationally, disgust would have been enough. The motivation
towards physical violence came from a much deeper layer of
David's mind. The whole relationship is held, electrically, in

the hand which Uriah closes upon David's. Then it slowly relaxes into genuine hatred, the kind of hatred rational causes can never generate. To the end, Dickens can never shake off the original feelings he had about Uriah, pile execration on his head as he may.

Mr. Wickfield's fixation on his daughter is another of the major themes of the novel. It is a grim example of an obsession with one person or idea which gradually stiffens into a fixation in which the original object ceases to have a part. Mr. Wickfield's later port-tippling has nothing to do with Agnes. The obsessively fixated end is displaced into an inner symbol that has lost its reference to reality. At the beginning he is in command enough to register disapproval of Dr. Strong's household; he seems to have felt that the relationship itself was wrong; and he deals efficiently with Jack Maldon's careless disrespect for the doctor. Yet at the end, he is a dotard and a moral bankrupt.

As for David, his blindness to Agnes is as grave, and as natural, a miscalculation as any in the book. That he should find himself attracted to Dora Spenlow is no more, but no less, inexcusable than that Emily should fall for Steerforth, or Steerforth for her (for he does fall in his casual way). Throughout the book David is consistently careless about Agnes's feelings, using their childhood confidence in each other to boast about his latest passion.

It is, of course, myopia one is dealing with here, not anything evil. It would be absurd to put David's blindness to Agnes on a level with Heep's treachery. Yet Heep is only trying to get by foul means what it seems so easy for others to get by fair; the end itself does not seem so extraordinarily vicious. There is moreover an element of sheer jealousy in David's anger at Heep's advances to Agnes, which is dog-in-the-manger-ish.[10] A more subtle and telling ambiguity, however, attaches to Dora's father, the proctor, Spenlow. Uriah Heep is a devil. But what about Mr. Spenlow? Though it would be odd to describe so respectable and inoffensive a man as evil, isn't he basically doing the same thing as Heep — draining as much financial fluid as he can from the common body? Not only is he as mercenary as Uriah, his use of his partner Jorkins as a shield from his own bad conscience is more insidious than Uriah's false humility, because more apt to take in the deceiver as well as the world it is meant to deceive. Dickens intimates as much in the scene in which Spenlow, aware of David's recent financial losses, reveals that he has uncovered the liaison with Dora, and discourages him more or less on the grounds that his own will and testament has been made and that his personal affairs are in such a serene order that David's interference would wreck them. This is, of course, a blatant rebuff for a financially undesirable suitor, but such is Spenlow's depth of feeling about it, that tears come into his eyes as he speaks, and David is almost moved himself. Neither an overdeveloped talent for amateur theatricals, nor ordinary insincerity, nor even the Pecksniffian cant, can quite explain this brilliant performance. The Spenlow syndrome lies close to the heart of the mature Dickens: no one has ever exceeded the penetration and deftness of Dickens's exposure of so many varieties of what existentialist philosophy has called *mauvaise foi*. The fiction and drama of Sartre and Camus are largely devoted to this type of exposure: usually the individual is held responsible for his own self-unmasking. Freedom, in fact, in the Sartrean sense consists in the perpetual unmasking of one's own biologico-social tilts towards *mauvaise foi*. *Mauvaise foi* (in the Dickensian as well as Sartrean sense) is not quite the same thing as self-deception in the ordinary sense of the term, since this normally assumes the participation of the individual's will, his connivance at his own delusion. *Mauvaise foi* concerns something more fundamental and functional, something which may seem natural, beyond the will. Like Freud's investigations of the psychopathology of everyday life, Husserl's attempt to break down "the natural standpoint" really amounts to an effort to defeat nature on its own terms — nature being the supersession of animal laziness over the superior quality of consciousness, upon which our attainment and assertion of our individuality and integrity depend.[11] Thus, *mauvaise foi* is, as it were, perfectly compatible with sincerity: sincerity, like laziness and stupidity, can be a form of natural bad faith. Sartre tries to demonstrate this thesis in his story "Portrait of an Anti-Semite", in which the hero's anti-semitism is shown to devolve not from any profound or serious convictions about race (these, Sartre's story implies, would be welcomely real) but from deficiencies in his own character. How much more powerful is Dickens's more natural and relaxed exposure of Mr. Spenlow's use of Jorkins, and his skilfully contrived case for refusing his daughter's hard-up suitor.

David Copperfield seems centrally important in the light of this account. A large number of its apparently unrelated themes are connected by this common preoccupation. David's attitude towards Agnes (even to Dora: this "wrong choice" is interesting from the phenomenological point of view); Mr. Micawber's "waiting for something to turn up", and his disingenuous exploitation of his own charm and rhetoric to put off paying his debts; Mr. Wickfield's abrogation of responsibility for himself and his business affairs — all these in different ways illustrate the novel's basic concern. Mr. Spenlow's use of Jorkins (a classic phenomenological syndrome) and his "sincere" fabrications on the head of David's suit to his daughter, are perhaps the subtlest examples of all, and are accomplished with fine judgment.

At about this stage of the affair, one becomes fully aware of a light satirical tone, which in fact crept into the writing when David first fell in love with Dora. It is easy to dismiss David's ravings about Dora and Love as romantic gush, and thereby to miss the subtle irony of a brilliant episode. For here Dickens is mocking himself and the whole cult of romantic love. As one progresses into the complications of the maze — the mediations of Miss Mills, an overtly satirical figure; the intervention of Miss Murdstone, now a more comically icy figure, shrunk by the reasoning eyes of David's adulthood; the superb pomp of Mr. Spenlow, the offended father; the distraction of David, the rejected lover — one becomes increasingly conscious of a tone increasingly frequent in the mature Dickens, both warm and ironic:

> Miss Mills had a wonderful flow of words, and liked to pour them out. I could not help feeling, though she mingled her tears with mine, that she had a dreadful luxury in our afflictions. She petted them, as I may say, and made the most of them. (Chapter 38, p. 555.)

It is not only Miss Mills he is laughing at. The same amused yet sympathetic tone is used in speaking of his own absurdities:

> I signed myself, hers distractedly; and I couldn't help feeling, while I read this composition over, before sending it by a porter, that it was something in the style of Mr. Micawber. (Chapter 38, p. 554.)

What one begins to enjoy as a masterpiece of romantic comedy, gradually works up to an almost surrealist pitch, and quite suddenly, with an abruptness thoroughly in keeping with the tone of the whole, reaches a farcical climax, amusing, yet serving a definite purpose in the progress of the novel: through a brilliant comic narration by the clerk Tiffey, we learn that Mr. Spenlow is dead.

David himself is neutral as far as Spenlow is concerned; as a possible father-in-law, he was always too remote and off-hand to arouse any sympathy or respect in his daughter's suitor. What does agitate David is the complexity of the situation created by the event. The obstacle to his union with Dora is now removed. For this he cannot but be glad. At the same time, he feels an uncomfortable abstract remorse for having been at variance with Dora's father, and for now appearing to stand to gain by his decease. Deeper still, he entertains a "lurking jealousy even of Death", that will distract Dora's attention from himself. He thus waits with some trepidation on the reading of the will. The ironic twist Dickens now gives to the whole episode — to Spenlow's life as well as to his death — shows more clearly than any other single quality, how far he has progressed from the time when he used deaths and coincidences to solve problems; it is also a harbinger of the profound ironies that govern the late novels. When Jorkins (Spenlow's "obdurate" partner) and David go through the dead man's effects, it is discovered that he has not only made no will, but that he has left his affairs in a state of deliberate anarchy, and wasted his entire income on keeping up his personal appearance, so that Tiffey wouldn't give a thousand pounds for the remaining effects. The severity of the judgment passed here surpasses the treatment even of Uriah Heep. Heep at least tries to involve others in himself; Spenlow has existed in a vacuum of his own vanity. The whole trend of Dickens's art is apparent in this episode. For it is *hollowness* (rather than malignancy) that is beginning to interest him.

The death of Mr. Spenlow serves to complicate, then, not to simplify: it leads directly to the marriage of David and Dora, and this brings with it a new range of complexities. There is a school of criticism which insists that the real "moral" of *David Copperfield* is to be studied in the "mistake" David makes in the process, the mistake he blunders into because of his "undisciplined heart".[12] If we reject such a thesis more or less out of hand, it is less because we feel like trusting the tale rather than the teller here (in both cases it's the tale we are concerned with), than for the sort of reason Theodor Adorno gave for rejecting "interpretation" *via* "concepts invoked from above" — the "deadly aesthetic error of equating the philosophy an author pumps into his work with its metaphysical substance".[13] The "metaphysical substance" (= the basis of the art-experience) in *David Copperfield* is that the love between David and Dora is marvellous, miraculous, life-enhancing, but precisely *not* a relationship. And this is the opposition Dickens spells out so beautifully in his exquisitely articulated scenes, with a wide dynamic range of tenderness and irony. It is not so much that Agnes will be a *pis aller* (as Chesterton observed),[14] as that the two situations, the love and the relationship, are presented severally as making up a whole life's possibilities.

Certainly, Dickens did nothing better than the domestic anarchy of David and Dora's so-called marriage. It would be impossible to exaggerate the consistent brilliance of the wit with which this tender farce is retailed. It achieves a kind of meticulous vivacity somehow set apart from the Gothic exuberance of Dickens's most popular comic vein. As with the courtship mediated by Miss Mills and the death of Dora's father, Dickens graduates easily from innocent humour ("fun", simply) to *comédie noire*. For the domestic life of the young Copperfields is to be dominated by their servants. At first it seems that the purpose of this is merely to highlight the irresponsible charm of the young couple. But it is not long before the transparent charm (they play at mothers and fathers) reveals a rather horrible *Angst* behind it. It simply is not funny — though Dickens makes us laugh at it — that Paragon's cousin in the Life Guards is more or less quartered on the Copperfields, so that their evenings are dominated by his continuous growling the other side of the wall; or that the spoons disappear; or that inexplicable bills are run up at the local inn in Dora's name; or that the cousin in the Life Guards is eventually arrested for desertion at the Copperfields' house. There is nothing like this in the earlier Dickens, though there is much like it in the darker novels to come: Dickens makes of the dishonest servant a disturbing image of anxiety, a nightmare or vampire, sucking the healthy blood of the *bon bourgeois*.

But, of course, the *bourgeois* are also responsible, and this is only one of many examples in *David Copperfield* where the question of assigning responsibility and failure assumes supreme importance. The masters, after all, are as culpable as the servants who prey on them, because their laxity and carelessness — laxity and carelessness they could not have afforded without the economic backing of the class-system itself — make it possible to rob them, and even encourage the servants to take advantage of them. This aspect of the matter is brought out superlatively well in the fate of the little page the Copperfields acquire. David admits that when they engaged this page — "in an evil hour" — they had already given up the housekeeping as a bad job. This is a significant admission: quite simply, the property-owning class had no right to shelve its responsibilities in this way; the master serves the servant as well as the servant the master. The chilling history of the page confirms this. Interestingly enough, Dickens does not give the boy a name: even Mr.

Topsawyer — who never appeared in the book, and was dead even when spoken of — was given a name. But this page, for some reason, Dickens desists from naming. Instead he calls him a "perfect Whittington" in respect of quarrelling with the cook though in no other: his story is a grimly realistic version of the old folk tale that Dickens so often returned to in clarifying his own experience. This boy has no relatives, and battens onto the Copperfields emotionally as well as materially. Dickens rapidly converts him also into an objectified neurosis:

> I watched him as he grew — and he grew like scarlet beans — with painful apprehensions of the time when he would begin to shave; even of the days when he would be bald or grey. I saw no prospect of ever getting rid of him; and, projecting myself into the future, used to think what an inconvenience he would be when he was an old man. (Chapter 48, p. 691.)

The boy has become something like the old man of the sea; David's attitude towards him is helpless and resigned: "I'll never get rid of him". Such situations are radical to Dickens's art and the feeling of life it embodies. Taken only a little further, and shorn of the huge capacity for joy, exuberance, and common-sense which in fact brace and sustain it, it would turn easily into the inexplicable obsessiveness so characteristic of Strindberg and Kafka. But in Dickens, the facts are never allowed to degenerate into the entirely interior, malignant and personal as they are: the situation remains objectively real. Moreover, it has its other aspect: the Copperfields are responsible for their servants. There could be no better illustrations of the peculiarly subtle balance of humour and anxiety that consistently informs *David Copperfield* than the history of the boy who, through the Copperfields' negligence, steals, gets himself arrested, and — stricken with remorse — keeps divulging details of more and yet more thefts he has committed during his service. Finally, David remarks, "I got to be so ashamed of being such a victim that I would have given him any money to hold his tongue." (Chapter 48, p. 692.) The story ends with the boy being transported and made "a shepherd of, up the country somewhere, I have no geographical idea where" (p. 692).

This last clause is significant: it is an understandably weary dismissal of a wearisome subject; but it is not the old careless humour of the Pickwick days that attends this dismissal of a juvenile Magwitch whose case history Dickens by this time cannot treat lightly. A little further on, David explicitly acknowledges his complicity in the case: " 'My dear,' said I, 'it is painful to me to think our want of system and management involves not only ourselves (which we have got used to), but other people.' " (Chapter 48, p. 692.) Dickens pivots brilliantly here onto the subject of Dora's general unfitness, and David's general responsibility for that. The preoccupations are indissolubly connected, and once again we can see in the fact the source of the novel's unique quality. For the writing never for a moment loses its charm: as far as Dora is concerned Dickens is blessed with artistic infallibility. It is safe to say that with any other novelist we would be in the position of having to dismiss a sentimental flaw in a major novel. The tone of the David-Dora episodes is affectionate and warm, yet it is as far from the sentimental as it could well be. It is an illustration of that general law Chesterton noted of Dickens: "if sentimentalism be held to mean something artificial or theatrical, then in the core of his character Dickens was the very reverse of a sentimentalist."[15]

Yet this charm — and this is curiously characteristic of the novel — soon enough loses its unsullied quality, and becomes the mask of an anxiety that gradually infects everything. The servants become parasitic not only on David's pocket but on his peace of mind; he in turn, in attempting to "form Dora's mind", infects her with his own anxiety. He casts a shadow across her: his "responsible" attitude towards things threatens to destroy that life in her that he had found so irresistible. Realizing this, he comes to understand also that the marriage is from certain points of view a mistake: he cannot have Dora and what she means to him, and at the same time have what Agnes is to mean later. So there develops that sense of loss so often referred to in the pages narrating the progress of their marriage. Dora, after all, had been always what she was — wholly and to the last degree.

She is one of the few wholly undeceived and unfraudulent characters in a book teeming with the niceties of bad faith and self-deception. It is David who has leeway to make up — leeway between what he wants and what he has committed himself to having by free choice. He has first to abandon an invalid solution: the attempt to coerce Dora into being something else, to force her into a role she cannot play. Then comes the resignation, the acceptance of "resolving henceforth to be satisfied with my child-wife, and to try to change her into nothing else by any process". (Chapter 48, p. 695.) But then, following this resigned acceptance, comes the phase of regretting Agnes, and this is where the "undisciplined heart" motif is heard so often — too often, it might appear, except that Dickens has a further permutation up his sleeve. We think we have the situation well in hand now, that we have merely to survive the discreet extermination of Dora so that David can enjoy the right choice as well as the wrong one. What a boring and heartless book that would be! But Dickens nowhere else in his *oeuvre* shows anything but contempt for the notion of "discipline" and the *disciplined* heart in the Dickens world is simply a contradiction in terms. In *David Copperfield*, moreover, death always serves to complicate not to simplify. The fundamental message of the book — if we insist upon extracting one — is certainly not to be couched in terms of the "disciplining" of the heart. It is much closer to that "that's the way it is" Theodor Adorno saw as so importantly operative in the clauses of Kafka.[16] Nor is this to flout Dickens's own directives. On the contrary, it is to observe them more rigorously.

For the "dead blank feeling" that comes upon David as he approaches that "frozen region yet unseen" which is Dora's imminent death is certainly not a convenient preparation for the disencumbrance of the newly disciplined David. David in fact is to be shaken by Dora's death — his refusal to think about it forewarns us of the fact — as by nothing else. How can we say then that the marriage is a mistake at all? Only again by superimposing our own need for clear mandates upon a design that is as delicate yet as strong as life itself. To be sure, Dickens leads the "undisciplined heart" moralists a long way before delivering the *coup de grâce*. In the last and most beautiful of the four retrospects, the one which ends with Dora's death, David is paid in full for all those secret doubts and regrets:

> I sit down by the fire, thinking with a blind remorse of all those secret feelings I have nourished since my marriage. I think of every little trifle between me and Dora, and feel the truth, that trifles make the sum of life. Ever rising from this sea of my remembrance is the image of the dear child as I knew her first, graced by my love and by her own, with every fascination wherein such love is rich. Would it, indeed, have been better if we had loved each other as a boy and girl, and forgotten it? Undisciplined heart, reply! (Chapter 53, p. 768.)

Well, what is the answer to that question? An affirmative answer is explicitly negated by the previous words, the purpose of which is precisely to lead the reader to see the fallacy of his own reasoning. The "that's how it is" here accepts the necessity of the regret, of the error accepted; but it as certainly bids us deny the denial of experience implicit in the "undisciplined heart" thesis. The remorse here is the reverse of the regret for the "mistake": the rectification of which confronts him in the figure of Agnes, who is present in the house at the moment of Dora's death. The remorse is for the blasphemy against life involved in breeding and brooding on those regrets and the sense of loss, and in falsifying the very substance of what is most marvellous in life. The corresponding blasphemy open to the reader is to cancel this marvellous episode in seeing it as a moralistic mock-up, intended to bring out by contrast the rightness of the Agnes relationship.

Dickens now has to bring his novel to its logical climax. Dora's death occurs one hundred pages before the end of the novel. What follows seems to me one of the most remarkable achievements in nineteenth century fiction. The impact of the blow on David is delayed: from the point of view of the action this is required for Dickens to be able to consummate the other major themes in his huge design — the death of Steerforth and the branding of Heep. But in fact, the delayed action of the shock of Dora's death could only work at all in psychological terms: a purely strategic delay would be callous bathos. We have had too many instances already of David's character not to feel the rightness of Dickens's treatment of the matter. We remember the curious duplicity, above all, with which he felt his mother's death: his temperament, we understand by now, is one which experiences intensely and immediately, but which holds the fact at arm's length in order to be able to survive its impact, and then absorb it at leisure. He weeps, but can watch himself weep. In the same way, before Dora's death, his prescience refrigerates the future: the frozen region is an emotional necessity for him, a North Pole he dreads to enter, but which will preserve him from a too intense emotional suffering.

So now, after the death, he cannot at once accept what has happened at its full significance:

> As it was, an interval occurred before I fully knew my own distress; an interval in which I even supposed that its severest pangs were past; and when my mind could soothe itself by resting on all that was most innocent and beautiful, in the tender story that was closed for ever. (Chapter 54, p. 769.)

It is at this stage that David mentions the plan of a trip abroad. In the subtleties of Dickens's narrative we don't quite remember at what point and for what reasons the suggestion is shelved; but it begins the process which is to end in the full impact of the grief's being experienced without diminution. Self-awareness, the book teaches us again and again, is not simply a matter of noting our impulses towards self-deception, and admitting when we are wrong or unkind. It is not the wrong choice of mate David has to become aware of now, but the nature of his own suffering.

Dickens makes it appear inevitable and natural that David should leave his wife at a critical stage of her illness, witness the explosion into authenticity of Mr. Micawber, return to endure her death, endure almost immediately after this the heavy blow of Steerforth's and Ham's deaths, and only then go on the promised trip abroad to accept the full experience of Dora's death itself. There is not so much a climax to the book as a cluster of climaxes, a staggered peripeteia, cruel yet emancipating, which consummates the whole work. What is most interesting perhaps is that the cruel private blow — the death of Dora — takes place in two phases, the initial shock and the later absorption of its implications, which are punctuated by the great shipwreck scene. Without question this scene is the formal crisis of the novel, like the great storm that consummates *Martin Chuzzlewit*. Everything tells us so, the building momentum of the prose, the sheer intensity of the description of the storm, the fact of the last trip along the road to the sea; this is a crescendo of all the novel's symbolic motifs. And this peripeteia depends for its force not so much upon the actual death of the dear friends, but upon the great message of forgiveness which the whole episode enacts. It is indeed an excellent example of Dickens's functional use of action: the action supplies the meaning, not the words or the stated intentions of author or character.

The source of this meaning is in the common ground Ham and Steerforth share as human beings. Steerforth is now not the seducer, nor Ham the offended lover. Ham responds to a deeper call than his hurt: Ham dies without knowing for whom he dies, and this is important. We are concerned not with a psychologically motivated change of mind, such as we witness when Mr. Pickwick forgives Jingle and Mrs. Bardell, but with a deeper ethic of forgiveness. Dickens makes Ham forgive Steerforth on the ground of a greater humanity that transcends and undercuts the personal situation in which they happen to have been locked. To punch home the meaning, Dickens exploits to the maximum his incomparable powers of narrative and description. It is the storm which consummates the fable, and in its preternatural violence all animosities and hostilities are blown out.

Finally, the whole ethic of the novel is implicit in the character and career of David himself. It is this unity of character and morality that makes this in some ways the most satisfying of all Dickens's novels. The fullness of *David Copperfield* is the fullness of life lived to the utmost. There is no other work in the language, I believe, in which this profound commonplace — that life is the sum of what happens to us, and should be lived to the fullest, without evasion or question — is so irresistibly urged. Dickens closes on a calm that is well-based on firmness and industry. Much of the poignance with which this serene ending is conveyed derives from an inspired last word from Mr. Micawber, his own unreality suggested by banishment to Australia. Mr. Peggotty returns from the colony, with a newspaper in which there is a letter adressed to David himself ("the eminent author"). There is an indescribable sadness in this voice — the self-same voice of innumerable convivialities in London — coming from a vast distance, not only of space but of time and dream, as though it were heard in the innermost recesses of the memory. David remains to the end the friend and companion of Mr. Micawber's youth.

8 *Bleak House*

Technically, in an admittedly suspect sense of an always suspect word,[1] *Bleak House* displays a greater virtuosity and a more startling originality than any other Dickens novel. This much could be gathered from a simple statistical account of its structure. It is told in two distinct and interwoven parts. There are sixty-seven chapters in all, of which thirty-four are in the third person present tense (what has been called the omniscient narrative),[2] and thirty-three in the first person past tense of "Esther's Narrative". The reader may find a tabulation of the distribution of these chapters helpful in envisaging the structure of the novel:

Omniscient Narrative	*Esther's Narrative*
1, 2;	3, 4, 6;
7;	8, 9;
10, 11, 12;	13, 14, 15;
16;	17, 18;
19, 20, 21, 22;	23, 24;
25, 26, 27, 28, 29;	30, 31;
32, 33, 34;	35, 36, 37, 38;
39, 40, 41, 42;	43, 44, 45;
46, 47, 48, 49;	50, 51, 52;
53, 54, 55, 56;	57;
58;	59, 60, 61, 62;
63;	64, 65;
66;	67.

It is only when one reflects how irritating an idiom the present tense narrative usually is, and how rarely two different angles of narration are used to focus a subject clearly, without sleight of hand, that one realizes what an extraordinary book *Bleak House* is: at no point in the story is one aware of technical carpentry or narrative manipulation. Dickens has chosen exactly the right medium to convey a vision of growing complexity: *Bleak House* is at the same time a satire on the law, a detective story, a social tract, a psychological model, and a tragic metaphor of the human condition. On each of its five levels the novel is explicit and detailed, yet never did Dickens combine the threads of his narrative with greater mastery. Like *David Copperfield, Bleak House* is polyphonic in the only sense in which that over-used adjective can really be applied to literature: the effect of one thread (or more) of the story is carried over in the mind while others are presented to it, so that one's attention, though never distracted, is enriched by the harmony of simultaneously existent ideas.

A detailed breakdown of the interweaving of the two narratives would be extraneous to the present context. Broadly speaking, however, it is true to say that the omniscient narrative concerns itself with one main theme, to which there are several tributaries. The main theme is the disgrace of the house of Dedlock through the discovery of an illicit liaison between Lady Dedlock and a dead army officer, known as Mr. Nemo. This liaison resulted in the birth of a child, and the child is known to us as Esther Summerson. The action of this part of the novel involves the hunt for Esther's identity by a clerk called Guppy, the discovery of Lady Dedlock's secret by her lawyer Tulkinghorn, the murder of Tulkinghorn by Lady Dedlock's maid Hortense, and the unjust incrimination of the soldier George. This part of the novel is linked to the other by the figure of Esther Summerson herself, cunningly planted by Dickens in the heart of the other main theme, the Jarndyce and Jarndyce lawsuit. As a ward of court, with Ada Clare and Richard Carstone, Esther is in an ideal position to document the

progress of the lawsuit, or rather its disastrous effect upon
Richard Carstone, while remaining ignorant of the progress of
the other action, in which she is the unwitting key-figure.
The two narratives are wide apart at the start, gradually con-
verging from about chapter 28.

Paradoxically, the present tense narrative as Dickens
exploits it here creates a static lifeless effect — the effect of
the inventory, the stage direction, or the Robbe-Grillet anti-
novel. The present tense narration evokes the image of a vast
dead edifice on the point of collapse, and an atmosphere of
strange unreality. This is especially true of the celebrated fog
passages at the beginning. What is observed in the present
tense stays where it is put. Thus, the fog "rolls defined
among the tiers of shipping"; if Dickens had said "rolled", a
voice would whisper at some level of the reader's mind,
"what did it do then?" simply because the tense implies that
it stopped rolling at some time or other. Confirming the
analogy with the inventory, Dickens uses main verbs very
sparingly in the first few pages. Sentence after sentence goes
by without a verb at all: "Fog on the Essex marshes, fog on
the Kentish heights. Fog creeping into the cabooses of collier-
brigs; fog lying out on the yards, and hovering in the rigging
of great ships; fog drooping on the gunwales of barges and
small boats." (Chapter 1, p. 1.) — And so on. The present
tense, too, enables the writer to be everywhere; the past tense
always suggests an observer who has to be hidden away somewhere. This is, of course, a property habitually exploited in
poetry, and in a sense *Bleak House* is a vast symbolic poem,
in which Dickens displays all the preternatural animistic
power he possessed for imaginatively inhabiting things and
people and causing them to live.

But there is another property of the present tense which is
equally relevant to Dickens's ultimate intentions. For the
past tense narrative can always be — in fact, is always
nominally claiming to be — a faithful record of what actually
took place, such as one finds in newspapers and court
records. This is why prose fiction is *the* medium for popular
wish-fulfilment: it is a convincing sort of record, and there-

fore satisfying to identify with. Once the writer commits himself to the present tense, he has lost this pretence of verisimilitude, and appeals to a different capacity in the reader. We can never quite believe in a present tense narrative: it immediately sets up an irritated awareness of a trick the writer is trying to put over on us. Dickens takes just this fact about the present tense narrative to create an atmosphere of deceit, sham, unreality; and, moreover, to convey a sense of his own ironical attitude towards what he is describing. It is in combining thse two qualities — the poetic "thereness" (and yet deadness) and the sense of irony — that he succeeds. The whole narrative has an air of subtle mockery that could not be conveyed in the past tense, and which contrasts most movingly with the earnestness of Esther Summerson's story.

Of all the aspects of Dickens's art which have received wrongful abuse over the past seventy years, none has received more than his conception of a certain kind of feminine "virtue". Most critics seem to loathe Amy Dorrit, Little Nell, Esther Summerson, Agnes Wickfield, Ruth Pinch, and the rest of them, with a psychopathic intensity. From the first (innocently chosen) volume to hand, I quote: "[*Bleak House*] contains the most detestable of all Dickens' heroines. Esther Summerson is odious, so sweet, so sweetly spiteful — especially about Mr. Skimpole — so tenderly cocksure, so coy and sub-acid."[3] This kind of amateurism is admittedly too light-weight to require serious attention — though when, if one has the fortitude to continue, one later learns that Harold Skimpole with his "exquisite conversation" is the writer's favourite character, the cattiness of his judgment on Miss Summerson stands revealed as the predictable reaction of a man, the exact wrongness of whose reading is a tribute to the uncompromising thoroughness with which Dickens has done his job: Miss Summerson's shrewd judgment of Skimpole is anything but "sub-acid", and the more biting for her having generously praised his undeniable charm.

However, the point could be made from almost any critique of Dickens,[4] and these young ladies he so evidently admired and cared for excite a powerfully hostile indifference in many of his readers. Yet this seems to me a wrong reaction, often difficult to understand, except as the result of lazy submission to anti-Victorian conditioning. In the first place, it is necessary to return to the text, to return, that is, to the artistic actuality underlying the miasma of sentimentality and cant that has gradually obscured our own vision of the Victorians in general and Dickens in particular. The truth that then confronts us, I believe, is that Esther Summerson has a function in the novel which makes her successful realization a technical necessity. Her narrative seems, more and more, to be a remarkable, sustained achievement. It is of course the master himself reporting: nobody but Dickens could have conceived Mr. Turveydrop, for instance: "He had such a neckcloth on (puffing his very eyes out of their natural shape), and his chin and even his ears so sunk into it, that it seemed as though he must inevitably double up, if it were cast loose." (Chapter 14, p. 190.) This is the Dickens animism at its most pregnant, its exact energy beyond not only Miss Summerson (from whose pen the description allegedly comes) but any other novelist in the world. And when we turn to the omniscient narrative it is, of course, to find the same exuberant skill in evidence. Yet how cunningly the two narratives are cumulatively made to differ, so that the focus of their refections amounts to a total vision neither could have aspired to alone. This is managed in part by a wide difference in tone. The omniscient narrative is careless towards people and their sufferings, at times almost cynically callous. The description of Guster, the Snagsby family servant, is a far cry from the pathos of Dickens's earlier social portraiture:

> Guster, really aged three or four and twenty, but looking a round ten years older, goes cheap with this unnaccountable drawback of fits; and is so apprehensive of being returned to the hands of the patron saint, that except when she is found with her head in the pail, or the sink, or the copper, or the dinner, or anything else that happens to be near her at the time of her seizure, she is always at work. (Chapter 10, p. 129.)

Funny? Of course not. In case we should think that the lovable Boz has lost his compassion, we return to Esther Summerson's sympathetic intelligence, and remind ourselves that she is the moral touchstone of the novel. We shall find then that the style of her narrative, though still Dickensian, is plausibly muted, modulated to create the illusion of a memoir written by a shrewd and likeable, if sometimes arch, woman. Esther's narration of her illness by itself should allay any doubts about the quality of the art invested in her:

> My hair had not been cut off, though it had been in danger more than once. It was long and thick. I let it down, and shook it out, and went up to the glass upon the dressing-table. There was a little muslin curtain drawn across it. I drew it back: and stood for a moment looking through such a veil of my own hair, that I could see nothing else. Then I put my hair aside, and looked at the reflection in the mirror; encouraged by seeing how placidly it looked at me. I was very much changed — O very much. (Chapter 36, p. 504.)

Clarity and understatement of this order make Esther's narrative throughout a sober, purposeful comment on the rest of the book. She has, moreover, a fund of industry and charity that is a feminine equivalent of David Copperfield's energy.

Her falling a victim to disease is typical of the sombre tone that colours the whole, and is integral to its deepest purposes. That Dickens should choose for his heroine a bastard disfigured by smallpox, and for him *not* to exploit the pathos inherent in the disfigurement, in itself suggests the moral climate he is working in. For Esther's disfigurement, like her parentage, is essential to the meaning of the whole work, the disease being metaphysical and moral as well as physical and social.

The nature of the contagion can be understood from the number of different elements and social *milieux* it involves. Esther catches the disease from Jo, the crossing-sweeper, who is given shelter in John Jarndyce's household. Jo is also used as a guide by Lady Dedlock, Esther's mother, when she visits the grave of her lover, Captain Hawdon, Esther's father. The crossing-sweeper mediates between Esther and her parents, and the scene in which he does so is remarkable for a peculiar ferocity of tone:

> With houses looking on, on every side, save where a reeking
> little tunnel of a court gives access to the iron gate — with every
> villainy of life in action close on death, and every poisonous
> element of death in action close on life — here, they lower our
> dear brother down a foot or two: here, sow him in corruption, to
> be raised in corruption: an avenging ghost at many a sick bedside:
> a shameful testimony to future ages, how civilisation and
> barbarism walked this boastful island together. (Chapter 11, p.
> 151.)

This seems to strike a note we are accustomed to attribute to
social anger in Dickens: it is to be found in *Oliver Twist,* in
Nicholas Nickleby, in *A Christmas Carol,* and it is normally
set down as the outraged indignation of the reformer. But in
point of fact there is an important connection between the
anger of the social reformer and the most serious concerns of
the great artist in Dickens. The reformer, certainly, is concerned with what can be changed — with the ephemerally,
rather than with the eternally offensive. But it is likely that a
great artist's awareness of what can be changed, with what is
disfiguring the world now, will deepen into a consciousness
of what cannot be altered: what started as reformist anger
will turn slowly into a much more tenacious disgust. In
Dickens, this deepening of vision replaces the usual
reformer's drift into reaction and complacency. The indignation stays on, but it is transformed into the deep fury of the
tragic poet: it is the human condition which enrages Dickens
in *Bleak House,* not any ephemeral injustice.

What we have here, it seems to me, is a phenomenon which
can perhaps be more easily understood by reference to other
major tragic writers. For the smallpox that attacks Esther
Summerson has the force of a punitive visitation: it is as
though she is being punished for the sins of her parents,
much as Osvald is destroyed *for and by* Captain Alving's sins
in *Ghosts.*[5] There is, in Ibsen's play and Dickens's novel,
evidence of that deep ineradicable association of sex and
disease, of carnal pleasure and guilt, which occurs in so much
great tragedy, and which is perhaps its *raison d'être.* The
plague in *Oedipus Rex,* Hamlet's obsessive disease imagery,
the congenital syphillis in *Ghosts,* the insanity of the captain
in *The Father* — it is more than accident which relates these

manifestations of the tragic curse. The curse is simply being human — an animal dependent upon the life of the body and the procreative function. This profound discomfort — deepening in some works, such as *Gulliver's Travels* and *The Waste Land,* to an almost neurotic revulsion — is really the core of all tragic art. This surely is what explains the horror at physical existence which is so powerful in *Hamlet,* in *Ghosts,* in *Oedipus Rex.* It is also what explains what we can call simply the Freudian basis of tragic art — the origination of so much of our emotional life in our parentage and the persisting preoccupation with the Oedipal elements of the family situation. This, at any rate, is the postulation underlying the present thesis, that there is in *Bleak House* a profound association between procreation (Esther's illegitimate birth) and disease (her disfigurement by smallpox). There is throughout a disgust which transcends its origination and a sense of waste which by far exceeds the inadequacies of the legal system. One of the most remarkable things about the book in fact is that its great societal thesis — a nation is a unity in which the higher strata dangerously depend upon the lower, and must fall through the corruption created by social injustice and alienation — becomes the text not so much for reformist propaganda as for a religious diatribe on the evils of the human organism:

> There is not a drop of Tom's corrupted blood but propagates infection and contagion somewhere. It shall pollute, this very night, the choice stream (in which chemists on analysis would find the genuine nobility) of a Norman house, and his Grace shall not be able to say Nay to the infamous alliance. There is not an atom of Tom's slime, not a cubic inch of any pestilential gas in which he lives, not one obscenity or degradation about him, not an ignorance, not a wickedness, not a brutality of his committing, but shall work its retribution, through every order of society, up to the proudest of the proud, and to the highest of the high. Verily, what with tainting, plundering, and spoiling, Tom has his revenge. (Chapter 46, pp. 627–28.)

If we tried to read this as social protest, we should have to discount it: we could not accept evidence from a source so patently incapable of detachment and objectivity. This "reformer" has become almost paranoiacally involved with his subject-matter, convinced of the hopelessness of his task, certain to the point of neurosis of punitive retribution. He simply goes too far — unless we read him as we read the great prophetic poets of the Old Testament. In which case he stands revealed as a visionary: this speaker's tone moves us to deplore the inadequacies of ourselves as human animals, and the intensity of his voice, unpalatable to the social reformer (things after all were being done in 1852), testifies so strongly to his vision of human potentiality, that our feeling about life is heightened and chastened. We experience not transient indignation but tragic catharsis.

In the same way, the house of the Dedlocks becomes, over the course of the novel, a symbol of our human society. (Sir Leicester, like the Tite Barnacles of *Little Dorrit*, likes to assume a patron's responsibility for the state of England.) Some such expansion of the family or house takes place, probably, in all great tragedy: the root of tragedy is in the family, and it is sexual, but the family/House generally assumes a representative status. "Something is rotten," Hamlet observes, not in his family alone, but "in the state of Denmark". In the same way, the curse on the House of Atreus is symbolized by a plague upon the city of Thebes, and the dishonesty of Karsten Bernick by a shipwreck. We miss a whole dimension of meaning in *Bleak House* if we fail to observe the general relevance of the curse of the Dedlocks. Initially, this curse is dramatized in Mrs. Rouncewell's wonderful narration of the old romance of the ghost's walk: " 'I will die here where I have walked. And I will walk here, though I am in my grave. I will walk here, until the pride of this house is humbled. And when calamity, or when disgrace is coming to it, let the Dedlocks listen for my step!' " (Chapter 7, p. 90.) The hubris which so automatically invites destruction in Attic drama is embodied in Sir Leicester Dedlock himself, with his total inability to comprehend the realities of recent history and contemporary society. For it is a historical case Dickens is arguing here: the aristocrats have simply lost touch not only with economic and social realities, but with their own emotional requirements. Some such emotional impasse is suggested in the family name itself; it is also embodied in the coldness and hauteur of Lady Dedlock. But the hubris of the great House is most dangerously trumpeted by the faithful retainer, Mrs. Rouncewell, almost immediately after the passage just cited: " 'But it comes back, from time to time; and so sure as there is sickness or death in the family, it will be heard then.' " Her grandson Watt reminds her of her omission: the lady in the legend, in pronouncing the curse on the house, had spoken not only of sickness and death but also of disgrace: " 'And disgrace grandmother — ' Watt says. — 'Disgrace never comes to Chesney Wold,' returns the housekeeper." It is almost a parody of the dramatic irony of the Greeks.

It is in relation to the curse of the Dedlocks, too, that Esther Summerson's function in the book is to be determined. In her own narrative, concerned as it is with the documentation of Richard Carstone's deterioration, she appears in a negative role, as a kind of moral salvage agent, sweetening and tidying the lives of those around her. But this role is significantly related to her predestined role as the agent for the destruction of the Dedlocks. For it is in coming to an awareness of herself in this capacity that she most deeply understands herself. Like a criminal returning to the scene of the crime, she haunts Chesney Wold:

> Stopping to look at nothing, but seeing all I did see as I went, I was passing quickly on, and in a few moments should have passed the lighted window, when my echoing footsteps brought it suddenly into my mind that there was a dreadful truth in the legend of the Ghost's Walk; that it was I, who was to bring calamity upon the stately house; and that my warning feet were haunting it even then. Seized with an augmented terror of myself which turned my blood cold, I ran from myself and everything, retraced the way by which I had come, and never paused until I had gained the lodge-gate, and the park lay sullen and black behind me. (Chapter 36, p. 515.)

This fear of oneself is something we encounter again in *Great Expectations,* and it is impossible to exaggerate its importance here: the profound sense of fatality, of inexorability, which is so impressive and moving a part of Dickens's greatest writing, derives perhaps from some such ineradicable conviction of complicity in human evil, even when there is no rational cause for it.

Esther seems to accept the disease in a spirit less of self-sacrifice than of obeisance — of sacrifice in the stricter liturgical sense of the word. She stands in for Ada Clare. But she also, as I have observed, seems to earn the disfigurement as the price of her parents' guilt. It is of the essence of the thing of course that she is herself innocent: the peculiar sense of damnation which is so powerful in *Bleak House* could not have been realized without this spectacle of irrationally afflicted innocence. As so often in Dickens's most inward writing, the reader is *taken through* the experience: it is a question not of the criticism of life, in Arnold's terms, but of the enforced participation in the enlarging imaginative experience. Esther's voyage through fever and near-death to disfigurement and eventual peace is really the great central imaginative fact of *Bleak House:* "In falling ill," she writes, "I seemed to have crossed a dark lake, and to have left all my experience, mingled together by the great distance, on the healthy shore." (Chapter 35, p. 488.) It is the habit of thinking naturally in metaphoric and symbolic terms that most distinguishes Dickens from his great contemporaries. The "dark lake" in this passage is inset deep in the imaginative substance of the novel, much as the incidents in epic and allegoric poetry present and enact in themselves the poet's meaning. The account of sickness and hallucination which follows, with its preternaturally vivid dream sequences and labouring flagging prose-rhythm, belongs to the highest level of Dickens's art. It is, once again, the intensity of the imaginative participation the reader is asked to make that is so remarkable: "For the same reason," she observes, "I am almost afraid to hint at that time in my disorder — it seemed one long night, but I believe there were both nights and days in it — when I laboured up colossal staircases, ever striving to reach the top, and ever turned, as I have seen a worm in a garden path, by some obstruction and labouring again." There is an eerie echo here of the Chancery experiences of Carstone and the others, and it is significant that the chapter in which these experiences are related also includes Miss Flite's great account of the Chancery hell: it is characteristic of *Bleak House* that it constantly seems to be about more than the immediate narrative facts. Everything in it is related to everything else. This same chapter also tells us of Alan Woodcourt's journey, shipwreck, and heroism, and ends with Esther's hope that she and he should meet "at the journey's end".

There is, then, no doubt either that Esther's role in the novel is of the greatest significance, or that it is not confined to observing and sympathizing. Her experiences must be ours for the book to succeed at all, and this is nowhere more true than in her evaluation of the Chancery disease, which is, from one point of view, the novel's main subject.

Chancery, incorporating the Jarndyce and Jarndyce suit, is one of those pieces of symbolism so simple and so excellent that they explain themselves and are done violence to by being labelled. The most obvious temptation is to equate Chancery with The Law, or Institution; in other words, to limit it to its explicit designation. Dickens possessed to an extraordinary degree that quality which it is perhaps more important that a great artist possess than any other: I mean that fierce awareness of his contemporary world, which penetrates by sheer intensity to a deeper layer of meaning in whatever he beholds. For this reason we may expect a steady climb in his reputation as the particular evils of his time recede into the past. *Bleak House* stands to gain more than any other Dickens novel from this process. To express what it was he had to convey at the time he wrote the book, Dickens used the imagery and symbolism of the Law: he had had some professional experience of the legal machine, of course, and detested its inefficiencies and inhumanities. At one level, *Bleak House* is about the Law and its effects. But to describe it exclusively in terms of its immediate legal concerns, or, what is hardly less narrow, to see it as a satire on Institution, is absurdly inadequate:[6] there is a sense of complexity and resonance in the reading of *Bleak House* which is not satisfied by a resumé of its overt facts. There is a residuum of "meaning", which requires interpretation. To say that it is a satire on the Law or on Institution is to refuse symbolic interpretation. Yet we have an impression, upon putting the book down, of something that touches all our lives, and which is nothing to do with the law itself. This is why, I say, we must interpret the story as an allegory: it really says, Life in general is like this.

It was apparent from the complex moral ambiguities of *David Copperfield* that nothing so narrow as a satire on "legal machinery" could occupy Dickens thereafter; and, in fact, the great themes of *Bleak House* are substantially foreshadowed in the earlier work. I refer principally to the satire on "Expectations" in the treatment of Mr. Micawber, and to the irony associated with Mr. Spenlow's *mauvaise foi*. What was there treated as ironic comedy here assumes a tragic intensity and scale. The mockery of *Bleak House* reaches down to the bases of the self and of society, leaving nothing untouched. The nature and range of the symbolism can now be appreciated. Its poetic intensity — poetic not in any grace of expression but in its soldering depth — is suggested in the speech mad Miss Flite makes when she is explaining to Esther what the power of Chancery is, and how she herself got drawn into it:

> "First, our father was drawn — slowly. Home was drawn with him. In a few years, he was a fierce, sour, angry bankrupt, without a kind word or a kind look for anyone. He had been so different, Fitz-Jarndyce. He was drawn to a debtors' prison. There he died. Then our brother was drawn — swiftly — to drunkenness. And rags. And death. Then my sister was drawn. Hush! Never ask to what! Then I was ill, and in misery; and heard, as I had often heard before, that this was all the work of Chancery. When I got better, I went to look at the Monster. And then I found out how it was, and I was drawn to stay there." (Chapter 35, p. 499.)

And when Esther asks Miss Flite what Mace and Seal can do, upon her mentioning the words,

> "Draw," returned Miss Flite. "Draw people on, my dear. Draw peace out of them. Sense out of them. Good looks out of them. Good qualities out of them. I have felt them even drawing my rest away in the night. Cold and glittering devils!"

Miss Flite, in fact, is one of the most terrible victims of Chancery, with her little bag of "documents" (nothing but paper matches and dried lavender), and her attic full of birds with symbolic names. The whole scene with Esther Summerson deserves extensive quotation; for in it Miss Flite reveals that lucid yet helpless awareness of her condition that makes any form of obsession or addiction terrifying to the uninitiated. Wouldn't it be better simply to stay away from Chancery (which Miss Flite attends every day, in the hope of a judgment in her favour), Miss Summerson asks her. Of course it would, comes the reply: " 'Very wearing to be always in expectation of what never comes, my dear Fitz-Jarndyce! Wearing, I assure you, to the bone!' " (P. 498.) Mad little Miss Flite is very close here to the centre of the whole novel. It is precisely this wearing to the bone, which Dickens is at pains to show. In Miss Flite's case the transformation of external reality into private symbol has long since translated her life to a quasi-religious plane. When she leaves, it is with a cheerful anticipation: " 'Yes, my dear, as I was saying, I expect a Judgment. Shortly. Then I shall release my birds, you know, and confer estates.' " It is obvious not only that no judgment is ever going to come for Miss Flite (except death), but that any judgment which did come would deprive her of her *raison d'être*. With her lucid awareness of her condition there has come a strange metamorphosis of her entire being: she has admitted to herself that the judgment is never coming. Her expectations then are on a kind of immanence: yet it is without any exaltation. She has in fact ceased to be a live human being: she has become her expectation.

This central thesis is expressed still more dramatically in the figure of Krook, the so-called "marine-dealer" offered to us as a parody version of the Lord Chancellor. Just how wholly Dickens conceived this novel in symbolic terms can be gleaned from the first description of Krook's premises. A kind of grubby disorder had always been an essential part of the Dickens universe. He was as fascinated by chaos and squalor as he was himself tidy and clean. But he was repelled by the imposition of insane order upon an actual untidiness. When Miss Flite, showing Krook's house to the Jarndyce wards, tells them that Krook is called among the neighbours the Lord Chancellor, and that his shop is called the Court of Chancery, we begin to feel a deep discomfort in the presence of the piles of bones, picked clean, and neatly stacked together, and even more discomfort from the three sacks of ladies' hair Krook tells them he has stacked below. We have met this quirky combination of anarchy and system before — in the mind of Nazi Germany; it is disturbing to realize that Dickens has provided us here with a subtle parody of the actual Court of Chancery and is reminding us of a terrible madness in our great social institutions. If we add the superbly casual detail of the "one-legged scale, hanging without any counterpoise from a beam," and the ghost of Tom Jarndyce driven insane by the cause, we have here an image of the *Bleak House* hell, complete with broken justice and devoured humanity.

But it is not only the suitors and plaintiffs who fall victim to the madness: the Chancellor himself is ignorant of why he is doing what he is doing, and the tons of legal rubbish Krook collects in the hope of coming across something valuable parallel the documents accumulated in the great court itself. The expectation that has worn Miss Flite to the bone takes a still more sinister form in Krook. There can be few images in literature more farcically chilling than that of Krook chalking up the memorized characters of the name Jarndyce, one by one, erasing the last before writing the next, or pasting up "several large printed alphabets in several plain hands". Krook's whole condition is plainly central to the meaning of the entire novel. "I cannot imagine," Esther writes, "a countenance more singularly expressive of caution and indecision, and a perpetual impulse to do something he could not resolve to venture on, than Mr. Krook's was, that day." The magnificent portrait Dickens gives us confirms the impression of arrested will. Like some denizen of a mythological underworld, Krook appears frozen in his own indecision:

He was short, cadaverous, and withered: with his head sunk sideways between his shoulders, and the breath issuing in visible
smoke from his mouth, as if he were on fire within. His throat,
chin and eyebrows were so frosted with white hairs, and so
gnarled with veins and puckered skin, that he looked from his
breast upward, like some old root in a fall of snow. (Chapter 5, p.
50.)

His end is one of the most daring strokes in the whole
book. Within the symbolic schema of *Bleak House,* Krook's
death by spontaneous combustion convinces: it is deeply consistent with the tone of the whole. For Krook's obsession
with the will and his incessant hovering on the brink of some
statement or action he can never bring himself to make create
within him a vacuum of meaninglessness. It is Life which
Krook can never quite force himself into, and it is Life which
exacts his death: he bursts like a tumefied frog. The incident
is narrated with appalling realism:

"What, in the Devil's name," [Guppy] says, "is this! Look at
my fingers!"
A thick, yellow liquor defiles them, which is offensive to the
smell. A stagnant, sickening oil, with some natural repulsion in it
that makes them both shudder. (Chapter 32, p. 454.)

That such a passage can fit so naturally into the background
of the novel alone testifies to its overtly symbolic character.
In fact, the same dreadful sapping process is at work throughout the novel. There is, for instance, Gridley, the man from
Shropshire. We meet Gridley early on in the book, on the
third page of the first chapter, as the man who "Periodically
appears from Shropshire and breaks out into efforts to
address the Chancellor at the close of the day's business, and
who can by no means be made to understand that the
Chancellor is legally ignorant of his existence after making it
desolate for a quarter of a century." (Chapter 1, p. 3.) His
subsequent "case", and his death after pursuit and arrest by
Inspector Bucket, forms a complete sub-plot in its own right,
a sub-plot which underscores the meaning of the whole book.
It is given to Gridley both to state the case against the
"system" and to anticipate the end of the Jarndyce suit
itself: "My whole estate left to me in that will of my father's
has gone in costs." Gridley has been destroyed by his

exasperations, distorted into rage and irritation; his self-diagnosis — not at all a bad one in the circumstances — is that giving way to ire saved him from turning imbecile. But we may take leave to doubt the gain in the long run; on his death-bed Gridley is an appalling piece of evidence for the "drawing power" Miss Flite attributed to the court:

> His voice had faded, with the old expression of his face, with his strength, with his anger, with his resistance to the wrongs that had at last subdued him. The faintest shadow of an object full of form and colour, is such a picture of it, as he was of the man from Shropshire whom we had spoken with before. (Chapter 24, p. 351.)

Perhaps the greatest triumph of *Bleak House* is the careful documentation of the process which led up to this kind of decline in the person of Richard Carstone. It seems incredible — if we bear Carstone in mind — that critics used to charge Dickens with being unable to show people changing. They were thinking of course of the great comic monsters — characters whose essence is their imperviousness to external influences of any kind. In fact, no novelist has ever surpassed Dickens in the ability to portray the deterioration of character with growth. People do not basically change: but their attitudes, capacities, vitality, responsiveness — all these can and do change. No one knew this better than Dickens.

What happened to Krook, Miss Flite, Gridley (the man from Shropshire), and a host of Chancery ghosts, a generation before, happens to Carstone in front of us. When someone so initially vigorous, fresh, and optimistic falls to the devouring worm of Chancery, the degeneration is all the more terrible. When Alan Woodcourt calls on his friend, Carstone's greeting is very like Steerforth's to David, upon being startled by him in the boat-house: " 'Woodcourt, my dear fellow!' cried Richard, starting up with extended hands, 'you come upon my vision like a ghost.' " (P. 692.)

Carstone is, of course, the same type as Steerforth entirely. Unsuited by a stultifying classical education for any modern career, and lacking the "character" to acquire more relevant qualifications, he knocks about the world from profession to profession, unable to work up any enthusiasm that will last for more than a few months. He is less beloved of his creator than Steerforth, and a much grimmer case. There is nothing Byronic about his end; his inability to concentrate his undoubted intelligence onto some worthwhile task leads him by an inexorable process into the hellish treadmill of Chancery: " 'To make short of a long story [he explains to Woodcourt] , I am afraid I have wanted an object; but I have an object now — or it has me — and it is too late to discuss it. Take me as I am, and make the best of me.' " (P. 692.) He already has the addict's lucidity about his obsession: he is irrevocably caught between the perpetual expectation that nothing can disabuse him of, and the growing sense of the unutterable waste within himself.

In no respect is this horrible indecision shown more subtly than in Carstone's relations with his guardian John Jarndyce. Up to a point, there seems to me a similarity between Jarndyce's function in *Bleak House* and that of the Elector in Kleist's *Prinz von Homburg.* Both characters have an ambiguous relationship with the young hero, and a generally godlike role in the entire action. In a sense John Jarndyce becomes for Carstone the surrogate of the case which bears his name, almost as Christ becomes surrogate for the Father and the "embodied antagonist and oppressor" for a baffled humanity. This suggests what may in a very distant final analysis turn out to be true — that the lawsuit, and Chancery itself, have a transcendent identity, their malignancy being projected onto them by the suitors. (This at any rate is what Kafka made of the novel.) John Jarndyce serves to crystallize Richard Carstone's growing absorption in the case. There is, to my mind, no grimmer figure in fiction than Richard Carstone — who had bounded along so enthusiastically at the beginning of the novel — seen lounging through the inns of court, "biting his nails and brooding", in the later stages of the story: "On many such loungers have the speckled shadows of those trees often fallen; on the like bent head, the bitten nail, the lowering eye, the lingering step, the purposeless and dreamy air, the good consuming and consumed, the life turned sour. This lounger is not shabby yet, but that may come." (Chapter 39, p. 555.) In a still more penetrating and general phrase, Dickens speaks of the cause as "resolving his existence into itself". In a nutshell, that is the essence of *Bleak House.*

The chapter from which these passages come — an important one, and the first to involve Carstone in the omniscient narrative — began with a chilling interview between Carstone and his attorney, Vholes. Mention of Vholes brings us to an important thing about *Bleak House.* This is that it shows more clearly than any other Dickens novel the kind of structural relations obtaining between evil and innocence in the later Dickens. We remember that in the first novels there was a strict dynamic relationship between the demonic villains and the mesmerized but incorruptible waifs, and that this relationship was crucially important in the life of the enterprise. It must now be observed that Dickens's changing vision is revealed in structural terms as much as in terms of "content". Indeed, that content is not only to be described in structural terms, but is framed in them; that is to say, in terms that relate to the *Weltanschauung* as a whole, and to the work of art as a whole.

If the "victims" of *Bleak House* are no longer strictly victims at all (as Oliver, Nell, Smike, and even Paul Dombey were), but really victims of themselves, so the villains are not strictly villains, but rather devourers, in the Blakean sense of the word. That which seeks to devour existence is a definition of evil which *Bleak House* and the later Dickens in general might be said to body forth. *Bleak House* has no Carker or Heep, but in recompense it has a greater variety of spongers and parasites than even *Dombey and Son.* There are two main groups of devourers in *Bleak House,* lawyers and others. Dickens's attitude towards the law and lawyers is particularly significant here, and again in a structural sense. Lawyers had always been sterile and counter-productive members of society in the Dickens world; futile, and living only off the distress of others. Now this emerges in a new structural relation to the meaning of the whole: Dickens's general sense of the law as parasitic on human indignity and anxiety now emerges as a deep insight into the actual nature of social man in the nineteenth century. In some way, the law seemed to provide Dickens with the perfect model for the peculiar state of affairs in the modern world, with its apparently insoluble anxieties, tensions, delusions. and addictions. We are approaching the essential meaning of Dickens's later work, and indeed of his work as a whole: in the indefinitely postponed decisions of the legal system, in its consuming, wasteful processes and its self-perpetuating dynamic of hope and disillusion, Dickens saw a model for modern society. Thus, necessarily, the suitors wasting away in futile hope attract to themselves the devouring attorneys and solicitors who create and produce nothing, but consume the life of others. Thus the lawyers in *Bleak House* — Tulkinghorn, Kenge, and Vholes — complete a total account of human behaviour in society subject to new and as yet less than half-understood strains and tensions. The lawyers are inevitable, *even indispensable,* members of society, for their constant availability and inexhaustible serviceability is in a sinister way necessary to the existence of the clients: the victims need the devourers.

This is most spectacularly true of the relationship — symbiotic as it almost becomes — between Richard Carstone and Vholes. (It is a brilliant name, by the way, with a suggestion of small rodent life from which the "h" is drying the warmth.) Vholes is purely a bloodsucker, horribly industrious in seeking out a receptive host, and consuming his life away. This he does as naturally as another man might look for a post in a bank or try to sell bread, and with as little misgiving that there might be something wrong in what he is doing. He pulls Carstone on step by step, watching him grow thinner without the slightest flicker of emotion or understanding. When he explains the situation to Carstone, his aims and motives are quite plain:

> "It is my duty to attend to your interests with a cool head, and I can quite understand that to your excited feelings I may appear, at such times as the present, insensible. My daughters may know

me better. But they have known me longer than you have, and the confiding eye of affection is not the distrustful eye of business. Not that I complain, sir, of the eye of business being distrustful; quite the contrary. In attending to your interests, I wish to have all possible checks upon me; it is right that I should be cool and methodical, Mr. Carstone; and I cannot be otherwise — no, sir, not even to please you." (Chapter 39, pp. 550–51.)

This kind of profession of honesty is a familiar element of Dickens's account of villainy: we remember the exchanges between Jonas Chuzzlewit and Montague Tigg. But it is not the self-righteousness of the hypocrite nor the "innocence of evil" that we are asked to recognize in Vholes. Vholes is not justifying himself here, he is explaining and describing, without any tell-tale over-emphasis. Yet what he is doing is itself evil: of this the omniscient narrator leaves us in no doubt: "As though, Mr. Vholes and his relations being minor cannibal chiefs, and its being proposed to abolish cannibalism, indignant champions were to put the case thus: Make man-eating unlawful, and you starve the Vholeses!" (Chapter 39, p. 549.) Moreover, Vholes is described often in terms suggesting a vampire bat. He takes off his gloves "as if he were skinning himself", his hat as if "he were scalping himself". He has "an inward manner of speech and a bloodless quietude". It is Carstone's blood that he needs of course, and Dickens doesn't hesitate to emphasize the point: Vholes speaks "as if there were an unclean spirit in him that will neither come out nor speak out", and looks at his client as if "he were making a lingering meal of him with his eyes as well as with his professional appetite". This last image suggests if not the erotic at least the curiously intimate emotional involvement of the attorney and his client. I have called it symbiotic; it is, certainly, a genuine growing together, a relationship of the most uncomfortable kind. And what is perhaps the most deeply disturbing suggestion of *Bleak House* as a whole is that this kind of relationship — evil in the Blakean sense of the word — is a common and perhaps ineradicable element of our societal organization. As we live together, we necessarily practise emotional and economic cannibalism. This is of course not observed and annotated complacently or deterministically; on the contrary, as I have already emphasized, Dickens's indignation and disgust are fiercer here than in any earlier or indeed later novel. But structurally and dynamically, the role and function of evil have been transformed so much that it seems invidious to retain the word, at least in its older significance of malignancy.

What, for instance, is one to make of Tulkinghorn? There are cultivated and intelligent readers who actually admire him, and he does share a puritanic cleanliness with characters like Jarvis Lorry of *A Tale of Two Cities,* and a stately dignity with a character like Dr. Strong of *David Copperfield.* Both of these latter characters are strongly approved by Dickens, though there are involuntary reservations in the handling of Dr. Strong. Tulkinghorn undoubtedly has the interests of the Dedlocks at heart: his motivation is indeed unusually disinterested: " 'The sole consideration in this unhappy case,' " he tells Lady Dedlock (and we believe him), " 'is Sir Leicester.' " Sir Leicester being, as he later adds, for his purposes, identifiable with the Dedlock name, honour, and estate. Yet he is "an oyster of the old school, whom nobody can open" (p. 131), "a larger species of rook" (p. 162), and, most damning of all, "the trustiest one of the Law's representatives" (p. 305). He is "close, dry, and silent" and "repressed". In another significant image, he is associated with a millstone: "Look at a millstone, Mr. George, for some change in its expression, and you will find it quite as soon as in the face of Mr. Tulkinghorn . . . " (p. 485). Tulkinghorn acts in this capacity towards George himself and also towards Gridley; in his dry fastidious way he harries and persecutes honest life as much as Vholes does, and his key-role in the whole narrative is as the tracker-down of Lady Dedlock. The ambiguities in the characterization are fairly sturdily dispelled here, though with an extraordinary detachment on Dickens's part:

> It may be that he pursues her doggedly and steadily, with no touch of compunction, remorse, or pity. It may be that her beauty, and all the state and brilliancy surrounding her, only gives

him the greater zest for what he is set upon, and makes him the more inflexible in it. Whether he be cold and cruel, whether immovable in what he has made his duty, whether absorbed in love of power, whether determined to have nothing hidden from him in ground where he has burrowed among secrets all his life, whether he in his heart despises the splendour of which he is a distant beam, whether he is always treasuring up slights and offences in the affability of his gorgeous clients — whether he be any of this, or all of this, it may be that my Lady had better have five thousand pairs of fashionable eyes upon her, in distrustful vigilance, than the two eyes of this rusty lawyer, with his wisp of neckcloth and his dull black breeches tied with ribbons at the knees. (Chapter 29, p. 402.)

This is the most important passage in the treatment of Tulkinghorn, and it is remarkable on many counts. First, in that it gives us a brilliant instance of the general law set forth at the beginning of *A Tale of Two Cities* that "every human creature is constituted to be that profound secret and mystery to every other". Dickens really believed this, and the belief explains, as it is explained by, his consistently behaviourist approach to characterization: as far as others are concerned, people are what they do and the way they do it. This does not mean, as Mr. Robert Garis takes it to mean, that Dickens is some kind of inspired mime, a cross between Marcel Marceau and Charlie Chaplin. It means simply that he was sure that the gestures and actions of which behaviour is composed do not so much "betray" or "reveal" emotional states, as set them forth: they *are* those states. And modern philosophy, both in England and on the Continent, has backed him up in this. The passage is secondly remarkable in the way it deepens our understanding of the lawyer by raising hypotheses and possibilities about him. The narrator does not commit himself to any of them, though we are intended to accept each as part of our conception of Tulkinghorn's "character". Thirdly, the passage is significant in the actual content of these speculations, and the relations that hold among them. Tulkinghorn is all these things — cold, immovable, power-loving, jealous of the Dedlock honour, concerned about it, and, most interestingly of all, quite simply resentful of the "slights and offences" he has had to endure from a higher class. At the base of this complex characterization, then, is a consciousness of class and caste with all its ambiguities and unarticulated grudges. Thus, it is natural enough that Lady Dedlock should draw his fire: for she epitomizes the upper-class negligence that insults the industrious burgher, and yet she is that worst of all social offenders, the upstart — no better than Tulkinghorn himself. So he begins to play the part of the blackmailer, and meets the blackmailer's fate at the hands of Lady Dedlock's passionately slighted maid, Hortense. There is no room here to go into the subtleties of Dickens's handling of the murder and of the lawyer's whole environment. But I must at least mention in passing the significance of those cellars in Lincoln's Inn fields, of that echo beneath Tulkinghorn's rooms, and of the fresh, cool port wine he lovingly descends into them to bring up. The enjoyment of his wine is the only refreshing thing about Tulkinghorn, and it seems strangely implicated in his life and death. As indeed does one other detail which ought to be mentioned in any account of Tulkinghorn: in his tower bedroom at Chesney Wold, Tulkinghorn is said to sleep "in his turret, with a complaining flag-staff over his head . . . " (Chapter 12, p. 162.) Much rhetorical play is made of the Roman allegory that eventually gesticulates towards Tulkinghorn's dead body in Lincoln's Inn; yet this subtle, passing observation prepares us far more sinisterly for his doom.

What Tulkinghorn shares with the other lawyers and solicitors in the book is an absence of moral realism. In Tulkinghorn's case, this is complicated by the workings of a subtle intelligence brooding upon a variety of different causes and stirred by a variety of conflicting motives. In the final analysis, however, he is as guilty of the displacement of moral by professional drives which is so conspicuously present in much more absurd men, such as Conversation Kenge. The human implications of the winding-up of the Jarndyce suit mean nothing whatever to Kenge. He is lost in admiration for its professional aspects: " ' . . . on the numerous difficulties, contingencies, masterly fictions, and forms of procedure in this great cause, there has been expended study, ability, eloquence, knowledge, intellect, Mr. Woodcourt, high intellect.' " (Chapter 65, p. 866.) — Gammon and spinach, we are tempted to add, for Kenge's list oddly echoes Miss Flite's list of birds.

Apart from the lawyers and their victims, there is a whole gallery of other parasites and victims. Among the most repellent are the ridiculous Smallweeds: this brilliantly evoked gaggle of gargoyles has a special role in *Bleak House*. The first Smallweed we meet, the young friend of Messrs. Jobling and Guppy, appears initially as a detailed portrait in the vein of acrid realistic reportage that had been an important element of Dickens's art since *Sketches by Boz*. This is the kind of absurd, self-preoccupied, dessicated and atrophied pseudo-dandy that Dickens had always loved to describe:

> ... he is a weird changeling, to whom years are nothing. He stands precociously possessed of centuries of owlish wisdom. If he ever lay in a cradle, it seems as if he must have lain there in a tail-coat. He has an old, old eye, has Smallwood: and he drinks and smokes, in a monkeyish way; and his neck is stiff in his collar: and he is never to be taken in: and he knows all about it, whatever it is. (Chapter 20, p. 275.)

The transformation with time of Dickens's comic sense is nowhere more alarmingly apparent than here: absurd, pretentious, pitiful, the young Smallweed arouses none of the laughter that comes so often and so easily to the reader of *Nicholas Nickleby* or *Martin Chuzzlewit*. By a natural extension of the perceptions invested in Smallweed, Dickens arrives at those weird, grotesque automata, his parents and sister. Grandfather and Grandmother Smallweed represent a logically final reduction of Dickensian man to his physiopsychological essentials: pathetic, acquisitive, mechanistically at the mercy of stimuli, and predictable in his comical responses. This is a bald parody of the human family, one which left a powerful imprint in the writing of some of Dickens's great expressionist successors, such as Strindberg. But the reality of which it is a parody contains a disturbingly high proportion of the Smallweed characteristics. For they are engaged in an arid search for the Jarndyce will and

Captain Hawdon's letters, and therefore offer a typically Dickensian parody of the main themes of the novel. In their genteel and human ways, Richard Carstone and lawyer Tulkinghorn are doing no more.

Nevertheless, the Smallweeds are brilliantly utilized caricatures, and the parasite theme of the novel is counterpointed more painfully in the more "normal" domestic situations. There is, for instance, old Turveydrop, making his gentility a pretext for living a life of idleness at the expense of his son, Prince. It is an indication of the engrossing fecundity of *Bleak House* that the horrible nature of this situation can so easily pass unremarked among the more dramatically highlighted horrors of the Jarndyce and Dedlock affairs. Prince's labours to sustain his father's expensive tastes and at the same time to provide for his own family make him a grim archetype of the social animal in the technological, urbanized world of the capitalist era. Through the wife he takes in the course of the story, Caddy Jellyby, Prince Turveydrop is related to the other outstanding example of domestic parasitism in the novel, the "telescopic philanthropy" of Caddy's mother. Mrs. Jellyby remains the classic original of a type of socio-political do-gooder who remains all too active in our own society. Yet her idealism is not a consequence of natural asceticism or purity, but a dislocation of her own proper interests. Her worn-out husband and her tribe of unwashed children are evidence of a fundamental physical sanity which has simply been perverted. Dickens shows great skill here in finding convincing domestic equivalents for acute anxiety-states and for intricate moral dilemmas. One thinks of the later Strindberg, of the evilly tyrannical cook who wastes the life of the young couple in *The Ghost Sonata*: Dickens had touched on this humorously in the succession of pillages, thefts, and liberties perpetrated by the domestics at the expense of David and Dora in *David Copperfield*; he was to again in *Great Expectations*.

If the comic sense of the earlier novels appears transformed in the aridly absurd Smallweeds, it manifests a more sadly satiric form in the figure of Harold Skimpole, the last

of the novel's parasites I want to deal with. Here, surely, is
the cousin of Mr. Micawber, the professional charmer, forever
in debt, forever depending on his friends to get him out of
trouble. The parasitism is here openly confessed, even
flaunted as a way of life, poetic rather than prosily industrious. Yet Micawber was a deeply experienced character,
whose appearances were awaited and welcomed. Skimpole is
a non-experience, his vitality mere froth, his evasiveness
repulsive in its "honesty". This honesty is of course a further
development of what I earlier described as the *mauvaise foi*
of Micawber and Spenlow. No strategy or moral dodge in the
whole novel is more wholly dishonest than Skimpole's
professions of honest parasitism. The sheer nastiness it conceals, and no doubt increases out of inverted guilt, is revealed
when his notes towards a memoir are finally published after
his death. Esther registers the appropriate contempt when she
reads of John Jarndyce — Skimpole's endlessly generous
patron — " 'J. in common with most other men I have
known, is the Incarnation of Selfishness.' " (Chapter 61, p.
831.)

It is obvious that to describe a work, in which the implications are so deep and terrible as those I have been analyzing,
as a "detective-story with social relevance,"[7] is, to say the
least of it, inadequate. It is equally obvious that the "satire"
refers to something of vastly greater generality than the Law,
or Institution. What Dickens has done, in fact, in creating an
institution upon which so many different people are help-
lessly fixated, is to find a universal symbol for the human
refusal or inability to live. The relationship to *David
Copperfield* is obvious. What Dickens defines so minutely in
the degeneration of Richard Carstone, the drying-up of
Gridley, the withering to insanity of Miss Flite, the lunatic
suspicion of Krook, the proliferation on top of all this helpless self-destruction of mushroom-forests of parasitism, is
nothing less than the destruction of existence to which Blake
refers in the "Marriage of Heaven and Hell". The parasites
and the machinators (Tulkinghorn and the Smallweeds, for
example) only breed upon a decay which itself derives from

the inward confusion and self-maiming of others. The responsibility of these others for their souls is entirely their own. Carstone is his own victim; Vholes only sniffs out the corpse-to-be, and battens on to it in good time. Chancery itself is a monument to human self-destruction, to expectation, hope, illusion, whatever name we care to give to the process which prevents men from seeing that life *is* now, around them, and not in some imaginary future or condition still unrealized. Hell has its officers — the lawyers, here — but itself exists only by virtue of the candidates eligible for it. It is hope, the refusal to take life as it is, without special privilege, that destroys Richard Carstone. The implication of the whole book is that we refuse at our peril to accept the responsibility for our own destinies.

The resolution of this huge design, the most elaborately polyphonic in all Dickens, I think, depends on a profound stroke of irony that is inherent in the initial conception. Jarndyce and Jarndyce, the law suit that has been in progress for so long that generations have been born into it and outlived by it, is ended: it is over, not for the day, but "over for good" (p. 865). Esther Summerson and her husband Allan arrive at Chancery at the beginning of the new session, interested to see what will be the effect of the new will, found in Krook's shop by the Smallweeds, sold to John Jarndyce, and considered by Conversation Kenge to be of outstanding relevance to the Cause. They are surprised to find clerks carrying out bundles of paper: "bundles in bags, bundles too large to be got into any bags, immense masses of papers of all shapes and no shapes . . . " (Chapter 65, p. 865.) This is the dog-eared corpse of Jarndyce and Jarndyce, the legal fiction on which so much life and energy has been wasted throughout its existence. On being asked by Allan what has been the outcome of the cause, Conversation Kenge reveals that the whole estate has been consumed in costs.

The effect upon Carstone is, as Woodcourt predicts, catastrophic. Ada Clare, Richard's wife and co-ward in the cause, tells Esther that Allan found Carstone "sitting in the corner of the Court, like a stone figure. On being roused, he had broken away, and made as if he would have spoken in a fierce voice to the Judge. He was stopped by his mouth being full of blood." (P. 868.) Carstone dies of the shock; and Miss Flite releases the birds in her attic. The death of Jarndyce and Jarndyce by slow combustion parallels the explosion of Krook and consummates the process which has carried the whole novel along, so turgidly and painfully. The final expulsion of the cause from Chancery, symbolized in the ejection of the bundles of paper, is like the purgation of a worm from the bowels. Irony — implicit earlier in that often sardonic throw-away facetiousness of the humour — has now become a property of Dickens's vision. The human enterprise itself is now seen as a sick comedy. That the entire estate upon which so many expectations have so long been fixed should have been consumed in costs seems the only appropriate end for so protracted a sick joke as Jarndyce and Jarndyce. (*Jarndyce—jaundice,* of course, echoes perpetually in the back of the mind.)

It is plain what position *Bleak House* occupies in the developing scheme of Dickens's *oeuvre.* The novel is a critique of the Dickensian expectations, their ultimate illusoriness and destructive power. Such a critique was satirically hinted at in the handling of Mr. Micawber. Something of the inward self-exhaustion of Carstone and the other Chancery ghosts, too, was visible in the unfunny saga of the Micawber family life, with its endless removals and arrests. Now, the theme of the expectations emerges as the central concern of all Dickens's work, taking as its natural expressive device the legacy — hidden, lost, or unexpectedly turning up — that is so familiar an element in the popular and serious art of the high capitalist era, from *Middlemarch* to *Juno and the Paycock.*

What Chancery and the Jarndyce suit offer together is a whole psychological model, an allegory and a metaphor for human existence. The fixation upon the judgment of the suit becomes, like the warren dug by the industrious animal narrator of Kafka's story, *The Burrow,* at once a refuge from reality and a source of inward erosion. Kafka's animal constructs his earth fortress, with its endless ramifications, false tunnels, sancta within sancta, in order to buttress against reality and emotional contact with others a self which becomes progressively less secure. Like the super-powers today, the creature, never safe from doubt, undermines its sense of security with its own precautionary measures: the safer it becomes, the less safe it feels. Dickens's novel, like Kafka's story, translates naturally into emotional or social terms, and is not the less allegorical for being realistically presented. Richard Carstone, Miss Flite, Krook, the man from Shropshire, all the Chancery ghosts are victims of their own *mauvaise foi* before they are victims of the system: in each case, the decisions they have taken about life shield them from the perpetual adjustment to reality that life demands, if it is to be lived effectually. Richard Carstone, for instance, could have succeeded in the army, at medicine, in the law, in any of the careers to which he so fitfully applies himself, had it not been for the worm of the Chancery illusion inside him. He believes in the golden fruit of the Jarndyce law suit, and hence persuades himself that no career can satisfy him. His economic system, a weird parody of Mr. Micawber's, beautifully typifies the subtle self-deceptions with which he has entangled himself: " 'My jewel of a dear cousin, you hear this old woman! Why does she say that? Because I gave eight pounds odd (or whatever it was) for a certain neat waistcoat and buttons a few days ago. Now, if I had stayed at Badger's I should have been obliged to spend twelve pounds at a blow, for some heart-breaking lecture-fees. So, I make four pounds — in a lump — by the transaction!' " (Chapter 18, p. 234.)

The whole novel is, at one level, a psychological system. It was Kafka who took the Dickens novel, pruned it of its social relevance, and turned it into psycho-spiritual allegory. Yet Dickens's mature novels, for all their intense realistic social relevance, are no less allegorical. But if *Bleak House* presents a psychological allegory, it also presents a concealed metaphor, and it is one of the great mythic works of literature. Just as *King Lear* suggests that, *au fond,* life is a wind-swept heath upon which naked lunatics play charades, and *Waiting for Godot* that it is the bored conversation of tramps waiting for something they know will never come, so *Bleak House* argues that human existence is most like a protracted waiting for a legacy that bequeaths us nothing. It is of course much else besides; but this, I submit, is its great underlying metaphor, a metaphor which served Dickens for the rest of his life.

The vision of *Bleak House* is, I have argued, tragic. It is not tragic in the Bradleyan sense: it does not concern the fall of a great man. But it is full of the pity of human waste, the wearing to nothing of human tissue, the waste of energies and potential, the gnawing away of life. This — one concedes, as Dickens winds up his great tale — is the truth about the way most of us in fact live and die; and that this is a tragic fact is borne out by that most searching of all the acid tests that undercut the critic's theorizing: in laying down the book one has the sensation of having passed across a battlefield.

9 Hard Times

Hard Times is certainly the most externally conceived of all Dickens's works, with none of the identification-from-within which usually provides the consciousness of the enterprise. It is a novel "about" something, instead of being a vehicle for the artist's self-projection and analysis. This externality in conception accounts for both the weaknesses and the strengths of the book. Without the involvement in the world of his narrative guaranteed by the myth, Dickens tends to fall back upon caricature: Bounderby, Mrs. Sparsit, James Harthouse, Slackbridge, even Stephen Blackpool, are social emblems or caricatures rather than "real" people. Yet *Hard Times* is ultimately a great piece of prophecy, and Dickens's grasp on the social, political, and moral realities involved is sure and deep. Only Dickens could have written *Hard Times,* which is to say more than that the aliveness of texture, the wealth of invention, and the brilliance of metaphor are beyond the abilities of any of his contemporaries. It is to say that Dickens alone could have grasped the moral and social issues concerned, and bodied them forth in terms of scene, character, and event.

Yet this very act of fictional bodying forth could only have been achieved through means which transcended the laws of realist fiction: caricature, we may say, or the use of emblematic rather than unique, naturalistic characterization, was essential to Dickens's achievement here. To this extent, the treatment of Bounderby, for instance, and of Stephen

Blackpool and Bitzer, is perfectly judicious. The meanings could not have been conveyed in any other way, since the presentation presupposed and depended upon a vast act of simplification, which would have been jeopardized by any greater degree of individuation. The difficulties arise only when Dickens needs to combine these emblematic or class-typical elements of his fable with the "private" action by which the parable is also effected.

Initially, the problem does not worry Dickens. The whole Book the First (the first third of the novel) is more or less completely successful. Here Dickens is setting out his plan. Gradgrindery is to be contrasted with Sleary-ism, which is to say, the world of the severe Benthamite pedagogue with the world of a travelling circus. Associated with Gradgrind's educational system — based upon quantification of all experience and a total elimination of what the uninitiated call the life of the spirit and the emotions — is industry, the world of Josiah Bounderby. Bounderby and Gradgrind appear aligned in the first scene of the novel, and are associated by what seems a common philosophy. The Bounderby's upon the coarse awareness that a soft heart and profit, is seemingly aligned with Gradgrind's fact-founded educational system, as it has been expounded in the brilliant opening chapter. Yet as the novel proceeds, we see that Dickens has in fact worked a clever sleight upon us: Gradgrind and Bounderby have actually little in common. Even their common contempt for sentiment and fancy is based upon differing premises: Gradgrind's upon genuine intellectual conviction, of the sort practised by James Mill; Bounderby's upon the coarse awareness that a good heart and a lively imagination never led anybody to a good bank balance. After the initial association in the opening chapters, the two men go their own ways. The sleight works: when Bounderby and Gradgrind together visit Mr. Sleary with the intention of requesting him to remove Sissy Jupe from Gradgrind's school, the world of the circus folk immediately registers as a valid alternative to the life we have already learned to associate with both Gradgrind and Bounderby.

The clowns, acrobats, and dancers who crowd into Mr. Sleary's room to witness the confrontation with Gradgrind and Bounderby, embody precisely those qualities outlawed by the pedagogue and the industrialist — waywardness, unpredictability, earthy good sense, and a tolerance based upon recognition of a need to help and be helped. To Bounderby, these people are fools who might keep his hands from their work. (A better industrial psychologist might have seen their value as entertainment.) To Gradgrind they are a distinct moral menace, loose-living, subversive, free, dionysiac.

Dickens expends all his genius in creating the rich wayward stink of the horse-riding ambience. Dr. Leavis has made the connexion between Sissy Jupe and certain characters of D. H. Lawrence.[1] In reading the account of the horse-riding folk, we are reminded again of Lawrence, this time through one of the later poems, "When I went to the Circus":

> It was full of uneasy people
> Frightened of the bare earth and the temporary canvas
> And the smell of horses and other beasts . .[2]

It is just this sense of exposed reality, of a pungency too strong for cerebralized, industrialized man, that makes Dickens's treatment of the Slearly circus so significant. He is, in fact, taking up something he had let drop at an earlier stage of his creative career, the fascination with low-life characters in *Nicholas Nickleby* and *The Old Curiosity Shop*; in taking it up, he has raised it to a higher level of meaning. Sleary's horse-riding is used, quite consciously and with full appreciation of its significance, to represent a way of living in many ways superior not simply to the system of fact and utility, but to civilization itself, with all the exclusions and prohibitions of impulse, rudeness, and instinct the concept implies.

This surely is the great significance of *Hard Times* in Dickens's *oeuvre*. Its quite conscious application of something once merely loved and felt, now fully comprehended, marks a new stage in Dickens's development. From *Hard Times* onwards, we see Dickens reversing the direction of the early dream novels: in *Oliver Twist,* for instance, the hero has to be rescued from the proletarian-criminal class, and proved to be of good bourgeois stock; but Estella in *Great Expectations* is shown to be not the bourgeoise she had always seemed, but the daughter of a convict and a murderess. *Hard Times* stands halfway between these two stages. Sissy Jupe, the travelling acrobat's daughter, provides the humanizing strength lacking in the children of the good bourgeois Gradgrind, while, in a curious inversion of the Oliver Twist situation, Bounderby, the bully of humility, the proletarian braggart forever proclaiming the horrors of his own up-bringing, is revealed as a liar whose childhood had been quite comfortable.

Thus, *Hard Times* brings to full consciousness something half-consummated in *Dombey and Son* and *David Copperfield* — Dickens's deep love and compassion for the submerged and outlawed energies of modern civilization. Florence Dombey had fled to the proletarians for comfort, the Peggottys were David Copperfield's only true friends. Yet in these books the workers are still semi-ideal, sturdy retainers who respect the gentry and "know their place", even to the occasional forelock-tug. From *Hard Times* stems the much profounder love for the working class we see maturing in *Great Expectations* and *Our Mutual Friend,* and we cannot divorce this process from the parallel diminution of the ogreous glamour of evil itself. " 'It's aw a muddle,' " Stephen Blackpool says, and the muddle, Dickens argues, comes from above and within, from the misdirections and mis-government of the ruling class, but also from the options on serious and deep living that are open to the individual himself, and not taken up by him. If we trace the development of the Dickens hero from Oliver Twist to David Copperfield, I have observed, we see this dual process at work — the diminution of ambivalently conceived evil, and the transformation of the working class from hag-ridden semi-criminal mobs to a source of vitality denied the civilized classes. As the base of the class pyramid, the proletariat is in touch with the soil, from which the higher classes are divided. Thus, Dickens turns increasingly to the best and strongest feelings of those who, however they may be brutalized by over-work and bad conditions, have not been perverted by the need to exercise an authority unearned and misunderstood, and who therefore retain their hold upon the deeper instincts the rulers have found unprofitable or embarrassing, and in consequence have outlawed. When, late in life, D. H. Lawrence lamented that "the middle-class cut off some of my vital vibration", he was referring to a situation Dickens knew well. "Class," Lawrence wrote, "makes a gulf across which all the best human flow is lost."[3] All Dickens's later work is an attempt to restore this "best human flow". It is for this reason that the great tradition of the English novel moves through Dickens to Lawrence, for both men saw and felt the necessity of breaking down all the crippling barriers of prohibition and inhibition implicit in what Lawrence stigmatized as "the middle class *thing*". (The phrasing is important: Lawrence makes it clear that it is not the middle class itself, a body of human beings, that is in question, but the *thing*, the consciousness of caste and barrier.)

Gradgrind's system of fact and Bounderby's business cult equally check and etiolate this best human flow. But the two men are totally different and stand for different things. And this difference causes an imbalance never wholly set at rest in the book. Bounderby, for plot reasons, has to marry Gradgrind's daughter, Louisa; in other words, the life streams of the two men have to merge. This process merely reveals that Bounderby, the bully of humility, is caricature, and nothing but caricature. As a class-emblem (and this point is important), he is magnificent: every detail is perfect, and he remains the prototype of the self-made man, the tycoon who still exists and still plays his part in fiction as in life. Yet he resists integration into an emotional fabric meant to be taken seriously. Bounderby the noisy braggart is an apt comment on the vulgar quality of life his "values" lead to. Bounderby as hurt husband is an absurdity, a fictional disaster.

Bounderby's refusal to integrate himself in the genuine emotional life of the novel only reveals what the shrewder reader had suspected: that the artistic means by which he is characterized differ widely from those used to define Gradgrind. For if Bounderby is superb social caricature, an emblem of the kind we associate with the art of Daumier, Gradgrind is a real and sympathetic human being: "The emphasis was helped by the speaker's square wall of a forehead, which had his eyebrows for its base, while his eyes found commodious cellarage in two dark caves, overshadowed by the wall. The emphasis was helped by the speaker's mouth, which was wide, thin, and hard set." (P. 1.) The metaphor of the caves and the commodious cellarage is one of several in the book, deployed at strategic moments, which show a new trenchancy in Dickens's modes of characterization: here the figure suggests the combination of depth and stoniness eventually to bring Gradgrind to his knees. We forget neither the gloomy ring of that "cellarage", nor the vulnerability of those "commodious" depths, nor yet the suggestion of spidery movement in the brilliant use of the active verb "found" to describe the eyes. Consistently, Gradgrind holds our attention as a serious man, seriously misguided, Bounderby on the other hand is from first to last a *tour de force* of plosives — a remarkable achievement, but in a quite different literary mode.

But it was two or three novels before Dickens was to learn to keep his modes distinct, to keep characters like Bounderby clear of any emotional engagement meant to be taken seriously. The Podsnaps and Veneerings of *Our Mutual Friend* inhabit a separate plane of reality, related to the rest of the novel by their function of providing commentary on it: they remain essentially apart, in the action but not of it, hectoring and bellowing in their emblematic universe. The idea that Veneering, for example, or Boots or Brewer, should have a private life is absurd, a form of artistic suicide. At that late stage of his career, Dickens was perfectly aware that such characters belonged to a particular artistic mode, and that this mode, while of great use and adaptability, did not lend itself to involvement with other more private modes *on their terms.* This is nowhere so well revealed as in the sensitive and subtle treatment of Podsnap's daughter, Georgiana, who acts as a liaison between the Podsnap-Veneering satiric mode and the mode of real relationship and individuated characterization. Georgiana's realistically conveyed dread of the elegible suitors her father throws her way acts as a commentary on her father's values, just as her father's emblematically expressed values comment on and set off the activities and purposes of people like the Lammles and Fascination Fledgeby, who are not class-caricature, but "real" people, caught up in the class-history net.

At the stage of writing *Hard Times,* Dickens had not yet acquired this sort of tact, nor the technical expertise to keep separate the different modes represented by Bounderby and Gradgrind. He was, as it were, misled, by his own initial alignment of the two men, into believing them similar characters. Thus, Gradgrind himself has to move uneasily between the modes, between satiric caricature and psychological realism. From the first description of him we are never allowed to forget the human being within the system; a little later in the first book, we are explicitly told that he "was by no means so rough a man as Mr. Bounderby. His character was not unkind, all things considered; it might have been a very kind one indeed, if he had only made some round mistake in the arithmetic that balanced it, years ago" (p. 27). Now in fact Dickens does not, I think, quite succeed in keeping *this* Gradgrind, the real father of Tom and Louisa, separate from "Thomas Gradgrind, Sir. A man of realities. A man of facts and calculations." (P. 3.) His purpose, of course, demanded that the real Gradgrind should suffer because of the heartless Benthamism he has allowed to alienate him from his own deeper impulses, his children from theirs, himself from his children. The children must come to grief to demonstrate the thesis that a thorough-going utilitarianism is destructive of the best and most real life. This is the novel's great fable, its great prophetic parable. Edmund Wilson has pointed out that Dickens's message was demonstrated with almost staggering fullness in the *Autobiography* of John Stuart Mill.[4] Mill underwent precisely the kind of crisis experienced by Louisa Gradgrind after the botched elopement with James Harthouse. At the age of early maturity, when a young man should be emerging into the best of his intellectual and sexual life, Mill underwent a terrifying apathy, a numbness, of the kind described by Coleridge:

> A grief without a pang, void, dark, and drear,
> A stifled, drowsy, unimpassioned grief,
> Which finds no natural outlet, no relief,
> In word, or sigh, or tear —

Louisa Gradgrind, after her marriage to Bounderby, experiences "A curious passive inattention" (p. 220), and she turns against her only ally, Sissy Jupe: "the strongest qualities she possessed, long turned upon themselves, became a heap of obduracy, that rose against a friend." (P. 224.)

The treatment of Louisa and of Gradgrind himself in this chapter (the first of Book the Third), is impeccable. It is moreover, part of an ambitious design adumbrated in the titles Dickens gave to his three books — *Sowing, Reaping* and *Garnering.* This causal schema itself indicates that the novel was written at a transitional stage. In *Hard Times,* Dickens is moving from a fiction which, however dazzlingly expressionist in his hands, conformed to the narrative laws of realist practice, to an altogether more daring idiom, in which natural symbolism, emblem, and metaphor function as integral elements in the narrative design. I have already noted the greater self-consciousness of the treatment of the Sleary horse-riding, which, if we contrast it with Mrs. Jarley's waxworks, appears quite consciously set up for symbolic contrast with Gradgrindery. We could extend this observation to the methods of characterization which range from penetrating realism to brilliant social caricature.

Unfortunately, however, the anomalous involvement of Bounderby in Louisa's emotional life is paralleled by certain frictions within the treatment of Gradgrind himself. For he is forced to parrot his own system in a mechanically comic way, which cuts across the realities of the superb passages in the third book in which he confesses his fundamental guilt before his daughter. As a result, it is difficult to keep the man in the mind as a consistent entity, without consciously or unconsciously excluding one or other of his aspects. Certainly, Dickens had thrown Gradgrind up into brilliantly distorted relief as the ogre of his children's nursery days: "The first object with which they had an association, or of which they had a remembrance, was a large black board with a dry Ogre chalking ghastly white figures on it." (P. 9.) And it had already been Dickens's purpose to show the diminution of childhood ogres into normal, harmless grown-ups, as for example in the dwindling of Betsey Trotwood in *David Copperfield*. But here it is not merely childhood distortion that created the ogre. The ogre is presented to us, with Dickens's approval, in quasi-mechanistic terms:

> Indeed, as he eagerly sparkled at them from the cellarage before mentioned, he seemed a kind of cannon loaded to the muzzle with facts, and prepared to blow them clean out of the regions of childhood at one discharge. He seemed a galvanizing apparatus, too, charged with a grim mechanical substitute for the tender young imaginations that were to be stormed away. (Book 1, chapter 2, p. 3.)

Dickens's general accuracy as a psychologist has, of course, been confirmed by behaviourism, just as the success of his comic method anticipated the gist of Bergson's account of laughter in terms of the mechanistic behaviour of the human organism.[5] But the brilliant behaviourist organism who mouths "Facts, nothing but Facts" is not the same artistic entity as the man who has a daughter he loves, and who has to admit finally the failure of his whole life's work. So that when Gradgrind, informing Louisa of Bounderby's offer for her hand in marriage, hears her say, " 'Life is very short' ", he replies — with absurd feelinglessness — according to the system: " 'It is short, no doubt, my dear. Still, the average duration of human life is proved to have increased of late years. The calculations of various life assurance and annuity offices, among other figures which cannot go wrong, have established the fact.' " (P. 100.) Even more outrageous is his response to Louisa's gentle rejoinder, " 'I speak of my own life, Father.' — 'O indeed? Still,' said Mr. Gradgrind, 'I need not point out to you, Louisa, that it is governed by the laws which govern lives in the aggregate.' " (P. 100.) Dr. Leavis finds this scene masterly in its irony;[6] and looked at from a certain point of view perhaps it is; yet it is to me unthinkable that a man as intelligent and humane as Gradgrind should have remained so insensitive to his favourite daughter's thinly veiled reluctance, to her hurt dumb insolence in the face of Bounderby's preposterous offer. Dickens has confused his modes here: he is treating Gradgrind as the ogre of Louisa's nursery, as the "canon loaded to the muzzle with facts", after having suggested so much more.

The error is exactly inverted in the treatment of Bounderby. A magnificent and trenchant satiric figure, Bounderby is ludicrously incapable of entering into real human relations. As the bully of humility, forever harping on his mythically ghastly upbringing, Bounderby is perfectly polarized by the genteel Mrs. Sparsit, the fallen gentlewoman who acts as housekeeper-companion to him: indeed the respective hubris of the two characters — her affectation of humility suggests her ineradicable class-superiority as much as his claims to have been spawned in a ditch are meant to emphasize his greatness in getting on — keeps them perfectly equipoised. But married to Louisa, Bounderby collapses, and Dickens has to pervert the evidence to rescue his creation: Bounderby must not only bray his self-made braggartry, he must also, when occasion demands, snivel and whine. The characterization collapses at a touch and Dickens flounders so badly that the whole central book of the novel — "Reaping" — is probably the most tedious and unreal tract of its length in the whole of Dickens. The offence is compounded in the deterioration of Mrs. Sparsit — a Gorgon of the type beautifully pilloried later in *Little Dorrit* — from an efficiently kept up social Grande Dame to a more authentically Dickensian but outrageously improbable pantomime dame floundering about Lancashire in the rain, peeping through curtains and collecting evidence.

Of the two flaws — the falsification of Bounderby and the metamorphosis of Mrs. Sparsit — the second is the more interesting. For it reveals the truth that Dickens really felt bored by the lady, as indeed he was bored by the upper classes throughout his life. Mrs. Sparsit is adequately defined in terms of her "Coriolanean" nose and her stony dignity. Her collapse into a "vulgar" demonstrativeness suggests, I think, that Dickens really required more from his characters, as from people in reality, than civility and "superbness": his very failure in the depiction of the aristocracy testifies to his great love of vitality and a certain exhibitionist generosity in behaviour which he judged (I think rightly) to be eliminated by the code of the *morgue Anglaise*. Dickens was no gentleman, and we in part owe to the fact the persistence of his enormous life and fecundity.

Mrs. Sparsit becomes human then, only as Dickens's hold on the initial characterization begins to falter: the less authentically she behaves, the more human she shows herself to be. This lies close to the heart of *Hard Times* and, again, pinpoints the novel's place in Dickens's *oeuvre*: he had used the myth to lever himself up out of the clutches of the workers. Now, he begins to find the altitude chilling.

So, Dickens was bored to death by Mrs. Sparsit in her Coriolanean vein, and by the *mores* she embodied. Her civility and good breeding, her "knowing her place" — knowing it to lie above Bounderby's, even in her dependence — all this produced a deadness which Dickens allowed his imagination to distort into life, or at least into a fair semblance of it. And this is much more serious a "critique" of upper class insouciance than the somewhat laboured *exposé* of its falsity we see at work elsewhere in this and in other novels. Dickens finds their inward coldness and their stifled vitality to be much graver faults than the *Vanity Fair* "spuriousness" he so often falls back upon when he attacks his betters. There is, I think, only one exception — in *A Tale of Two Cities* — to the rule that in Dickens the upper classes are cold (or arrogant) and boring. This attitude towards good manners is obviously consistent with the tremendous vivacity and grotesquerie of his own creative invention. It is the absence of this vivacity that vitiates the central book of *Hard Times,* dedicated as it is to the dull James Harthouse and his lifeless and unreal attempt to seduce Louisa Bounderby.

To a considerable extent, Dickens shared George Eliot's puritanic distrust of aristocratic insouciance. Harthouse, like Henleigh Grandcourt, is civil, effortlessly well-mannered, and unscrupulously bent on conquest. Like George Eliot, Dickens, with his essentially middle-class energy, disliked the casualness and coolness of such men, who, he felt, "must be up to something". Anyway, whatever the reasons for Dickens's attitudes, the episode of the failed seduction is extraordinarily dull. No serious indication is given of any real emotion in either party, so that Dickens is forced to make the best of a bad job by thwarting Harthouse's attempt with a massive display of novelistic *légerdemain*: the seduction flops, Louisa falls sick, Harthouse lets himself be fobbed off by Sissy, and Bounderby strides out of Louisa's life. The purpose of the whole affair of course was to bring home to Louisa's father just what a mess he has made of his daughter; as soon as Harthouse is got rid of, interest revives. There follows the breaking of Thomas Gradgrind's belief in his system, and with it the basis of his whole life. It says much for Dickens's genius that neither the dullness of the Harthouse episodes, nor the previous errors in the treatment of Gradgrind himself detract from the power of the fable he has been elaborating: the crushing of Gradgrind is one of the finest things in Dickens and, as with Mr. Dombey, the effect is achieved by a skilful use of metaphor.

Suggestions of depth, of a vertical dimension in personality immeasurable by rational means, form an important part of the characterization throughout the novel. Depth is suggested in the "commodious cellarage" of Gradgrind's eyes; Louisa is explicitly described as "unfathomed" (p. 10), and from the start displays a repressed unpredictability evidently at loggerheads with the utilitarianism forced upon her by her father's educational ideas. When Gradgrind almost "understands" her — when he "bent his deep-set eyes upon her in his turn, perhaps he might have seen one wavering moment in her . . . " — his failure to grasp those "subtle essences of humanity" (p. 99) is described again in terms of depth: "he hardened her again, and the moment shot away into the plumbless depths of the past, to mingle with all the lost opportunities that are drowned there." (P. 100.)

We can easily recognize in these hints and indications of depth and concealment the master-hand of *Dombey and Son*; and from one point of view, the case argued in that novel is paralleled here. Gradgrind like Dombey is brought down by his refusal and inability to acknowledge his own deeper requirements. Moreover, as the coldness of Dombey's marbled household was pointedly contrasted with the warmth of Solomon Gills' Ships' Instruments Shop and the salty good-heartedness of Captain Cuttle, so in *Hard Times* the Gradgrind dryness and repression are set against the mire and vitality of the Sleary horse-riding. If *Hard Times* is less successful than *Dombey,* it is certainly in part because of the experimental nature of the later work. It is true that Dombey's downfall was described in terms of "ground long undermined", but the metaphor is enlightening rather than functional; in the main, *Dombey and Son* keeps to the realist track. *Hard Times* breaks new ground. It eschews full dramatization in favour of a more economic symbolic and emblematic shorthand. A "case" can now be argued in a figure of speech; a whole phase of social reality symbolized in a character or a predicament. It is not to be wondered at that at this stage Dickens made his mistakes. Later books like *A Tale of Two Cities* show complete absorption of the new methods, and step decades ahead of the contemporary realists and naturalists in the direction of Kafka and Conrad.

Sleary's circus appears only at the very beginning and the very end of the book. Over the intervening two hundred pages, Sleary's horse-riding is represented by Sissy Jupe — "girl Number twenty". Nobody, since Dr. Leavis's essay appeared, can have doubted that Sissy — "so dark-eyed and dark-haired, that she seemed to receive a deeper and more lustrous colour from the sun, when it shone upon her" (p. 4) — stands for something serious and vital in Dickens's world. Dr. Leavis's "Lawrentian" ascription has, however, been disputed by Mr. Robert Garis: "It seems an exaggeration, then, to single out for crucial quotation a description of a character which is not in fact made anything of later by this highly repetitive artist."[7] But we are not here concerned with the behavioural traits Dickens loved to vary and ring changes on; it is a matter of a persisting quality of being; nor is the story that of Sissy at all, basically, but that of the Gradgrinds. The hints Dickens drops throughout the book serve their purpose. It is Sissy who is "run after" by that awful blinking Marx Brother, Bitzer. Bitzer was caught initially, in a typically inspired moment, at the other end of the same sunbeam as enriched Sissy Jupe. We never forget the relationship established by that sunbeam: in contrast to Sissy, Bitzer "was so light-eyed and light-haired that the self-same rays appeared to draw out of him what little colour he possessed" (pp. 4—5). So that when Sissy bumps panting into Gradgrind and palpitatingly professes herself "run after", it is not surprising to find that the pursuer is "the colourless boy" Bitzer. (P. 25.) When Gradgrind observes that Sissy is "serviceable" in the family (in a "generally pervading way"), he really puts his finger on her role in the book as a whole. It is Sissy who knows what Louisa feels when she accepts Bounderby's offer of marriage: she "looked, in wonder, in pity, in sorrow, in doubt, in a multitude of emotions, towards Louisa" (p. 103). Gradgrind himself is "possessed by an idea that there was something in this girl which could hardly be set forth in a tabular form" (p. 92). High praise indeed!

So *Hard Times* is Louisa's rather than Sissy's book. But although Sissy really has only a passive "generally pervading" influence on matters, she is in fact the one truly "free" and therefore wholly authentic character in the novel, and Mr. Garis's scepticism on the subject can be set aside. No matter how slighted and put upon she is, she remains, like Amy Dorrit in a later novel, undetermined, beyond the reach of narrowing and constricting conditioning, a full and alive human being. This fact emerges most clearly in the novel's *dénouement,* when the Sleary horse-riding returns in the profoundly significant form of a refuge for the delinquent young Tom Gradgrind. It has been Dickens's purpose to "show" the effects of Gradgrind's Benthamite philosophy upon the two children exposed to its influence. Louisa collapses into emotional confusion, and Tom gets into debt and steals, letting the blame be put onto the ostracized working man, Stephen Blackpool. The air of demonstration still sits fairly heavily on the book: it was to be several years before Dickens could integrate the "case" to be argued into a fully imagined narrative. But the marshalling of the evidence is still impressive. For Dickens has aligned three different philosophies by means of a family resemblance obtaining among them, so that they come to assume a kind of syllogistic interrelation. Gradgrind, I have observed above, is really different from Bounderby; yet we can see how Dickens is able — fairly — to align the two men by virtue of their common scorn for emotion, wonder, and imagination. Gradgrind is an idealist, yet his rigorous Benthamism easily coalesces with the hard-tacks-and-no-nonsense of Bounderby's business cult. Similarly, Bounderby's harsh opportunism can be validly derived from Gradgrind's idealistic utilitarianism. This is the first part of Dickens's syllogism. The second part is the relationship of both philosophies to the cynicism of James Harthouse, which represents a yet further deterioration of the Gradgrind no-emotions-only-facts outlook. Louisa in fact falls a prey to Harthouse's facile cynicism precisely for the same reasons as her father found the young man politically plausible. Harthouse's cynicism, in fact, Dickens shows to be an inevitable consequence of the Gradgrind divorce between reason and emotion. Without emotional conviction, without faith, without a personal commitment which cannot be questioned or articulated, all the fact systems in the world can generate no binding power, and can therefore validly be taken in whatever spirit we like, to justify whatever interpretation of the situation we choose, no matter how "cynical" it may seem, so that it serves our interest. Indeed, the very notion of cynicism becomes obsolete: there is only factual rightness and wrongness, rationality and irrationality. Enlightened self-interest is all, in so far as this notion has not itself been invalidated in favour of sheer calculation. This is the significance of James Harthouse: if Gradgrind is right, so is Harthouse. If there are only quantifiable entities, then the statistics do our reasoning for us, and cynicism is as valid an ethic as any other. We begin to see the point of Dickens's otherwise dangerously philistine attacks on statistics: sooner or later we have to stop the computers, and take a stand, irrespective of whether or not later turns taken by the figures might change our perspective, and therefore invalidate the decision. Dickens's interpretation of sooner or later is, of course, right now.

But where does the moral binding-power come from? Sissy has no answer when Gradgrind and M'Choakumchild mock her emotional response to non-emotive, statistical questions which happen to involve people dying, and dependents being left. Dickens tried to supply the answer first by negatives: Gradgrind's Benthamism is psychological suicide, Bounderby's hell-for-leather capitalism brutal and destructive of humanity and environment alike.

It is curious, incidentally, how penetratingly lasting Dickens's prophecies are: he makes us aware of pollution as a threat to life and sanity a hundred years before society itself got around to considering the question:[8] "Down upon the river that was black and thick with dye, some Coketown boys who were at large — a rare sight there — rowed a crazy boat, which made a spumous track upon the water as it jogged along, while every dip of an oar stirred up vile smells" (pp. 11–12).

The evocation is of the very essence of the book, and we need only contrast this and other such passages of *Hard Times* with the Black Country nightmare of *The Old Curiosity Shop*, to see how far and in what direction Dickens has progressed. The factories of the early book are really internal, symbolic of Nell's nightmare experience; here they take place in the vaster objectified nightmare of society itself. Dickens has widened his symbolic powers to be able to construct a parable of the greatest social and moral relevance. For parallel with the Gradgrind story, and connected to it by the agency of Bounderby, is the story of Stephen Blackpool.

If the Gradgrind philosophy and Bounderby opportunism are alike evil, it might be thought that socialism and its doctrine of class brotherhood provided an answer, a means of arriving at "the best human flow" Lawrence spoke of. Lawrence himself in fact debated precisely this possibility in *Kangaroo*, and it is difficult to see how he could have arrived at his conclusion without Dickens's contribution to the question, seventy years earlier. Like Lawrence in *Kangaroo*, Dickens rejected the socialist solution, or at least the trade union alternative.

Again, we cannot help being struck by the penetrativeness of Dickens's treatment of the subject. Here, a century before films like *On the Waterfront* and *The Angry Silence,* is the unmasking of collective solidarity, the myth of the proletarian brotherhood. Brotherhood, Dickens argues, amounts in practice to the Slackbridges leading the sheep by the nose. When Slackbridge, the professional agitator and orator, persuades the Hands to send Stephen to Coventry, it is the triumph of the same philosophy as crushes Louisa Gradgrind and polluted the river: rationalist materialism, putting ends before means and ideas before people, forsaking emotions we know to be true for the theoretic considerations we have accepted as inevitable. These considerations, Dickens argues, do not bind the workers together, they bind them apart. It is true, as Dr. Leavis holds,[9] that Dickens did not seem to appreciate the necessity of trade union actions in the alleviation of workers' conditions. But he saw with the profound acumen of so much of his political insight, the evil of the trade union *mentality*. However great his understanding of the social organism, Dickens always in the end held to the persistent integrity of the individual as the only real mode of human and even of social salvation.

Blackpool himself is a further experiment in the direction of the fully achieved emblematicism of *A Tale of Two Cities*. In other words, he stands for a situation, a class, a predicament, without having to exist for us in quite the same way as Louisa or Sissy exist for us. We must avoid any temptation to condemn him as unreal, and recognize a perfectly valid literary mode. Dickens is doing something difficult and unprecedented here; he is creating a character real by the standards of Victorian realism, but capable of functioning as a symbolic, almost an abstract term in an argument: "A rather stooping man, with a knitted brow, a pondering expression of face, and a hard-looking head sufficiently capacious, on which his iron-grey hair lay long and thin, Old Stephen might have passed for a particularly intelligent man in his condition. Yet he was not." (Bk. 1, Ch. 10. pp. 63—64.) — "In his condition"; this is the phrase which alerts us to the symbolic, generalized function of this careful, detailed, realistic portrait. The point is reinforced by the summing up of Stephen as "a good power-loom weaver, and a man of perfect integrity" (p. 64). Brecht, it would appear, learned from Dickens the art of presenting a "good man" who is not idealized out of credibility, and who can therefore hold our interest without forsaking the ability to function in the development of a social thesis which would certainly be jeopardized by excessive individuation. The great limitation of much nineteenth century fiction was precisely its enormous strength in verisimilitudinous presentation of social man. Lacking any real rhetorical voice, it could achieve universality within the confines of its elaborately dramatized concreteness only by the adoption of the self-conscious authorial interjection.

With Stephen Blackpool, Dickens creates a type of "the good man", a man who can say "it's aw a muddle", without the statement's confining itself to a unique psychological complex. When Stephen and Bounderby confront each other in the mill owner's drawing-room, it is a meeting of two classes, capital and labour, we witness, not a clash of personalities, and Stephen's words express social alienation far more terribly than Slackbridge's rhetoric: " 'Let thousands upon thousands alone, aw leading the like lives and aw faw'en into the like muddle, and they will be as one, and yo will be as another, wi' a black unpassable world betwixt yo, just as long or short a time as sitch-like misery can last.' " (P. 151.) Alienation of man from himself by wrong-headed rationalism, and from his fellows by the absence of social sympathy, is the theme of *Hard Times*. Consistent with this theme, we can see how impossible it was for Dickens to endorse the kind of collective action which enhanced and heightened the alienation into overt class war. His way was to attack the conscience of the ruling class, not to encourage conflict. The alienation motif is beautifully consummated in Stephen's death: the accident by which he falls down a disused pit-shaft demonstrates the mastery Dickens had already achieved over the use of symbolic action. It is difficult to imagine a more effective means of dramatizing class-alienation. Stephen's death, or, rather, what he whispers while dying, is the agency of finally drawing together the separate threads of the story. When it is revealed that Gradgrind's son, Tom, not only committed the theft from Bounderby's bank for which Stephen himself was being hunted, but also deliberately implicated Stephen himself, Sissy Jupe, putting justice second, impulse first, in the appropriately anti-Gradgrindian way, spirits Tom away from retribution and secures sanctuary for him in Sleary's circus.

In *Hard Times,* to say it again, the Sleary horse-riding represents a quite conscious taking up of an option let fall in *Nicholas Nickleby* and *The Old Curiosity Shop.* The picaresque life, semi-outlawed, as free from organized authority as from puritan obsession with cleanliness, close to the soil, to manure, to dung — all this now assumes a distinct authority. Victorian man — overclothed, overblown with morality, and status-conscious — is stripped down to something approaching bare essentials: "Amazing creatures," Sissy now finds them, after so long a stay under Gradgrind's sterilized roof, "so white and pink of complexion, so scant of dress, and so demonstrative of leg." (P. 281.) From every point of view the *dénouement* Dickens contrives at Sleary's is a triumph of art, one of the finest episodes it seems to me in all fiction. Just as Sissy, after her sojourn among the hard-facters, is dazzled by the "amazing creatures", so, by an ironic inversion of roles, young Gradgrind is clothed as the clown he really is: "In a preposterous coat, like a beadle's, with cuffs and flaps exaggerated to an unspeakable extent; in an immense waistcoat, knee-breeches, buckled shoes, and a mad cocked hat; with nothing fitting him, and everything of coarse material, moth-eaten and full of holes; with seams in his black face, where fear and heat had started through the greasy composition daubed all over it." (P. 283.) This is the figure Gradgrind sees skulking in the back benches of the empty circus tent, afraid and ashamed to confront his father in his guilt and his absurdity. Aptly enough, the confrontation between Gradgrind's pretensions and the reality it has been revealed to be takes place in the sawdust ring of an empty circus tent. Dickens shows his genius in nothing so much as in his choice of location for this scene.

Thus, after a long and often wearisome sojourn among the Harthouses and Sparsits, the tale returns to Sleary and the circus, for a second look at the rich, grime-encrusted world that nurtured Sissy Jupe. The circus has of course provided background and symbol for a great deal of art, both before Dickens and since. Here, the great image of life as a fair or a circus receives an extra edge: there is something significant in the irruption of the motif in the closing years of the great commercial-industrial advance in the nineteenth century. Perhaps the work which best epitomizes the two aspects of this circus-*commedia dell' arte* cult is Djuna Barnes's *Nightwood,* which mates the life-giving pungency of *Hard Times* with the magic of *Le Grand Meaulnes.* Djuna Barnes, in fact, is quite explicit in her treatment. Her Dr. O'Connor's castigation of American puritanism dovetails with Lawrence's lines on the circus, and recalls the overpowering circus odour which pervades so many of the novel's early stages: " 'We wash away our sense of sin, and what does that bath secure us? Sin, shining bright and hard. In what does a Latin bathe? True dust.' "[10] The Latin way, as O'Connor describes it, resembles the earthiness Lawrence noted in the circus poem quoted above. It is in these circumstances that Gradgrind is forced to eat his own philosophy, first by Tom, who taunts him with his own worship of statistical laws — " 'So many people are employed in situations of trust; so many people

out of so many will be dishonest . . . How can I help laws?' "
(p. 284); then by Bitzer, who suddenly turns up to arrest
Tom quite candidly as a piece of self-help *à la* Gradgrind.

So, Gradgrind is caught out; and it remains for Sleary to
redeem the mess by practising *his* own lawless pragmatism.
With Tom safely out of the way, Sleary is at liberty to
propound his philosophy. But before he does so, he tells
Gradgrind of the death of Sissy's father, and in doing so
completes what must be one of the most moving fables in all
Dickens. We remember Signor Jupe as a man who had
" 'missed his tip at the banners, too, and was loose in the
ponging' "; who, in other words, was failing in his job of
equestrian acrobat. Jupe never appears in the book. We are
told that he had "cut", leaving Sissy on her own; as a result
of which action, Gradgrind (kindly, in fact) took the child
into his own home. It is difficult to imagine a stronger proof
of Dickens's supreme genius than the reflection that out of
this situation he can conjure a perfect little *novella,* no more
than two pages in the telling, those two pages separated by
two hundred others.

Sleary introduces the subject of Jupe by means of a
characteristic observation, " 'it ith athtonithing.' " he says,
" 'The way in whith a dog'll find you — the dithtanthe he'll
come!' " The rejoinder is predictably pedantic: " 'His scent,'
said Mr. Gradgrind, 'being so fine.' " (P. 291.) The punc-
tiliousness of the Benthamite pedagogue emerges once more
for the narrow ignorant thing it is. Just how much Gradgrind
has to learn about the more complex aspects of behaviour
Sleary now reveals by ignoring Gradgrind's facile rejoinder,
and narrating — with a wealth of wise compassion — the story
of Signor Jupe's dog:

> "We wath getting up our Children in the Wood one morning,
> when there cometh into our Ring, by the thtage door, a dog. He
> had travelled a long way, he wath in very bad condition, he wath
> lame, and pretty well blind. He went round to our children, one
> after another, as if he wath theeking for a child he knowed; and
> then he come to me, and throwd hithelf up behind, and thtood
> on hith two forelegth, weak ath he wath, and then he wagged hith
> tail and died. Thquire, that dog wath Merrylegth.'
> "Sissy's father's dog!" (Book 3, chapter 8, p. 292.)

We are ourselves jolted along with Gradgrind at this point, neither he nor we had bargained for emotional attachment at this level — and from a dog! " 'Tho, whether her father bathely detherted her; or whether he broke hith own heart alone, rather than pull her down along with him; never will be known, now, Thquire, till — no, not till we know how the dogth findth uth out!' " So, with three of four recollections and speculations about a man we never even see, Dickens can conjure a complete and moving life-history. We are in no position now to resist Sleary's marvellous moralizings: " 'there ith a love in the world, not all Thelf-interetht after all, but thomething very different ... it hath a way of ith own of calculating or not calculating, whith thomehow or another ith at leatht ath hard to give a name to, ath the wayth of the dogth ith!' " (Chapter 8, pp. 292–93.)

10 Little Dorrit

Little Dorrit, one of the most admired of Dickens's novels in modern times, begins with an ambitious piece of "atmospheric" writing that has become somewhat controversial. It is, one would have thought, impressive by any standard; Mr. Garis, however, chooses to use it as evidence for Dickens's theatricality. In fact, Dickens is doing something rather more interesting than scene painting here, something lost, I think, on Mr. Garis, who sees the Marseilles prison, the arid terrain, and the place of quarantine of the English travellers as a setting rather than an environment for the characters. The implication of this judgment is that they are more like characters before a theatre backdrop than in the artistically integrated world of a "serious" novel, and his reason for holding this view is that there is too much evidence of the Dickensian creative persona in the descriptive writing, so that the characters remain unaffected by or unresponsive to their environment: "The narrator alone remains conscious of the weather and offers occasional reminders to the reader. But the characters themselves are unaffected by these reminders, and when they have finished their encounters it is again the narrator alone who is conscious of the effects of that opening description . . . "[1] This raises a whole covey of questions: what is the law (and where is it stated? by whom?) regarding the relations of character to "setting" or "description" in fiction? *Should* the characters be affected by their environment? If so, how? Is it not possible for an artist to express a meaning by positing an indifference to surroundings in his characters? How, *enfin*, should a creative artist relate his characters to their environment? To which novelist ought we to turn for guidance? Mr. Garis's answer to this last question at least is George Eliot; and he cites as an example of "serious" art sufficient to reveal Dickens for the cheap but effective actor-manager he is that well-known passage from *Middlemarch* which recounts Dorothea's return to Lowick after the disillusionment of honeymoon. Her world-view is discoloured by her experiences, and the day of her return is appropriately "dull and dreary: the distant flat shrank in uniform whiteness and low-hanging uniformity of cloud. The very furniture in the room seemed to have shrunk since she saw it before . . . "[2] *This,* we are to understand, is how to do it; *this* is "descriptive" relevance: "We are interested only in the cold day", Mr. Garis observes, "in relation to the experiences of a created character in whose experiences we have become engaged. A concrete scene is evoked, as in Dickens's description, but every detail in it is relevant to Dorothea Casaubon."[3] What matters, in other words, is that "the perspective on the scene" is that of Dorothea, of the particular actor in the scene. It is interesting how Mr. Garis's argument relates to this opening section of *Little Dorrit.* For it would be the easiest thing in the world to cite literally hundreds of examples from Dickens in which this kind of personal colouring of a scene takes place, examples which in their brilliance, their poetry, and their ebullience, would reveal George Eliot's scene for the homely watercolour it is. More, it would be no less easy to show that it is precisely from Dickens that George Eliot learned this art. There are, in fact, two sorts of effects in the extract from *Middlemarch* I have quoted: one is the "appropriate" correspondence between the character's emotions and the weather (it was the "uniform whiteness and low-hanging uniformity of cloud"); the second is the character's sense of things having altered with her alterations ("the very furniture in the room *seemed* to have shrunk" — my italics). Now the first of these is what used to be called the pathetic fallacy: it is what we see in action in Keats's "La Belle Dame sans Merci", and in a thousand scenes of Scott, the Gothic novelists, and the Brontës. Scenes like this work in part at least because there are, as Rudolf Arnheim and other Gestalt psychologists have been suggesting for half a century, relations of isomorphy and congruence between human emotional states and objective structures in nature.[4] There is no point in trying to discredit Mr. Garis's account of this kind of artistic relevance. What is astounding is that he should adduce an instance of it as evidence against the novelist who is the greatest master of it in nineteenth century fiction. In a realistic art form such as the novel it is no less incumbent upon the novelist to make everything count than it is upon the dramatist or the epic poet. And since the property and furniture of his art largely consisted of actual streets, houses, chairs, and skies, it was as necessary as it was inevitable that in the true artist the realistic appurtenances should acquire symbolic status. We see this in action in the Ibsen drama, and we see it in the Dickens novel. Everything must indeed be relevant. This there is no disputing. What is disputable is both the extreme narrowness of Mr. Garis's criteria for establishing relevance and his blindness to the existence in Dickens of the sort of effect he praises in George Eliot and Henry James.

The narrowness of Mr. Garis's criterion leads him to misunderstand not only the passage in *Little Dorrit* he questions, but by implication a whole range of critically important scenes and descriptions throughout Dickens's *oeuvre.* For unless we accept Mr. Garis's strange stipulation that to be relevant in fiction description must be related to the immediate emotions of a character, as the dreariness of Lowick is to Dorothea Casaubon, we must see that in true art the descriptions are *part of the total art-work,* and the sum of all the effects makes up the whole. The storm in act 3 of *Lear,* the tempests in *Wuthering Heights,* the great shipwreck scene in *David Copperfield,* the magnificent sunset that accompanies the murder of Montague Tigg in *Martin Chuzzlewit,* the serenity of the summer night on which Michael Henchard sells his wife in *The Mayor of Casterbridge*

— are these scenes laid on for effect, for convenience, to whip up our interest? Of course not: they are themselves part of the emotion or the meaning that is conveyed; they are the work of art, taken in association with everything else around them. It would be a very rash critic who would presume to supply any single simple explanation of their workings. All one can say is that they are "scoring", instrumentation of idea and feeling, and that like all good effects of scoring or instrumentation they themselves also direct and modulate the progress of the work. Certainly, there are plenty of instances of the exploitation of such effects by inferior hands, who use them in an anti-structural way as pathetic leverage. In the same way, there are plenty of composers who make use of the current vocabulary of instrumentation and harmony merely to provide a frame for their melodic invention.[5]

"Relevance", in short, is not reducible to the simple psychological correlation Mr. Garis observes at work in the passage from *Middlemarch*: how miserable she was, and what a dreary day it was, and how dull everything seemed. Nor ought the characters necessarily to be "conscious" of the weather or the scene: it might, on the contrary, be the essence of the situation that they were not. Is La Gioconda *aware* of the awesome mountains and glaciers her creator has set at her back? No, but we are, along with Leonardo, and that is what matters. It is not always the character's response that matters, but ours, and our response is to the total field of vision, a field which includes the characters, the character's reactions, and the things around him of which he may not be and often cannot be aware. In the case of the opening of *Little Dorrit*, these considerations are of especial importance. For in those opening chapters the keynote of the whole book is given, surely and relentlessly in the oppressiveness of the heat: "Everything that lived or grew, was oppressed by the glare; except the lizard, passing swiftly over rough stone walls, and the cicala, chirping his hot dry chirp, like a rattle. The very dust was scorched brown, and something quivered in the atmosphere as if the air itself were panting." (Chapter 1, p. 2.) Already the vastness of the oppressive heat has prepared us for a canvas of the broadest scope. Dickens has made us feel, by the tense vibrancy and the relevant generality of the writing, that we are in the presence of matters that concern us deeply. This is a crude indication of the sort of relevance these opening chapters have for us, a relevance, one feels, that goes a long way beyond the operation of the pathetic fallacy at work in the little scene from *Middlemarch*.

The sense of accumulating significance conveyed in the tone and trenchancy of the descriptive writing of *Little Dorrit* — no novel I have ever read seems more deadly *serious* about things, serious in every line and paragraph — is not really satisfied by the narrative shoots that have been put out at this stage. We remain unengaged by Rigaud and Cavalletto in their jail and almost as unengaged by the quarantined English travellers in theirs. But the contrast between the oppressively expansive glare outside and the dank closeness of the prison cell has not been lost on us. We look out through the bars with Rigaud, and Dickens's panoramic descriptions of the white roads and a prostrated nature make sure that we experience already an obscure sense of absurdity in the complicated social machineries which have conspired to have these two men squat in a confined darkness under an illimitable sky. (It is Dickens's ability to make us experience the illimitability that makes the "descriptive" writing so much more than mere description.) Can it matter that these two men are not out on the roads, with the cicala and the lizards? The experienced Dickens reader, moreover, will already perhaps have caught, at some level of the verbal consciousness, a delicate assonantal likeness between the word Marseilles and the word that is to come so often later, Marshalsea. We know before picking up the book, probably, that this is to be *the* book about prisons in an *oeuvre* dominated by prisons: we begin in an unimportant provincial gaol in the *midi*, and now move across the harbour to another sort of prison, the prison of quarantine. Dickens's novel has already started to take shape.

All this has been by way of a prelude, a prelude on the

grandest scale and in the full musical sense. A prelude, properly used, does not merely touch on the themes and emotions we are to expect, it also gives the composer or dramatist the opportunity to anticipate the ultimate outcome, the end of it all, and to set what is to come in the longest perspective. If the two opening chapters make up a prelude, it is a prelude with two broad climaxes. At the end of the first chapter, Dickens anticipates a key-passage at the end of the whole novel:

> The wide stare stared itself out for one while; the sun went down in a red, green, golden glory; the stars came out in the heavens, and the fire-flies mimicked them in the lower air, as men may feebly imitate the goodness of a better order of beings; the long dusty roads and the interminable plains were in repose — and so deep a hush was on the sea, that it scarcely whispered of the time when it shall give up its dead. (Chapter 1, p. 14.)

The polarity of fire-fly and star here counterpoints the contrast between the grubby prisoners in their gaol and the vast expanses of the world outside. At the end of the second chapter, which concerns the sequestered travellers, Dickens again rises to a great height of contemplation to speak of "restless travellers through the pilgrimage of life" (p. 27). Perhaps the whole significance of *Little Dorrit* lies in its presentation of the human condition as being about equally composed of the restlessness of travel and the stasis of imprisonment. There is in fact almost as much travelling as imprisonment in the novel. The Meagles, Clennam, and Miss Wade seem to us in some way to be idling in the wings of life, as — in the second chapter — in the wings of the novel.

The full value of this expansive prelude is only fully apparent when chapter 3 lands us firmly and uncomfortably in a muddy London. London was always reality for Dickens, and the opening chapters have very much the air of taking place in an oddly pleasant illusory world: they are impregnated with a sense of returning. One now appreciates this curving run-in to have been a preparation for the filth and mire of the metropolis, a preparation which makes us experience the London miasma with a freshness which imparts a moral flavour to our distaste. This distaste — the distaste for a world in which "nothing is pleasant to the five senses" — now grows into the novel's first major theme, the brooding self-doubt of Arthur Clennam. On returning to the scenes of his childhood, re-experiencing the unutterable boredom of the English Sunday, in which he recognizes the deadness of his mother's religion, Clennam experiences an intolerable feeling of guilt: is it possible, he wonders, that his father has wronged someone in his arid commercial career, and that he, the son, inheriting the family business, inherits as well the responsibility and the guilt? The idea forces itself upon him irresistibly in the appalling gloom of his mother's bed-chamber. Everything about the house has the same haunted atmosphere; we are presented in fact with a symbol of Clennam's childhood and of the Oedipal guilt that obsesses him. Thus, the house is the House of the Clennams, as Chesney Wold was the House of the Dedlocks, and it too must fall. At the same time, of course, the house is clearly a societal emblem — a business House, and the doubt concerns the basis of commercial society as a whole. Clennam feels oppressed with a sense of his own complicity in this darkness and confusion. He is a kind of middle-aged Hamlet, a David Copperfield with a conscience.

It seems to me supremely significant that Dickens should have produced such a hero, with such preoccupations, at this stage of his career. Once again we are aware of the central function of the mythic hero. The Dickens myth, I have argued all along, is the representative myth for bourgeois man — for Western man, that is, at this particular stage of his technological, economic and social development, the stage reached in the capitalist, industrial era. Man in this situation suffers from unique and novel discomforts — from uncertainties as to purpose, identity, and status. But he suffers also from a new sense of guilt and responsibility, and it is modern man's attempts to establish the limits and extent of his own responsibilities that is Dickens's main subject.

No single character demonstrates this thesis more conclusively than Arthur Clennam. In him Dickens has raised, more disturbingly than any of his fellow novelists, the question of bourgeois man's self-division and his exploitation of his fellow men. That is to put it as a German neo-Marxist might like it put. In terms of Dickens's *oeuvre,* it means that the implicit assumptions within the mythic structuring of the earlier books — the hero's worthiness of the reward, the unearned golden fruit, the confidence in the retired godfather-capitalist, and the belief that somewhere there are enough material goods to sustain him in the secure well-being he assumes to be his birth-right — are now raised to the surface and subjected to questioning. We have seen this process taking place before — in the satire on the expectations in Mr. Micawber, in the new spiritual findings of *Bleak House.* Now we see Arthur Clennam inheriting the expectations so blithely looked to by Oliver Twist and Martin Chuzzlewit, and suddenly feeling uncomfortable in their possession. Clennam returns reluctantly to England, as though dragged back by some force.

Now much if not all of the force may be attributed directly to his (supposed) mother. Mrs. Clennam is a character conceived and presented with enormous power, and we have in her the first of a series of fierce female figures troublingly dominant in the later Dickens. Now that Erich Neumann[6] has popularized Jung's psycho-mythology, it is safe to assume a passing familiarity with the figure Jung called *die schreckliche Mutter.* It is extremely dangerous to allot to literary criticism the task merely of spotting archetypal figures as they occur in literature: that is rather the task of psychoanalysis or anthropology. In the first place, this kind of pattern-picking can easily take the place of the act of criticism itself — as though merely to establish the appearance of these archetypes were to have done the work that counts rather than to have begun it. In the second place, of course, the very generality and universality of such figures makes it likely that they will occur randomly in the second-rate as well as in the first-rate writer, and in the ramblings of psychosis as commonly as in either. In the third place, it is dangerous quite simply because of the dangers of feed-back; writers and critics primed with Neumann and Jung, as once with Freud and Frazer, will attempt to give classic status to writing which has perhaps no further claim to it than the presence of archetypes — archetypes which do, undeniably, have a terrific impact in so many great classic works. As we become conscious of the workings of the mind, and of the kind of function carried out by its symbols, so these symbols lose their utility for the creative artist.

Dickens's later work must, nevertheless, be described at least in part in terms of the dynamic power, at the same time attractive and repulsive, of Jung's *schreckliche Mutter,* and so long as we keep this description structural rather than specifically psychoanalytic — so long, that is, as we concern ourselves with certain structural relations without which the work cannot fully be understood, rather than with speculations on the character of Dickens himself — there is no need for us to fear substituting an irrelevant medical interest for the proper interest of literary criticism. Mrs. Clennam is the first appearance of the Terrible Mother in Dickens, and she is by any standard a formidable and fearsome personage. She is moreover profoundly concerned in Arthur's doubts and misgivings. Her influence over him is malign and it is she he must interrogate to get at the cause of his self-doubt: she in some way holds the secret of his guilt. The relationship is crystallized in a terrifying scene in the fifth chapter of the novel when Arthur reveals to her that he suspects his father's life of "grasping at money and driving hard bargains" to have involved himself and his family in some shame and guilt which must be expiated. Mrs. Clennam's reaction to the suggestion is Kafka-esque in its intensity:

> There was a bell-rope hanging on the panelled wall, some two or three yards from the cabinet. By a swift and sudden action of her foot, she drove her wheeled chair rapidly back to it and pulled it violently — still holding her arm up in its shield-like posture, as if he were striking her, and she warding off the blow. (Chapter 5, p. 49.)

This expression of the emotion in direct physical terms strongly recalls the most intense moments of Kafka's stories — the father's vindictive rejection of his beetle-son in *The Metamorphosis,* for instance: "His father knotted his fist

with a fierce expression on his face as if he meant to knock
Gregor back into the living-room"[7]. Mrs. Clennam's raised
arm and Herr Samsa's knotted fist almost ceremonially enact
the terrible parent's malediction of the child.

Yet neither the real implications of the *schreckliche
Mutter* nor of Arthur's brooding doubts, I believe — central
as both themes are to Dickens's *oeuvre* — are fully explored
in *Little Dorrit*. Paradoxically, the novel seriously falters with
the introduction of its eponymous heroine, Amy Dorrit;
paradoxically, because Little Dorrit is the great success in the
novel. She is never successfully integrated into the Clennam
household where she is retained to do needlework as a salve
to Mrs. Clennam's conscience. Later it is to be revealed that
the Dorrits were swindled by the Clennams, so that there is a
kind of ironic justice in Arthur's degradation to the Marshalsea and his eventual marriage to Amy. But in spite of this
conscientious grafting, Dickens does not, in my view,
persuade the two strands of the book satisfactorily to cohere.
The story begins to move in two worlds — the dark sin-ridden
world of the Clennams, and the oddly light world of the
Marshalsea. There is indeed evidence of a radical indecision,
an uncertainty about the true nature of the novel's fundamental concern. It seems to me that Dickens for once falls
foul of his economic bondage: a free writer would not, I
fancy, have embarked upon a long novel when he had the
materials for several shorter ones to hand. For there are at
least two novels here: the story of Arthur Clennam's dread
and guilt, and the story of the Dorrit family.

The Clennam theme is rendered with power and vividness,
but there are profound uncertainties in the later handling.
Affery's "dreams", for instance, have a Dostoievskian intensity, and always seem to be about to lead to something of
absorbing interest. What is it she sees and in her fear
persuades herself she dreams? What foul secret *does* the
house possess? Affery's torments take on a fearful graphic-
ness that is of a piece with the metaphysical atmosphere of
the whole household: inner and outer are totally confused,
and we along with Affery are unsure about where guilt and

nightmare end and horrible reality begins. Flintwinch ("the hanged man") and his mistress are bound together by something more radical than economic interest and service. Money and neurosis are inextricably entangled in them both. But all this, promising as it is, leads to anti-climax. Dickens has created a metaphysical horror which belongs to the vague haunted atmosphere of Poe and Dostoievsky, and this kind of atmospheric dread cannot be resolved in terms of rational motivation. Sensing this, Dickens contrives a foul enough secret, an actual incarceration. But the contriving of a twin brother for Flintwinch borders on the absurd, and even in retrospect drains some of the spiritual dread from Affery's dreams. Both as regards the Dorrits (quite superfluously dragged in here) and Arthur's own guilt, the inextricably involved business of Arthur's father's mistress's brother's son, and so on, is quite ineffectual. It is, I submit, impossible to follow the chapters dealing with the unravelling of the Clennam-Dorrit-Flintwinch-Rigaud intrigue with any sort of comprehension, unless one makes an effort of the will so great as to drown the intrinsic interest of the events in tedium. *Bleak House,* we note, with more structural complexity, has less narrative complication than *Little Dorrit.*

Dickens failed to consummate the Clennam theme partly, I think, because he had to work it in with the Dorrit material — this at least seems largely true of the technical aspect. It is not a question of too much plot or the invidiousness of concealed wills: the will discovered and sold in *Bleak House* functions effectively as a focus for the general obsessive mania which dominates the entire novel. Here, the impropriety is that of the yoking together of irreconcilable themes. Arthur's dread of his horrible mother is never satisfactorily resolved and never occupies the central place in the narrative, though it often usurps it at the expense of other interest. (The theme is better handled in *Great Expectations.*) Mrs. Clennam's role remains ambiguous; it is as if Dickens actually changed his mind about what the real subject of his novel was to be. Initially it seems to be about Clennam's guilt. The opening chapters deepen towards a promising tragic theme. Clennam's lacklustre joylessness begins to seem like the consequence of a deep insistent class-guilt, draining the energy as terribly as the legal obsessions of *Bleak House*. Mrs. Clennam's fierce ugliness and the *angst*-ridden gloom of the household suggest that this is so.

But at just the point when some development seems about to take place, Dickens drops the theme entirely, and follows another story. Clennam deserts a stage he never promised to occupy very interestingly anyway, and the Dorrits take over. The lameness that features often in the subsequent eight hundred pages is evident first of all at the close of the fifth chapter when Dickens first tries to graft the Dorrit onto the Clennam story and unite the two major themes of the book: "Influenced by his predominant idea, he even fell into a habit of discussing with himself the possibility of her being in some way associated with it. At last, he resolved to watch Little Dorrit and know more of her story." (Chapter 5, pp. 55—56.) This is bare-faced narrative engineering and is, anyway, far too hesitant and indecisive to maintain the reader's interest. (With how much more facination do we follow the old man at the beginning of *The Old Curiosity Shop*, and enter with him into Little Nell's story.) It is moreover quite shamelessly disingenuous: Clennam's guess would be a shrewd insight or a strange foreknowing in life; in a novel it is an artful attempt to appear to raise the possibility of what the writer knows perfectly well is to come.

As the novel proceeds, it becomes plain that Dickens cannot at this stage sustain the theme of Clennam's guilt; but he is artist enough to know it, and he allows a theme that does absorb his interest to take over the burden of the tale. The next time Clennam's doubts and guilts are referred to is some three hundred pages later, when it is no less hesitant and indecisive: "A frequently recurring doubt, whether Mr. Pancks's desire to collect information relative to the Dorrit family could have any possible bearing on the misgivings he had imparted to his mother on his return from his long exile, caused Arthur Clennam much uneasiness at this period." (Chapter 27, p. 319.) This is an artificial attempt to justify or revive the theme initiated in the opening chapters. Now the most convincing evidence for the argument that *Little Dorrit* is an artistic failure — evidence much needed in the face of what Dr. Leavis[8] and others have said about the book — is the intermittent and uncertain handling of this theme. As much is suggested by the wholly satisfactory treatment of the theme (or something very close to it) in *Great Expectations* and *Our Mutual Friend.* (John Rokesmith of the latter novel — the closest parallel to Clennam — is surely already conceived when Clennam passes the FOUND DROWNED notice on his way to his mother's house in chapter 3.) Dickens has, I think, quite simply come at the theme too baldly, snatching at it before the emotion had worked itself into satisfactory form. As the returning hero of Dickens's basic myth (David Copperfield with a conscience), Clennam represents, I have argued, a significant development of the myth's inward transformation. It is not only, Do I deserve this inheritance? that he asks himself so persistently, but more, Am I in some way put in the wrong by it? But Clennam's character is unable to sustain the theme adequately. The honest, pondering, groping inability to commit himself to any course of action on his own behalf (he intercedes for John Chivery to Little Dorrit, and cannot even let himself fall in love with Minnie Meagles), his foolish gambling of his partner's money, the styling himself Nobody — all this makes him too inert, too passive a character to perform the function Dickens seems to have meant him to perform. He is a significant and real character (as witness his inability to be generous about his rival Gowan and his flashes of anger with John Chivery), but not one through whom Dickens could carry out the exploration he needed to at this stage.

Now this inadequacy of Clennam is interestingly related to the *schreckliche Mutter* theme — or rather to Dickens's failure to consummate this theme. Clennam is unable to stand up to the wrath of his mother: he is transfixed by the Gorgon's stare (an emblem that recurs several times in the book). In this he resembles Pip, Sydney Carton, and John Jasper from later novels. At this stage the mythic hero is

robbed of his masculinity by the *schreckliche Mutter*. In the
end, she turns out not to have been his mother at all — a
revelation of some significance: Clennam is the natural child
of an actress and a guilt-stricken puritan. But this child of
nature has none of Edmund's zest and sensuality: he remains
listlessly oppressed, and he can do nothing that is not self-
deflating and ultimately self-destructive. Clennam in fact
loses no chance to do himself down: he not only insists on
going to prison instead of letting the solicitor Rugg salvage
something from the wreckage after the crash, he must
proclaim his guilt in public, thus making himself a scapegoat.
Finally he persists in his "taste" for the Marshalsea instead of
the more comfortable Kings Bench. This is not just honesty,
if it is honesty at all (he shows no regret for his creditors). It
is simple self-destructiveness. Clennam betrays from first to
last a need to abase and humiliate himself.

This drive towards self-abnegation is manifest, too, in his
relations with several other fierce female figures who are
interestingly prominent in the novel, Miss Wade, Mr. F.'s
aunt, and Mrs. General. No man in the book gets the better
of Miss Wade, the embittered lesbian who gains possession of
Tattycoram. But there is a marked difference between Mr.
Meagles's clumsily well-meaning attempt to get from her the
box thought to have been left with her by Rigaud, and
Clennam's request for information about Rigaud. Meagles
blunders from first to last, making things worse with each
ham-fisted effort to get on the right side of the lady; but he
leaves without loss of face or self-respect. Clennam on the
other hand is totally humiliated. Once Miss Wade has found
out his vulnerability to imputations against his family, it is a
simple matter for her to manipulate and incapacitate him:
"Wrung by her persistence in keeping that dark side of the
case before him, of which there was a half-hidden shadow in
his own breast, Clennam was silent." (Chapter 20, p. 658.)
Mr. F's aunt, on the other hand, is really a comic parody of
Mrs. Clennam: she attacks Arthur violently whenever they
meet in the most outrageous terms ("It is the voice of one of
the Parcae", as Lionel Trilling observes).[9] Ostensibly her

animosity is based upon Arthur's having been Mr. F's rival for Flora. But she becomes, as the novel progresses, another stony accusation, an indictment of his inadequacy; once she is described as "a malignant Chinese enchantress", and once as having a reticule so stony that it might have been "petrified by the Gorgon's head and had got it at that moment inside." This is a significantly casual reference. What Mr. F.'s aunt has in common with Miss Wade and Mrs. Clennam is the stony rigidity: the flow of life has been damned up within them. With Mrs. Clennam, of course, this process is presented explicitly as the psychosomatic paralysis which so brilliantly anticipates the findings of psychoanalysis.[10] We are close to a major psychological complex here. Edith Dombey, Rosa Dartle, Miss Wade, Mrs. Clennam, and Mr. F.'s aunt are different characters with different histories; but they share a common emotional frigidity, a blockage of impulse and a frustration of natural desire that either arrests their affective life altogether in a violent and unstable stasis, or perverts it into "unnatural" sexuality. This, I have suggested above, is one of the great secrets of *Dombey and Son*. In *Little Dorrit* the theme is best illustrated in Miss Wade's "History of a Self-Tormentor" (chapter 21 of Book the Second). This document plausibly presents a case-history of a particular kind of emotional inversion, "unnatural" indeed in its paranoid obsessiveness. A large enough number of modern psychiatrists would be found to support Dickens's general drift.

Even more interesting in this light is Flora Finching's description of herself as "the statue bride": "when rent asunder we turned to stone in which capacity Arthur went to China, and I became the statue bride of the late Mr. F." (Chapter 24, pp. 284–85.) Flora's panted monologues are full of brilliant phrases and rich surreal transitions, many of them — such as her description of her father, Christopher Casby, as "smoothly blundering" — pure Boz. But although this fertility is comic, and Flora is fundamentally an absurd creation, she is also responsible for some of the novel's most touching moments. The frustrated spinster-window is a stock figure of fun in the early Dickens, but there is nothing comical in Flora Finching's generous and impulsive response to Little Dorrit: "Flora taking [Amy's bonnet] off in the best-natured manner in the world, was so struck with the face disclosed that she said, 'Why, what a good little thing you are, my dear!' and pressed the face between her hands like the gentlest of women." (Chapter 24, p. 281.) This coming together of characters is the essence of good fiction, and it is in contrast with such moments that the Rigaud-Blandois-Flintwinch material, for instance, is revealed for the *Grand Guignol* it really is. The planting of Flora in the Casby household was almost as crafty a move on Dickens's part as the planting of Esther Summerson among the Jarndyces. Her casually irreverent attitude towards her father the Patriarch strips him of his spurious grandeur before Pancks gets to work with the shears. But more importantly than this, she shows quite simply how *not* to turn to stone: her description of herself as the statue bride is taken seriously by us — and the whole narration of her wedding with Mr. F. (with the break with Arthur and the wedding procession in "the glass-house" coach) is a fine example of Dickens's genius for the inserted narrative. She *was* the statue bride; there *was* a heart-break; she and Arthur suffered more perhaps than either could later have said. Moreover, Arthur, we remember, went off to China in the capacity of having been turned to stone: we have every reason to believe that he has come back in the same shape. Yet here is Flora, fat and forty, and full of good-humoured life. It is a deceptively simple piece of writing. The right placing of Miss Wade and Mrs. Clennam is effected more trenchantly through the presentation of Flora than through the awe-struck eyes of Arthur. For Flora strips the awful dignity from Mrs. Clennam as irreverently as she places her father: " 'Really?' she comments innocently, when Little Dorrit tells her of Mrs. Clennam's kindness to herself, " 'I am sure I am glad to hear it because as Arthur's mother it's naturally pleasant to my feelings to have a better opinion of her than I had before, though what she thinks of me when I run on as I am certain to do and she sits glowering at me like Fate in a go-cart — shocking comparison really — invalid and not her fault — I never know or can imagine.' " (Chapter 24, p. 284.)

We no longer take Mrs. Clennam quite so solemnly after we have seen her through Flora's eyes as "Fate in a go-cart". Rich in Beckettian elisions and Dadaesque irreverences, Flora's crazy monologues have a serious function in the book: certainly they are the only true comedy on show. The Plornishes are droll, and Casby's inane profundities funny enough. But only Flora's linguistic behaviour has the rich explosive density of the best of Dickens's comic writing — relating diverse areas of the story, melting one attitude or tone into another, disturbing solemn *parti pris,* yet coming up smiling all the time; flourishing absurdities that flash from time to time with stunning common sense, they recall the most inspired moments of Mrs. Gamp.

Paradoxically, although Clennam is embarrassed by her, Flora's vitality and sweetness seem more closely associated with life. By comparison with her breezy silliness, Clennam's fixation on his own abjectness is tedious. He remains entranced by the Gorgon's stare. It drew him back to the England in which "nothing was pleasant to the five senses". Within the Clennam house there is something which will not let him breathe freely, and the formal structure of the book in part rests upon his efforts to locate and exorcise the malign influence. Hence his lame enquiries after the Dorrit family. But of course there was something more troubling than the guilt incurred in the swindling of the Dorrit brothers — something in the house, some dark mystery, that hangs over his mother as over himself:

> The purpose he had brought home to his native country, and had ever since kept in view, was, with her greatest determination, defeated by his mother herself, at the time of all others when he feared that it pressed most. His advice, energy, activity, money, credit, all his resources whatsoever were all made useless. If she had been possessed by the old fabled influence, and had turned those who looked upon her into stone, she could not have rendered him more completely powerless (so it seemed to him in his distress of mind) than she did, when she turned her unyielding face to his, in her gloomy room. (Chapter 23, pp. 679—80.)

This is an important passage. It shows yet again the persistence of the Gorgon motif in the later Dickens; but it also shows more overtly than any other passage in the book, perhaps, the precise nature of the old woman's incapacitating influence over him. She annuls his masculinity, and he would have her gone. This physical complex is real and powerful in the novel. My argument with *Little Dorrit* is only that Dickens had not at this stage found the right imagery and narrative pattern to express it satisfactorily. For we note that there has been no advance or change from the fearful scene of Mrs. Clennam's malediction in chapter 5 to her "fabled influence" in chapter 23 — nearly six hundred pages later. There has been no development in this most important situation, and the novel's turgid progress reflects the fact.

Nor is there any satisfactory resolution. Mrs. Clennam is exorcised and Arthur is, at roughly the same stage of the story, released from bondage into a modestly useful life. More, the Clennam house itself literally crashes to the ground. Yet there is curiously little interaction between the two themes — none of the deeply satisfying formal resolution of *Great Expectations* or *A Tale of Two Cities*. Dickens fails to make Mrs. Clennam's transformation through confession important in the history of her son. The narrative at this stage indeed — obsessed and clogged as it is with Rigaud and Flintwinch — has little of the pressing onward movement that is characteristic of Dickens's greatest final movements. On the contrary, he almost wilfully contrives to obfuscate the situation by having Mrs. Clennam merely speak to Amy without a word to Arthur (who is thought too ill to see her). This merely confuses the issue, and the reader's efforts to follow what is going on preclude any deep involvement in the events.

This is true in spite of Dickens's exploitation of the strategic illness. Clennam falls sick with a "low, slow fever". The handling of his imprisonment has throughout been exemplary. The stages of his decline and demoralization under the shadow of the bars are documented with the precise yet compassionate detail that is so remarkable in all

Dickens's treatment of prison experiences. It is extraordinary to think that his own brief prison experience lay forty years behind him when he wrote these desolately atmospheric lines: "He had heard the gates open; and the badly shod feet that waited outside shuffle in; and the sweeping, and pumping, and moving about, begin, which commenced the prison morning." (Chapter 29, p. 755.) We are forced to experience Clennam's fever, too, as suffocatingly as Dickens always compels us to endure his heroes' illnesses. The sequence of weathers is especially remarkable. One would be hard put to account for the peculiar sense of "significance" in the succession of rain and sun and heat that makes up the course of Clennam's obscurely remembered fever; why it seems so "right" simply that he should be aware of a "hot misty Day" as the sixth of his prostration and that the sun should rise: "A blurred circle of yellow haze had risen up in the sky in lieu of the sun, and he had watched the patch it put upon his wall, like a bit of the prison's raggedness." (Shades of Mr. Garis's carping about Dickens's descriptions: is *this* a mere setting for a character, or is it part of a whole imaginative experience, in which we participate with the suffering character?) Eventually he wakes up to find around him "some abiding impression of a garden" — a "garden of flowers with a damp warm wind gently stirring their scents" — and, inevitably, Little Dorrit at his bedside.

The whole episode is so masterfully handled that I hesitate to suggest what I think I must — that the part it plays in the whole fable is of less significance than it ought to be; that it *does* less in the resolution of the narrative than, for instance, Esther's voyage across her "dark lake" does in *Bleak House,* or John Harmon's near-drowning in *Our Mutual Friend.* Yet I think the point should be made, if only to indicate the nature of the novel's peculiar strengths. For after the fever, and the final neutralization of Mrs. Clennam's influence (she of course loses her *mana* with her unpleasantness), Clennam owns himself under the power of a much greater feminine principle, Nature herself:

> Yet Clennam, listening to the voice as it read to him, heard in it all that great Nature was doing, heard in it all the soothing songs she sings to man. At no Mother's knees but hers, had he ever dwelt in his youth on hopeful promises, on playful fancies, on the harvests of tenderness and humility that lie hidden in the early-fostered seeds of the imagination; on the oaks of retreat from blighting winds, that have the germs of their strong roots in nursery acorns. (Chapter 34, p. 815.)

This is an explicit setting at nought of the "old fabled influence", and the identification of Amy with a greater maternal power in Nature, the goddess of the old religions, helps bring the fable to its sonorous close. The Marshalsea, we observe in these pages, has taken on some of the baleful feminine personality of Mrs. Clennam, like the prisons of *A Tale of Two Cities*: "Changeless, and barren, looking ignorantly at all the seasons with its fixed, pinched face of poverty and care, the prison had no touch of any of these beauties. Blossom what would, its bricks and bars bore uniformly the same dead crop." (Chapter 34, p. 815.) Like Mrs. Clennam, the gaol is sterile and fixed. The beauties referred to in the last passage, incidentally, are those of an autumn evoked, in the opening paragraph of this the last chapter of the whole novel, with the utmost richness. Although the year is dying, there is a great sense of resurgence in Nature here —

> the ocean was no longer to be seen lying asleep in the heat, but its thousand sparkling eyes were open, and its whole breadth was in joyful animation, from the cool sand on the beach to the little sails on the horizon, drifting away like autumn-tinted leaves that had drifted from the trees.

One thinks of the spring awakening of *The Old Curiosity Shop*. This is the autumn of Dickens's life, and his final cadence is bitterly serene:

> They went quietly down into the roaring streets, inseparable and blessed; and as they passed along in sunshine and shade, the noisy and the eager, and the arrogant and the forward and the vain, fretted, and chafed, and made their usual uproar.

Amy is not sacrificed as Nell was, but the strength of the novel's close owes more to her than to Clennam.

Now Amy must be the real force of the book: structurally, we have no choice but to accept this conclusion. As with Esther Summerson, the twentieth century reader has to contend with a certain amount of prejudice in his own mind. Once again, I believe, Dickens succeeds in the rare and difficult feat of interesting the reader in a character who must for her own consistency be all but devoid of the usual blemishes. It is remarkable — and significantly so — that after the initial brief references to her "pale transparent face, quick in expression, though not beautiful in feature, its soft hazel eyes excepted", Dickens never attempts to describe her. He often refers to her childlike size, but there are no further physical details used in the characterization. Instead he shows us every hesitation, blush, and sigh, so that the inward life is felt. This is in sharp contrast, for instance, to the characterization of Pancks, who is throughout insistently described in terms of tug-boat imagery, of his snuffling and grunting, and of his "coaly" nails and sharp black eyes, and, above all, of the hair he is always (somehow) causing to stand up like the bars on the prison wall. There is uncertainty in Dickens here. Pancks never becomes a real character, as is evident in the "bending" Dickens subjects him to: he has to be benevolent within the unpromising exterior. The sureness with which Amy is felt, on the other hand, is evident in precisely the absence of identifying mannerisms. There is nothing to her but her diffidence, her sweetness and her honesty, yet she never becomes boring or unconvincing.

The novel within the novel — the story of the Dorrits — is very nearly a perfect work. F. R. Leavis has remarked that *Little Dorrit* seems to him the most "highly organized" of the Dickens novels.[11] For myself I can see no good reason — appalling precedent apart — why the story of the Dorrits should not be excerpted and printed separately. From the two brilliantly condensed chapters (chapters 6 and 7 of *Book the First*) recounting their sequestration and early life in the Marshalsea, through the arrival of the fortune, to the final breakdown at the social dinner-party in Rome, the whole narrative is above praise, consistently intelligent, sympathetic and yet dispassionate. Now of course it is centrally related to the Dickens *oeuvre* as a whole. Here is the Dickens family (one parent dead, the other feckless), fallen on hard times and imprisoned for debt; along comes the golden fruit that was the birth-right of the early heroes and heroines, and, lo, instead of endless happiness and a vista of jolly Christmasses stretching into the future, nothing but nervous anxiety, uncertainty, petty snobbishness, shame, and ultimate disgrace. The Dorrit story is thus a profound satire on Dickens's basic myth, the myth of the expectations. The book shows parallels with an earlier novel I have already referred to more than once, *The Old Curiosity Shop*. William Dorrit has the fluttery nervous gentility of Grandfather Trent, and Little Dorrit clearly repeats Little Nell (with a good deal more realism). In both cases the girl is worn out by the man, and is devoted to him. (The pattern is to be repeated again in *A Tale of Two Cities,* where Dr. Manette — attended by Lucie — once again reincarnates John Dickens.) The parallel is underlined by the figure of Pancks, who seems like a straightened-out Quilp. He is saturnine and swarthy like the dwarf, and even develops an apparently voyeuristic interest in Little Dorrit: "As she glanced down into the yard, she saw Pancks come in, and leer up with the corners of his eye as he went by." (Chapter 24, p. 295.) Unfortunately Quilp's magnetic roguishness is replaced by a rather unreal benevolence, and this aspect of the story has no conviction behind it. This is particularly true of the detective work Pancks carries out on behalf of the Dorrits. The vagueness of his enquiries is experienced with some discomfort: we feel confident in neither the how nor the why of his efforts, and Dickens could surely have released the Dorrits from debt without all this mysterious coming and going. Pancks's unmotivated and implausible interest in the Dorrit fortunes smacks of a half-hearted return to the narrative methods of the early novels.

Such imperfections — there are yet others in the book — have no influence, fortunately, on the progress of the Dorrit story itself. The real irony of the tale I suppose is that the

Dorrits do not change at all after receiving the legacy. They simply have more money to indulge their vices of character. Tip and Fanny bloom as scapegrace and social climber respectively, but they only amplify the ways they had acquired — ironically enough through Amy's efforts — in the Marshalsea. (I should observe in passing, by the way, that Fanny Dorrit is another of the book's real successes: Dickens never surpassed the wit and point of this satire on the social *arriviste* living only to outdo her great rival, Mrs. Merdle.) The irony of Mr. Dorrit's situation is that he should have acquired his lordly manner in the prison at all. He makes it a whole world, in which his social advantages stand him in good stead, a world suited to his own weakness and dishonesty. This is illustrated in numerous small incidents — in the pretence of being surprised at receiving the gifts and tributes he in fact confidently expects from departing collegians, in the patronizing attitude he adopts towards his brother Frederick's so-called debility, in the assumption of ignorance towards the fact that Tip, Fanny, and Amy go out every day and work to support him. But these more obvious forms of self-deception fade into others less easily detectable, and eventually form part of a whole attitude towards life, a stance, a *modus vivendi,* which is itself quite simply inauthentic. At this point we can no longer say that Dorrit is deceiving himself, or even that he is choosing to deceive himself, although he is doing both things. In accepting the conditions of prison life and even making them desirable instead of continuing to protest in outrage, as Gridley did in *Bleak House,* he has become a completely inauthentic man. This began as a process of adaptation: he comes to find prison life agreeable, and it could be said that this prevented him from going mad or simply declining.[12] This is to some extent true, and part of the value of Dickens's presentation of the case is its general applicability. Evolution, in a sense, demands of us some such ability to adapt to our environment as Dorrit adapts to life in the Marshalsea. But it is at a terrible price, and we can use Dickens's treatment of Dorrit as a psychological model for human behaviour in general. Life offers many opportunities for such "adaptation": should we accept what we cannot resist, or assert our humanity by destroying ourselves in the name of a superior state?[13] One of the facts about the Gordon riots which had most struck Dickens when he was researching *Barnaby Rudge* was that after the destruction of Newgate some of the freed prisoners returned to the ruins of the prison as if drawn by some "indescribable fascination", and "seemed to have no object in view but to prowl and lounge about the old place: being often found asleep in the ruins, or sitting talking there, or even eating and drinking, as in a choice retreat." (*Barnaby Rudge*, p. 629.) Newgate, in other words, was their home, and they were frightened of liberty. This is an insight into prison mentality which Dickens was to adapt, universalize and deepen until the end of his life. When William Dorrit is told about the legacy, his violent physical reaction informs us of the huge lie his adaptation to the Marshalsea has been: "He yielded himself to her kisses and caresses, but did not return them, except that he put an arm about her. Neither did he say one word. His steadfast look was now divided between her and Clennam, and he began to shake as if he were very cold." (Chapter 35, p. 419.) He behaves then with the disturbing nervousness — a "feverish flutter" — which has characterized his behaviour from time to time hitherto, when he becomes aware of himself as he is. Significantly, it is now that he utters his only words of commiseration for the other prisoners — " 'Poor creatures!' in a tone of much pity for their miserable condition." (Chapter 35, p. 421.) We understand that he has known all the time not only how wretched his condition has been, but what sacrifices his children have had to make for him. And this is why Amy is as much a source of discomfort as a solace to him: her honesty again and again forces him to see the truth, and blocks the easy deceptions he likes to practise upon himself and upon others.

Such a man, it is obvious, will be subjected to tremendous strains in liberty. As a matter of fact, Dickens crystallizes the new position of the Dorrits by means of a brilliant stroke of narrative. At the end of the first part of the novel

("Poverty"), the Dorrits are shown taking their final triumphal leave of the Marshalsea. The second — "Riches" — starts halfway up the Alps. No proper names are used in this first chapter, and a complex social conjunction of English and French travellers is set forth with no blur or confusion. We recognize the Dorrits soon enough, and then the Gowans, yet not too easily to prevent our coming to know them again in their new state: Dickens makes us appraise them afresh in their new affluent personae. Even when we are sure to have recognized them, Dickens withholds their names: we have not been re-introduced, and so keep our distance. There are many sorts of symbolic device available to the realist novelist, but none more centrally relevant to his art then the exploitation of setting and action at which Dickens so often excels. Gradually it dawns upon us, as we read the opening chapter of the second part of *Little Dorrit* and absorb Dickens's marvellously crisp, precise descriptive writing, that the Dorrits are stranded halfway up the social as these travellers are up the geographical Alps. The scenery is dizzy, the water crystal clear, the air hard to breathe, everything is new, cold, rare. So it is with the Dorrits in their new social world.

Mr. Dorrit cannot grow. The only change he shows after the legacy has arrived is that the self-pity he displays so often in the prison now turns into touchiness. The shadow of the prison lies on him all the time; he is never free of the fear that someone *knows* about the Marshalsea days. Dickens therefore portrays in him the peculiarly acute discomfort of modern bourgeois man. The snob syndrome, I have already noted, is a crucially important element of Dickens's work. It is in one sense the fundamental situation of Dickensian man to be a snob, to be trapped in the anxieties and uncertainties of the snob consciousness. None of us is quite free of snobbishness except those who have no higher to rise in society, and those who have no lower to fall. William Dorrit therefore has an important significance for us: few characters in fiction have so precarious an existence as his becomes in "freedom", or communicate so profound a sense of uncertainty and anxiety. This nervous fear has corrupted all his social relations and insinuated itself into his innermost emotions. When Amy's girldhood admirer, John Chivery the son of the Marshalsea turnkey, visits Dorrit's London hotel to pay his respects in the old Marshalsea way (with a bunch of his father's cigars), it is apparent that Dorrit can see in the visit only a threat to his security (the boy must mean to expose him), and an insult to his gentility. Even when he has repented of his mistake, and apologized to Chivery, he must beg him not to mention anything of their former connexion to those dreaded characters, the flunkeys:

> 'Oh! I assure you, sir,' returned John Chivery, 'in my poor humble way, sir, I'm too proud and honourable to do it, sir.'
> Mr. Dorrit was not too proud and honourable to listen at the door, that he might ascertain for himself whether John really went straight out, or lingered to have any talk with anyone. (Chapter 18, p. 634.)

There is no more tormented image in fiction than that. The final breakdown at the Rome dinner comes almost as a relief: now at least he had no need to dread discovery. And in the end he gives himself away, as though the organism which has had to live so long with deceit, uncertainty, and cowardice has exacted its revenge.

The story of William Dorrit clearly expresses a central and enduring concern of Dickens's, a concern which is counterpointed by the Merdle thread of the novel. It must be said right away that there is a fatal vagueness in the handling of the great financier's affairs. To refer the sceptical reader to Trollope at this point is by no means to ask him to sacrifice artistic interests to documentary ones. On the contrary, *The Way We Live Now* is, in respect of its financial aspect, an artistic triumph, if of a low-keyed order. And the basis of its success is its consistent grasp upon not only the actualities of finance, investment, and speculation, but the psychological and emotional involvement of his characters in these actualities. Trollope has written a book about finance, or rather about the personalities involved in it, and to succeed in such a venture it is necessary to give the facts at least as interestingly as he does: we follow the rise and crash of his Melmotte with far more interest than that of Dickens's

Merdle, simply because Trollope sees to it that we are informed about and interested in the technicalities of investment and speculation, and Dickens does not. He is too general about it, and merely tells us about the crash, where Trollope makes us experience its tensions, fluctuations, and uncertainties. (The same point can be made about Doyce's inventing, which is simply not made intelligible to us.)

This is the more unfortunate because the Merdle theme is important in the life of the whole novel. The obsession with paper shares, the lunatic loss of a "centre of self," the self-commitment to illusions of wealth — all this is predictable from the earlier Dickens. What we have in the nation-wide faith in Merdle (= Fr. *merde,* of course), is a further version of the kind of syndrome treated in *Bleak House,* and radical to the Dickens myth. The people who pin their faith in Merdle are doing — *mutatis mutandis* — what Richard Carstone was doing in *Bleak House.* The investment in Merdle's schemes is simply gambling, a lottery, and it was inevitable that Dickens should arrive at the idea of a lottery sooner or later. The pathetic belief in the *Loterie nationale,* or the football pools, or the television quiz, is a delusion significantly characteristic of man in his bourgeois-capitalist phase. Looked at from one angle, Dickens's early heroes and heroines are lucky winners in the lottery of life, and this, as I have pointed out, was the secret of their tremendous appeal to Victorian England. My basic contention throughout these pages has been that this nucleus of preoccupations (crystallized in the form of the myth) is gradually raised to the surface of awareness as Dickens develops, and that his last novels provide us with the final critique of them. *Little Dorrit* takes up the thread of this critique where it had been dropped at the end of *Bleak House.*

The collapse of Merdle and the emptiness it reveals behind the speculation are especially relevant to our placing both of Arthur Clennam and of England itself, of which he is in many ways so typical. Clennam's major attempt to work off his guilt ends in disaster: he stakes the admirable Doyce's hard-earned money on Merdle. It is a significant blunder: Doyce's very solidity is based precisely upon the avoidance of such illusion-mongering as is spectacularly evident in the nation-wide mania for Merdle investment. This provides us with a criterion, very nearly, for judging people aright in *Little Dorrit,* one which helps us tell the solid from the hollow, the authentic from the inauthentic, the good, simply, from the bad — for the very villainous villain Rigaud is just such a gambler. Doyce, like Mr. Meagles, simply would not indulge in this kind of fantasy: Clennam would, and the fact is an important reflection of his inward confusion. The Wall Street crash is something Dickens would have grasped instantly and intuitively, for he had analyzed much of its psychological workings already.

We are close here to an appreciation of the novel's profound relevance to our own time. Lionel Trilling has suggested that "At no point, perhaps, do the particular abuses and absurdities upon which Dickens directed his terrible anger represent the problems of social life as we must now conceive them."[14] He then suggests that the book deals with a more general. problem — the nature of the essence of society itself. This is certainly at least in part true. Yet the social relevances of *Little Dorrit* are, as I have already indicated, at least as important as this more timeless significance. It is not only about man and society, but bourgeois man in capitalist society, and not only about bourgeois man in capitalist society, but bourgeois man in capitalist England. For the book has a very specific and troubling relevance for Englishmen: it suggests, I think, that England — the first and greatest society that emerged in a purely capitalist guise — had already reached a stage of terminal over-complexity. Its social inhibitions and taboos, its complicated legal and political customs and institutions, its refined and ancient sense of station and appropriateness, all these things, in combination with the great energy of its scientific and commercial genius, and its instinct for compromise and adaptation, had made England a stagnant yet overcrowded society even in Dickens's time. *Bleak House* had already sounded a note of contempt for "this boastful island", or rather for its conviction that everything was all right in a world in which so much was manifestly all wrong. But in *Bleak House* this scorn is swallowed up in the general disgust for the human animal. In *Little Dorrit* there is a quite specific implication that England, with its rapid urbanization, and its increasingly clogging democratization, was already in the process of being strangled by its own complexities. This is evident from a number of particular scenes and episodes — most spectacularly in the treatment of the Circumlocution Office, a bald-faced piece of work by *Bleak House* standards, but effective in its rough-handling way. Mr. Trilling rightly points out that the Circumlocution Office no longer has its counterpart in reality; it probably never did, quite. But there remains even today in England a residuum of Tite-Barnacle-ism: British officialdom retains much of the dead preoccupation with self-perpetuating machinery, and the treatment of Daniel Doyce, outstandingly, could be paralleled a dozen times in the twentieth century, from the rejection of Liddell Hart's tank strategy to the indifference towards Barnes Wallis's swing-wing jet. A refusal to make the most of its own inventive genius remains sadly characteristic of modern England.

This sense of England's decline pervades other areas of the novel. There is for instance Mr. Meagles, with his stupid, good-humoured intolerance of Doyce, his ignorant blindness to the civilization of France, his foolish patronage of Tatty-coram, and, worst of all, his involuntary reverence for Henry Gowan's blue blood. That the retired businessmen of the earliest Dickens should turn out on closer inspection to be stupid was one thing, for them to be arrant snobs quite another. Gowan himself, also, appears as *English, all-too-English.* It is interesting to see Dickens here taking over a character from the Thackeray world without resorting to crude satire. Gowan is seen very much from the *petit bourgeois* point of view: he is, like most aristocrats in Dickens, lazy and up to no good. But there is no suggestion of villainy here, and when Gowan is moved by Mr. Meagles's plea for Pet's well-being to retort "Don't be so broken-hearted, sir. By Heaven I will!", it is plain how far he is from the callow ruthless opportunists of the early Dickens. What makes Gowan tick — or not tick — is something far more insidious than self-interest: it is a fatal inability to take anything seriously, an ineradicable, reductive, good-humoured cynicism, an unexpungeable taint of the amateur. And again, I think, Dickens has diagnosed a specifically English phenomenon: Henry Gowan is the type of the English dilettante, incapacitated by a deep-seated scepticism from committing himself to the exploitation of even such talent as he has.

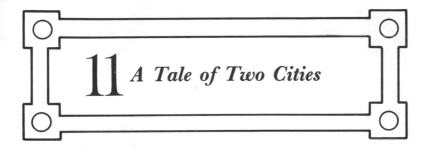

11 A Tale of Two Cities

A Tale of Two Cities extends the historical inevitability of *Barnaby Rudge* to include all human existence, whether private or public. To do this, Dickens resorts to a vast range of literary devices which transcend the confines of realism, and substantially replace the straight synthetic naturalism of the earlier book. Instead of setting unique individuals in a unique narrative, to imply a wider meaning, he now presses to their logical conclusion the new symbolic and emblematic techniques he has been perfecting since *Hard Times* to body forth a series of ideas apprehended at an abstract level. Thus, the later novel is more lucid, economical, and certain: what had been as it were stumbled upon in *Barnaby Rudge,* is here known and understood from without and above. Hence, the *Tale* of necessity abandons the old close realism: here we find personification, choric figures, deeply embedded symbol and metaphor, and a presiding cope of classical mythology.

This much is apparent from the brilliant second chapter. Like *Bleak House,* the novel begins in mud and fog, though the import is quite different. The mist here is "like an evil spirit, seeking rest and finding none". The horses are "mutinous", and steam into the mist "as if they had made it all". The mud clogs and impedes the horses, like the steep hill they labour up. The passengers are suspicious of each other and of the guard, who, in turn, suspects them. The atmosphere of the entire novel is thus created — suspicion, distrust, repression, an uphill struggle. For the horses are the French people, the hill history, the mud and the guard the oppressors. The book therefore begins with arrested effort: momentum is set up in the mind — there is a sense of something powerful being held in restraint. The action of the novel is to a considerable extent the unleashing of these still contained forces. The half-mutinous, clogged horses suggest the social phenomenon of unwilling servitude, rather as the wind at the beginning of *Martin Chuzzlewit* "suggests" the roistering turbulence that is to follow. But Dickens now works with far greater precision, and the quantities can be attributed quite confidently.

Throughout the work, metaphor and characterization interact; no longer does Dickens limit himself to the closely individuated methods of orthodox character-creation. "The central category and criterion of realist literature", observed Lukacs, "is the type, a peculiar synthesis which organically binds together the general and the particular both in characters and situations."[1] Paradoxically, Lukacs regards only the "type" as fully three-dimensional, the dimension missing from narrowly individualist fiction being the socio-historical. In no novel are these criteria more spectacularly vindicated than in *A Tale of Two Cities,* with its enormous variety of character modes, ranging from accurate realism, as in the portraits as Dr. Manette and Sydney Carton, to pure personification, as in the case of certain characters who, while able to play a part in the fabric of a realist narration, can "stand for" a class, or a class situation. In *Hard Times* it was observed that Dickens had not yet mastered this subtle and difficult art: Bounderby and Stephen Blackpool could not quite dwell harmoniously with Gradgrind and Sleary. Now Dickens stands forth as a great master of three-dimensional type creation.

So much is suggested by the initial description of Ernest Defarge, in whom we see the image of a whole class, a resentful proletariat, smouldering for revolution. He seemed, says Dickens, "a man not desirable to be met, rushing down a narrow pass with a gulf on either side, for nothing would turn the man". Defarge is both "unique" in keeping with orthodox criteria, and emblematic: he shows forth a historical and social predicament. "True great realism", Lukacs remarks, "thus depicts man and society as complete entities, instead of showing merely one or the other of their aspects."[2] Taking Flaubert and Zola respectively to exemplify an excessively private psychological fiction and an excessively "social" fiction, Lukacs chooses Balzac as his ideal artist, whose "types" convey the whole truth about man. He would have done better, I think, to take Dickens, the greater artist, the more penetrating analyst. What is true of Defarge is true of many characters in the *Tale*. His wife, for instance, is an equally ruthless emblem of class determinism, her steady knitting the perfect symbol for the grim vengeance-storing memory of the repressed class. Dickens creates Madame Defarge "realistically" without sacrificing her allegorical status. One remembers her, like some portrait of Daumier or Cézanne, as representative of her class, yet fixed unforgettably in terms of her own personal mannerisms — the "stern kind of coquetry" with which she flirts with Barsad, the eyebrow lifted "by the breadth of a line". She is thereby distinct from La Vengeance, who is pure personification. There is, in fact, an unbroken chain of characters, differentiated by varying shades of individuation: the roadmender for instance is totally private, and small, and occurs again and again, at different junctures of the narrative, wildly out of true with probability, until one learns to read him correctly, as a Brechtian choric figure, recording and witnessing the events of history. If the Defarges stand for the collective will of the proletariat, the mender of roads certainly represents the "little man", sheepishly following the dictates of what is supposed to be his own will. And what of the great apparition who appears on the roads to terrify the little man, "a shaggy-haired man, of almost barbarian aspect, tall, in wooden shoes that were clumsy even to the eyes of a mender of roads, grim, rough, swart, steeped in the mud and dust of many highways, dank with the marshy moisture of many low grounds, sprinkled with the thorns and leaves and moss of many byways through woods"? (Book 2, chapter 23, p. 217.)

No one, presumably, would deny that Dickens has created a breathing character here, yet this is another representative figure: it is the Revolution lying there on the bank, "the powerful frame attenuated by spare living, and the sullen and desperate compression of the lips in sleep" (p. 218).

The power of Dickens's imagination ensures that we "see", and are brought into contact with, a live human being: yet, if we go back through the description, we see that every detail applies as well to the *class,* to the socio-historical group he represents, as to the individual. It is by the most skillful and judicious use of these techniques and modes that Dickens is able to consummate his design, which is to convey the inexorability of the historical process and the inevitability of private involvement in it. He could not have aspired to the detachment that makes possible the book's general meanings had he confined himself to the closely worked naturalistic mode of *Barnaby Rudge*: the increase in philosophical breadth and depth in the later book is exactly proportionate to the greater freedom of its imaginative modes and styles.

If the characterization in *A Tale of Two Cities* ranges across the social spectrum, from the little roadmender to the Marquis St. Evrémonde, it ranges with equal breadth and skill across the imaginative spectrum, from figures who are emblems of a class, symbols in a historical process, to those who, like the Manettes and Sydney Carton, play, or rather wish to play, no part in the social process whatever, yet cannot escape it, and are drawn into it *against their will.* This might ultimately prove to be the book's greatest message. Its complex marriage of private and public destinies suggests the profound truth that we are not free to choose with respect to history and the social dynamism: we are part of it, we constitute it, and we have to try to understand our part in it.

In the *Tale,* the marriage of public and private themes is effected by means of a series of interlocking equivocations, ambiguities, and ambivalences. A typical example can be observed in the character of Ernest Defarge — "Good-humoured looking on the whole, but implacable-looking, too". Defarge's ambiguity goes farther than this: for he is on "our" side, the loyal servant who helps Dr. Manette — the victim of aristocratic oppression — to return to life. And the Defarges retain throughout an air of being on the side of "right", initially of Justice, later of Time and History. Yet by the end of the book, the Defarges — Madame rigorously, Ernest half-heartedly — themselves represent the repressive forces of persecution. Not only is there no inconsistency or swerve of sympathy in this, Dickens forces us to acknowledge an ambiguity in the process of history itself. Just as we are first for the Defarges as the saviours of the unknown political prisoners and the representatives of the oppressed, then against them, as themselves persecutors of what we, obedient to Dickens's directives, accept as the side of sanity and goodness, so history forces us to compromise any basic sense of right we might possess.

The whole novel is charged with similar ambiguities of loyalty and allegiance, cutting across the customary transversals. We can recognize in this perhaps a vestige of that ambivalence which led Dickens at once to celebrate and to deplore the sacking of Newgate Prison in *Barnaby Rudge*. But there is nothing in the earlier book to compare with the interaction of concealed antagonisms that exist in the *Tale*. These now operate at all levels. The brother of the faithful Miss Pross is the treacherous spy, Barsad. Mr. Lorry's servant, Jerry Cruncher, has tangled with the law, and bullies his religious wife; Jerry's hair reminds Dickens of blunted prison spikes, and at night he is a body snatcher. (Cruncher is an odd inversion of Gabriel Varden: Varden cures his wife of her bigoted "religion", where Jerry is himself cured of bullying his wife for her religion. On the other hand Varden, by virtue of his trade of locksmith, is a kind of custodian of the values of law and tradition which the Gordon rioters all but destroy: Jerry is an illicit, obscene practitioner of the process of disinterment represented in the recalling to life of Dr. Manette by Jerry's master, Jarvis Lorry. Both Varden and Jerry provide daring parodies of the major themes of their respective books.) These minor strands support and confirm the major theme, however, the theme round which the whole book revolves — the ambiguous relationship between Dr. Manette and Charles Darnay.

The unique power of the novel derives from the skill with which Dickens handles this theme, the paradigm of the basic inter-marriage of social and private life. For the doctor of Beauvais and the true heir to the St. Evrémonde dynasty are, in spite of themselves, locked in a deadly struggle. Fate made them enemies and at the same time pitched them together as father and son-in-law. Yet this is not all. The father son-in-law relationship has its own ambiguities: Dickens has contrived here a cleverly submerged Oedipal situation to exploit the antagonism between the father and the suitor who wishes to displace him in his daughter's emotional world. Dickens informs us that Darnay (D'Aulnais) is the nephew of the Marquis St. Evrémonde, Manette's persecutor, at a typically strategic moment — immediately after Darnay has asked Manette for his daughter's hand in marriage. The extent of the doctor's emotional dependence on his daughter, and the damaging effect upon his hard-won and precarious mental stability of any proposal, have been sufficiently emphasized for us to be ourselves alarmed at the hazards involved in Darnay's offer. But there is something more sinister at work. Darnay had met the Manettes casually on the Dover-Calais packet, when Darnay had comforted Lucie. Their first real encounter, however, is fraught with the cross-purposed ambiguity that pervades the whole story: Lucie is called by the crown to testify *against* Darnay in a trial in London at which he is accused of spying for France. After his acquittal has been secured through the brilliant intervention of Sydney Carton, Darnay is congratulated by the Manettes and by his lawyers. It is now that a sinister moment warns us of something horribly wrong: Jarvis Lorry catches sight of Manette "frozen, as it were, in a very curious look at Darnay: an intent look, deepening into a frown of dislike and distrust, not even unmixed with fear. With this strange expression on him his thoughts had wandered away" (book 2, chapter 4, p. 75) — to the Bastille, of course. The incident strikes hard and has a curious resonance. Shortly afterwards, we are introduced to Monseigneur, the Marquis St. Evrémonde; and it is on his enquiring after his "nephew Charles from England" that we realize that the man Lucie has testified against is blood of her father's persecutors.

The flash of fear Darnay inspires in Manette outside the Court intensifies to the point of break-down when Charles asks him for Lucie's hand. As always under severe emotional strain, the doctor reverts, sinisterly, to the bootmaking that kept him alive in the Bastille. When Lucie returns to the house in Soho, she finds his reading-chair empty:

> "My father!" she called to him. "Father dear!" Nothing was said in answer, but she heard a low hammering sound in his bedroom. Passing lightly across the intermediate room, she looked in at his door and came running back frightened, crying to herself, with her blood all chilled,
> "What shall I do! What shall I do!" (Book 2, chapter 10, p. 130.)

Doctor Manette's hammering, the most sinister of musical motifs, recurs throughout the book, which reads, at one level at least, as a brilliant study of traumatically induced amnesia.[3] Yet it is related by its origination in the Bastille to the historical narrative, with all its painful cross-purposes and paradoxical actions. For the boot-hammering is also the motto of the class vengeance. Darnay precipitates it in these scenes by asking Manette to part with his daughter: but he occasions it also as a St. Evremonde. Thus, just as the Defarges are friend and enemy, first helping Manette to escape, then accusing his son-in-law, and threatening even his daughter's safety, so Manette and Darnay behave like enemies and profess love: friends by acquaintance, they are deadly enemies by blood. Thus, when Manette is finally compelled to testify against Darnay, the bitter irony derives its thrust from a whole system of tensions: something in Manette's fibre cries out for Darnay's blood, as his instinctual revulsion outside the courtroom in London had shown. He, at the same time, wishes both to preserve Darnay as his daughter's husband and to destroy him as the rival for his own affections.

Darnay himself seems at first sight a harmlessly decent

young man, one of Dickens's straight romantic leads, the equivalent of Edward Chester in *Barnaby Rudge*. Yet this is a facile view, the result of ignoring the third dimension Dickens's characters have — that given by the socio-historical framework. If *A Tale of Two Cities* is the story of the innocent bourgeois doctor imprisoned by an unscrupulous élite, it is also the story of the responsible young aristocrat who disinherits himself out of disgust at his own class and tries to atone by a life of hard work. When we see Darnay as the representative of a class that needs to atone an historical culpability, he acquires new interest and depth. This representativeness emerges most plainly in the conversation he holds with his uncle, the marquis, after dinner in the chateau on the night of the marquis's murder. When the uncle deplores the decline of aristocratic privilege, Charles replies with a straight repudiation: if the estate ever falls to him, he says, " 'it shall be put into some hands better qualified to free it slowly (if such a thing is possible) from the weight that drags it down, so that the miserable people who cannot leave it and who have been long wrung to the last point of endurance, may, in another generation, suffer less; but it is not for me. There is a curse on it, and on all this land.' " (Book 2, chapter 9, p. 118.) Darnay's answer when his uncle sarcastically enquires how he intends to live " 'under your new philosophy' ", is characteristically Dickensian — " 'work' ". Thus, each man speaks for his philosophical position — St. Evrémonde unequivocally for the conservatism of *l'ancien régime*, Darnay for the new liberalism.

The relationship corresponds, point for point, with that between Edward and Sir John Chester in *Barnaby*; nothing indeed would serve better to illustrate the extent of Dickens's maturation as political and social philosopher than a detailed comparison of the two relationships. Edward Chester entirely lacks Darnay's social significance and is nothing more than a colourless romantic lead, complete with faithful retainer (Joe Willett) and fair lady (Emma Haredale); his father anticipates St. Evrémonde in his effeminacy, cruelty, and egocentric arrogance, but has nothing of his representative status. There might at first sight appear to be some loss of vitality involved here, in fact: Chester has his own wit and charm, and is individuated beyond those suspect dints in the nose which are all that serve to realize the petrified refinement of St. Evrémonde. Yet although the cross-tying divisions of loyalty are present in *Barnaby* (the Protestant Edward Chester loves the Catholic Emma Haredale), the characterization is strictly limited by the naturalistic technique used to embody them. Thus neither Edward Chester nor Sir John has any representative status. St. Evrémonde explicitly personifies the aristocracy in a way that goes far beyond the merely generalizable relevance of his nephew, Charles. Dickens shows considerable skill, in fact, in making these quite different styles of characterization cohere; Darnay can lead a private life, fall in love and have children, indeed it is important that he can, since he is one of the characters who demonstrate the inexorable involvement of the private in the general social destiny. His uncle, on the other hand, is called upon to do no more than stand for a class. Yet there is no awkwardness in his relations with Charles: he is integrated into the realistic texture with perfect literary tact. He can act therefore with "unbelievable" cruelty ride down a child, for example, in true aristocrat fashion. This Sir Jasper pose starts to make literary sense only when we see him not as a crudely drawn stereotype, but as an exquisitely presented personification of aristocracy, foreshortened and exaggerated by the only true master of the judicious caricature in Victorian fiction. Dickens sees to it, of course, that St. Evrémonde is "there", just as Defarge and the revolutionary agents were. St. Evrémonde's actions, broadly dramatized for demonstrative purposes, can validly stand for the mass of experiential data Dickens wishes to refer to and invoke as the background and dynamic process of the Revolution.

It is interesting that Dickens should at this stage of his career have chosen to treat the decline and deposition of the aristocracy. I have argued all along that Dickens's great significance and centrality in the scheme of nineteenth century fiction derive from the basic myth that dominates his *oeuvre,* that myth which enacts a personal nightmare at the same time as it mimics the dynamic logic of the societal process: the Dickens myth rehearses the upward striving that generated the energy of capitalism. In the two historical novels, he sets his great social theme in historical perspective. It must be remembered that an English novelist was in a uniquely privileged position to attempt this task. The social clash which is enacted in the *Tale* was much more a digested memory in England, with its more advanced social and economic structure, than in Russia or France — the first country still labouring under a sluggish feudalism, the second having precipitately transformed itself, within living memory, from feudal monarchy to bourgeoisified republic. This makes it virtually impossible to carry out meaningful comparison between, say, the Russian or French and the English novel. The English novel owes its supremacy in the nineteenth century to two things — being able to pull Dickens out of the hat at the right moment, and the technological and political advances that made the moment right. The novel in nineteenth century France enacts a state of intellectual exasperation, producing the introspectionism so characteristic of the Parisian *avant garde*; the Russian novel, if we restrict our compass, as I think we should, to Tolstoy and Turgenev, confronts a still feudal situation with an impotent ideology. Hence, the dynamism of the Russian novel is still the romance: one thinks of *On the Eve* and *Anna Karenina* with their basis in a "passionate" relationship romantically insoluble in accordance with the de Rougemont canon. Significantly, Tolstoy's attempts to gear his romance to historical reality resulted in the head-shaking impotence of Levin (in history, good intentions are not enough), and the overtly hopeless determinism of *War and Peace*. It may be that Tolstoy "knew" what was coming, and thought it should come; it may be, alternatively, that he merely reflects the Russian intellectual's characteristic abrogation of responsibility. Either way, he failed to provide a dynamic solution to the dilemma of the novelist in his time. Dickens, like Balzac, may have had the "wrong" political views (his reformist humanitariansim, founded upon right thinking and charity, being more "wrong" even than Balzac's high toryism),[3] but he understood history and the process of social change as Tolstoy never did, and this, because he was involved, and knew himself to be involved, in that restless upward drive that is modern history.

The decline of the aristocracy in France, therefore, provided Dickens with a political paradigm unavailable to him in recent English history. The progressive etiolation of the ruling élite which refuses — as the British aristocracy had never refused — to renew itself from below, had long been a theme of Dickens's. In *Hard Times* already he had shown his growing awareness of the phenomenon of over-civilization in its bourgeoisified form. Here in the treatment of the French Revolution, we have Dickens's most penetrating analysis of the question. When St. Evrémonde is murdered in his bed, Dickens exploits his gift for expressionist animism to suggest an analogy between the refinement of the marquis himself and the stone gargoyles decorating his chateau. These gargoyles, he says, have been "waiting through about two hundred years". In the same way, the marquis and his class have been turning into stone, inviting nemesis. The gargoyles become emblematic of the aristocratic petrification. Thus, the "mask" of the marquis's face (Dickens has used the image several times) is the consequence of a civilization of dissimulation and practised elegance, symbolizing at once the superficiality and fineness of the type. This mask turns into stone under the gorgon's stare. It is significant that at this point Dickens again uses classical myth: we shall see that there is a whole network of such mythological allusions running through the novel.

A later episode adumbrates the conception of the aristocracy from another angle — that of the professional revolutionaries. In chapter 15 of book 2, the Defarges take the little roadmender (summoned to Paris to give evidence to the revolutionary council) on a journey of ideological indoctrination to Versailles. The little man is, as the Defarges anticipate, ravished by the spectacle of the royal party, and cheers his head off. They lead him through his paces: they know that the popular gullibility that helps keep the monarchy in its seat also sucks out of it its marrow and reality: " 'You are the fellow we want,' said Defarge, in his ear; 'you make these fools believe that it will last for ever. Then, they are the more insolent, and it is the nearer ended.' " (Book 2, chapter 15, p. 166.) Madame Defarge completes the lesson with characteristic savagery: " 'If you were shown a great heap of dolls, and were set upon them to pluck them to pieces and despoil them for you own advantage, you would pick out the richest and gayest. Say! Would you not?' " He would, of course; and he agrees, too, that if he were shown a flock of birds, unable to fly, and were set upon them for his advantage, he would "set upon the birds of the finest feathers' ". Madame winds up with crashing finality: " 'You have seen both dolls and birds to-day . . . now, go home!' " (Book 2, chapter 15, p. 167.)

The monarchy is a show, a farce with a dark ending, its obliviousness to the coming disaster making that disaster all the more certain. Yet *A Tale of Two Cities* is not only *not* a revolutionary novel, it implicitly and explicitly condemns the "right" radicalism, with all its attendant horrors: in the end, the book intimates, the greater realities of basic human feeling are all we can depend on. Nowhere is the hideousness of class-covetousness more powerfully conveyed than in Madame Defarge's imagery of dolls and birds: we see in these pathetically gaudy creations all the piteousness of a class that has refined itself out of effectual contact with political reality, and in Madame Defarge's tone all the "passionate intensity" of those who have everything to gain and nothing to lose.

In this way, Dickens penetrates to a profound compassion for a class he had never before been anything but bored by. In the very interesting preface he wrote to the *Tale*, Dickens states "I have so far verified what is done and suffered in these pages, as that I have certainly done and suffered it all myself." How great this imaginative journey was, we can gauge from the scornful treatment of the aristocracy in his earlier books. He had shown abundantly his angry compassion for the poor and the down-trodden: the vision into the plight of the doomed aristocracy in the *Tales* marks, I think, a new and important landmark in his maturation.

By the time Darnay returns to revolutionary France in answer to Gabelle's appeal, the balance of sympathy has swung from the people to the aristocrats. The enraged peasants, bestialized by a brutal, effete aristocracy, have hardened into the uniformed surly bureaucrats of the proletarian dictatorship. Neither the peasants nor the citizens of St. Antoine had ever been remotely idealized. They were either stunted animals or credulous naifs. It is the handling of the aristocrats that changes. When Darnay arrives at La Force an amazing spectacle confronts him, the aristocrats in prison: "The women were seated at a long table, reading and writing, knitting, sewing, and embroidering; the men were for the most part standing behind their chairs, or lingering up and down the room" (book 3, chapter 1, p. 242). It might almost be a *levée*! "But the crowning unreality of [Darnay's] long unreal ride, was, their all at once rising to receive him, with every refinement of manner known to the time, and with all the engaging graces and courtesies of life" (book 3, chapter 1, p. 242).

For the first time in Dickens's work, the positive concomitants of status, tradition, and privilege are allowed to exist. Instead of the degeneracy of St. Evrémonde, whose refinement expressed itself negatively as a mask that concealed only a moral callousness, Darnay sees elegance and fineness. Throughout Darnay's journey through revolutionary France, the proletarians strike a chord of strident coarseness, which merely displaces the arrogance of the *ancien régime* without improving on it. Darnay, as usual, is the book's centre of gravity, its moral touch-stone; we see things substantially through his eyes, and his self-sufficient middle-class doctrine of work is, in the context, "authentic". Thus, far from touching him with its courtly *gentillesse,* the gestures of the aristocrats in La Force appear to him only a charade of the qualities that died with the real values of the class:

> So strangely clouded were these refinements by the prison manners and gloom, so spectral did they become in the inappropriate squalor and misery through which they were seen, that Charles Darnay seemed to stand in a company of the dead. Ghosts all! The ghost of beauty, the ghost of stateliness, the ghost of elegance, the ghost of pride, the ghost of frivolity, the ghost of wit, the ghost of youth, the ghost of age, all waiting their dismissal from the desolate shore, all turning on him eyes that were changed by the death they had died in coming there. It struck him motionless. (Book 3, chapter 1, pp. 242–43.)

As well it might, and us with him. For by this time our response to the aristocrats has become a complex amalgam of pity, scorn, regret, nostalgia, and dislike. The callousness of St. Evrémonde is shown in fact to be no more than a by-product of the withering, the atrophying of the imagination, that accompanies the corruption of absolute power. Earlier, Dickens had associated the two aspects of the case in a single metaphor — "The leprosy of unreality".

Disraeli probably knew the aristocracy better than any other Victorian novelist; but his retailing of its mores, like James's later romanticizations, lacks a placing awareness of its historical position. Dickens, on the other hand, saw the aristocracy as condemned by its own unreality, and saw in this, moreover, a paradigm of the class process. Thus, he saw the phenomenon in depth, even though from the outside. Dickens's social spectrum tends to fade away into caricature or idealization at either extreme, yet in both cases, at top and bottom of the social ladder, his historical insight was unerring. The foreshortening of the social depiction in the earlier stages of the book — its at times almost cartoon world of bestialized workers and decadent aristocrats — serves a fundamentally correct historical vision.

The centrality of the novel in Dickens's output derives however from more than its socio-historical vision. The imprisonment of Darnay for the second time reminds us of the obsession with captivity that began, improbably, in *Pickwick,* and asserts itself in almost all Dickens's major novels. In *Barnaby Rudge* twenty years earlier, he had attempted exorcism with a ritualistic destruction of Newgate. In the *Tale,* he re-enacts the fall of the Bastille; and still the demon will not let him rest. He has Charles Darnay arrested not once, not twice, but three times. The first time in London he is saved by Sydney Carton's wit; the second, in Paris, he is released amid a raucous popular rejoicing somehow more frightening than anger. Dickens has placed himself in a tricky position now: to have your hero tried for his life and released once seems orthodox wish-fulfilment practice; to have him tried and released a second time, peculiar, or just bad construction, the return of a none too interesting major chord. Dickens redeems the situation by a brilliant tonal *volte face*: Darnay is immediately re-arrested, so that the release preceding it appears not a point of rest but a transition, a means of modulation preparing the return of a perhaps forgotten minor theme, the redemption of Sydney Carton. It is a daring move. For it is in fact another repetition: Carton again exploits the physical likeness between himself and Darnay to facilitate a substitution, so that Darney can be spirited away under the eyes of the Revolution.

Yet the difference between the two similar acts measures the spiritual progress of the entire novel: for what had earlier flickered idly through Carton's slovenly brilliance now asserts itself as a means of spiritual salvation. Through his love of Lucie, Carton is now able to perform the "far far better thing", which is to say, nothing less than the non-absurd act, the act one would not wish reversed, which cannot be devalued by time. Carton and Darnay are of course one and the same man, twin halves of one personality — the earnest and the dissipated aspects, perhaps, of the original conception of Walter Gay. Perhaps the most important implication of a brilliantly executed literary manoeuvre, is that the hardworking, responsible Darnay is almost entirely passive: it is the drunken Carton who finally makes the sense-conferring decision to act. The "far far better thing" is almost the only action in the book which transcends the all-powerful determinism Dickens is at such pains to convey. Dr. Manette was recalled to life, independently of his own volition. Every other character in the book, almost without exception, acts according to the dictates of time and history: the aristocrats exploit the privilege chance has conferred upon them, the proletarians bay for blood like hungry wolves, Darnay walks into traps with his eyes open, the Manettes testify against him without wanting to, the lawyers scheme like termites. Darnay, to be sure, had chosen to step out of his class. Yet his earnest, politically conscious decision to become Mr. Charles Darnay, *bon bourgeois,* is significantly negative, and is punished with confusion and misunderstanding. Carton alone steps outside the laws of time and history to break into the realm of existential significance with his act of deliberate choice. Yet the greatest irony in this is that Carton, supremely the anarcho-individualist, saves himself from absurdity by choosing to participate in the great historical process. When he steps out onto the scaffold and places his head in the mouth of La Guillotine, Carton walks onto the stage of history, out of the meaningless wings, where he had brooded so long and so unprofitably. Thus, the complex inter-marriage of private and social destiny, the dependence of every element of society upon every other, is consummated in this final act.

It is important that the man who comforts the little seamstress on the way to execution and finally puts his head on the block be the same *débauché* as idled moodily round Lucie Manette, and, bitterly regretting the "Waste forces within him, and a desert all around", is tormented by a vision of a "fair city", with "airy galleries from which the loves and graces looked upon him, gardens in which the fruits of life hung ripening, waters of Hope that sparkled in his sight" (book 2, chapter 5, p. 85). In the middle sections of the book, a lofty tone begins to usurp Carton's attractive negligence: for a while Dickens tries to reform Carton, to pretend that he was "really" decent. In other words, he manifests the characteristic Victorian revulsion against "sin": the Victorians simply could not stomach the soiled man. George Eliot's characters do not sin, they make mistakes, for which their creator forgives them. Thackeray tells us in advance not to expect a hero in his greatest novel, and there is a significant relation between the decline of the hero in Victorian fiction and the characteristic bourgeois inability to accept the fact of consciously chosen "evil", sin, or vice. Something crucially important seems to hang on the tragic hero's bent towards self-destruction, expressed either in demonic evil (the Byronic satanism, fostered perhaps by Blake's re-reading of *Paradise Lost*), or in some other conscious act of self-committal that brings him face to face with reality. Tragedy in the Victorian age happens in spite of the artist: *Moby Dick, Wuthering Heights, The Mayor of Casterbridge* — such works as this are tragic because their heroes, Ahab, Heathcliff, Henchard, pursue what emerges as their "destiny" across the lines of respectable behaviour. The tragic myth is not a recipe for safe living, a catalogue of errors to be avoided. It reflects the truth about the human condition, not the psychological quirks of spectacular power-mongers. Adam has chosen, and we are fallen.

Unable to accept this fact, yet equally unable to deny it, the Victorians created a series of schizoid studies, culminating in Stevenson's *Dr. Jekyll and Mr. Hyde,* of which Dickens's Carton-Darnay duality is perhaps the most penetrating. Just as the ape and the angel fight it out in the person of Dr. Jekyll, so Carton and Darnay express the twin aspects of the Victorian personality: Carton plays out the Victorian fantasy of the free life of the libido, wasteful, yet irresistibly attractive, which is repressed in Darnay's life of sober atonement through work. The line between Stryver's dissipated jackal and the existential hero of the last chapter is unbroken, though lost sight of in the middle sections of the novel: Carton never quite sinks under the nobility Dickens tries to heap upon him, so that the discomforts experienced in such episodes as the death of the Darnays' little son ("Remember me to dear Carton") are minor blemishes of texture rather than major faults of conception. He goes down, in the end, into an abyss where he knows his way: he does not sacrifice himself, so much as make a journey of self-finding, and this is a journey only the soiled man can make.

The death of Sydney Carton serves, however, a second purpose, which expresses itself throughout the novel in a series of semi-allegorical figures and emblems, giving the tale an underlying mythic basis. Many of these figures are drawn from classical myth, and much of the novel's detached serenity derives, I think, from them. The golden thread, for example, that leads Manette out of the labyrinth is Lucie's hair, but also reminds us of the thread Ariadne lends Theseus to lead him out of the Cretan maze. Several mythological archetypes are conflated by the power of Dickens's imagination, which dissolves the classical allusions and re-constitues them for its own ends without losing contact with the primitive emotions served by those myths. The thread image occurs everywhere: the roads are like threads, seen from a great height in chapter 16 of book 2, and the whole of France in an exalted vision is seen "concentrated into a faint hair-breadth line", the same hair-breadth by which Madame Defarge raised her eyebrows at her knitting. For all the powers in the novel, all the deities and demons are female. The furies are omnipresent, hounding the aristocrats until they appear as if "waiting their dismissal from the desolate shore". The gorgon's stare killed St. Evrémonde, and before it did his coach was attended by gnats and whips that snake about it like avenging furies. When the Revolution breaks out, Madame Defarge receives a fearful aide, La Vengeance; the furies who had attended St. Evrémonde break out in earnest: "The Vengeance, uttering terrific shrieks, and flinging her arms about her head like all the forty Furies at once, was tearing from house to house, rousing the women." (Book 3, chapter 2, p. 212.) The women outdo the men. "The men", Dickens observes (p. 212), "were terrible . . . but the women were a sight to chill the boldest." Madame Defarge breaks loose, prowling through the streets after the Manettes like a tigress. The men are swept aside: Defarge himself, now trying to shield his old master, is suspected of treason, and disregarded. In the streets an awful band of girls and women perform the frenetic ritualistic dance, *La Carmagnole.*

Such grace as was visible in it, made it the uglier, showing how warped and perverted all things good by nature were become. The maidenly bosom bared to this, the pretty almost-child's head thus distracted, the delicate foot mincing in this slough of blood and dirt, were types of the disjointed time. (Book 3, chapter 5, pp. 264–65.)

"Types of the disjointed time" — the phrase, and indeed the whole passage, reminds us of the basic determinism argued in the book. Its strange power indeed derives from the politico-economic plausibility given to the underlying fatalism: and this fatalism is bound up with the vengefulness of the feminine powers that govern the book's action. It is no accident that the three ideals of the Revolution — *Liberté, Egalité,* and *Fraternité* — are all feminine (grammatically speaking), nor that the great prisons have feminine names — *La Force* and *La Bastille.*

All this feminine imagery reaches a natural climax with the final sacrifice to the ultimate feminine deity in the book, *La Guillotine* herself (humourized by the Parisians out of deference to her sexuality). If Madame Defarge is Clotho, the Fate who spins the cloth of life, *La Guillotine* is Atropos, with the shears, "she who cannot be turned". Carton, the hero, must be devoured by the Terrible Mother, in whose maw he places his head. It is plain that some fundamental psychic process is being furthered here, a process continued in Pip's final conquest of Miss Havisham, and perhaps ended in the multiple arms of Kali, the most fearful of all the Terrible Mother images, in the (presumed) Thuggee slaying of *Edwin Drood.*

(Some indication of the depth of Dickens's imagery in this novel is revealed by comparison with, say, Zola's *Germinal,* where so many of Dickens's revolutionary metaphors and camera angles appear, shorn of their acute poetic relevance, if pushed to more violent extremes. The underlying sexuality of the predominance of the women in the proletarian rising erupts furiously in Zola's hands: where Carton is offered as a sacrifice to the devouring sexual goddess, Maigrat, the odious class-traitor who runs the settlement shop and sells goods to the miners' wives in return for the use of their bodies, is literally castrated by the haggard proletarian witches, crazed with hunger and seeking revenge on the whole world of men.)

Thus, the journey Sydney Carton makes in the tumbril at the end of the novel consummates a complex design, a design worked with a metaphoric power incomparably superior to the plodding carefulness of Zola. The tumbril moves "like a plough", and once again Dickens exploits his great gift for poetic image to thrust his ideas through to their conclusion. The marriage of the psychic process to the historical thesis, which is the great achievement of *A Tale of Two Cities,* is managed very largely through such metaphors, sunk in the texture of the narrative. At the very beginning of the story, when Jarvis Lorry, on his way to rescue Dr. Manette, muses upon the fate of the doctor through the window of the Dover coach in the morning light, he sees a "ridge of ploughed land, with a plough upon it where it had been left last night when the horses were unyoked" (book 1, chapter 3, p. 13). The Revolution has harnessed the plough to the team again, and Sydney Carton is crushed by it. Paradoxically, the ancient symbol of purpose and peaceful husbandry is now used to consummate a story of bitterness and revenge: "As the sombre wheels of the six carts go round, they seem to plough up a long crooked furrow among the populace in the streets. Ridges of faces are thrown to this side and to that, and the ploughs go steadily onward." (Book 3, chapter 15, p. 353.) Thus the great classical image of purpose and construction stands also for time and the passage of history: " . . . the great magician", Dickens observes, with a characteristic deviation from determinism to fatalism, "who majestically works out the appointed order of the Creator, never reverses his transformations" (p. 353). So the image of inexorability is consummated in an act of sacrificial atonement that at once transcends and fuses with the historicism the novel also argues:

> All the devouring and insatiate Monsters imagined since imagination could record itself, are fused in the one realisation, Guillotine. And yet there is not in France, with its rich variety of soil and climate, a blade, a leaf, a root, a sprig, a peppercorn, which will grow to maturity under conditions more certain than

those that have produced this horror. Crush humanity out of shape once more, under similar hammers, and it will twist itself into the same tortured forms. (Book 3, chapter 15, p. 353.)

Inevitably, one thinks of Russia at this point; later, of Mao's China, when the little seamstress, in a scene of wonderful tenderness, puts her question to Sydney Carton as they move towards their execution. *Is* all this, horrible as it is, necessary? " 'If the Republic really does good to the poor, and they come to be less hungry, and in all ways to suffer less, she may live a long time: she may even live to be old.' " (P. 356.)

Nothing was more abhorrent to Dickens's mind than the justified lie, the explained brutality. As is indicated in his treatment of Madame Defarge, he regarded any form of thinking that loses contact with the only realities we have (those of actual and present human experience) as subtle and less subtle self-deception. Ideology, in fact, he had come to think of as rationalized bad faith, whence comes his consistent ridiculing of any institutionalized charity. Nevertheless, the historical objectivity rigorously held throughout *A Tale of Two Cities* was not to be pawned for his cherished private benevolence. Instead of condemning the terror outright, as would have seemed consistent with his life-long horror of violence and brutality, and indeed with the meaning of the novel itself, Dickens rises to what remained perhaps his greatest moment of political vision and prophecy. He sees in the wake of the terror not a cynical regression (how easy that would have been for a less distinguished mind — "Plus ça change . . . "), but the possibility of atonement, of redemption, in fact, very like that of Sydney Carton whose earlier personal vision is strangely paralleled here:

"I see a beautiful city and a brilliant people rising from the abyss, and, in their struggles to be truly free, in their triumphs and defeats, through long long years to come, I see the evil of this time and of the previous time of which this is the natural birth, gradually making expiation for itself and wearing out." (Book 3, chapter 15, p. 357.)

12 *Great Expectations*

Towards the end of *A Tale of Two Cities,* Dickens speaks of "the great magician", who never reverses his transformations. The tumbril that carries Sydney Carton to the guillotine moves with the inexorability of a plough, the plough of history, of time, even of some "fate". Yet the whole novel has also sought to demonstrate the necessity of private involvement in history, and Carton actually redeems himself — makes sense of existence — by choosing to participate meaningfully in its action. In *Great Expectations* Dickens continues to explore the sense of inexorability with which the *Tale* had been so deeply imbued, and plunges right to the heart of the basic myth governing all his work to define with great exactitude the nature of the individual's responsibility for himself *vis-à-vis* the societal scheme of which he is, whether he likes it or not, a part. If we can see in Carton the man who finally exercises significant choice in order to cancel his own absurdity, we see in Pip the man whose choice involves him in a life of bad faith from which reality, or the self-declaration of reality, delivers him in spite of himself. Thus, Carton discovers himself by the positive act of self-commitment, which redeems his past life, although it does so only by destroying him; Pip's involuntary progress, the enforced revelation of himself to himself, on the other hand, invalidates his past life, though he is able now to live a life free of absurdity. Is the implication that we can only choose positively in destroying ourselves? Perhaps. But Dickens's imagery suggests as much of Pip's passivity: at the end of the second stage of his expectations, immediately before Magwitch appears to shatter his world, Dickens again invokes the fatalistic spirit of the *Arabian Nights* and makes a direct parallel with his own life: "So in my case; all the work, near and afar, that tended to the end, had been accomplished; and in an instant the blow was struck, and the roof of my stronghold dropped upon me." (Chapter 38, p. 297.)

It is significant that Pip refers here to his life as a "stronghold"; reality or truth is to make itself known by smashing in a defensively conceived edifice. The stronghold is Pip's bad faith. The stripping away of the hero's pretensions or delusions, and the accession of reality has, I suppose, formed the peripeteia of most of the major dramatic or fictional works of the post-Romantic era. Sometimes the revelation takes the form of a public admission of a guilt or culpability the hero has long acknowledged to himself. The pillars of the community are revealed to be hollow by the guilty hero himself, the whited sepulchre hitherto held in great esteem by the society he serves but also exploits. Ibsen's hero Bernick, for instance, moves through the guests assembled to pay him homage, like a man walking through a forest, towards the confession which will unburden him of his respectability and his guilt at the same time. Some such denuding of hitherto concealed purpose and motive provides the basis of most nineteenth century works of fiction or drama that aspire to major status; the nineteenth century imaginative literature dictates the content and direction of twentieth century existentialism, which differs, where at all, only in its more sophisticated conception of bad faith. Existentialism is concerned with a more fundamental form of bad faith than the conscious deception of Bernick in *Pillars of the Community*. We can, it is true, distinguish in nineteenth century fiction many shades of bad faith, ranging from the conscious dishonesty of Ibsen's hero, to the hypocrisy of Pecksniff and Bulstrode, men who are taken in by their own cant. On the extreme opposite wing from Bernick is Phillip Pirrip, who did not at any stage of his expectations know exactly what he was doing, but who, in choosing to believe that Miss Havisham was his benefactress, expressed the basis of his thinking about people and the world, and in doing so betrayed his own deepest requirements. Pip's decision is such a fundamental form of bad faith that the English expression, self-deception, no longer quite serves to categorize it. Pip deceives himself, as he tells us, when he persuades himself that he will be putting Joe and Biddy to great inconvenience in asking them to put him up for Mrs. Joe's funeral, when he "really" knows that nothing would please them more. This shallow kind of self-deception never fully takes in the self-deceiver, it merely supplies him with sufficient rational assistance to justify him in doing something he really intends to do, with or without the self-deception: "All other swindlers upon earth are nothing to the self-swindlers, and with such pretences did I cheat myself." (Chapter 28, p. 213.)

Self-deceivers of this kind are common in Dickens. One thinks of Mrs. Mantalini, for instance, and the ease with which her husband can flatter her into belief in his love for her: Mrs. Mantalini's gullibility is a function of her need to believe Mantalini. But this kind of shallow self-deception which procures a needed peace of mind, easily shades into a more serious variety. The fecundity of Mr. Mantalini's invention makes of his systematic deception of his wife and his wife's equally systematic credulity a game we are glad to enjoy. A bridge from these lighter comic self-deceptions to the darker delusions of the later novels is provided by Mr. Micawber. Mr. Micawber's faith that something is bound to turn up is only in part a testimony to his bounteous optimism; equally, it is the systematic pretence of the self-deceiver who doesn't want to face reality.

In *Bleak House,* Richard Carstone's economic theories more subtly repeat Mr. Micawber's in their self-deluding adaptability; and Miss Flite's "belief" that one day judgment will be pronounced in her favour goes along with a perfectly frank acknowledgment that such a judgment will never materialize. With these disturbing cases from *Bleak House* — among which we must, I think, class John Jarndyce's ostrich act in the Growlery — we come close to the world of *Little Dorrit* and *Great Expectations*. Here, the self-deceptions have grown so deeply into the personality, or are so integrally intertwined in the fabric of the personality itself, that we can really no longer use the phrase self-deception at all without altering its meaning. Pip "knew" that Joe and Biddy would love more than anything to have him put up with them at the forge, just as Mrs. Mantalini "knew" that all Mantalini's outrageous hyperboles were pure bluff: both agreed with themselves to turn a blind eye on what they knew to be the case. We can with less ease state that Mr. Micawber "knew" that nothing would ever turn up, without his doing something to make sure it did. Still less, that Richard Carstone "knew" that Esther Summerson was right in urging him to get on with the job of living, to make his own way and forget the Jarndyce suit. With these cases we approach the point at which such decisions about life — Micawber's refusal to put his shoulder to the wheel, Carstone's inability to accept life as it came, with the necessity of starting on an equal footing with everyone else — are no longer easily accessible to consciousness. Miss Flite's lucidity pin-points the difficulties in describing such situations in the conventional terms: she knows that she is deceiving herself — which is logically impossible, and yet seems the only way to describe the case. In these cases, we must say that personality itself expresses and enacts a fundamental decision about life which may itself be either evasive or stultifying.

To discuss Dickens's later novels in these terms is not to hitch Dickens to a fashionable band-wagon, but on the contrary to point out how that band-wagon — existential analysis — itself follows the thought and practice of Dickens and the other great Victorian masters. This analysis culminates in *Great Expectations*. It is Dickens's greatest novel because in it the myth that underpins all his work is brought to the surface and itself made the subject, the thematic content of the work. There is no gap, in other words, between the mythic content behind the story and the actual details of the narrative. No longer can we posit the shadow plot, which the details of the actual story disguise or criticize: in describing the elements of the submerged myth, we perforce describe the plot itself, what would be abstracted and *résumé* by the blurb writers or a sub-editor for *The Oxford Companion.* The outer and inner narrative are at last merged together perfectly and finally.

It is a rare feat in literature. Only Sophocles's *Oedipus Rex* seems comparable. *Oedipus Rex* is unique because its narrative details seem to summarize the submerged content of all tragedy: a man slays his father in order to sleep with his mother. *Great Expectations* is unique because it encapsulates the fable of every modern novel, and raises to the surface the motive force of all major art of the capitalist era. Both works are profoundly ironical: each posits an ignorance of self and a conflict at the root of personality which will slowly and inevitably destroy the fragile construction of the ego. The life of each hero, Pip and Oedipus, is early dominated by a father figure, to whom the son is hostile (Oedipus murders his father at a cross-roads; Pip — though helpful to him — inwardly rejects Magwitch at what is later shown to have been the cross-roads of his own life), and a version of the Terrible Mother — the sphinx and Miss Havisham. Miss Havisham behaves like a sphinx — enigmatically refusing to disabuse him of his illusion; her silence, like the sphinx's riddle, appears to beckon Pip onwards. Between these two ogres the hero is trapped. It is the error about the source of his expectations, of course, the mistaken attribution of benefit to Miss Havisham, which is at the root of Pip's bad faith, just as the misplaced trust and happiness in Jocasta lies at the root of Oedipus's misfortune. But this isn't to say much. *Great Expectations* is concerned with more than a simple confusion in values, a blindness to the manifest goodness of Biddy and Joe in favour of the coldness of Miss Havisham and Estella; this would have been a simpler story, the story, in fact, without Magwitch — that "progress of a snob" some critics have reduced it to. According to this account, Pip should have gone back to the forge, his lesson well-learnt, Dickens's dishonest desire to have his cake and

eat it alone standing in the way of this harmonious solution.[1]
Then it would have been easier to place the novel — somewhere between Warwick Deeping and H. G. Wells. But *Great
Expectations* is major art, and has the recalcitrance of major
art. It has, in other words, a conflict within itself, which it is
the purpose of the writing to resolve. This conflict is the
tension between Miss Havisham up in Satis House and
Magwitch out on "th'meshes".

It is part of Miss Havisham's cult to keep Pip in a teasing
suspense. At any moment she could have revealed the
negative truth, but she enjoyed being thought his
benefactress, and so kept quiet, partly out of whimsical
malice against the world, partly out of a rather petty class-
superiority. But Miss Havisham is more than this — she is a
major figure in the book, one who affects the dynamism and
balance of the whole narrative until she is at last destroyed.
Like Arthur Clennam's mother, of whom she is a direct
descendant, she is a constant source of disquiet to the hero.
But where Mrs. Clennam actively deceived Arthur and so can
be held responsible for his guilt feelings, Miss Havisham is the
focus of Pip's own least creditable emotions, and does
nothing active to deceive him. The gain in power is characteristic of the advance upon the never fully articulated guilt
that pervades the earlier novel. Miss Havisham makes Pip
ashamed of the old home on the "meshes", even of Joe
Gargery, whose industrious good-heartedness stands out so
boldly against her corrupt deadness. Joe and Miss Havisham
at this stage of the book are diametrically opposed — hard
work and kindness being set against atrophy and malice.
They also represent fairly unequivocally the class relations,
which are indeed already implicit in their places of residence,
the forge and Satis House.

The morbid airlessness of Satis House insists upon overtly
symbolic interpretation of the sort required also in understanding *A Tale of Two Cities*, to which *Great Expectations*
is in many respects a sister novel. The windowless house is a
familiar image in psychoanalysis for withdrawal of a neurotic
severity.[2] What Dickens has done in Miss Havisham is to

perfect what he had earlier attempted with Mrs. Clennam — the physical effect of profound emotional shock and quiet. But at the same time, Satis House itself is patently symbolic of stagnant commercialism:

> The brewery buildings had a little lane of communication with it; and the wooden gates of that lane stood open, and all the brewery beyond stood open, away to the high enclosing wall; and all was empty and disused. The cold wind seemed to blow colder there, than outside the gate; and it made a shrill noise in howling in and out at the open sides of the brewery, like the noise of wind in the rigging of a ship at sea. (Chapter 8, p. 51.)

The loving description of the Maypole Inn Dickens had written exactly twenty years earlier in *Barnaby Rudge,* contrasts strikingly with this magical evocation of decay: as in the earlier passage, Dickens uses the image of the wind at sea to suggest impermanence and hazard. Soon after this passage, Estella discourses airily on the implications of the house's name.

> "Enough House!" said I: "that's a curious name, miss." "Yes," she replied; "but it meant more than it said. It meant, when it was given, that whoever had this house, could want nothing else. They must have been easily satisfied in those days, I should think." (Chapter 8, p. 51.)

The guilt of the successful bourgeoisie, symbolized in the decaying brewery which has had enough, but which is also the victim of its own complacency (as Estella's hint about the equivocal name suggests), is set against the steady industry at the forge. A typically sly intimation of this allegoric content is the name of the game — *Beggar my neighbour* — Pip and Estella are required to play for Miss Havisham's amusement. And the nostalgia of the "parasitic" classes for the industry of the workers is beautifully captured in the scenes in which Miss Havisham and Estella join in the round "Old Clem" (the blacksmiths' anvil song) which Pip is commanded to sing for them.

Joe Gargery might be thought to stand more or less unambiguously for a life of productive industry, directly opposed to the useless repressiveness of the old brewery. But though he is primarily a maker of horseshoes, his trade brings him naturally into contact with the law that sees to the retention of malefactors. His initial role in the story is as the (unwitting) provider of the file Magwitch uses to remove his leg-iron. Later, on Christmas morning, he has to repair a faulty pair of handcuffs for the military. Emotionally, Joe is on the side of the prisoner he later sees wallowing in freezing water and mud; but it is not accidental that he has already helped recapture Magwitch. Both the file and the leg-iron appear later in the story in a way recent criticism has not hesitated to underline.[3] The man who signs to Pip by stirring his drink with a file in The Jolly Bargeman, and the leg-iron used by the unknown assailant to fell Mrs. Joe, do, certainly, play their part in the process of Pip's ambiguously guilty consciousness. What has not perhaps been sufficiently emphasized is the strange significance of Joe's trade itself, and the beautifully ambiguous use Dickens puts it to. Both file and leg-iron function much more significantly than as appurtenances of the "hero's guilt": they are connected with the very fibre of the story's social allegory. Unlike Gabriel Varden, the old Tory, Joe is loyal to his class: he expresses nothing but sympathy for the convict, "poor miserable fellow-creature", is distrustful of Miss Havisham, antagonistic to Jaggers, and quietly hostile to his wife's ghastly *petit bourgeois* relation, Pumblechook. This new adjustment of the social prism is symptomatic of the book's moral climate.

Mrs. Joe herself plays a leading part in perverting Pip's life. It is she who is so keen for him to make a good impression on Miss Havisham, and plants in his mind the germ of class-consciousness. Without her and Uncle Pumblechook's influence, it would hardly have been possible for Pip to draw the wrong conclusion about the source of his income. She despises Joe, fawns upon Pumblechook, and implicitly accepts his criteria of judgment on all social and human matters. She is, as Joe observes, " 'Given to government' ", and, significantly enough, " 'would not be over partial to my being a scholar, for fear as I might rise. Like a sort of rebel, don't you see?' " (Chapter 7, p. 44.) So that when she is finally struck down (by Orlick, as we are led to believe), Pip's immediate feeling of guilt is based upon more than the knocks he received from her in being brought up by hand. The social discontent she has implanted in his mind rankles much more.

The acidity, for example, of the awful Christmas dinner — one of two big convivial scenes in the book, each of them important — derives from the bullying moralizing to which Pumblechook and Mrs. Joe subject Pip and Joe together, but also from the insinuation into the homely forge atmosphere of *petit bourgeois* pretensions. Apart from Mr. Hubble, the wheelwright, the guests are from a higher social grade than Joe: Mr. Wopsle is the clerk of church, and Pumblechook himself a modestly well-to-do corn-chandler. Joe, moreover, wears his Sunday best, and they adjourn after the meal to the parlour. Later in the book, Joe's discomfiture on his London visit to the newly bourgeoisified Pip is again signalized in his awkwardly donned best suit. Pumblechook presents the ritual bottle of sherry to complete the class transformation, so that the scene — a far cry from the dreamy wish-fulfilment of Christmas with the Cratchets — becomes itself microcosmic of the entire novel. Throughout the book, the characters are consistently given territorial rights related to their social position. At the bottom of the pyramid is Magwitch, the outcast who stays out on the marshes; next comes Orlick, the half-skilled labourer, who penetrates only as far as the forge itself and sometimes to the kitchen; next comes Joe, who takes his place here in the parlour, awkwardly out of his element; next comes Mrs. Joe, who gets as far as Mr. Uncle Pumblechook's house; next, Pumblechook himself, who gets as far as the gates of Satis House, where he is stopped by Estella's imperious scorn.

Pip's being allowed free access of Satis House can, without too much strain, be made to stand for his own agonizing transformation from one self to another. So that the spiritual act of finding at the end of the novel is inextricably and essentially connected with the class-stratification and the offences against it. The only exception to the territorial delimitation of class-privilege listed above is Joe's weird visit to Satis House, on the occasion of Pip's apprenticeship, when, again dressed ridiculously in his Sunday best, he finds it impossible even to address Miss Havisham, but insists on speaking to her through Pip, as though it were Pip who had spoken the questions uttered by Miss Havisham. Even in Miss Havisham's territory, Joe remains in a different sphere, out of context.

It is at Satis House, too, that Pip sees Jaggers for the first time — another link in the weak chain of inference which leads to Pip's life of bad faith. Joe, again, reveals his nature in his relations with Jaggers. The lawyer is involved in the illusions Pip grows to live by, and in the crisis when they are revealed. The evening he comes down to the Jolly Bargeman to break the news of the expectations to Pip, Jaggers insults Joe by suggesting that he accept some financial compensation for the loss of his apprentice. The offer is in fact quite reasonable; but Jaggers cuts a poor figure. He remains quite blind to the fineness of Joe's reaction, and insensitive to his quality. To Jaggers, Joe is just a fool who doesn't know when he is well off. It is remarkable that Jaggers is the only person in the novel who can make Joe — gentlest of Christians — angry to the point of violence: even Orlick could not do that. Jaggers straddles the novel's various locales and sectors in an interesting way. His insensitivity to Joe is paralleled in his treatment of Estella's mother, his servant, a murderess he has got off. Although he gives the woman a livelihood and sanctuary in his house, he treats her as a kind of prize specimen, to be shown off to dinner guests. Getting people off — whether guilty or not — is Jagger's life; it is also his hobby, and it does not do to enquire too closely into his motives. His whole manner suggests the detached amused cynic, getting his own way more for his own satisfaction than for any deep concern for what he clearly regards as a miserable affair. Jaggers is the disinterested connoisseur of crime and behaviour, slightly vain, and aggressively "masculine", with his creaking leather boots and his paternalistic attitude towards Pip. It is this disinterest of his which makes him insensitive to Joe's manly response to his offer of compensa-

tion for the lost apprentice: it is inhuman, basically, as this
scene incontestably demonstrates, for it cuts him off from
the human emotions that matter (to Dickens, at any rate).
For these reasons, it is hard to accept Mr. Robert Stange's
view of Jaggers as "a physician who treats moral
malignancy".[4] Surely Jaggers doesn't *treat* moral malignancy
at all: he gets people off whether they're guilty or not. And
the soap, which Mr. Stange sees as antispetic, is not in fact
antiseptic but *scented*: the Pontius Pilate routine is one he
knows becomes him very well. There is too much vanity,
arrogance and, yes, cruelty (as witness the housekeeper's disregarded pleas at the dinner party), to justify Mr. Stange's
vision of Jaggers as a kind of moral sage. The Pilate parallel
itself suggests this reading: Jaggers can "wash his hands of
it", though he would have answered Pilate's famous question
with his own formula: "Truth is evidence". Anything further
from the inwardness Dickens demanded of moral judgment
could hardly be imagined. Thus when Mr. Stange observes
that "Jaggers has a complete understanding of evil",[5] one is
entitled, surely, to reject the equation of evil with crime: he
knows a lot about *crime,* but shows no interest whatever in
the moral ambiguities of behaviour. Keeping the murderess in
his house is on a par with the death-masks on the wall and
the tall-but-true anecdotes with which he magnetizes the
young men at dinner: she is a rare collector's piece, a real live
human being, a strangler! There is more of the big-game
hunter than the moralist about Jaggers. Certainly he is a
complex character. But Dickens possessed the ability denied
to George Eliot, to leave a character in the air — completely
"realized", completely "there", but fundamentally
ambiguous and mystifying. For I do not pretend to be doing
more than Mr. Stange is doing, or from a more privileged
position. And if I cannot without protest accept Mr. Stange's
assertion that Jaggers is "like a god (dispensing) justice",[6] I
grant that the same disinterest which makes the lawyer
repellent and amoral also makes him attractive. More, that it
saves him from the "bad faith" which in various ways dogs
most of the other characters in the book. When he meets

Bentley Drummle for the first time, his response is intuitive
— he sniffs violence and felony, something that attracts him
as the acted-upon violence of the strangler had attracted him:
"Bentley Drummle is his name is it? I like the look of that
fellow.'." (P. 200.) This has nothing to do with Drummle's
"good breeding": Jaggers's detachment from "feeling" is
matched by an equivalent un-interest in class, money, or
"background". His authenticity contrasts sharply with the
inauthenticity of so many of the other characters in the
book, geared as that is to the money-class blockage.

What slowly begins to emerge from the book, in fact, is the
truth that class itself in the modern world expresses and
reflects a kind of bad faith which was not inherent in the
older master-servant relationship. At the centre of the see-saw
that rises with Pip's expectations and falls with his disillusionment, is the second of the two big dinner party scenes which
throw so much light on the novel's progress. The petty class-
consciousness of Mrs. Joe and Pumblechook that permeated
the Christmas dinner party in the early stages of the story, is
matched at a higher social level by Mrs. Matthew Pocket's
morbid interest in "blood". The Pockets, of course, have an
important role in the story: their name indicates their
principal preoccupation, and we come across them first
mooning about Satis House waiting for Miss Havisham to die.
Herbert himself and his father are themselves genuinely
decent men: Herbert is one of the few real "gentlemen" in
Dickens. But Mrs. Matthew Pocket substitutes for her
relations' vulgar interest in money an even more appalling
concern for breeding. At first glance, the dinner party at the
Pockets' Thames-side home presents us with the knockabout
comedy and facetious disaster of the earlier Dickens:

> "Here! Give me your fork, Mum, and take the baby," said
> Flopson. "Don't take it that way, or you'll get its head under the
> table."
> Thus advised, Mrs. Pocket took it the other way, and got its
> head upon the table; which was announced to all present by a
> prodigious concussion. (Chapter 23, p. 182.)

A second glance reveals the same deadly relevance, the

same amused bitterness, that control the entire novel. What Pip sees at Mrs. Pocket's in fact is truly horrible: Mrs. Pocket's concern for blood and breeding leads her to admire the slovenly cad, Drummle, and to delegate her household duties to the two comically named but otherwise sinister servants, Flopson and Millers. Again, as in *David Copperfield* and *Bleak House,* Dickens uses the below-stairs tyrants, devouring the marrow out of the household, to symbolize waste and menace. Here, the episode has a plain societal relevance: Dickens offers us a parable of class-relations which it is important for us to grasp if we wish to comprehend the social meaning of the whole. Matthew Pocket's "desolate desperation" and his entire helplessness in the face of his wife's maddening nonchalance and the domestics' cynical exploitation of things, reaches it apogée when the only honest servant in the house tells him that the cook is lying insensibly drunk on the kitchen floor, with a large bundle of fresh butter made up to sell for grease. His wife refuses to believe ill of her cook, discredits the informant, and utterly frustrates Matthew's efforts to impose some order on the chaos with a high-handed appeal to her noble birth. The domestic anarchy is grim in itself, yet it suggests a broader implication in terms of English social development: the vicious exploitation of addled good-breeding by a drunken dishonest proletariat is another of the ugly by-products of class-consciousness. (The situation is paralleled in Turgenev's *Fathers and Sons,* where Arkady's well-meaning uncle, and the typical enlightened land-owner, dissipates his patrimony in ill-conceived reform. Some of the more brilliant sketches in *A Sportsman's Notebook,* Turgenev's *Sketches by Boz,* such as "The Bailiff" and "The Estate Office", also treat the theme.)

Pip registers all this; and it is important for us to acknowledge what vices his snobbishness does not lead him into. He does not, for instance, acquire pompous or overbearing manners; he does not ever court Bentley Drummle; he does not substitute cash values for human ones. None of these perennial traits of the *nouveau riche* snob does he display.

The point of the book is lost if we find it hard to comprehend how Dickens retained sympathy for the progress of a snob. We might as well be surprised at Shakespeare's maintaining interest in the progress of a murderer in *Macbeth*. Pip does not become unpleasant, nor does the money corrupt him in a simple way. It is rather that he grows up with a conflict inside him, a conflict which has parallels in the contemporary social structure. Experience forces this conflict to a crisis: in enjoying Pip's downfall, the Victorian bourgeoisie became aware of its own internal contradictions. The dynamo of this inner turmoil is that same class-creating, class-conscious drive upwards from life and mire as supplies the Dickens myth with its energy. The critique of class and of snobbishness in *Great Expectations* is inseparable from the close investigation into the hero's responsibility, or rather of his refusal to accept this responsibility, that we have observed to be increasingly the thematic core of Dickens's mature writing. *Great Expectations* is, essentially, the Dickens myth raised to the surface, laid upon the table, dissected, criticized: in it, all the assumptions implicitly made in the myth's earlier projections are exposed to light. This is what I intend by calling it Dickens's greatest study of bad faith. We can see in its fable a model of the individual's participation in the societal organism of capitalism, such as we cannot see, I think, in the case of Dickens's great French counterpart. Indeed, one of the most striking features of Dickens's development is best illustrated by contrast with the mature Balzac. I refer to the transmutation of evil, which I have several times observed to be of great significance in the evolution of Dickens's art from *Oliver Twist* to *Our Mutual Friend*. In *Illusions Perdues,* the story of Lucien de Rubempré, an aspirant poet frustrated by the corruption of Paris, parallels in certain fundamental mythic ways the story of Pip. In the same novel, the provincial inventor Séchard, swindled out of his invention by the capitalist sharks, parallels the artisan inventor of *Little Dorrit,* Daniel Doyce. The differences between Balzac and the mature Dickens, however, are striking and crucial. The dynamic of the mature

Balzac remains by and large the manichean conflict so characteristic of the early Dickens, the Dickens of *Nicholas
Nickleby,* for instance, and even *Martin Chuzzlewit.*
Certainly, Balzac is at this stage much the more sophisticated
artist. Dickens in the early novels (it is, I have argued, their
secret and their charm) hardly raises the relevant questions as
to the nature and influence of capitalism and its institutions.
On the contrary, the hero is rescued by magically empowered
capitalist father-figures such as the Cheerybles, Mr. Garland,
and Mr. Brownlow. But this is the immature Dickens. Later,
the Balzacian dialectic — radically critical of capitalism,
though from the high tory point of view — is outgrown by
Dickens so thoroughly that Marxian and neo-Marxian
criticism has never really been able to get to grips with him.
It is not charity, or sentimentalism, or the "change of heart",
that makes Dickens heterodox from the leftist viewpoint, but
the fact that as an older man he could no longer believe in
the manichean dichotomies that gave the early barnstorming
broadsides against money and the system their force. The
world of *Little Dorrit* is so confused that it is "Nobody's
Fault" — nobody's fault, everybody's responsibility. This
really is the progression of Dickens. On what might be called
the ecology of moral confusion Dickens is, I submit, the
greatest master in European literature. No one, I think,
questions his supremacy in the evocation of the chaos caused
by the rapidity of nineteenth century urbanization. But
Dickens differs from Balzac in precisely the evaluation of this
chaos: he is no longer, as an older man, willing or able to
make the straight satiric indictment which governs the
morality of *Illusions Perdues.* Séchard is swindled out of his
invention (or rather the profit he should have derived from
it) by villainous businessmen; Daniel Doyce is "swindled" not
by practice or evil, but by the well-meaning bungling of his
patron, Arthur Clennam, who is in turn exasperated by the
terminal complexity of the social organism, of which the
Circumlocution Office is only a brilliant satiric reduction. In
Great Expectations the focus is changed, so that the hero
himself is placed in the position occupied by the Dorrit

family in the earlier book. Pip is exasperated not by capitalism or the system, but by himself. Thus, although Satis House and the Pockets seem to represent the deterioration of social and private morality under capitalism, the point of the novel is lost if it is not understood that Pip is directly and fully responsible for his own progress. Thus, where in Balzac "Evil" is still the swindling and the corruption of bosses and businessmen, even when abetted by the hero's own personal limitations, in Dickens it has become something rather more complicated. Evil still exists; violence, malice, envy, and the rest of the deadly sins all persist, and resist both reform and amelioration. But the relation of these phenomena to the individual is now subtle and difficult. Numerous examples prove this point in the book; none, perhaps, is more apt than that of Orlick, especially in his relations to Mrs. Joe.

The most striking feature of Dickens's treatment of Mrs. Joe, and the best instance in the book of his uncanny insight into disease and pathology, is her violent change of attitude after the attack towards Orlick, her presumed assailant. Dickens's nose for uncomfortable nuances of violence and malice was always acute. Yet nothing in his long series of homicidal studies from Bill Sikes to John Jasper quite equals the sinister quality of Mrs. Joe's new-found and half-imbecilic affection for her old antagonist. "I confess that I expected to see my sister denounce him," Pip observes, when Biddy, with characteristic acumen, guesses that it is Orlick Mrs. Joe is trying to refer to with the hammers she scrawls on the slate;

> and that I was disappointed by the different result. She manifested the greatest anxiety to be on good terms with him, was evidently much pleased by his being at length produced, and motioned that she would have him given something to drink. She watched his countenance as if she were particularly wishful to be assured that he took kindly to his reception, she showed every possible desire to conciliate him, and there was an air of humble propitiation in all she did, such as I have seen pervade the bearing of a child towards a hard master. After that day, a day rarely passed without her drawing the hammer on her slate, and without Orlick's slouching in and standing doggedly before her, as if he knew no more than I did what to make of it. (Chapter 16, pp. 116–17.)

— Waiting to be denounced, of course: it must have been a gruelling trial, even for one of Orlick's sullen, churlish disposition.

Orlick plays a persistently pertinent part in the action. He fights Joe, abuses and assaults Mrs. Joe, flirts — grotesquely — with Biddy, hates Pip, and eventually turns up in Miss Havisham's employ. Pip gets him dismissed from his post, whereupon he reappears in association with Bentley Drummle. Mr. Garis thinks that Orlick represents some of that virile manhood Dickens and Pip feel themselves to have lost: "We can now define Orlick as the embodiment of pure and uninhibited libido."[7] But there is nothing libidinous (in the conventional sense of the word) in Orlick: he is powerful and violent, but it is a clumsy, shambling, round-shouldered sort of power he wields. There is more of the masturbator than the rapist about him, and his behaviour is consistently comic:

> "Well, then," said he, "I'm jiggered if I don't see you home!" This penalty of being jiggered was a favourite suppositious case of his. He attached no definite meaning to the word that I am aware of, but used it, like his own pretended Christian name [Dolge!], to affront mankind, and convey an idea of something savagely damaging. When I was younger, I had had a general belief that if he had jiggered me personally, he would have done it with a sharp and twisted hook. (Chapter 17, p. 124.)

Certainly, there is nothing in Orlick of the satyr-like strength and grace that attends Hugh in *Barnaby Rudge,* and I do not think this is his function. These dreamlike recurrences of Orlick's, coupled with the novel's strictly monothematic nature, are presumably what have prompted many critics to regard *Great Expectations* as the saga of "the Hero's guilt". Mr. Julian Moynahan — whose title I have used to introduce discussion of the theme — argues that Pip is indeed guilty, and is in fact responsible for the crime by which he is apparently obsessed: "Snobbery is a crime. Why should Pip feel like a criminal?"[8] The answer is that he doesn't, and it is only by a play upon words that we can say, as Mr. Moynahan does, that Pip's "callous" treatment of Joe is "criminal". Even callousness is only tendentiously to be called criminal, and we could argue (indeed we should) that Pip doesn't treat

Joe "callously" at all. This is precisely the sort of reading American critics — set on by Humphry House — have forced upon the novel. To adopt this sort of attitude towards Pip is to sabotage the novel's effectiveness: it is to narrow a universal fable down to a moralistic treatise. Mr. Moynahan's thesis leads him to especially strained parallels with Dostoievsky: "In the *Brothers Karamazov* Ivan comes to recognise during the course of three tense interviews with his half-brother Smerdyakov, how he shares with that brother a criminal responsibility for the murder of their father, although Smerdyakov alone wielded the weapon."[9] Such a reading is made plausible by Mr. Moynahan only by arbitrarily yoking together the characters of Pip and Orlick (a procedure in which he is followed by Mr. Garis). I can see no justification whatever for the conflation of two characters in this case — no two characters seem free of conflation, given such licence as Mr. Moynahan's. But even so, the parallel with the Dostoievsky situation is to say the least of it obscure. Ivan Karamazov is guilty of the murder of his father because without his destructive intellectual analyses it would never have occurred to Smerdyakov to commit the crime. Pip is entirely guiltless, judged from this standpoint: if we do not keep a tight hold on our words, they will betray us into all sorts of nonsense. Ivan is directly responsible for an actual crime; Pip just is not, and we must keep these distinctions clear. In point of fact fear rather than guilt seems to be the driving force behind the nightmarish apparitions of Orlick, and indeed behind the novel in general. To be caught and implicated in a criminal or near criminal offence meant only one thing for Dickens — prison, and that for him was the greatest of all earthly catastrophes. Pip's sense of guilt, for example, at his secret association with Magwitch and with the leg-iron used to assail Mrs. Joe, yields well to this explanation. This is even more true of that strangely melodramatic episode towards the end of the book when, having lured Pip out onto the marshes, Orlick all but "does for" him. In a terrifying vision, Pip imagines he sees Orlick, having murdered him, slouching about the ale-houses to establish an alibi in the town, and "contrasted its light and life with the lonely marsh and the white vapour creeping over it, *into which I should have dissolved*" (chapter 53, p. 405 — my italics). Dissolved, of course, in quicklime: for it is crucially important that Orlick should have lured Pip into a lime-kiln. Mr. Garis finds the episode "curiously self-defeating".[10] This is presumably because of his own insistence upon Orlick's role as pure libido, whose purpose in the scene is the "draining off" of Pip's violence. If we don't insist on some subjective interpretation which cuts across Dickens's own purposes, the episode doesn't seem so self-defeating. For the scene parallels not Krook's spontaneous combustion in *Bleak House,* but rather the presumed dissolution of Edwin Drood's corpse in quicklime in Dickens's last novel. When Pip approaches the kiln to meet his assignment, the lime "was burning with a sluggish stifling smell"; later, face to face with his own death, he remembers the white vapour that had crept towards him over the marsh, "like my own warning ghost" (p. 405.) Again, while approaching the kiln, he had felt that the marshes "were very dismal. A stranger would have found them insupportable, and even to me they were so oppressive that I hesitated, half-inclined to go back" (chapter 53, p. 400). His back, at this moment, is turned "towards the distant Hulks . . . " — the hulks, the repository of so much of his early imagining, evil, sordid, as grimily fascinating to Pip as they were to Rimbaud, who had imagined the horror of swimming "sous les yeux horribles des pontons". At this moment the hulks seem friendly, almost like the old home. There follows the horrific death-dance of Orlick, more violent than ever, drinking himself into a frenzy.

Orlick's role here can be satisfactorily explained only in teleological terms: his function is to reduce Pip to mist, much as the button-moulder in *Peer Gynt* has the task of boiling Peer down to primal matter again. Just as the button-moulder lets Peer off time after time, always promising a rendezvous at the next cross-roads, so Orlick delays destroying Pip until rescue arrives: the hero survives, endures the still more overtly teleological trials of *Our Mutual Friend,* finally to perish in the unearthly cathedral environs of *Edwin Drood.* For we must never forget that all the Dickens novels together make up one vast drama, the *Höhepunkt* of which is *Great Expectations.*

In *Great Expectations,* the nervous fear that permeates all Dickens's writing reaches almost neurotic intensity. Pip is severely frightened in three key-scenes: by Orlick in the lime-kiln, by Miss Havisham in Satis House, and, at the beginning of the book, by Magwitch on the marshes. In the lime-kiln scene, we find, I think, the closest approximation to Dickens's own voice of any moment in all his work:

> It was not only that I could have summed up years and years and years while he said a dozen words, but that what he did say presented pictures to me, and not mere words. In the excited and exalted state of my brain, I could not think of a place without seeing it, or of persons without seeing them. It is impossible to over-state the vividness of these images, and yet I was so intent, all the time, upon him himself — who would not be intent on the tiger crouching to spring! — that I knew of the slightest action of his fingers. (P. 405.)

Phrases like "impossible to overstate" — offending as they do against the criteria of presentation Dickens always adhered to so rigorously — themselves tell us how seriously Dickens means us to accept his word for what he is attesting: what he is attesting is the action of the mind under extreme stress, and not just any mind but the mind of an imaginative genius. Dickens is here describing how he himself came by his own fantastic store of images and impressions.

It is one of the rare glimpses Dickens offers us of his own creative processes: the preternatural brilliance of his writing clearly derives from the instantaneous verbalization of image described in this paragraph. In this as in many other respects, it might be said, *Great Expectations* approaches closer to autobiography than any other Dickens novel except *David Copperfield*: he is himself of course, diffused and concentrated (both) throughout his entire *oeuvre,* which therefore constitutes one long act of autobiography. The overtly mythic novels merely afford him greater opportunity for putting a specific image of himself onto the page. The diffidence of character confessed to by David Copperfield is paralleled most interestingly by Herbert Pocket's affectionate summing up of his friend's character: " 'a good fellow, if you want a phrase . . . a good fellow, with impetuosity and hesitation, boldness and diffidence, action and dreaming, curiously mixed in him.' " (Chapter 30, p. 234.) Much like many of us, in short: the fact that Dickens does not dwell endlessly upon the details of his own character should not lead us into thinking him unaware of himself. His whole canon makes up a self-projection: and yet the action of this self-projection does not limit itself to the peculiarities of his own personality. What Dickens's sort of genius does is more interesting than what it is. The integrity of Dickens's work depends very largely on the thoroughness with which his own personal drama is enacted, and the intensity of the lime-kiln scene connects up with the other two scenes in which Pip is terrified to an almost hallucinatory pitch.

In one, Pip spends a whole night up and awake in Satis House, scared to move, while upstairs Miss Havisham moans and gropes her way about. First she haunts him so that he cannot sleep: "A thousand Miss Havishams haunted me. She was on this side of my pillow, on that, at the head of the bed, at the foot, behind the half-opened door of the dressing-room, in the dressing-room, in the room overhead, in the room beneath — everywhere." (P. 292.) Pip gets up trying to tire himself out; puts on his clothes and goes towards the door to the outside world, only to be cut off and trapped by the errant old woman:

> After a time, I tried in the dark both to get out and to go back, but I could do neither until some streaks of day strayed in and showed me where to lay my hands. During the whole interval, whenever I went to the bottom of the staircase, I heard her footstep, saw her candle pass above, and heard her ceaseless low cry. (Chapter 38, p. 293.)

Anyone unfortunate enough to be the victim of arachnephobia will recognize the phenomenon Dickens has evoked here so powerfully; the fear itself serves as a factory endlessly producing the hated image, and freezes the will so that even the slightest movement is impossible.

Miss Havisham is never actually likened to a spider, but she behaves like one, spending her whole life in the dark, prowling around at night and laying her hands on whatever food she comes across. I have already discussed the societal significance of Satis House, and Miss Havisham's role as a repository of Pip's worst errors about life and people. That she means very much more than this is apparent from the above considerations. No one who is aware of Jung's work in this territory can avoid associating the significance of the emotion invested in Miss Havisham with the multitude of comparable figures Jung culls from the world's mythologies. What we have here in fact is another of those fearsome female figures which dominate Dickens's later work. In the case of Miss Havisham, an outstanding parallel is Rochester's mad wife, always present, locked up in the attic, and occasionally emerging, with terrific results, in *Jane Eyre*. Like Charlotte Brontë, Dickens uses fire in a ritualistic exorcism of the dark ugly monster which acts as a check or paralysis on the hero's progress. Rochester is not free to marry Jane until his wife is dead; though even when he is, it is in a crippled state. Pip damages his right arm in the exorcism — a tribute to the maiming powers of the clinging mother. In *Great Expectations*, the resolution is more complex than in *Jane Eyre,* and more specific than in *Crime and Punishment*, where the moneylender's relation to Raskolnikov is always ambiguous. In all three novels the overall sense is that once the horrible old spider-woman has been burned out, the world will be all right. In *Jane Eyre* the exorcism is made to turn upon a technicality — Rochester now being legally free to marry Jane — which accounts for but does not explain the emotional intensity generated in the episode. In *Great Expectations,* the exorcism coincides with Pip's own self-revelation, his final discovery of his own paltriness. Significantly, the only time he feels on equal terms with Miss Havisham is in the scene immediately before the burning, where, now knowing the truth about the source of his expectations, he upbraids her for fostering his mistake. More, he actually feels pity for her: he is for the first time superior to her. Her power, which had been inextricably involved with Pip's delusions about people and class, has already gone when she is ritualistically expunged. The great power of the book derives largely from this close marriage of the story's psychical and societal dimensions, a quality it shares with *Crime and Punishment,* where the ritualistic expulsion of the Terrible Mother also involves the moral eradication of money, as the venom in the veins of capitalism.

What has happened is that Pip has come to terms with a conflict within him — the conflict between the convict and the lady, the feared father and the Terrible Mother. For the last of Pip's three traumatic experiences — the first in the book — establishes his relations with Magwitch, the feared father. As the book moves to its conclusion, the hero slowly begins to overcome the mother, and to accept the father. Now, Magwitch is all that most horrified Dickens in the proletariat: he is dirty, loud, violent, over-demonstrative of emotion, and, last and most important, an actual criminal. His name — *magic witch* — suggests a diabolic dimension. He arrives, with tremendous force, cursing and dirty, and in distress, on the first page of the book: " 'Hold your noise!' cried a terrible voice, as a man started up from among the graves at the side of the church porch. 'Keep still, you little devil, or I'll cut your throat!' " (Chapter 1, pp. 1—2.) The Magwitch trauma *is* the book, in essence, for Pip's conflict starts right there among the graves, when the hirsute, muddy, bleeding convict startles him into awareness of himself, or rather of a conception of himself. It is important that Magwitch's first great roar of "Hold your noise!" follows immediately upon Pip's own first awareness of his own identity. The words leading up to Magwitch's cry are "At such a time I found out for certain, that . . . the small bundle of shivers growing afraid of it all and beginning to cry, was Pip." Thus, Magwitch's terrific appearance has a decisive impact. Magwitch is more than "unaccommodated" man: he had been "soaked in water, and smothered in mud, and lamed by stones, and cut by flints, and stung by nettles, and torn by briars." Being a convict, moreover, he is below the condition of a beggar, even of a lunatic. He is, in fact, the most dramatic and powerful image Dickens had yet conceived of the proletarian — which is to say, of Man himself. With this tremendous spectre — a strange recrudescence of the ogres of the early novels — Pip has to come to terms.

Or rather, he has to be made to come to terms. For the import of the book is not satiric, but tragic. Which is to say that the hero is broken by his own decision, yet broken in spite of himself. Pip's first moves towards the reconciliation of himself with himself (that, I think, is what is involved) are negative: he strives away from Magwitch, and later from Joe, as hard as he can, and as long as he can.

Yet the real irony of the book is that Pip's life is *not* based upon something malignant and vicious: to a large extent, Dickens reverses the conventional direction of the nineteenth century moral stripping. Bernick and Bulstrode, the typical whited sepulchres of mercantile morality, are finally revealed as hypocritical imposters, whose outward show of probity is a sham. The beauty of *Great Expectations* is that Pip's wealth, and more than his wealth, his entire moral orientation and identification, are shown not to derive from the caprice of a malignant old lady, but to be the consequence of an act of kindness and charity. Pip could have betrayed Magwitch on the marshes: and we believe that it was not so much the fear of the young man but an instinctive good faith, an unwillingness to betray his word given to a human being at the end of his tether, which prevented him from doing so. This initial act of charity launches the book, and lies at the root of Pip's character, uncomfortably consorting with his revulsion from the man. In so far as one person, without working for it, can deserve money worked for by another, Pip deserves Magwitch's. He certainly would not have deserved anything he might have inherited from Miss Havisham (over and above the few guineas she actually pays him for wheeling her around). Yet he immediately assumes that she is the benefactress, and builds his life upon the assumption. Thus, the novel presents Dickens's final summing up of the legacy and the hopes and expectation built upon it:

Pip welcomes the role of parasite. Thus, Pip's "self-discovery" is of a more complex and interesting kind than that of Bulstrode or Bernick. At one level, it should surely have been welcome: looked at objectively, Pip emerges as a nicer person after the revelation of the source of the expectations than before it. The young buck living off Miss Havisham's capriciously endowed wealth was nothing more than a parasite, who made his affiliation to the bourgeoisie as complete as possible. Magwitch's reappearance reveals him again as the good-hearted blacksmith's boy who kept good faith with a "miserable fellow-creetur" he could easily (and even with an appearance of moral uprightness) have betrayed.

Yet he would still have been a parasite — Magwitch's little doll, dressed and refined at his pleasure. Which is presumably why Dickens makes Pip refuse to take any more of the money. The shock of having to acknowledge himself a parasite, dependent upon the sweat and toil of a man who pulled himself up from a convict ship to a position of responsibility and wealth, drives him out of his own bad faith. He feels free of Miss Havisham for the first time, and free even to give up the idea of Estella, though with pardonable regret. Estella — the star — ignorant of her origins, and morphined out of emotional life by Miss Havisham's unhealthy possessiveness, sums up in her exquisitely untouchable beauty the major implications of the whole fable. That fundamental alienation from the deeper strata of the self which Pip's conscious choice of Miss Havisham's class-values brought to him works at a far more radical level in Estella: she exists in a social, sexual, and moral void, declassed, uprooted. And we may be sure that Dickens yielded to Bulwer Lytton's plea for a gentler ending because he knew that Estella had already paid in full, not only by being married to the boorish Drummle, but by having missed "life" more or less completely. The woman Pip marries at the close is already sadly resigned to a penitential existence. The contrast with the happy endings of the early novels could hardly be more stark: in those first fantasies, the hero was rescued from the company of thieves and workers, claimed for gentility, and given in happiness to the bourgeois girl. Now, on the contrary, the beautiful bourgeoise is shown to be the illegitimate child of a convict and a murderess, and the hero reacknowledges his kinship with the lowest strata of humanity.

For all his straining away from the proletariat, Dickens could never escape them. We remember David Copperfield's sense of being dogged by the Peggottys: whenever he wants to appear a real gentleman before Steerforth or Steerforth's mother or the acid Miss Dartle, the good old fisher-folk materialize to claim him for one of themselves. The neurotic fear of the abyss drives him to disown them, as in the scene when he hurriedly assures Steerforth that the humble working men with him are relatives of Peggotty. Of this neurosis — a national neurosis, its trauma the violent and painful transition to high capitalism — snobbishness is merely a symptom. The snob is guilty of a particular variety of bad faith, a vicious denial of part of himself that craves vindication. Only the very highest and the very lowest in society are quite free from snobbishness; hence, I feel, Dickens's late acknowledgment of aristocratic *vertu* in *A Tale of Two Cities,* and his concern in *Great Expectations* with those who are less than the lowest — the criminals, those who, having forfeited the societal structure, are free of its values. Magwitch's magnanimity cannot be explained away in terms of gratification. The depth of Pip's *bouleversement* on Magwitch's revelation of the truth is partly owing to the sheer magnitude of his act. Paradoxically — and paradox of this kind is right at the heart of *Great Expectations* — Pip was quite content to be set up by Miss Havisham in the approved way: *she,* being rich and wayward, has the right to her whims and even her gigolos, and besides, there were always the Pockets to be spited. With all this, ugly and narrow as it is, Pip is quite content, though he is not happy, as we know: he confesses that he used to think "that I should have been happier and better if I had never seen Miss Havisham's face" (chapter 34, p. 258). But Magwitch's munificence exceeds all bounds: it is gargantuan, inhuman, it expects no reward, it has no motive. This is what shatters Pip. For if the act had no

NB

motive, it had motivation, and he knows that the simple child had been so much better than the man he grew up to be. How many of us are proof against that reflection?

Now, Pip moves from a sudden and abrupt shock towards a reconciliation with what he is. It is important to remember that the process is more fundamental than a moral "self-awareness": Pip was fully aware of what he had become under the influence of the money and the fixation on Miss Havisham and Estella before Magwitch ever returned. He had castigated himself quite sufficiently for his behaviour towards Joe and Biddy, and the sheer senselessness of his life among the Finches of the Grove. And if we yield at all to the temptation to describe the novel as a movement towards self-knowledge, it must be understood that we designate by the phrase something a little different from what it usually denotes: Pip's awareness of his snobbishness, of his misplacement of values, is not brought on or even noticeably increased by the arrival of Magwitch and the breaking of the awful news. The point is of some importance. In much the same way, Lear is brought to see himself not so much as a selfish and possessive old man, but as a *human animal,* and this process is somewhat more fundamental than the moralist's reading would have us accept of the play. The purpose of tragedy is not to teach us lessons, or to give us moral guides and landmarks. Its effects and processes are altogether more basic. There is little in *Oedipus Rex* for the moralist. We cannot *blame* Oedipus: everything lay outside his conscious control. Yet we feel that his final breaking does bring him to a profound knowledge of the nature of reality and of human experience within that reality. (It is doubtful in fact if we could understand the play fully without the choric directives.) So, in *Great Expectations* Pip's unmasking is very much more fundamental than the revelation of his snobbishness, of which, as I have stressed, he was already perfectly well aware. What it amounts to is a revelation of what really lay behind that snobbishness, of the profounder bad faith that used the petty self-deceptions (like not wanting to put out Biddy and Joe) merely to effect its purposes. The knowledge Pip finally comes to is more profound and more broadly meaningful than the moralist's cherished "self-awareness": it is that much rarer and more important consciousness of man's place in the world and his relations with his fellows. For the final impact of *Great Expectations* is at once personal and subjective, and social and objective: Pip is led to see his own nature in Magwitch, and to embrace what he had in himself abjured, as part of a profound process of moral reorientation towards himself and the meaning of his life. Yet this process is of its very nature bound up with society, the social relation, since what Pip had denied had been Magwitch's spectacularly proletarian nature — his coarseness, his animality, his gross emotionalism, his violence.

It is no accident that at the height of the marvellous journey down river at the end of the book, the boat in which Pip and Herbert are taking Magwitch towards safety passes beneath a "large transport with troops on the forecastle looking down on us". One remembers the earlier glimpse of the hulks at the beginning of the book: "like a wicked Noah's ark. Cribbed and barred and moored by massive rusty chains . . . " (chapter 5, p. 36). The animals in the ark, of whom Magwitch was one, call out to something feminine in Pip, just as Jaggers had before, creating an emotion not dissimilar to Rimbaud's "Bateau Ivre" and even the overtly sexual "Mon Coeur bave a la poupe". Rimbaud's self-immolation began with his ordeal with the soldiers; so, Pip, recoiling from Magwitch as long as he can, finally comes to accept him, and cancels the disjunctions between Miss Havisham and Magwitch, illusion and reality, mother and father, gentility and actuality, the feminine and the masculine, of which the mind-body is composed. In the transition from repugnance from Magwitch to a deep love for him, Pip — and Dickens through him — finally resolves a block within himself.

The quality of the writing in these pages, with its compact ease and intricate clarity, itself testifies to the depth of the reconciliation which has taken place within Pip and within his creator, reconciliation with himself, with his past, with his father: "It was like my own marsh country," he observes of the Thames-side they pass through, "flat and monotonous, and with a dim horizon; while the winding river turned and turned, and the great floating buoys upon it turned and turned, and everything else seemed stranded and still." (Chapter 54, p. 416.) At the opening of the book, just at that moment of self-identification when Magwitch roared into Pip's life, he records also his awareness of his country, "the dark flat wilderness beyond the churchyard, intersected with dykes and mounds and gates, with scattered cattle feeding on it . . . and the low leaden line beyond . . . the river; and . . . the distant savage lair from which the wind was rushing . . . the sea." (Chapter 1, p. 1.) When Magwitch arrived back from Australia on that dark and stormy night he had come along with an "eternity of cloud and wind". Now, the storm spent and Magwitch accepted, Pip passes "all the stages of his age and youth entering the whirlpool", for the river, we note, is "turning and turning" and again, "turning and turning". The whole of the trip down river is a miracle of narrative and atmospheric evocation and pure inner line, touching the pulse of emotion, and gently letting its beat come through. Pip's observation that "It was like my own marsh country" falls with ambiguous force: it is his own country in being a landscape reclaimed from his own earliest recollected experiences, experiences which had had an element of rejection and negation, but which are now embraced, so that the landscape is, though recognized, as if seen for the first time.

Yet the serenity of Magwitch (" 'Ay, I s'pose so, dear boy. We'd be puzzled to be more quiet and easy-going than we are at present' ") is broken directly, not by Compeyson and the ignorant forces of law (a mockery here as everywhere else in Dickens), but by an agent the more inexorable for being totally unrelated to the personalities concerned. The steamer that comes "driving down upon us irresistibly" and leaves them in a "troubled wake of water" carries out here the function carried out in *A Tale of Two Cities* by the tumbril-plough of history.

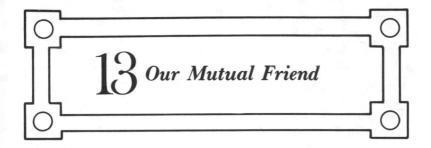

13 *Our Mutual Friend*

Our Mutual Friend takes to its conclusion the ironical treat-ment of the legacy, the expectations, which has preoccupied Dickens since *Bleak House*. *Great Expectations* may have seemed to sum up the theme with some finality: the money is given to the hero, as to the Dorrits, and instead of solving all his problems, it creates new ones by bringing him face to face with himself. Yet *Our Mutual Friend* goes further. It has a quality which can hardly be compared with any earlier Dickens novel. It is a last period work, in a more than chronological sense. The same is true of *Edwin Drood*: the etherial purity of atmosphere in the unfinished novel is dis-tinctly super-real. Nor is it by chance that it is set in the environs of a cathedral. "Religious", in fact, might be applied to both of the last works, though to *Our Mutual Friend* in a didactic rather than mystical sense. It is the quality of experience that is religious in *Edwin Drood*: we seem to breath with difficulty in a sharpness of air. *Our Mutual Friend* presents the more instantly recognizable London of so much Dickens — dirty, turgid, ridden with disease. Dickens is concerned here not with rendering a quality of experience, but with drawing up a metaphysical constitution, a teleology.

What we have here is familiar enough in the creative lives of major artists — a last period which resolves the apparently insoluble in religious allegory, and transmutes tragedy into comedy. Ibsen and Shakespeare offer comparison with Dickens: *Our Mutual Friend* and *Edwin Drood* correspond, roughly speaking, to Shakespeare's *Winter's Tale* and *Tempest*, and to Ibsen's *John Gabriel Borkmann* and *When we dead awaken*, respectively. Like Ibsen, Dickens sinks his religious allegory in the commercial environment of his time. The dust heaps and river-rats of *Our Mutual Friend* correspond, roughly, to the dark commercial guilt and symbolic silver-mines of *John Gabriel Borkmann*; the frost and moonlit ruins of *Edwin Drood* to the glaciers and avalanches of *When we dead awaken*. The title of the latter play suggests the dominant preoccupation of all these great last-period works: rebirth, redemption, revival, renewal. It has become something of a critical cliché to posit these motifs in the later Shakespeare, but this should not deter us from observing their presence in Dickens.

In *Our Mutual Friend* the moralistic drive towards an ultimate ethical ordering — the characteristically Blakean insistence on discriminating between the devouring and the prolific elements of existence — results in a didactic pattern, which has clear analogies with the cyclical resurgences of the late Shakespeare. A still more appropriate comparison presents itself in Mozart's *Die Zauberflöte*, which shares the rebirth theme and also the didactic schematicism of *Our Mutual Friend*. In both cases, too, there seems at first sight to be some loss of artistic power. Henry James's reaction to *Our Mutual Friend* is significantly typical: "*Our Mutual Friend* is, to our perception, the poorest of Mr. Dickens' works. And it is poor with the poverty not of momentary embarrassment; but of permanent exhaustion . . . Seldom, we reflected, had we read a book so intensely *written*, so little seen, known, or felt."[1]

What James objected to in *Our Mutual Friend*, Bernard Shaw indicated in *Die Zauberflöte* by calling it "an allegorical music-play"[2] — as opposed, that is, to fully fledged opera. To convey new meanings, Mozart resorted to methods which to some extent fractured the sturdy fine realism of his earlier operas. In *Die Zauberflöte* Mozart sacrifices the close tight sophistication of *Le Nozze di Figaro* and the realism of *Don Giovanni* for a new allegorical clarity. So, in *Our Mutual*

Friend, Dickens imposes upon the wealth of his naturalistic observation a sometimes artificial design, which affords him the degree of transcendence required to express his new meanings. A similar sacrifice of realism is made by Shakespeare in setting his last comedy on a remote island, and by Ibsen in setting his last play halfway up a mountain. In each case transcendence was the object.

There is no denying a degree of engineering in the proving of Bella Wilfer, for example: she is guided through her paces by her creator, represented by John Harmon-Rokesmith, much as the travellers are steered through their various trials and quests by Prospero in *The Tempest.* And Noddy Boffin's feigned miserhood (so real that some critics have thought Dickens's final revelation itself a cheat)[3] makes its point not in spite of but by means of its non-realistic mode of presentation: the creator here is acting directly as instructor. The survival of Hermione in close proximity to her husband for sixteen years in *The Winter's Tale* is much more wildly improbable than anything in *Our Mutual Friend*: but we accept it without demur as a paradigm of rebirth, as we should Boffin's demonstrated reform. We allow Shakespeare the right to proffer meaning in this instructional way, and should allow Dickens his. This kind of didacticism, in fact, is a regular property of last-period comedy and romance. It is part of its import. Shakespeare and Dickens manipulate their characters through the movements of a transcendental dance. If we see *Our Mutal Friend* in this way, as typical last-period comedy, with patterned dance-figure often replacing realistic psychological action, and redemption as its main motif, its anomalies will often emerge as strengths, and its curious similarities to the very earliest of Dickens's novels appear as the impressive closing of a circle.

Too much indiscriminate symbol-mongering over the past decade has tended to obscure the significance of the really powerful, deeply embedded symbols that do lie at the heart of the later novels of Dickens. The dust heaps of *Our Mutual Friend* gather in resonance when we see them as the culmination of Dickens's exhaustive investigation into the

moral and psychological implications of the legacy underlying his basic myth. In *Our Mutual Friend* Dickens objec-
tifies the legacy, the estate, the expectations, in the form of
the mounds of dust which represent the wealth amassed by
the Golden Dustman. It is a vast act of purgation and defeca-
tion: this is the waste produce of the capitalist organism. For
the Golden Dustman acquires gradually a representative
status, finally to stand for any and every capitalist. Thus,
although the subject of the Harmon inheritance is introduced
by Mortimer Lightwood at a Podsnap dinner as a conversa-
tional oddity, the very graphic description offered of the
mounds and the process of their accumulation immediately
assumes an emblematic status:

> "he grew rich as a Dust Contractor, and lived in a hollow in a
> hilly country entirely composed of Dust. On his own small estate
> the growling old vagabond threw up his own mountain range, like
> an old volcano, and its geological formation was Dust. Coal-dust,
> vegetable-dust, bone-dust, crockery dust, rough dust, and sifted
> dust — all manner of Dust." (Book 1, chapter 2, p. 13.)

It is Dickens's very special genius, of course, to be able to
give to the commonplace and the grimily realistic a mythological status, and in so doing to confer upon the real and the
ordinary a mythological identity. Thus *Great Expectations*
was, at one level, a folk tale, in which the poor orphan
expelled the old witch from the palace which had gone to
sleep for a hundred years. So, *Our Mutual Friend* presents the
fairy tale of capitalism: the landscape of dust, now lit by the
moon, now dry and arid under wind, is like the Harz Mountains, in which bewitched wanderers look for purpose and
magic charms. With almost perverse skill, almost as though to
prove to us that a thing is beautiful or ugly, fair or foul, only
as we behold it, Dickens conjures around the dust heaps a
strange magic, in the very irony with which, for instance,
Noddy Boffin speaks of " 'the beauty of the landscape' ",
and through the crazy prism of Silas Wegg's curiously
Blakean poetic genius —

"Weep for the hour,
When to Boffin's Bower,
The Lord of the valley with offers came;
Neither does the moon hide her light
From the heavens to-night,
And weep behind her clouds o'er any individual in the present
Company's shame." (Book 1, chapter 15, p. 188.)

Now the point, ultimately, is this. The fortune itself is neutral; it can corrupt only the corruptible. Just as the old fairy stories and allegories turned upon finding the true inheritor to the throne, the real king's son or daughter long lost among the shepherds, so the nineteenth century morality concerns the right to the inheritance and, then, the value of the inheritance itself. It is fatuous to pretend that money can remain irrelevant in the spiritual cosmology of the modern world. If money is rejected, then man himself is rejected. This is perhaps why the nineteenth century developed such a neurosis about it. The vices and wonder of modern industrial life existed side by side, mountains of gold overpeering abysses of degradation and vice. The twentieth century has toned this down to a kind of grey uniformity. The contrasts are more discreetly hidden (at least in Europe) and sometimes even ironed out. It is therefore more difficult for us to take money so seriously as a symbol. The fact remains that to reject the power for good money represents is to decide that man is not worth working for. Fortune in Dickens occupies a place not unlike that of kingship in Shakespeare. *Henry V* for instance presents Shakespeare's fully endorsed commendation of experience within the social machine, much as *David Copperfield* embodied Dickens's. In the tragedies Shakespeare saw this dissolve before his eyes, as Dickens saw the fullness and solidity of *David Copperfield* disintegrate into the random chaos of *Bleak House* and *Little Dorrit*. Towards the end of their lives both Dickens's and Shakespeare's very ironically qualified approval emerged in figures who had decided to withdraw from the "usual uproar", only, finally, to reaccept the admittedly not too rosy enterprise in an act of transcendence. Prospero's resumption of his dukedom and John Rokesmith's resumption of his name and identity and fortune reflect a similar turning back to man and society. This is the sense in which we must read *Our Mutual Friend* as religious comedy, as teleological pantomime.

The action of the novel is begun by John Harmon's fake death, and his assumption of the provisional identity of Rokesmith alias Julius Handford, the secretary. This strategy of Harmon's governs the whole novel in a far more organic way than old Martin's deception governed *Martin Chuzzlewit*. Rokesmith is a moral investigator, a private eye moving warily through a gloomy symbolic landscape, one who might, should the case prove intractable, remain inside his new identity, and cease to operate. But he is himself the descendant of Arthur Clennam, first cousin to John Gabriel Borkmann. At the dead centre of the novel — towards the end of the second book — Harmon's "solo" confesses quite explicitly the obscure sense that persecutes him as it had persecuted Arthur Clennam:

> "When I came back to England, attracted to the country with which I had none but most miserable associations, by the accounts of my fine inheritance that found me abroad, I came back, shrinking from my father's money, shrinking from my father's memory, mistrustful of being forced on a mercenary wife, mistrustful of my father's intention in thrusting that marriage on me, mistrustful that I was already growing avaricious . . . " (Book 2, chapter 13, p. 266.)

Harmon's soliloquy is perhaps the most important single passage in the entire novel, both explaining the mainspring of the action, and placing the hero in the succession of all the Dickens heroes, from Oliver Twist to Edwin Drood. Here is the mythic hero confronting the legacy, the expectations, and coolly deliberating on its implications. *Great Expectations* had brought the myth to full consciousness. Now, with a final turn, Dickens's evolution brings him to those equivocal mounds, which present the expectations in concrete form, and also demand interpretation and response. The fortune had seemed mystical in *Oliver Twist*; it tortured and tantalized Richard Carstone; it brought Pip face to face with himself. Now it stands in the moonlight, meaningless and repulsive yet potentially fertile.

It is the essential action of *Our Mutual Friend,* therefore, that is encapsulated in Harmon's "solo". He stands aside from himself and weighs the values of renunciation and commitment. In keeping with the didactic mode of the novel, these ponderings are presented schematically: there is no attempt to insinuate them in a dramatized, "rendered" form. What follows these initial deliberations, however, is a brilliant and graphic account of what is in effect a "ritual" drowning, one of several in the book which are crucially important in the scheme of the novel's meaning.[4] It is this passage which most emphatically prompts an archetypal reading of *Our Mutual Friend*: what we have here is something as ritualistic as the Thuggee murder rehearsed in *Edwin Drood,* or the Masonic rites in *Die Zauberflöte.* For these deliberations of Harmon's are essentially those of a "dead" man: what he is really debating is whether or not to return to life, to resume his identity. And this gains enormously in significance as we see it in its place in the long single drama made up by the totality of the Dickens *oeuvre.* Mozart's freemasonry provides a narrative paradigm for all the last-period works, among which I have suggested *Our Mutual Friend* should be numbered. The shipwreck in *The Tempest,* the avalanche in *When we dead awaken,* Harmon's near-drowning in *Our Mutual Friend* — all these incidents are symbolic of the hero's rebirth, his shedding of the old self and his emergence into the new. The process is deliberately travestied in the Masonic initiation ceremony, as it is in Christian baptism. In the *Zauberflöte.* the last test Tamino undergoes is the water-cave, and it is at this point that the parallel with Dickens's novel becomes most interesting. The trial by water is present in the shipwreck in *The Tempest,* and also in the *Purgatorio* of Dante, where the poet-pilgrim drinks of the waters of Lethe and is then cleansed in the stream of Eunoe. In *Our Mutual Friend,* the trial by water becomes almost obsessive. The two most important near-drownings in the story are those of John Harmon and of Eugene Wrayburn, and the essential fable of the book is the rebirth of these two characters. (Apart from these two incidents, there are three other important drownings — those of Bradley Headstone, Roger Riderhood, and Gaffer Hexam.) Harmon exploits the belief that the corpse Gaffer Hexam fishes out of the Thames on the opening page of the book is himself in order to stand aside from his own identity, and to prove the character of Bella Wilfer. Thus, the trial by water, the initiation by a form of drowning, is suspended for a while. It is as though Dickens has collapsed the roles of Sarastro and Tamino: Harmon is at once the guiding master, who conceals his identity like the Duke in *Measure for Measure,* and indeed like Prospero himself, and a lost spirit in search of an identity, who hesitates before resuming life. As we shall see later, this ambiguity of function applies especially to his relationship with Bella Wilfer.

Harmon's account of the process could not be plainer. First, he falls in with the sailor Radfoot who is, clearly, his *alter ego*: the two men are mistaken for each other, and they finally exchange clothes in a London rooming-house, thus completing the identity switch. Radfoot is murdered *as* Harmon, and both men are thrown into the Thames. Harmon himself survives, but Radfoot perishes: the new Harmon, in other words, is born with the death of the old, for Radfoot has taken on Harmon's identity with his clothes. He has also, in a sense, exculpated Harmon, since he had intended to murder the heir to the Harmon estate, and present himself in his place. This leaves Harmon free *not* to be himself, to subsist in Limbo, while he makes up his mind. One detail enhances this account: Radfoot had arranged to meet Harmon at *Lime*house Church. The church precincts throw upon the narrative the quasi-liturgical tone that pervades *Edwin Drood,* while the name of the district inevitably suggests one of the more sinister, nagging obsessions of the later Dickens, an obsession already lightly touched on by the inspector — " 'You can't do better' ", he adjures Lightwood and Wrayburn, *à propos* of the missing Harmon heir, " 'than be interested in some lime works anywhere down about Northfleet, and doubtful whether some of your lime don't get into bad company, as it comes up in barges.' " (Book 1, chapter 12, p. 159.) The significance of lime in *Great Expectations* has already been noted. Pip underwent trials by water and fire and was threatened with annihilation in quicklime by Orlick. In *Edwin Drood,* the hero might have been both drowned *and* consumed in quicklime. Harmon's assignation at Limehouse Church, therefore, has an indubitably ritualistic significance: he is going to attend at the dissolution of himself.

In the event, Radfoot is mistaken for Harmon, and Harmon himself, though beaten up and thrown into the Thames, revives in the water. Yet he has, as I have noted already, died to his old self: John Harmon went into the river but Julius Handford came out of it. The actual account of the beating and the near-drowning is really the central fictional event in the entire tale. Robert Garis has depreciated the relative weakness of the account Dickens gives us of Eugene Wrayburn's experience of Headstone's attack: "Not only is it not enough" he says, "it is really nothing."[5] The general drift of Mr. Garis's argument there is every reason for rejecting, though he is more right than wrong here. But the real reason for Dickens's (relative) failure in describing Wrayburn's experience of Headstone's attack, and the subsequent "drowning", is that it was something he had already done, with tremendous force and convincingness, in the attack Harmon endured in the room in Limehouse, and his escape from drowning afterwards. All this is done "from the inside", and nobody, I should have thought, could deny the authenticity and the impact of the writing. It is important for Dickens to succeed at this point: it is Harmon's trial by water he must convey, with all its spiritual import, and his rebirth into another self. The most interesting point in the passage is precisely the way the beating-up enables Harmon to escape from his old self. Dickens exploits here his uncanny sense of physical violence: the attack is experienced as though by someone else — " 'I heard a noise of blows, and thought it was a wood-cutter cutting down a tree. I could not have said that my name was John Harmon — I could not have thought it — I didn't know it — but when I heard the blows, I thought of the wood-cutter and his axe, and had some dead idea that I was lying in a forest' ". (Book 2, chapter 13, p. 369.) The journey that begins in the forest continues in " 'a downward slide through something like a tube' ", by which time Harmon feels that " 'There was no such thing as I, within my knowledge.' " (P. 369.) He comes to, feeling " 'frightfully oppressed with drowsiness, and driving fast with the tide.' " He lands (mysteriously, as he afterwards thinks) *on the other side of the water,* and, almost at once, decides to accept his death and assume another identity. Dickens could hardly have made his allegorical point more clearly.

Immediately after this long soliloquy Rokesmith proposes to Bella, and is, as he expects, rejected. It is not just Bella's mercenary flightiness that dictates her answer. For this is the period of Harmon-Rokesmith's suspended identity. He is in Limbo, neither living nor dead: the richness of the parable is lost if we do not feel with Bella that Harmon-Rokesmith is deficient in human vitality. On his face, "there was a nameless cloud . . . on his manner there was a shadow equally indefinable" (book 1, chapter 16, p. 193). Bella's ironical description of him, too, calls to mind John Gabriel Borkmann in the first act of Ibsen's play: " 'a haunting Secretary, stump — stump — stumping overhead in the dark, like a Ghost' ". He is, she says irritably, like a "hermit-crab or oyster". It is appropriate then, that Harmon's body is for long believed to have been fished out of the river in the opening scene of the book: when Bella says he is like a ghost she is putting her finger on something central in his character. For he needs resurrecting: he has undergone a symbolic dying, and has yet to emerge into new life. Although he is the examiner, the tester, he is also himself in need of life and body. Indeed, his search itself is motivated not so much by a disinterested concern for goodness, as by a need to believe, a need for life. Harmon himself is to be restored to life by Bella. He may teach her the lesson of disinterest, of charity, of adult awareness of others, but she teaches him the more difficult lesson of vitality.

This vitality of Bella's redeems what might so easily have been uninteresting didacticism. Indeed, many readers may have felt that far too much was conceded, above, to hostile criticism. Bella's wilful selfishness is vividly enough presented for this thread of the narrative to stand in no need of apology or defence. Harmon needs her as much as she needs him, and this equilibrium of psychological forces holds good throughout the novel.

It is possible that Henry James, failing to perceive the place the novel occupies in the Dickens canon, reacted over-strongly to the functional grotesquerie of some of the river characters, and to the somewhat mechanical treatment of the Wilfers. There is little doubt that, one or two good strokes excepted, the Wilfers are a parody rather than an apotheosis of the Dickens family: here, once more, we have the basic family units of the wish-fulfilment nucleus — the unsym-pathetic mother, the pleasant but helpless father, the child, though not orphaned, still whisked away into the security of middle-class adoption. Certain elements of the Wilfer material are indeed intolerable. Mr. Wilfer, complete with playful incompetence and darling sleepiness, is sentimentalized in a way that recalls the worst excesses of *Nicholas Nickleby,* especially *vis à vis* Bella, who calls him "cherub" and throughout cossets him in a way that would be incestuous if it were not so ignoble for the father:

> "Well, dear Pa," said Bella, "the anniversary may be con-sidered over."
> "Yes, my dear," returned the cherub, "there's another of 'em gone."
> Bella drew his arm closer through hers as they walked along, and give it a number of consolatory pats.
> "Thank you, my dear", he said, as if she had spoken, "I am all right, my dear . . . " (Book 3, chapter 4, p. 457.)

If there were very much Dickens like this there would be good reason for the early reaction against him. This kind of tone, outrageous in its indulgence of a *petit-bourgeois* senti-mentality, has stuck in the throats of many critics, preventing further digestion, and has come even to "stand for" his quality, yet it is in fact more or less confined to indiscipline in his early manhood, and these pages of *Our Mutual Friend.*

What is true of the treatment of the Wilfers as a group may seem to apply to that part of the novel as a whole. The testing of Bella Wilfer by Rokesmith is partly formalistic: it is necessary in the novel's development, and, but for a more minute fullness in the observation of Bella, compares with the come-uppance of Martin Chuzzlewit.

Parallel with this theme, and beautifully inverse to it, is the redemption of Eugene Wrayburn by Lizzie Hexam. I have hinted above that one of the reasons why the Bella-Rokesmith material holds together so well is the ambiguity in the redemptive process: they redeem each other. Both Harmon and Wrayburn are purgatorial figures. Both are subjected to the water-rite; both are lost in a limbo of suspended existence — Harmon because of his guilt and his inability to take a strong decision about himself; Wrayburn because of his boredom, his aimlessness, his lack of a sense of the urgent and the imperative. There is a parallel between the Limehouse attack on Harmon and Bradley Headstone's attack on Wrayburn, followed at once by his near-drowning. Wrayburn survives, both physically and spiritually, through the skill of the water-rat's daughter, Lizzie Hexam. Wrayburn needs Lizzie Hexam's serious purity, but also her knowledge: she is the fisher of the deep, and Wrayburn, also like Harmon symbolically drowned, rises again to a new fullness of life through her. We touch here of course upon the novel's great societal schema, a schema implicit in the programme of *Great Expectations,* one that logically terminates Dickens's lengthy meditation on the issues of money, class, and man in society. For just as Estella was shown to be the offspring of a convict and a murderess, so Lizzie Hexam, in defiance of the class-consciousness of the age, is shown to possess a depth of virtue capable of redeeming the irresponsible middle-class wastrel, Eugene Wrayburn. The structural implications of the novel demand that we accept Lizzie's origination in the fundamental mire of society as part of her gift to Wrayburn: the reasons for breaking through the class-barrier are more basic, more peremptory than the mere need for kindness and good form advocated by Thackeray in *The Book of Snobs.*

Wrayburn of course descends from Sydney Carton and Henry Gowan. His bored charm, his casual wit, mask a degeneracy of feeling that has gone beyond Gowan's dilettante detachment, or Carton's self-destructiveness. He would be more sympathetic, in fact, if he showed a tendency to destroy himself more and others less. For he displays his worst qualities in his taunting of the schoolmaster, Bradley Headstone, who is also in love with Lizzie:

> "I stroll out after dark, stroll a little way, look in at a window and furtively look out for the schoolmaster. Sooner or later, I perceive the schoolmaster on the watch; sometimes accompanied by his hopeful pupil; oftener pupilless. Having made sure of his watching me, I tempt him on, all over London. One night I go east, another night north, in a few nights I go all round the compass. Sometimes, I walk; sometimes, I proceed in cabs, draining the pocket of the schoolmaster, who then follows in cabs. I study and get up abstruse No Thoroughfares in the course of the day. With Venetian mystery I seek those No Thoroughfares at night, glide into them by means of dark courts, tempt the schoolmaster to follow, turn suddenly, and catch him before he can retreat. Then we face one another, and I pass him as unaware of his existence, and he undergoes grinding torments. Similarly, I walk at a great pace down a short street, rapidly turn the corner, and, getting out of his view, as rapidly turn back. I catch him coming on past, again pass him as unaware of his existence, and again he undergoes grinding torments. Night after night his disappointment is acute, but hope springs eternal in the scholastic breast, and he follows me again to-morrow." (Book 3, chapter 11, pp. 542–43.)

No one in the book, not Silas Wegg himself, or Rogue Riderhood, behaves more repellently than this. Mortimer Lightwood's comment is unequivocal: " 'I don't like it.' " No man ever asked to be punished more fully than Wrayburn does here. Immediately after this brilliant description of his "amiable occupation", Wrayburn takes Lightwood out walking to see the thing itself. Sure enough, Headstone blunders into them, and Wrayburn, as though oblivious to the teacher's existence, taunts him aloud about the "grinding torments" he is so obviously undergoing:

> Looking like the hunted, and not the hunter, baffled, worn, with the exhaustion of deferred hope and consuming hate and anger in his face, white-lipped, wild-eyed, draggle-haired, seamed with

> jealousy and anger, and torturing himself with the conviction that he showed it all and they exulted in it, he went by them in the dark, like a haggard head suspended in the air: so completely did the force of his expression cancel his figure. (Book 3, chapter 10, p. 544.)

When Mortimer and Eugene go to bed that night, Mortimer finds that he " 'cannot lose sight of that fellow's face' ". Wrayburn's "light laugh" at this, his boast that *he* can, is flaunted a little too airily for conviction. What was it, after all, that drove him so elaborately to plan his nocturnal walks and cab rides? What gave him such penetrating insight into the psychology of torment? Why is it that the only thing on earth that goads him to any sort of effort is this hellish game of roasting poor Headstone on his own jealousy? The tormentors of the early Dickens were sadists like Daniel Quilp, who derived a positive pleasure from inflicting pain. But Wrayburn simply grills himself along with Headstone, almost as though to prove himself alive. His viciousness derives directly from the pointlessness of his existence, and this is largely social: for we accept him at all times as being, beneath the insouciance and the indifference, worthy of Lizzie's efforts to redeem him.

Dickens never surpassed the accuracy of the rendering of class division and class hatred displayed in these chapters. Bradley Headstone is an inflexible boor, for whom education, in fact, is not an end in itself. He manifests practically no disinterested concern for knowledge or truth and the learning he acquires so arduously is simply a means of raising himself. He is therefore central in the Dickens scheme of things, in himself a comment on the confusions that beset the social organism. His school itself is a more pointed version of all Dickens schools and of the spiritual confusion they express — "An exceedingly and confoundingly perplexing jumble of a school, in fact, where black spirits and grey, red spirits and white, jumbled jumbled jumbled jumbled, jumbled every night." (Book 2, chapter 1, p. 215.)

Headstone's inflexibility of temperament is suggested in his name, as is so often the case in Dickens. But though of "sluggish intelligence", he is a man of strong, in the end of insensate, passion. This is the key to his personality. His capacity for violence emerges for the first time in the very beautiful scene where Lizzie refuses his offer of marriage:

> "Are you quite decided, and is there no chance of any change in my favour?"
> "I am quite decided, Mr. Headstone, and I am bound to answer I am certain there is none."
> "Then," said he, suddenly changing his tone and turning to her, and bringing his clenched hand down upon the stone with a force that laid the knuckles raw and bleeding; "then I hope that I may never kill him!" (Book 2, chapter 15, p. 398.)

Headstone's abrupt change of tone is interesting here: it is part of his nature that there are no even graduations of feeling or tone for him.

Paradoxically, he is never really in control of himself. For all that he represents will and purpose, he is quite incapable of governing himself, of riding any situation. Wrayburn is equally doomed to be a victim. He draws the hostility of Headstone, Charley Hexam, and Roger Riderhood alike, and his careless arrogance loses its charm when it is contrasted with the seriousness of Headstone's involvement in his passion for Lizzie. Headstone is described as being "chained heavily to the idea of his hatred and his vengeance" — to the *idea*, it should be stressed: Dickens has indicated the nature of the inflexible will in the phrase. Yet the unsuccessful attack on Wrayburn is as decisive for the victim as for the assailant. Only when Headstone shows the ultimate fury of his passion does Wrayburn really understand that there is a level at which life ought to be taken seriously. He has deserved the attack: it reveals how much more in earnest Headstone is about life and about Lizzie than he is himself. So Wrayburn receives his symbolic drowning, survives, and is reborn.

Headstone is himself actually drowned, along with the man he had tried to implicate in the attack on Wrayburn, Rogue Riderhood. Riderhood himself, one of the water-rats, had also already survived one drowning, and had also been frustrated by the actual drowning of Lizzie's father, Gaffer Hexam, upon whom Riderhood had cast the blame for a murder committed by himself.

Wrayburn and Headstone had in common only one thing — a love that undercut and bypassed the class-structure of the society they lived in. Headstone's love for Lizzie, in fact, did him more credit than Wrayburn's does him. For Headstone was closer to her in class, and hence more likely to repudiate contact with her. What begins to emerge from the book is a pattern of relationships and sympathies that transcends and cuts through class.[6] The fixation on class or on the money-values enshrined in class and snob-feeling is explicitly and implicitly damned as causing and being caused by societal self-division. The house which, divided unto itself, cannot stand, is the house of society: we remember that in *Little Dorrit* the Clennam household collapsed, for no apparent reason, and we may see in the event a symbolic paradigm of the societal condition in advanced capitalist societies. It is significant that the condemned characters in *Our Mutual Friend* are defined in terms of their attitude towards class and station. Headstone, in spite of his disinterested love for Lizzie, is placed specifically in relation to his striving upwards through education towards a higher station. The same is true of his pupil, Lizzie's brother Charley, a whining cur, worsened by his little learning: "There was a curious mixture in the boy, of uncompleted savagery, and uncompleted civilisation. His voice was hoarse and coarse, and his face was coarse, and his stunted figure was coarse; but he was cleaner than other boys of his type; and his writing, though large and round, was good . . . " (Book 1, chapter 3, p. 18.) — Barbarism, in short, in the process of metamorphosis to civilization. The ugliness of Charley's type is paralleled more rudely in Rogue Riderhood, who, in spite of his bucolic fairy-tale name, is probably as ugly a proletarian boor as Dickens ever created. The point is important, because Dickens clearly did, still, regard the working class as having remained in contact with something positive lost by the middle classes in the course of their self-improvement. In Joe Gargery and Magwitch, Dickens had already indicated something of this surviving warmth and open-heartedness. But it would be a mistake to think that Dickens idealized the workers, or glamourized them. His uncomfortable sense of being almost one of them made this impossible. In *Our Mutual Friend,* Lizzie indicates and "stands for" the fundamental, pre-class naturalness he admired. Riderhood and Charley Hexam show how aware he was of the actual ugliness of a vast amount of proletarian life. Riderhood is churlish and sullen, no longer the simple workman, but a lout, harsh and servile, treacherous and insubordinate at once. "Last period" in Dickens does not, clearly, mean all-forgiving: no amount of social reform or Christian sympathy is going to eradicate or mollify people like Riderhood. It is the existence of people like him, paralleled across the class divide by the Podsnaps and Veneerings, that makes it essential for us to treat Dickens's class-orientation carefully. There is no slackening in the rigour of his judgments, nor of the basic determinism that is part of his vision: the significance, indeed, of the process by which exceptional characters like Lizzie and Wrayburn step outside the class-framework is lost if we do not see it as an evasion of what seems natural and inevitable. Bad faith, in this context, means accepting or not sufficiently questioning the pressures of money and class. Not only the Podsnaps and the Veneerings — characters who for all their brilliance are really "lay figures expressing certain aspects of the social reality he wants to present"[7] — but Headstone, Riderhood, Charley Hexam, and, until his awakening through near-drowning, Eugene Wrayburn himself, all offend against what Dickens felt to be a deep requirement of humanity. The human hells of people like Riderhood and Headstone, and the purgatorial trials of vacillating doubters and non-choosers like Wrayburn and Rokesmith, are rendered side by side.

Riderhood's is the sin of covetous hatred, Headstone's of destructive ire. The end they meet recalls Dante's description of Ugolino and Archbishop Rogiero (his murderer), locked together and frozen in a final embrace of hatred:[8] " . . . the two were found, lying under the ooze and scum behind one of the rotting gates. Riderhood's hold had relaxed, probably in falling, and his eyes were staring upward." (Book 4,

chapter 15, p. 802.) Ugolino betrayed his own side in the
Ghibbeline-Guelf strife: in the same way, Riderhood had
betrayed his own work-mate, Gaffer Hexam. He also had been
given a chance of redeeming whatever was good in himself,
by being symbolically drowned. Riderhood's response on
being saved by his mates is to curse the steamer that ran his
boat down, and to chide his mates and his daughter Pleasant
for too much "poll-parrotting". The whole episode is
narrated with a beautiful balance of mockery and compassion:

> See! A token of life! An indubitable token of life! The spark may
> smoulder and go out, or it may glow and expand, but see! four
> rough fellows seeing, shed tears. Neither Riderhood in this world,
> nor Riderhood in the other, could draw tears from them: but a
> striving human soul between the two can do it easily. (Book 3,
> chapter 3, p. 444.)

How profoundly true this observation is. Riderhood is
odious, a truly horrible character, yet between life and death
he acquires a kind of solemnity, a touch of the sublime. The
whole scene is at once gratitous — it adds nothing to the
action — and essential, of the essence of the whole. For the
whole novel is about a quality of the tender, the potentially
divine — presence or absence of which distinguishes the sheep
from the goats. Hexam had it once, but so waterlogged and
sodden that it has died, a contour in him, which is revealed
perhaps in his strange probity and in his love for Lizzie. The
beautiful elegy Dickens writes for him is one of the many
places in the novel where the greater spiritual dimension of
the whole is overtly disclosed:

> Soon the form of the bird of prey, dead some hours, lay stretched
> upon the shore, with a new blast storming at it and clotting the
> wet hair with hailstones.
> Father, was that you calling me? Father! I thought I heard
> you call me twice before! Words never to be answered those,
> upon the earth side of the grave. The wind sweeps jeeringly over
> Father, whips him with the frayed ends of his dress and his jagged
> hair, tries to turn him where he lies stark on his back, and force
> his face towards the rising sun, that we may be shamed the more.
> A lull, and the wind is secret and prying with him; lifts and lets
> fall a rag; hides palpitating under another rag; runs nimbly
> through his hair and beard. Then, in a rush, it cruelly taunts him.

> Father, was that you calling me? Was it you, the voiceless and the dead? Was it you, thus buffeted as you lie here in a heap? Was it you, thus baptized unto Death, with these flying impurities now flung upon your face? Why not speak, Father? Soaking into this filthy ground as you lie here, in your own shape. (Book 1, chapter 14, p. 174.)

At which point, of course, we recall that shape in the bottom of Gaffer's boat from the opening pages of the novel, "which bore some resemblance to the outline of a muffled human form . . . " (p. 2). Dickens has used all the power of his animism here to make the wind a spirit, an emissary of a great force, and it is to such an end that all his creative life has at last arrived: the supernal dimension of *Our Mutual Friend* represents the final self-identification of Dickens's imagination. Having for so long located and created life and spirit in inanimate objects and buildings, and in the behaviour of men, what was more natural than that it should finally find presence and life in the universe itself, and contact a presiding spirit?

This dimension — what I have called the religious nature of the novel — is what principally distinguishes Dickens from Balzac, of whose whole cycle of novels we can observe what Lukacs observes of *Illusions Perdues,* that "the ultimate integrating principle . . . is the social process itself and its real subject the advance and victory of capitalism."[9] This would describe *Our Mutual Friend* perfectly, without the redemptive theme that runs through the whole narrative. Jenny Wren, now quite overtly transfigured on the roof of Riah's house, sums up the theme of the book, speaking from out of a "glory of her long bright radiant hair" — " 'Come up and be dead!' " I have already observed that the key to the novel is John Harmon's strategem, the strategem by which he steps out of his identity, and goes through the process of deciding whether to step back again. This quest provides the motive force of the whole tale, and holds together and makes sense of the novel's vast proportions, its episodes, scenes, symbols, and interrelations. Harmon is the touchstone of the story, the structural key and the moral light. Yet he has his aides and himself needs assurance. And characters like Sloppy, Jenny

Wren, Riah, and Lizzie provide it. But his own education of Bella, and the life which in return he receives from her, would be impossible without the participation of Noddy Boffin and his wife. What Boffin does, in fact, is to clear Rokesmith-Harmon of any guilt: in burying the will in which Harmon's "unhappy self-tormenting father" reviled and dispossessed Harmon himself and his sister, Boffin cleared them ("What have we done to be dispossessed?") of any slur, and, symbolically, of any of the dark commercial guilt that hung over him, as over Arthur Clennam. Harmon refers to his "miserable youth", and the prospect of a life as dull and dutifully guilt-stricken as Clennam's confronted him. Thus, in a sense, his own stratagem in assuming a false identity is subordinate to the feigned miserhood of Noddy Boffin it parallels. So that the decisive act of the book is the munificence of Mr. Boffin, just as the overwhelming, the inexplicable act of *Great Expectations* was the altogether incomprehensible munificence of Magwitch. " 'I owe everything I possess,' " Harmon tells Silas Wegg, " 'solely to the disinterestedness, uprightness, tenderness, goodness . . . of Mr. and Mrs. Boffin.' " (Book 4, chapter 14, p. 788.) The point is of course that Harmon now possesses much more than a fortune: it is a belief — acquired through Boffin's munificence — in an order of humanity that neutralizes the fortune. Like Clennam, Harmon needed above all to lose the guilt, the "nameless cloud", the "indefinable shadow". The man who knocks Silas Wegg's head against the wall at the end of the book displays as it were a new strength and vigour: his "seafaring hold was like that of a vice". This physical forcefulness is so rare in any Dickens hero that it comes almost as a fracture of characterization. But Harmon has of course been reborn; he feels free, — and Dickens is with him — to take up the option on the fortune. The mounds have revealed themselves to him as compost, and it is in virtue of their regenerative power that the redemptive theme is consummated. It is important to recognize that *Our Mutual Friend* is a novel, finally, of acceptance.

Rokesmith's decision to become Harmon(y) again means

deciding for rather than against life itself and society. This is why it is futile to take Dickens to task, as some modern critics have,[10] for allowing Harmon to set Bella up in financial security at the end, thus aligning himself (so this argument runs) with the values he has been exposing throughout the book. This accusation only makes sense if we assume that the novel is just a realistic satire on Victorian commercialism: it is realistic, it is satiric, it is supremely relevant to its time. But it is something over and above all this, a distinctly super-real allegory on life itself, the situation which does not change, and yet which, changing incessantly, must be apprehended in its actual manifestation. It is not Victorian society and values that are being exposed, but the human condition. Thus, the money, the gold, the dust, is neutral in itself: to "reject" it would be a distinct turning away from life, a conscious act of rejection as partial and as damaging as the greed Dickens is at such pains to expose.

Indeed, not to take up the option would have been to make money the determinant by negation. It would be what D. H. Lawrence called "anti-Forsytism", "a vast grudge against property. And the thing a man has a vast grudge against is the man's determinant."[11] Not to see the significance of Harmon's resumption of his "property" is, in fact, to have misread the whole book, and to have failed to observe its true relation to the earlier novels. Harmon's having found something left in people that was not reached by money — Bella's final reformation, Riah's roof garden, Jenny Wren's pertinent incorruptibility — was the best and only reason for allowing money and property back into the system. Now it is harmless.

An allegorical reading of the book is suggested as soon as we see Rokesmith in Spenserian terms as touchstone and as moral investigator, as questing knight. But it is also necessitated by innumerable episodes and incidents throughout the novel. The proving of Bella, the assumed miserhood of Boffin, the uncertainty of Harmon himself, the trial by water of himself and Eugene Wrayburn — all these parallel and interwoven themes enforce a common explanation upon us.

If *Bleak House* is Dickens's inferno, *Our Mutual Friend* is his purgatorio, where all are tried, some coming through, others going under. Of the latter group, we must, I think, go not to the horrible Podsnaps and Veneerings (caricatures, in the final analysis), but to Headstone, Riderhood, and Silas Wegg. In the Wegg-Venus material, we find the ultimate proof of the novel's allegorical nature. From the first page of the book, the Thames has been Styx, Hexam Charon. London becomes a vast filthy wharf, upon which the drawn-faced crowds wait to be ferried downstream, or scrabble to get themselves fitted out for the last journey. Of this process Silas Wegg's search for a leg to perfect and complete him is only the most audaciously literal instance.

Wegg, the man with the wooden leg, is himself slowly turning into wood: he is defined constantly by metaphors — screwing, for example — that enforce this idea. Hence, he searches for a real leg to complete himself, so that he will be ready for the trip across the Styx. His self-dehumanization, of course, equally audaciously parallels the degeneration of the Podsnaps and Veneerings, Fledgeby, and the rest of them. "Come up and be dead!" Jenny Wren urged — die to this life, this scramble for money, position, prestige, in order to arise to another, better. The theme had been touched in — with typical casualness — by Charley Hexam in the third chapter of the book, when he tells Mortimer Lightwood that the corpse his father fished out of the river is deader than Lazarus. The reference is ironical, of course: Charley doesn't really believe Lazarus was reborn to life, and the following eight hundred pages tell us why he doesn't. In the same way Silas Wegg, treated to the sight of Noddy Boffin turned miser, growls, "He's grown too fond of money", and it fits perfectly with his own view of things. Whereas Bella Wilfer is shocked by the demonstration into a new sanity: is *this* what I want to be like?

Dickens was always a cruel writer: only the palpable force of his conviction and the rightness of his revulsion makes his treatment of many of his characters at all acceptable to us. One remembers the awful fantasies of poor Miss Miggs in

Barnaby Rudge — "I wouldn't have a husband with one arm, anyways. I would have two arms. I would have two arms, if it was me, though instead of hands they'd only got hooks at the end, like our dustman!" (*Barnaby Rudge*, chapter 80, p. 766.) And Pip's fearful speculation about being jiggered by Orlick — "with a sharp and twisted hook". This savagery corresponds either to an inner hell in which people live, or to an inner dread inspired by the malevolence of such people. Silas Wegg surpasses everyone in the aridity of his obsession:

> For when a man with a wooden leg lies prone on his stomach to peep under bedsteads; and hops up ladders, like some extinct bird, to survey the tops of presses and cupboards; and provides himself with an iron rod which he is always poking and prodding into dust-mounds; the probability is that he expects to find something. (Book 1, chapter 17, p. 213.)

Wegg's prodding and poking around in garbage provides an audaciously literal parody of the entire societal theme of the novel, and indeed of the legacy-expectations theme in general. For Richard Carstone was doing much the same thing in *Bleak House*. This daringly literal realization of metaphysical ideas is one of Dickens's most brilliant and original contributions to the novel as an art form. The *dénouement* he contrives in this instance is comparably literal and outrageous. The mounds having been cleared away, Silas Wegg is pitched out of the novel directly into a passing scavenger's cart — "A somewhat difficult feat, achieved with great dexterity and with a prodigious splash." (Book 4, chapter 14, p. 790.) When Silas Wegg returns to the garbage, the novel itself has come full circle. What we had in the mounds was a profound irony of indifference: the wealth of man, the end of his aspirations, is garbage, detritus, itself neutral; taken in its components, repulsive. This, Dickens intimates, is what life in our society amounts to. It is plain that this fundamental symbolism must undercut and offset every other pretension in the novel. The Podsnap-Veneering satire, in itself farcical, derived its vitality from the existence of this basic symbolic core: what, indeed, had they to be so vainglorious about? Silas Wegg's end symmetrically inverts the redemptions and rebirths with which the closing stages of the book are resonant. His end is as appositely Dantesque a damnation as the drowning of Bradley Headstone and Roger Riderhood.

If *Our Mutual Friend* comes full circle with Wegg's return to the mire, Dickens's entire *oeuvre* approaches, if it does not quite attain, full circle with *Our Mutual Friend.* The hero has repossessed the legacy, worked for by others, and been awarded the beautiful girl, exactly as in the earliest of Dickens's fantasies. In this he has been aided by the reappearance, after two decades, of the fairy godfather, the benign father-substitute, who looks after things while the hero is lost: Noddy Boffin is the direct equivalent of the Cheerybles and Mr. Brownlow. Yet the whole process has been transformed by the profound inward workings of consciousness. Every element in the myth has been reworked. Each ingredient possesses a different moral value. It was for Dickens's last and never-to-be-finished book to complete the evolution.

14 *Edwin Drood*

The literature on the mystery of *The Mystery of Edwin Drood* seems at first sight disproportionate to the novel's intrinsic worth. It takes its place logically in the Dickens canon, and as the final work in it holds special interest. But the vast majority of the critical matter on the novel is really irrelevant to its real issues and purposes, and ignores what cannot be ignored without stultification — its relation to the novels that immediately precede it. Most critics treat *Edwin Drood* as a detective story, and set about unravelling the mystery: who is Datchery? Is Drood really dead? And so on. None of this speculation is quite irrelevant; yet the fragment we have is interesting enough in itself, and lacks the kind of interest an unfinished Sherlock Holmes story might have. Neither *Bleak House* nor *Edwin Drood* succeeds very well in the genre mastered so effortlessly by Poe and Conan Doyle. The real interest of the action is never in the detection of the crime, but elsewhere.

My own conception of *Edwin Drood* as a last-period work of extreme religious intensity, set in the environs of a cathedral and bathed in a sequence of unearthly lights, has already been indicated above. Its rare purity of texture has been noted before. Longfellow, as poet, responded to its beauty, and Edmund Wilson spoke of its "vivid colours": "In this new novel, which is to be his last, Dickens has found a new intensity. The descriptions of Cloisterham are among the best written in all his fiction: they have a nervous concentration and economy (nervous in the old-fashioned sense) that produce a rather different effect from anything one remembers in the work of his previous phases."[1] Wilson has described the work well here, but he does not go further and explain its eerie power: the atmospherics of *Edwin Drood* — insistently meaningful, cold moonlight succeeding to flawless sunlight — can only properly be understood in terms of the novel's place in Dickens's development. The last act in the total drama of the *oeuvre, Edwin Drood* carries to their conclusion the preoccupations of the preceding works, *Our Mutual Friend, A Tale of Two Cities,* and *Great Expectations.*

Our Mutual Friend, I have observed above, in certain respects appears to regress to the formulae of *Oliver Twist.* This apparent regression is in fact a *pro*gression, and earlier elements are recapitulated at a higher level of integration and comprehension. This tendency continues in *Edwin Drood.* In the first place, Edwin Drood himself plainly repeats, almost parodistically, the focal figures — Oliver, Nell, Nicholas — of the early novels: his entire situation beautifully travesties that of these innocent mythic heroes and heroines. One would have thought Dickens had extracted the utmost from his myth, that he had examined exhaustively the ironies underlying its presuppositions. Yet here once more is the mythic hero, placed in a curiously cruel light, and aware of the oddities of his situation: " 'Isn't it unsatisfactory to be cut off from choice in such a matter?' " Edwin complains to Jasper of his betrothal to Rosa, to whom he has been promised by mutual agreement of both their dead fathers. " 'If I could choose, I would choose Pussy [Rosa] from all the pretty girls in the world.' 'But you have not got to choose.' 'That's what I complain of.' " (Chapter 2, p. 12.) The Pip situation, in other words, has been taken still further: Pip yearned for, and eventually received, the golden fruit, only to find it turn sour on him. Edwin Drood is guaranteed the certitude and freedom from material and emotional insecurity from the start, and finds the resultant state intolerably imprisoning:

"Yes, Jack, it's all very well for *you*. *You* can take it easily. *Your* life is not laid down to scale, and lined and dotted out for you, like a surveyor's plan . . . *You* can choose for yourself. Life, for *you*, is a plum with the natural bloom on it; it hasn't been over-carefully wiped off for *you* — " (Chapter 2, p. 12.)

This is the Edwin Drood situation. It is of course a logical development of the basic myth: Rosa and Edwin are the golden-haired children of the early stages of the myth, only they are imprisoned by it. Significantly enough, Jasper himself uses the image which really underlies the whole Dickens canon in order to define their situation: " 'See how little he heeds it all!' Jasper proceeds in a bantering vein. 'It is hardly worth his while to pluck the golden fruit that hangs ripe on the tree for him . . . ' " (p. 75). It has been obvious for a long while that the myth concerns life, the human condition. The myth is both an image of the human condition, and the means by which Dickens carries out his investigation of experience. In the present case, both Rosa and Edwin are alive enough to find the guarantees galling, and intelligent enough to end the situation by mutual agreement before they hurt each other more. Dickens's handling of this phase of the novel is exemplary, and Edmund Wilson is seriously misguided to find Rosa (and other "healthy, bright and good" characters in the book) "almost as two-dimensional as coloured paper-dolls".[2] Edwin's reaction after the agreement to end the relationship with Rosa is intelligent and mature: having found the situation with Rosa intolerable, he now — quite unexpectedly — regrets it: "Something of deeper moment than he had thought has gone out of his life; and in the silence of his own chamber he wept for it last night." (Chapter 14, p. 159.) Yet all the time his touchingly young vanity keeps Helena Landless hovering in the background.

Thus, the mythic lovers are at the centre of things in the book: it is their situation which precipitates the action. Rosa and Edwin are in fact curiously alike: they are equally blithe, fair and extrovert, and might almost be brother and sister, or even the twin halves of one personality. The mutually agreed dissolution of the betrothal seems to reflect some sense of unfitness in the match that might possibly be explained in

Jungian terms: there is almost a refusal of an archetypal incest in their balking at marriage.[3] And this view of things is reinforced by the appearance of the Landless twins.

The very name Landless suggests their inverted relationship to Rosa-Edwin. They are in every way the opposites of the mythic pair, not only in being propertyless, and in lacking the expectations of their opposites, but in physical type. Where Rosa and Edwin are fair, blue-eyed and sanguine, the Landlesses are dark — swarthy almost — and inclined to melancholia; where Edwin and Rosa are optimistic and light-hearted, the twins are "tigerish", and passionate. So that the arrival of the twins from the east is like the complementing of Rosa and Edwin with their darker halves: the Landlesses are the shadows of the mythic heroes. The reactions of the two pairs to each other are also symmetrically inverted: Rosa and Helena fall in love, Edwin and Neville fall in hate. Here, plainly, is a powerful square of tension, a psychological situation of considerable pregnancy: the rest of the book really emanates outwards from it.

The light and the dark couples are balanced by a dark and a light presence: Crisparkle — like his name, all clarity and effervescence — is the good angel; Jasper, with his music-hall villain name, the evil angel. The projected matings continue the symmetrical structuring of the book's psychology: the dark evil Jasper desires Rosa, and wants to destroy Edwin; the light optimist, Crisparkle, will (eventually) marry Helena Landless. What makes this fascinating energy-system the more interesting is the appearance in the book of Tartar. Tartar — Tartarus — is, like Jasper's good half, related, as his name suggests, to darkness and the unknown. (He is a sailor, and comes from strange parts.) Tartar helps in the anti-Jasper plan, and was to have married Rosa, in the end. We have, then, Crisparkle-Helena, Tartar-Rosa, with Jasper cancelling Edwin, and being himself destroyed by Neville, who is (presumably) in turn sacrificed in the effort. This makes a powerful and compact piece of typological psychology, at the centre of which a wrestle takes place between darkness and light, love and hate, optimism and despair.

If Edwin and Rosa are a clear counterpart of the early mythic couples — Martin and Mary Graham, Walter Gay and Florence, Edward Chester and Emma Haredale — Jasper and Crisparkle are as plainly regenerated versions of the evil ogre and the benevolent godfather of those pristine fantasies. Like Mr. Murdstone — whose beautiful hair he has — Jasper is a sadist, which is to say, a lover who derives positive and powerful pleasure from hurting the beloved. More, he is that most extreme form of the phenomenon, the lover who can only derive the complete satisfaction from actually murdering his beloved. If this is not so, how are we to explain the moment in the "confession" poured out under opium to the Princess Puffer, in which he laments the disappointment he experienced in the actual event itself?

> "What do I say? I did it millions and billions of times. I did it so often, and through such vast expanses of time, that when it was really done, it seemed not worth the doing, it was done so soon." (Chapter 23, p. 266.)

— " 'It seemed not worth the doing, it was done so soon' ". And later he says, cryptically, that " 'When it comes to be real at last, it is so short that it seems unreal for the first time.' " (P. 268.) It is hardly possible to exaggerate the intensity of Jasper's chagrin on finding that the actual event — the long-looked-forward-to slaying of the beloved Edwin — fails to come up to the voluptuous pleasure of the best of the opium visions. The opium affords Jasper an almost masturbatory indulgence of the fantasy of murdering Edwin, and, like many an adolescent before him and since, he discovers that the actual event falls short of the orgasmic intensity of fantasy. This, it seems to me, is the least inconsistent way of regarding John Jasper.

The murder was, as we are by now justified in assuming, performed as a Thuggee ritual. (Howard Duffield's thesis cannot, I think, seriously be questioned, although it still is.)[4] This means that Edwin is sacrificed to the goddess Kali. This follows naturally enough from the progressive thought of the books written immediately before *Edwin Drood,* and indeed consummates it. Kali is the last and the most fearful of all

Terrible Mother images — as fierce and implacable as Atropos/Guillotine, as horrible, with her many arms, as the arachnoid Miss Havisham. Thus, Edwin Drood (dread-Druid), the last of all Dickens's mythic heroes, is devoured by the last of the Terrible Mothers. This, at one level, is the fundamental psychic action of the novel. I say psychic, rather than psychological. The careful balancing of emotional and psychological quantities in the central nucleus of the novel constitutes its *psychological* action. By psychic action I intend rather the function the enactment of the narrative may have had for Dickens himself, and has therefore for us, his readers. For it seems that the Terrible Mother was an ineradicable element of reality for Dickens. But there is another factor here which I have so far only hinted at: Jasper worships Kali not only because he is a sadist, but because he is a homosexual.

Jasper's homosexuality has aroused little attention from the critics presumably because it is never shielded or disguised. His doting uncle act cannot, I think, be dismissed, as it is by Mr. Dyson,[5] as a clever front for the murderous act he intends to commit. This is to over-simplify and indeed to sabotage the complex psychology of the character: it leaves one with the unpalatable necessity of accounting for Jasper's actions by positing sheer evil. But evil, though it is not to be explained *away,* is at least to be explained — somehow. And we owe as much to Dickens of our ability to explain it as we owe to anyone. The proof of the love Jasper flaunts so boldly is the fact that it is Edwin, and Edwin alone, who must be sacrificed, that it is Edwin alone who can provide Jasper with the maximum thrill. A good parallel for Jasper in fact would be Melville's Claggart, whose conception Jasper probably influenced. These reflections are not disproved by the fact that he never mentions the pleasure of the act in the opium confession of chapter 23: we know that he is talking about the murder, and he does not mention that, either. He only says that whatever it is that happens on the journey disappoints him. Nor is Jasper's homosexuality disproved by the "mad" love he confesses for Rosa in the sundial scene.

On the contrary. In the first place, there is nothing necessarily exclusive about homosexuality: Rosa and Edwin are like brother and sister, and in loving one, Jasper could be loving the other. But there is more to the sundial scene than is at first apparent: there is no doubting the intensity of *some* emotion seizing Jasper here, but what it really is, is obscure. He is possessed, he is giving a brilliant performance (by which I do not mean "putting on an act"), such as he gives in the cathedral. Life for Jasper has to have a ritualistic dimension before it is interesting to him. Besides, although he *professes* love in the sundial scene, nothing in his behaviour testifies to love, but on the contrary to the most intense hatred: "I don't ask you for your love; give me yourself and your hatred", he says to her. He taunts her, makes her cry, and enjoys her tears, just as earlier, in the equally sinister piano scene, he had enjoyed the Svengali-type power he knows he has over her. Both these key-scenes support rather than confute the thesis of Jasper's jealous homosexuality.[6]

Jasper is a central character in Victorian fiction. Dickens is coming close to the heart of something that haunts the whole century: John Jasper needs opium to make existence tolerable. Contrary to what Edmund Wilson suggests, Dickens is not dressing up a Dostoievskian "war of the members" with a "whole machinery of mystification: of drugs, of telepathic powers, of remote oriental cults".[7] The oriental-occidental antithesis is essential to the story: in the east, or in his own imaginative version of the east, Jasper finds both abandonment and a more severe discipline than is offered by the Church of England. The opium, too, associates the east with release and dedication: it is noteworthy that Jasper uses opium not only to intensify and ease a tedious existence, but to devote himself to a passionate duty. There is little conventional escapism in his addiction, and the experiences he divulges resemble more the heightened visions of *Les Illuminations* than the idle fantasies of de Quincey. But boredom, or the need to escape from it, is of course part of Jasper's predicament. Again, this makes him supremely representative of his time, and indeed of ours. To condemn

Jasper out of hand is to commit the moralistic fallacy. Jasper is in all essential respects an aesthete. But it would be absurdly shortsighted to set down *Edwin Drood* as a satire on, or a critique of, the aesthete: the book *is,* by and large, a vehicle for the exploration of Jasper's consciousness, and Dickens has done a far more valuable job of work than any puritan sermon could have afforded us.

Thus the east means religious intensity of experience, and an amoral eschewal of New Testament values for Jasper: the excellence of the book is very much bound up with the balance of Dickens's condemnation of and interest in Jasper's attitudes. All these things are essential to the scheme of the novel as a whole, and to our understanding of Jasper and what he represents. Jasper is not to be exhausted in a list of his characteristics: he stands for, we might say, more than he is. It is wrong to suggest, as Mr. Wilson does,[8] that Jasper is a less clear and less honest version of Raskolnikov: the two characters are quite different and represent different things. Raskolnikov is, by comparison with Jasper, a confused moralist. He has none of Jasper's diabolism (to say nothing of the homosexuality), but is, on the contrary, a fanatical utopian. Jasper is the richer, if the less sympathetic, character — the prototype of Claggart, and a whole series of homosexual hero-villains in the twentieth century, from those of Proust, through Gide and Hesse, to William Burroughs.

Mr. Dyson thinks Jasper symptomatic of our moral decline, and savages Edmund Wilson for regarding him as a self-portrait:

> Dickens depicts in Jasper a path of despair and damnation which stands in its relevance to the individual much as the Terror in *A Tale of Two Cities* does to society at large. His final novel is his most striking picture of the human situation in its starkest relationship to good and evil.[9]

I am not sure what the last sentence means, but I take it (along with the context in which it is set) to mean that Jasper represents come kind of terminal madness, a private equivalent of the dehumanized insanity of the French

Revolution; that Jasper is what happens when we forsake "reason and sanity . . . the true pearls beyond price."[10] And "Decency, sanity, wisdom: these above all are the healing things". Of course: yet this formulation seems to me supremely useless, the type of the moralistic statement — a description of a perfect state of affairs, with no hint about how we get there.

It may have been crude of Edmund Wilson to suggest that Jasper was intended as self-portraiture, and worse than crude to suggest that his Kali worship is somehow redeemed in a far land ("And yet in another land there is another point of view from which Jasper is a good and faithful servant").[11] No, Jasper is not to be regarded as a sectarian Thug, but merely as a westerner who, for his own psychological and sexual purposes, has exploited the cult. Nevertheless, Wilson is right to indicate the element of Dickens that there is in Jasper: the vein of cruelty and lust that runs through his novels, from *The Old Curiosity Shop* onwards, makes it impossible to deny that Jasper's demonic ruthlessness, as well as his ennui and despair, correspond to something important in Dickens. Wilson is surely correct, therefore, in suggesting that Dickens must here to some extent at least be projecting himself: how else could the writing have such potency? "Is it not damnable," Mr. Dyson expostulates, "to imagine that a murdering scoundrel like Jasper can in any serious manner be compared with one of the greatest creative minds of his own or any other age?"[12] This is surely naive: nobody suggests that Shakespeare harboured a mass murderer within himself, or Milton the Prince of Darkness; but don't we believe that Macbeth and Satan could not have been conceived and realized without inside information? We all "know" what is good and right: but how are we to achieve them unless we first unravel the tangle of envy, desire, and hatred within ourselves?

It seems especially important not to adopt the moralist's stance at this point. The real "morality" of *Edwin Drood* seems to me to suffer fatal fracture if we condemn Jasper out of hand as a villain or a lunatic. There is a great gap between

Jasper and Bradley Headstone: Headstone, though excellently presented, is observed from the outside. Jasper, on the other hand, is projected from within: we start the novel inside Jasper's head, and his moods and despairs colour the world of the narrative in a way inconceivable with a "case" like Headstone. We accept from Dickens that Jasper is "wicked" all right. This is not the point. What matters is what we, now, bring to the book. In spite of Dickens's horror at Jasper, he sees to it that we experience his consciousness, his world: his ennuis and despair are ours, and we contain and bottle up his passions and endure his horrid hangovers and awakenings. It is not quite accurate to say that there is something of Jasper inside all of us; but his torments and disillusions, his belief in release, his capacity for ecstasy — these are states we are made to experience, and, in some sense, to take seriously and sympathize with. These are the facts of creative literature which accompany the moral attitudes the novelist *also* asks us to adopt. This is not to say that the pointers the artist gives — and Dickens, notoriously, gives us many — are not also part of the imaginative facts. But if we take them alone and combine them with moralistic directives of our own, it is possible for us to fail the artist in the journey he asks us to make through the world of his work. Mr. Dyson's attempt to set Jasper down as totally deranged seems to me to spring from this kind of unbalanced response.

Mr. Dyson implies that Jasper is a "Romantic" figure, in a pejorative sense of the term. There is not really much basic difference between Mr. Wilson's summary of *Edwin Drood* as an attempt by Dickens to fuse two sides of his own personality — the respectable and the demonic — into one, and Mr. Dyson's view of the book as a picture of "the human situation in its starkest relationship to good and evil", except the all-important one that Mr. Dyson insists that *Dickens* insists that the solution is for sane, wise, decent people (like ourselves) to wage war on evil romantics like Jasper. In this issue it seems to me that we should side with Mr. Wilson: the whole mechanism of the Dickens novel involves our participation in its ebbs and flows. And if we do not allow ourselves to *feel-into* the violence, the cupidity, the lust, the destructiveness, then it seems to me that our reading is shallow and even corrupt. If we merely condemn Jasper we fail to see the real part he plays in the novel's action: the fact is that Edwin must yield to the superior power of love. Jasper's passion is a more potent force than Edwin's affection, and this is not to be set aside by calling Jasper's love unnatural or perverted. It is unnatural only in its strength, and this is a comment on Edwin and the values he represents as much as on Jasper. Edwin has in fact been made to see this inadequacy of his love by Mr. Grewgious. In a scene of considerably ingenuity, Dickens holds up to Edwin Drood a cleverly parodied picture of "romantic love", an ideal relationship, which, offered seriously by a novelist, would certainly appear absurdly stylized and unreal: " ' . . . I figure to myself (subject, as before, to Mr. Edwin's correction), that there can be no coolness, no lassitude, no doubt, no indifference, no half fire and half smoke state of mind, in a real lover. Pray am I at all near the mark in my picture?' " (Chapter 11, p. 122.) This is a crafty piece of work: Grewgious, continually reminding everyone of his angularity and dryness, is in fact flagrantly romantic, yet he succeeds, merely by describing the mood, and values of the old romances, in making Edwin admit to himself that his own feeling for Rosa is grossly inadequate: " ' . . . my picture does represent the true lover as having no existence separable from that of the beloved object of his affections, and as living at once a doubled life and a halved life.' " This makes Edwin turn red and white, and he is intelligent enough to concede that his lukewarm, intermittent affection for Rosa — apparent to him now, since Grewgious has made him really look at it — simply is not enough to build a life on. The scene is thoroughly characteristic of Dickens's eccentric and wayward methods: he offers us a parody version of romantic love that makes us see the inadequacies of most of our relationships more clearly than the most painstaking introspective analysis could have. The point is clinched by the sequence of the following scenes: the next chapter shows us the intensity of Jasper (now planning his sacrificial murder, and making the ritual ascent of the tower with Durdles), and the one after that, the very tender and mature scene in which Edwin and Rosa agree to part as lovers.

Grewgious's stylization of love in the scene with Edwin (at which Bazzard the strange clerk is significantly in attendance) connects up with another of the novel's great underlying themes. *Edwin Drood* is in certain ways a stylized novel; so, in a related though slightly different way, was *Our Mutual Friend*. There the stylization was in the dance-rhythm of the relationships and the general symmetry of the narrative orderings. Here it is in the form of ritual: in *Edwin Drood* the phases and realities of life are offered as ceremonial. Jasper's Thug murder is the most spectacular instance of this, for it shows the sex-relation itself being enjoyed in an enhanced form: Jasper requires sex to be experienced as a game, as theatre, almost. In the same way, he and Crisparkle carry on their Manichean struggle in the stylized manoeuvres of church ritual. At moments of triumph, Jasper sings like an angel; Crisparkle for his part trains like a middle-weight preparing for a title fight.

The ceremonialization of life presented in these examples appears in the Grewgious-Edwin scene not only through the prism of Grewgious's chivalric romanticism, but in the terms of an initiation ceremony witnessed by Bazzard. Bazzard, *(Buzzard)* is the angel of death — but also a carrion fowl with an eye for bright things such as jewels. For the centre of the scene takes the form of a presentation. Grewgious hands over to Edwin the ring, the "rose of diamonds and rubies delicately set in gold", that somehow lies at the very centre of *Edwin Drood*. It is this ring which is to seal the marriage of Edwin and Rosa, and which in the event is to trap Jasper: Jasper was so confident of Edwin's notorious puritanism about valuables (everyone in Cloisterham knows that he wears only a gold-watch and a shirt-pin) that he failed to spot the ring in Edwin's pocket after he had killed him. The Thugs had the superstition that it was bad luck to kill a man with gold on his person. This would account for Jasper's failure in the murder. But it is also consistent with another of the novel's singularities — the preoccupation throughout with the basic constituents of matter. The ring leads to Jasper's capture (we are to presume) because gold does not dissolve in quicklime. Now in the ceremonial presentation scene, Grewgious has sufficiently stressed the enduring nature of the jewels — " 'See how bright these stones shine!' opening the case. 'And yet the eyes that were so much brighter, and that so often looked upon them with a light and a proud heart, have been ashes among ashes, and dust among dust, some years! If I had any imagination (which it is needless to say I have not), I might imagine that the lasting beauty of these stones was almost cruel.' " (Chapter 11, p. 124.) Following these words, Grewgious presents the ring to Edwin with full ceremony: " 'I charge you once more, by the living and by the dead, to bring that ring back to me!' " (It is to be noted that Grewgious has succeeded, presumably by the force of his tedious oratory, in putting Bazzard to sleep during this scene.)

The scene makes clear beyond any possible doubt the close association in the novel of ceremony, death, and ontology. For if *Our Mutual Friend* could be described as teleological pantomime, *Edwin Drood* can be called ontological fairytale: *Our Mutual Friend* asks, to what end? *Edwin Drood* asks, of what composed?

Fairytale, as I have hinted throughout, always forms part of the Dickens novel, with its underlying mythic properties — striving hero, angry giant, witch, ogre, good and bad fairy. In *Edwin Drood* Dickens makes explicit reference to one particular fairytale, *Jack and the Beanstalk*. In chapter 21, following Rosa's flight from Jasper and Cloisterham, Dickens begins to expand Tartar's window-box garden in Holborn into a strangely unworldly paradise:

> This a little confused Rosebud, and may account for her never afterwards quite knowing how she ascended (with his help) to his garden in the air, and seemed to get into a marvellous country that came into sudden bloom like the country on the summit of the magic bean-stalk. May it flourish for ever! Chapter 21, p. 241.)

Rosa has started to fall in love with Tartar, and the whole Holborn set-up has begun to assume typically Dickensian status as safe harbourage for destitute and fleeing orphans: the Landlesses are already ensconced there under the patronage of Grewgious and Crisparkle. Now the Staple's Inn rooms take on an extra-terrestrial air — ironically, in view of the fog and the under-privileged sparrows and trees there. In the next chapter, Tartar's ship-shape chambers with their magical window-boxes emerge in all their glory, like particularly delectable poop-deck quarters on some old galleon:

> On this bright summer day, a neat awning was rigged over Mr. Tartar's flower-garden as only a sailor could rig it; and there was a sea-going air upon the whole effect, so delightfully complete, that the flower-garden might have appertained to stern-windows afloat, and the whole concern might have bowled away gallantly with all on board . . . (Chapter 22, p. 243.)

Even by Dickens's standards, isn't this unusually rosy? No; because the chambers in Holborn have a deliberate unreality, signalled by the appearance of Tartar's flowers, and confirmed by the *Jack and the Beanstalk* reference. Rosa has had to flee from Jasper, and seek out Grewgious in London. The mechanism is familiar: at a certain stage in many of the earlier novels, Dickens leaves his heroine abandoned among enemies: like Florence Dombey, Rosa decamps and flees to safe harbourage. Now Dickens outdoes himself in the thoroughness of the campaign against evil. Grewgious sets Rosa up in Bloomsbury so that she can commune with Helena across Tartar's flowers (a fascinating and obscure piece of symbolism): there is a general digging-in, with elaborate planning to confute Jasper's spies. There never was such a ganging-up, even in Dickens. But there is an air of a final show-down about it that cancels any possible unction in the proceedings: Tartar's room begins to take on a lambent super-reality.

Immediately after the Jack and the Beanstalk reference, Rosa, Grewgious, Tartar, and Tartar's "man", Lobley, make a memorable and idyllic trip up the river, that same river that pulled its turgid way through *Great Expectations* and *Our Mutual Friend*. This event seems, on retrospect, one of the two or three key scenes in the novel, for, far upstream, the travellers reach a destination Dickens refuses to specify: "The tide bore them on in the gayest and most sparkling manner, until they stopped to dine in some everlastingly-green garden, needing no matter-of-fact identification . . . " (Chapter 22, p. 253.) This must be the first time Dickens has ever withheld information about one of his locales! The reason is apparent: the delicious passage is throughout lifted onto an other-worldly level. There is a seraphic quality to the verbal harmony hereabouts, a distinctly immanent atmosphere, equivalent to the "light that never was on sea or land" bathing the cathedral ruins in the earlier chapters of the book. Tartar's rooms are constantly referred to as ship-like, and Rosa is being prepared for a journey, in some obscure parallel with her dead counterpart, Edwin. Edwin who was about to voyage to Egypt (to the pyramids) was prepared by Jasper to make a rather longer trip, and Rosa here is taken to glimpse "some everlastingly green garden". On the trip back down the river from Eden, the great black bridges cast their shadows on the waters, as they do in *Our Mutual Friend*. The bridges, Dickens says, "spanned the river as death spans life". This makes it perfectly clear why the state of things in this chapter (23) is so gritty: the city, the world of man in general, is intrinsically gritty, because Dickens is now concerned with the sphere of the "everlastingly green garden", from which we have come, and to which we hope to return.

The day after this river trip — so important in the scheme of the book — Rosa wonders whether life can be got through without gritty stages: "No. She began to think that, now the Cloisterham schooldays had glided past and gone, the gritty stages would begin to set in at intervals and make themselves wearily known!" (Chapter 23, p. 254.) What is uncomfortable of course is simply the world itself, the material jacket of existence. This is the sense in which Dickens's fairytale is ontological: the book is riddled with speculations about matter, about the nature of reality, but also with a deep weariness of physical and terrestrial actuality. This explains the obsession throughout the story with the actual substance of which people are made up, which in turn expresses a strong sense of discomfort. The world is an uncomfortable place in *Edwin Drood,* either fiercely cold and raw, or stiflingly hot (as in the superb summer passage at the beginning of chapter 10), or, in London, gritty with dust and heavy with fog. Dickens's sense of the physical nature of things (always precise and intense) here gives rise to a disgust at the very nature of physical existence. Thus, the book is continually evoking physical discomfort (at the same time, often, as it evokes ecstatic beauty). And this sense of material contingency — the world, in *Edwin Drood,* is *de trop* — gives rise in turn to the curious speculations about people's basic substance. The basic image of *Edwin Drood* really is the mill, the mill in which human matter will be ground down to its constituent matter. The most striking example of the use of the image occurs in the description of Mr. Grewgious: "Mr. Grewgious had been well selected for his trust, as a man of incorruptible integrity. He was an arid, sandy man, who, if he had been put into a grinding-mill, looked as if he would have ground immediately into high-dried snuff." (Chapter 9, p. 84.) This kind of macabre speculation becomes, over the course of the novel, a modus of psychological and ontological analysis. Dickens finds himself continually going beyond the given human facts to a small pile of dust. A preoccupation with mortality can be traced throughout ,Dickens's *oeuvre,* from *The Old Curiosity Shop* onwards. Yet there is a world of difference between the wonderful closing sections of *The Old Curiosity Shop,* when the schoolmaster tutors Nell in the ways of time, and *Edwin Drood.* In the early book the speculation about an after-life was used to promote a spring-time resurgence, bought somehow with the sacrifice of Nell, who is reconciled to death in an almost Tennysonian rapture. In the last book, death has ceased to function as the source of easeful hope. Cloisterham Cathedral is rotting on its damp foundations — "Old Time heaved a mouldy sigh from tomb and arch and vault; and gloomy shadows began to deepen in corners; and damp began to rise from green patches of stone; and jewels, cast upon the pavement of the nave from stained glass by the declining sun, began to perish." (Chapter 9, p. 93.) Cloisterham itself is really a dead city; even the tramps "quicken their limp a little, that they may the sooner get beyond the confines of its oppressive respectability" (Chapter 3, p. 18). A city, Dickens sums up, "of another and a bygone time" — a dead city, in fact, in which "Fragments of old wall, saint's chapel, chapter-house, convent and monastery, have got incongruously or obstructively built into many of its houses and gardens . . . All things in it are of the past." (Chapter 3, p. 19.) There is something anticipatory of science fiction in the description of the city in chapter 3, even down to the detail of the pawnbroker who takes no more pledges. Time has stopped in Cloisterham, sinisterly, as though the world were waiting for some judgment. As of course it is: this is the point of the book. So continuous and insistent is this preoccupation that it even obtrudes into the flippant speech of Rosa and Edwin in the interview which immediately follows this descriptive writing. A trivial altercation about Edwin's ideal woman (who doesn't exist of course, except as a foil for Rosa) turns, by means of Edwin's forthcoming trip to Egypt, into a speculation about the pyramids and death: " 'Tiresome old burying-grounds . . . Isises, and Ibises, and Cheopses, and Pharaohses; who cares about them? And then there was Belzoni, or somebody, dragged out by the legs, half-choked with bats and dust.' " (Chapter 3, pp. 27–28.) Miss Twinkleton's ill-digested information is introduced by Rosa to spite Edwin, and the tone of the exchange is pettish; yet again, insistently, she returns later to the pyramids and death. ("And as to Belzoni, I suppose he's dead; — I'm sure I hope he is — and how can his legs or chokes concern you?" — How indeed!)

It is clear that for Dickens, Egypt meant one thing only — the pyramids, and the strange burial preparations of the pharoahs. So he associates Edwin's voyage to Egypt with the ancient knowledge of death: by the time Edwin disappears from the book, his coming journey has a very specific significance. He is going, not to an engineering job, but towards that dust that half-choked Belzoni. This idea is underscored by the activities of the officer of death in Cloisterham, Durdles. It is Durdles who is chosen by Jasper to initiate him into the ways of death. Durdles is the one comic character in the book. It is the more significant that he should be so insistently associated with the mortality-consciousness, the ontological preoccupation that is the book's core. Durdles is first cousin to Rogue Riderhood, surly and continuously drunk, and, most important of all, actually seeming to be composed of stone: Jasper tells Durdles that the choir boys call him Stony Durdles, referring either to his calling or to his name, which (Jasper would like to think) could be Stephen. Durdles disdains a straight answer. But the name is nicely appropriate — a sly hagiological reference to the Protomartyr, for the outstanding fact about Durdles's domestic life is that he is nightly stoned home by a hideous "Baby-devil" (Jasper's term), Deputy.

The relation of Durdles to the scavengers (Riderhood and Hexam) of *Our Mutual Friend* is obvious: they fished bodies out of the river, Durdles locates ancient corpses in the vaults, crypt, and walls of the cathedral. When Durdles finds a tomb and opens it, the body turns (or returns) to its basic substance: " 'Durdles came upon the old chap . . . by striking right into the coffin with his pick. The old chap gave Durdles a look with his open eyes . . . And then he turned to powder.' " (Chapter 4, p. 37.) So his basic function is to impress upon us the nature of our constituent matter. He suffers from "Tombatism", lives in a half-finished hole approached through "a petrified grove of tombstones, urns, draperies, and broken columns, in all stages of sculpture" (Chapter 4, p. 38); he is, as it were, impregnated with death and prowls about "among old graves, and ruins, like a Ghoule" (Chapter 12, p. 132). This surly expert on tombs and their inmates is attended by a strange parasite, Deputy, and it is probably the scenes in which Deputy appears, stoning Durdles, that would first apprise even the most placid reader of the book that something more fundamental than a good detective-story was before him. Deputy stoning Durdles home in the moonlight is beyond the weirdest surrealism, harsh, cruel, yet meticulously clear, and — when one considers that Durdles's tips keep Deputy alive, and Deputy's stoning gets Durdles to bed — instinct with its own queer charity. We know, too, that Deputy is to play a part in bringing Jasper to book: Jasper's reaction to him, indeed, is neurotically intense. He hoists the baby-devil up by the throat, and threatens later to kill him. Dickens too is mesmerized by Deputy: here more sharply and harshly focussed than ever, is the cockney kid of *Oliver Twist* and *Pickwick,* a last haunting appearance, perhaps, of Mealy Potatoes or Bob Fagin. Dickens never surpassed the accuracy of the class-speech of Deputy (with his "Kin-free-der-el" and "I-ket-ches-Im-out-ar-ter-ten"), and Jasper's shudder of horror is fully justified. Yet the baby-devil is also a pitiful little piece of economic stunting, reminiscent of the horrible world of Maxim Gorki. Even now Dickens cannot escape the proletarians, and it seems deeply significant that at the very last Christmas party Dickens ever lived to enjoy he contributed to a family word-game the meaningless address, "Warren's Blacking, 30, Strand", with, his son tells us, "an odd twinkle and strange inflection in his voice".[13]

Thus, the world in *Edwin Drood* is really already dead, awaiting some apocalyptic restoration to the "everlastingly green garden", to which Rosa was ferried by Tartar(-us). Edwin is to be sacrificed, it seems, in order that Rosa shall complete her journey. This, it is to be noted, is at once Jasper's and Dickens's intention, and the great irony of the story turns on this duplication of motive. The ring Edwin does not hand over to Rosa survives him as it were in virtue of his new maturity: had he given it her, it would have been in bad faith (he not only doesn't love her, he knows he doesn't), and so he would have perished in the quicklime without trace. The ring is what Jasper hasn't reckoned on, and so, equally, is Edwin's surprising good faith. Thus the contingency of things is gainsaid by "those sorrowful jewels": the rose of diamonds and rubies is really the most important symbolic property in the entire novel.

The notion of sacrifice is connected with the ceremonial

attitude towards emotions and the life of the emotions consistently adopted in the book. The central act of the story is the murder of Edwin by Jasper: the world of *Edwin Drood* is a draughty Druid temple, in which Jasper sacrifices to the great goddess, Kali, but also to something else — the awful pain and pointlessness of life itself. Edwin is to be sacrificed in order that Rosa shall fulfil herself, and the purposes of the fructifying world in her. This is from one point of view even Jasper's conscious aim. He sacrifices the beloved Edwin so that he shall enjoy him in Rosa. Yet it is himself Jasper is really sacrificing: the real immolation is not that of Edwin but of Jasper. One remembers the terrible scream heard by Durdles the year before the Christmas with which the novel's action opens — " 'The ghost of a cry. The ghost of one terrific shriek, which shriek was followed by the ghost of the howl of a dog: a long dismal woeful howl, such as a dog gives when a person's dead.' " (Chapter 12, p. 136.) This scream is connected with Jasper, as his over-hasty response to Durdles testifies, and as indeed Durdles already suspects. What was Jasper doing *last* Christmas Eve? Another sacrifice? Another victim? A Thug or Druid slaying? And is this what Durdles is tapping after in his prowling around the crypt? Durdles suspects Jasper of something: " 'Yours is a curious existence", Jasper ventures at one point: " 'Yours is another' " Durdles retorts.

A sacrifice of some kind is at the centre of the novel: its greatest irony may well be that it is of another kind than the high priest, Jasper, thinks. This much is suggested by the ironical and ambiguous part played by those "sorrowful jewels" in the ring that survives the quicklime burning of the corpse. The jewels and the ring testify to a different renewal: bearing testimony to Edwin's good faith and honesty, they forecast the rebirth of what is good and hopeful. Thus in a curious way Jasper's sacrifice is successful. But the consequences of the sacrifice may be even more spectacular than this.

We have noted throughout the book the desperate comfortlessness of Dickens's world now. He really reaches the nadir of weariness. In a passage of almost unbelievable cynicism, Dickens pillories the coming circus that will enliven the Cloisterham Christmas, and ends with the words, "quite as large as life, and almost as miserably"! This, from the creator of Pickwick and Vincent Crummles and Mr. Micawber! It is almost blasphemous, a sacrilege, comparable to Jasper's desire to murder in order to appease the terrible goddess of futility and pointlessness. Yet the passage is only a particularly vicious thrust; it is quite typical of the whole. How moving, then, and powerful, is the resurgence that gets under way in the last chapter Dickens ever wrote, "The Dawn Again". Here, again, in the final two pages he was to complete, Dickens celebrates the ravishing beauty of the world:

> A brilliant morning shines on the old city. Its antiquities and ruins are surpassingly beautiful, with a lusty ivy gleaming in the sun, and the rich trees waving in the balmy air. Changes of glorious light from moving boughs, songs of birds, scents from gardens, woods, and fields — or, rather, from the one great garden of the whole cultivated island in its yielding time — penetrate into the Cathedral, subdue its earthy odour, and preach the Resurrection and the Life. The cold stone tombs of centuries ago grow warm; and flecks of brightness dart into the sternest marble corners of the building, fluttering there like wings. (Chapter 23, p. 277.)

The beauty of the natural world, seraphically transfigured here with a hint of angel's wings, subdues the "earthy odour" that has impregnated the world of the novel, and makes possible the Resurrection and the Life. This is the direction of *Edwin Drood*.

Perhaps the richest irony attaching to *The Mystery of Edwin Drood* is the fact that the resurrection of the hero — the consummation of Dickens's entire *oeuvre* — has been achieved and effected, in the face of direct contradiction from Dickens himself, by his readers and critics.[14] Critical opinion has moved steadily towards acceptance of the fact that Edwin Drood is not in fact dead, although Jasper still thinks he is. More critics than not — I think it is possible to say — now believe that Dickens must have intended Edwin to survive Jasper's attack. Dickens himself told Forster quite categorically that Jasper murdered Drood, and we really are without any strong reason to disbelieve him. And yet, as I say, many students and critics of the novel feel that Edwin is to be resurrected. I think so myself: the literal resurrection of Edwin Drood completes, I think, the pattern of Dickens's work. It is more important to make up our minds on this score than it is to set about proving the thesis from the evidence, or rather the lack of it. What it does seem relevant to note at this stage is the pertinent possibility of Datchery being in fact Edwin, sunburned from six months in Egypt and intent on bringing Jasper to book. This makes sense of the entire symbolic plan of the book: the symbolic journey undertaken by Rosa up the Thames is undertaken also by Edwin; in Egypt, Edwin comes to knowledge of the pyramids and returns as the risen Osiris.

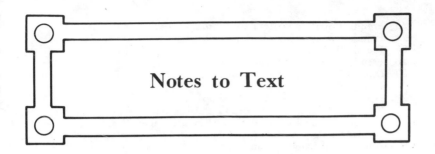

Notes to Text

1. INTRODUCTION: IN SEARCH OF CHARLES DICKENS

1. John Gross and Gabriel Pearson, eds., *Dickens and the Twentieth Century* (London, 1960).
2. G. Pearson, "The Old Curiosity Shop", Ibid., p. 90.
3. J. Jones, "David Copperfield", ibid., p. 143.
4. J. Holloway, "Hard Times", ibid., p. 173.
5. J. Gross, "A Tale of Two Cities", ibid., p. 195.
6. J. Taylor Stoehr, *Dickens: the Dreamer's Stance* (Cornell, 1964).
7. R. Garis, *The Dickens Theatre* (Oxford, 1964).
8. Harvey P. Sucksmith, *The Narrative Art of Charles Dickens* (Oxford, 1970).
9. C. G. Jung, *Psychological Types*, trans. H. G. Baynes (London, 1923), p. 51.
10. L. Trilling, *The Opposing Self* (New York, 1955), p. 64.
11. Sucksmith, *Narrative Art of Charles Dickens*, p. 345.
12. Ibid.
13. Garis, *Dickens Theatre*, p. 167.
14. Jung, *Psychological Types*, p. 481.
15. F. R. Leavis and Q. D. Leavis, *Dickens the Novelist* (London, 1970).
16. L. N. Tolstoy, *Anna Karenina*, trans. R. S. Townsend (London, 1912), 1:60. Tolstoy's Russian — *blestyaschtchy* — is not superior, and the example could be repeated ad nauseam without falsification.
17. See K. Koffka, *Principles of Gestalt Psychology* (London, 1936).
18. Garis, *Dickens Theatre*, p. 46.
19. D. Van Ghent, *The English Novel: Form and Function* (New York, 1956), p. 129. Mrs. Van Ghent's work had a decisive influence upon the younger American critics, though in point of fact the origin of Mr. Garis's work in particular is certainly a passage in Orwell: "It is because Dickens's characters have no mental life". (G. Orwell, *Collected Essays*, London, 1961, p. 82).
20. E. M. Forster, *Aspects of the Novel* (London, 1927), p. 98.
21. S. Freud, "Creative Writers and Day dreaming", *Complete Psychological Works*, trans. J. Strachey (London, 1953–), Vol. 4, p. 150.
22. Freud, "Creative Writers and day-dreaming", p. 149.

23. Freud, "Creative Writers", p. 150.
24. Freud, "Creative Writers", p. 150.
25. Freud, "Creative Writers", p. 148.
26. Freud, "Creative Writers", p. 148.
27. D.de Rougemont, *Passion and Society*, trans.M.Belgion (London, 1940), p. 27.
28. Pearson, "The Old Curiosity Shop", p. 83.
29. I have attempted — in broad outline only — an account of the growth and decline of the novel in my paper "Narrative Myths in the Novel" given at the twenty second congress of the Australian Universities Language and Literature Association, Adelaide, 1974. See also G. Lukacs, *Die Theorie der Romans*, Berlin, 1963.
30. Stoehr, *Dickens: the Dreamer's Stance*, passim, but especially pp. 114—195.
31. Garis, *Dickens Theatre*, p. 174.
32. Garis, *Dickens Theatre*, p. 175.
33. G. K. Chesterton, *Appreciations and Criticisms of the Works of Charles Dickens* (London, 1911).
34. Chesterton, *Charles Dickens' Works*, p. 204.
35. Chesterton, *Charles Dickens' Works*, p. 111.
36. Chesterton, *Charles Dickens' Works*, p. 200.
37. See for instance J. Ruskin, *Unto This Last*, Complete Works, (London, 1903—10), xvii, p. 31, n.
38. For an extensive treatment of this particular fallacy see W. H. Desmonde's *Magic, Myth and Money* (Glencoe, 1962).
39. G. Lukacs, *La Théorie du Roman*, trans. J. Clairvoye (Paris, 1963). This edition contains an "introduction aux premiers écrits de Georges Lukacs par Lucien Goldmann".
40. L. Goldmann, *Le Dieu Caché* (Paris 1955).

2. OLIVER TWIST

1. G. K. Chesterton, "Dickens, Charles", *Encyclopaedia Britannica*, Vol. 7, 1970.
2. See also J. Hillis Miller, *Dickens: the World of his Novels*, (Cambridge, Mass., 1958), p. 48.
3. See for instance John Bayley, "Oliver Twist" in *Dickens and the Twentieth Century* (London, 1960).
4. Chesterton, article in *Encyclopaedia Britannica*, Vol. 7, 1970.
5. M. Praz, *The Hero in Eclipse in Victorian Fiction*, trans. A. Davidson (London, 1946), p. 157.
6. In particular by C. Harvey Sucksmith, *The Narrative Art of Charles Dickens* (Oxford, 1970).
7. I have dealt with this question in my book *The Psychology of Hardy's Novels: The Nervous and the Statuesque* (University of Queensland Press, 1974), p. 10—11, and pp. 130—39.

3. THE OLD CURIOSITY SHOP

1. It is difficult not to believe that Günter Grass had in mind Quilp's monologue with the figure-head in Chapter 62, for instance, when he wrote *The Tin Drum.*
2. See however Gabriel Pearson's suggestion about the grandfather's gambling in "The Old Curiosity Shop", *Dickens and the Twentieth Century*, (London, 1960), p. 83.

4. BARNABY RUDGE

1. However in his book *The Historical Novel* (trans. H. and S. Mitchell, London, 1962), George Lukacs remarks that Dickens' *A Tale of Two Cities* by "giving pre-eminence to the purely moral aspects of causes and effects weakens the connection between the problems of the characters' times and the events of the French Revolution " (p. 243).
2. G. K. Chesterton, *Appreciations and Criticisms of the Works of Charles Dickens* (London, 1911), p. 75. Edmund Wilson also remarks on the ambivalence of Dickens's treatment of the riots in "The Two Scrooges", *The Wound and the Bow* (London, 1941), p. 19.
3. Chesterton, *Charles Dickens' Works*, p. 75.
4. See Charles Dickens, *Letters,* ed. M. House and G. Storey (Oxford, 1964) Vol.2, p. 377 (letter to J. Forster).

5. MARTIN CHUZZLEWIT

1. B. Hardy, "Martin Chuzzlewit", in John Gross and Gabriel Pearson, *Dickens and the Twentieth Century*, p. 114.
2. J.-P. Sartre, *Being and Nothingness,* trans. H. E. Barnes (New York, 1956), especially the chapter on "Bad Faith", Chapter 2 of Part One.
3. Wilson, *The Wound and the Bow*, p. 31.
4. D. Van Ghent, *The English Novel: Form and Function* (New York, 1956), p. 129.
5. R. Arnheim, *Towards a Psychology of Art* (London, 1967), p. 53.
6. Van Ghent, *The English Novel*, p. 129.
7. Van Ghent, *The English Novel*, p. 130.
8. Van Ghent, *The English Novel*, p. 130.
9. I can find no actual reference to *Martin Chuzzlewit* in Dostoievsky. The influence is not to be doubted, but one should perhaps be as circumspect about noting it as Edmund Wilson, who merely observes that Dostoievsky was "probably influenced by the murder in *Martin Chuzzlewit*". (*The Wound and the Bow*, p. 99.)
10. P. Rahv, "Crime and Punishment", in R. Welleck, ed., *Twentieth Century views: Dostoievsky*, (New Jersey, 1962), p. 19.
11. See J. Hillis Miller, *Dickens: the World of his Novels* (Cambridge, Mass., 1956) pp. 118–121.

12. The theory set forward here (such as it is) belongs with superiority theories of humour. See P. Keith-Spiegel, "Early Conceptions of Humor: Varieties and Issues." pp. 6—7, in J. H. Goldstein and P. E. McGhee, *The Psychology of Humor* (New York and London, 1972).
13. W. H. Auden, "The Prince's Dog", *Selected Essays* (London, 1956), p. 68.
14. Auden, ibid., p. 67.
15. Auden, ibid., p. 68.
16. Auden, ibid. Auden concedes this point by calling the scene on the battle-field a mistake on Shakespeare's part. The mistake was, one would have thought, Falstaff's. It is characteristic of such people never to know when the joke is inapposite.

6. DOMBEY AND SON

1. J. Forster, *Life of Charles Dickens* (London, 1922) Vol. 2, pp. 26—27.
2. Forster, ibid., p. 19.
3. Quoted in Forster, ibid.
4. Forster, ibid.
5. Chesterton has some interesting things to say on this matter in *Appreciation and Criticism of Dickens' Works:* "How far can an author tell a truth without seeing it himself?" (p. 59).
6. H. Taine, *History of English Literature,* trans. von Klaun (Edinburgh, 1871), Vol. 2, Book 5, p. 363.
7. E. Wilson, *The Wound and the Bow* (London, 1941), p. 62.
8. C. Dickens, *Dombey and Son* (London, 1860), Introduction.
9. K. Tillotson, "Dombey and Son", *Novels of the Eighteen-Forties* (Oxford, 1954), pp. 166—7.
10. J. —P. Sartre, *The Age of Reason,* trans. E. Sutton (London, 1947), p. 71.

7. DAVID COPPERFIELD

1. E. Wilson, *The Wound and the Bow* (London, 1941), p. 43.
2. J.-P. Sartre, *L'Etre et le Néant* (Paris, 1943), pp. 98—99.
3. J. Jones, "David Copperfield", in John Gross and Gabriel Pearson, *Dickens and the Twentieth Century* (London, 1960), p. 136.
4. Jones, "David Copperfield", p. 136.
5. S. Joyce, *My Brother's Keeper* (London, 1958).
6. See for instance John Jones' essay in *Dickens and the Twentieth Century.*
7. G. K. Chesterton, *Appreciation and Criticism of Dickens' Works* (London, 1911), p. 139.
8. Chesterton, *Charles Dickens' Works,* p. 138.
9. Chesterton, *Charles Dickens' Works,* p. 139.
10. See. G. Orwell, *Collected Essays* (London, 1961), p. 33.

11. See E. Husserl, *Ideas*, trans. W. R. Boyce Gibson (London, 1931), Chapter I.
12. Gwendolyn Needham ("The Undisciplined Heart of David Copperfield", *Nineteenth-Century Fiction*, Sept. 1954) writes: "The whole episode (the Yarmouth seduction and elopement) teaches the important lesson i.e. the real nature of love, truth, and the disciplined heart." (p. 92) Thus, Steerforth becomes an example, whose fatal end teaches David the folly of his love for Steerforth (which is shown up by contrast with a superior brand of love). According to this account, David's worship of his hero is a product only of undisciplined naiveté and inexperience. I shudder to think of this kind of "Holier-than-Thou" criticism being applied to Shakespeare. "Thus, the deaths of Romeo and Juliet doubly teach us the folly of hasty affection." In the first place, art does not instruct in this way. In the second, Indiscipline (like Selfishness, as I shall argue later *à propos* of *Chuzzlewit*) is a crude moral category which does violence to the exquisite subtlety and complexity of Dickens' treatment of his major theme. Mrs. Needham is reduced to reading the novel like taking Dickens' most superficial and laborious repetition of "Blind, blind, blind", the exclamations of "Ah! Undisciplined heart!" — to guide her along the autobahns, only fleetingly aware of the verdant country going past. David's (and Dickens') attitude to Steerforth is an especially delicate piece of the landscape. Steerforth himself is the closest Dickens ever came to a tragic hero in the full-blooded Romantic sense. Take away the Dickensian sense of proportion and social context and Steerforth becomes Stavrogin, whose birth he certainly danced over. Stavrogin is what Dostoievsky made of him: the young god, of great gifts, beauty and charm, yet tragically out of true with the world he lived in. And for all the implied criticism, not a breath of censure passes David's lips. The final glimpse of him lying dead on the Yarmouth sands suggests the drowned Shelley, and the entire episode — one of the most magnificently built-up dramatic narratives in the language — is full of the sustained turbulence and vivid sombreness we see in Turner. Dan Peggotty is allowed his vengeance: David is too aware of the tragic waste of Steerforth's own life, too conscious of the complexity of the web he is caught in, to pass judgment.
13. T. W. Adorno, *Prisms*, trans. S. and S. Weber (London, 1967), p. 247.
14. Chesterton, *Charles Dickens' Works*, pp. 134–36.
15. Chesterton, *Charles Dickens' Works*, p. 205.
16. Adorno, *Prisms*, p. 246.

8. BLEAK HOUSE

1. The suspect sense is the one suggesting that technique exists apart from meaning. *David Copperfield* is just as "good" a novel technically and in every other way as *Bleak House*. But we couldn't

show off as much in laying bare its mechanics. One might of course be driven to the same sort of ruse in trying to define the peculiar excellence of Bach's Kunst der Fuge without wanting to suggest some sort of intrinsic superiority over the Matthaus-Passion.

2. See W. J. Harvey, "Bleak House", in John Gross and Gabriel Pearson, *Dickens and the Twentieth Century* (London, 1960), p. 146.

3. O. Sitwell, Introduction to *Bleak House*, New Oxford Illustrated Dickens, p. viii.

4. Angus Wilson ("The Heroes and Heroines of Dickens", *Review of English Literature* 2 (1964): 134—35) lets off the usual broadside. Jack Lindsay (*Charles Dickens: a Biographical and Critical Study*, London 1950, pp. 134—5) gives a quasi-psychoanalytical explanation of what he calls Dickens' "psychotic fixation" on young girls. That seems to me a good instance of the abuse of half-grasped psychology. George Ford (*Dickens and his Readers*, Princeton and Oxford 1951) surveys the ground thoroughly.

5. J. Hillis Miller, *Dickens: the World of his Novels* (Cambridge, Mass., 1956) discusses Esther as sacrificial victim.

6. E. Wilson, *The Wound and the Bow*, (London, 1941) writes: "The fog stands for Chancery and Chancery stands for the whole web of clotted, antiquated institutions in which England stifles and decays". The fog cannot *stand for* Chancery any more than the actual thunder can *stand for* Lear's madness. In both cases the use of natural observation to enhance meaning must be distinguished from symbolism which has a quite different structure. Wilson's interpretation in general suffers from the narrowness of the social critic who would, for instance, confine the import of *The Trial* to a satire on Prague bureaucracy.

7. Wilson says more about *Bleak House*, but nothing to suggest that the novel does more than dramatise social issues. Shaw's debt to Dickens is mentioned as if it did Dickens credit.

9. *HARD TIMES*

1. F. R. Leavis, "Hard Times, an analytic Note", *The Great Tradition* (London 1950). I cannot remember when I did not know Dr. Leavis's great essay, and fully acknowledge by indebtedness to it, though this is not, needless to add, to say that I think he would approve of what I have said about the novel.

2. D. H. Lawrence, "When I went to the Circus". *Collected Poems*, vol.2, ed. by V. de Sola Pinto and Warren Roberts (London, 1964), p. 444.

3. D. H. Lawrence, "An Autobiographical Study", *Selected Literary Criticism* (London, 1956), p. 4.

4. E. Wilson, *The Wound and the Bow* (London, 1941), p. 32.

5. H. L. Bergson, *Laughter: an Essay on the Meaning of the Comic*, trans. C. Brereton and F. Rothwell (London, 1911).

6. Leavis, "Hard Times: an analytic note", p. 238.
7. R. Garis, *The Dickens Theatre* (Oxford, 1964), p. 153.
8. No earlier novel, neither *Oliver Twist* nor *Alton Locke*, makes the pollution point quite so precisely as this passage.
9. Leavis, "Hard Times: an analytic Note", p. 245.
10. Djuna Barnes, *Nightwood* (London, 1963), p. 130.

10. LITTLE DORRIT

1. R. Garis, *The Dickens Theatre*, (Oxford, 1964), p. 11.
2. G. Eliot, *Middlemarch* (London, 1950), p. 150.
3. Garis, *Dickens Theatre*, pp. 10–11.
4. See R. Arnheim, *Towards a Psychology of Art* (London, 1967), p. 16.
5. See H. Searle, *Twentieth Century Counterpoint* (London, 1954).
6. See E. Neumann, *The Great Mother*, trans. R. Manheim (London, 1955). Also, of course, C. G. Jung, *The Psychology of the Unconscious*, trans. B. Hinkle (London, 1916), of which Chapter 4 deals with the Terrible Mother. Erich Neumann's earlier book *The Origins and History of Consciousness* (trans. R. F. Hull, New York, 1954), deals with the Terrible Father as well and with the heroic mythology which is so relevant to a consideration of the Dickens hero himself.
7. F. Kafka, "The Metamorphosis", *Metamorphosis and Other Stories*, Trans. E. and W. Muir, Harmondsworth, 1961, p. 21.
8. F. R. Leavis and Q. D. Leavis, *Dickens the Novelist* (London, 1970), p. 282.
9. L. Trilling, Introduction to the New Oxford Illustrated Edition of *Little Dorrit* (Oxford, 1956), p. vii.
10. L. Trilling, "Little Dorrit", p. vi.
11. F. R. Leavis, "Luddites? Or, There is only one culture", *Lectures in America* (London, 1969), p. 9.
12. Jung offers an astute portrait of the "William Dorrit" type. Such a type finds, Jung observes, "adequate and appropriate play within the limits of the objective situation." – *Psychological Types* (London, 1923), p. 418.
13. See also Sartre's analysis of the national bad faith of France in *Les Chemins de la Liberté*: Sartre interprets the French acceptance of defeat – in a spirit of realism – as evidence of inward dishonesty. At the same time, of course, Sartre's French soldiers are Micawberish – waiting for something (repatriation, demobilisation) to turn up.
14. L. Trilling, "Little Dorrit", p. vi.

11. A TALE OF TWO CITIES

1. G. Lukacs, *Studies in European Realism*, Trans. E. Bone (London, 1950), p. 6.

2. Lukacs, *European Realism*, p. 6.
3. "This contradiction in his experience Balzac attempted to force into a system based on a Catholic legitimism and tricked out with Utopian conceptions of English Toryism. But this system was contradicted all the time by the social realities of his day and the Balzacian vision which mirrored them. This contradiction itself clearly expressed, however, the real truth: Balzac's profound comprehension of the contradictorily progressive character of capitalist development." — Lukacs, *European Realism*, p. 13.

12.   GREAT EXPECTATIONS

1. See for instance J. Taylor Stoehr, *Dickens: the Dreamer's Stance* (Cornell, 1964), p. 126.
2. The implicit assumption here — that psychoanalysis works with and from a dictionary of symbols — is one specifically repudiated by Freud himself. See *Psychological Works*, Vol. 5, Ch. 6 (London 1953), trans. J. Strachey.
3. See especially J. Moynahan, "The Hero's Guilt: the Case of Great Expectations", *Essays in Criticism*, Vol. 10, 1960.
4. G. R. Stange, "Expectations well lost", in G. H. Ford and L. Lane, eds., *The Dickens Critics* (Cornell, 1961), p. 304.
5. Stange, "Expectations well lost", p. 305.
6. Stange, "Expectations well lost", p. 305.
7. R. Garis, *The Dickens Theatre* (Oxford, 1964), p. 218.
8. Moynahan, "The Hero's Guilt", p. 70.
9. Moynahan, "The Hero's Guilt", p. 70.
10. See Chapter 10. Note 6.

13.   OUR MUTUAL FRIEND

1. H. James, "Our Mutual Friend", *Selected Literary Criticism*, Ed. M. Shapiro (London, 1963), p. 6.
2. G. B. Shaw, *How to become a Musical Critic* (London, 1960), p. 91.
3. See for instance G. Smith, *Dickens, Money and Society* (Cambridge, 1968), p. 183. In general, though, this view — based on rather simple notions of fictional probability — was commoner among the older Dickens critics. Arnold Kettle's strong statement of the opposite view ("Our Mutual Friend," *Dickens and the Twentieth Century*) is more typical of current critical thought.
4. A. O. J. Cockshut (*The Imagination of Charles Dickens*, London, 1961), who was written what still seems the most brilliant account of *Our Mutual Friend*, discusses the ritual and sacramental significance of the drownings and near-drownings in the book with far more subtle understanding than is manifest in the American neo-Jungian school.
5. R. Garis, *The Dickens Theatre* (Oxford, 1964), p. 231.

6. Edmund Wilson also notes the new alignment of sympathies: "Dickens has aligned himself in *Our Mutual Friend* with a new combination of social forces" (*The Wound and the Bow*, London, 1941, p. 80). See also Cockshut, *Imagination of Charles Dickens*, p. 182.
7. G. Lukacs, *Studies in European Realism*, (London, 1950), p. 53.
8. Dante Alighieri, *Divine Comedy*, "Inferno", Cantos 32—33.
9. Lukacs, *European Realism*, p. 53.
10. See for instance Taylor Stoehr: " . . . with folktale justice her patience is rewarded with all those riches she has renounced . . . and even their house, gotten up like a childish palace." *Dickens: the Dreamer's Stance* (Cornell, 1964), p. 208.
11. D. H. Lawrence, "John Galsworthy", *Selected Literary Criticism*, (London, 1956), p. 124.

14. EDWIN DROOD

1. E. Wilson, *The Wound and the Bow*, (London, 1941), p. 100.
2. E. Wilson, *Wound and the Bow*, p. 101.
3. E. Neumann, *The Origins and History of Consciousness*, "The Slaying of the Mother" and "The Hero Myth". trans. R. F. C. Hull (New York, 1954).
4. H. Duffield, "John Jasper, Strangler", *American Bookman*, February, 1931. His thesis is disputed by A. O. J. Cockshutt, "Edwin Drood" in Gross and Pearson, *Dickens and the Twentieth Century*.
5. A. E. Dyson, *The Inimitable Dickens* (London, 1970), p. 288.
6. In talking about Jasper's homosexuality one is, of course, up against moral inhibition of the severest kind. Dickens would have been shocked at the suggestion of any implied "beastliness"; hence, one imagines, Jasper's smoke-screens (flaunting the homosexual and concealing the heterosexual passion) are Dickens'. Nevertheless, we must swallow this and as ever respond to what the artist within the man lays bare. (This isn't of course to deny that there is, in this particularly fascinating case, a good deal of dispute about what this is.)
7. E. Wilson, *The Wound and the Bow*, p. 99.
8. Wilson, *Wound and the Bow*, p. 99.
9. A. E. Dyson, *Inimitable Dickens*, p. 293.
10. Dyson, *Inimitable Dickens*, p. 293.
11. Wilson, *Wound and the Bow*, p. 102.
12. Dyson, *Inimitable Dickens*, p. 291.
13. Quoted in E. Wilson, *The Wound and the Bow*, p. 98.
14. Forster implies that there was no doubt about the conclusion: "the discovery of the murderer was to be baffled till towards the close." (*Life of Charles Dickens*. London, 1922, p. 891.) But there was to be no doubt about Edwin's being dead: "So much was told to me before any of the book was written." (*Life of Charles Dickens*, p. 891.) But books have a habit of changing under execution.

Select Bibliography

CHARLES DICKENS

1. Novels

The Posthumous Papers of the Pickwick Club. Monthly numbers Apr. 1836–Nov. 1837. London 1837.

Oliver Twist; or The Parish Boy's Progress. Monthly numbers in *Bentley's Miscellany*, Feb. 1837–Mar. 1839. London, 1838.

Life and Adventures of Nicholas Nickleby. Monthly numbers Apr. 1838–Oct. 1839. London, 1839.

The Old Curiosity Shop. Weekly numbers in *Master Humphrey's Clock*, Apr. 1840–Feb. 1841. London, 1841.

Barnaby Rudge: A Tale of the Riots of 'Eighty. Weekly numbers in *Master Humphrey's Clock*, Feb. –Nov. 1841. London, 1841.

Life and Adventures of Martin Chuzzlewit. Monthly numbers Jan. 1843–July 1844. London, 1844.

Dealings with the Firm of Dombey and Son, Wholesale, Retail and for Exportation. Monthly numbers Oct. 1846 Apr. 1848. London, 1848.

The Personal History of David Copperfield. Monthly numbers May 1849–Nov. 1850. London, 1850.

Bleak House. Monthly numbers Mar. 1852–Sept. 1853. London, 1853.

Hard Times for These Times. Weekly numbers in *Household Words*, Apr. –Aug. 1854. London, 1854.

Little Dorrit. Monthly numbers in *Household Words*, Dec. 1855–June 1857. London, 1857.

A Tale of Two Cities. Weekly numbers in *All The Year Round*, Apr.–Nov. 1859. London, 1859.

Great Expectations. Weekly numbers in *All The Year Round*, Dec. 1860–Aug. 1861. London, 1862.

Our Mutual Friend. Monthly numbers May 1864–Nov. 1865. London, 1865.

The Mystery of Edwin Drood. Monthly numbers Apr.–Sept. 1870. (Six numbers of an anticipated twelve). London, 1870.

2. Lesser Fiction

Sketches by Boz. London 1836.

Christmas Books. London 1852.
Christmas Stories. London 1871.
The Uncommercial Traveller. London, 1861, 1868, 1875.

3. Miscellaneous Writings

American Notes. London 1842.
Pictures from Italy. London 1846.
A Child's History of England. Weekly numbers in *Household Words*,
    Jan. 1851–Dec. 1853. London 3 vols. 1852–4.
Letters. Vol. I (1820–39), ed. Madeline House and Graham Storey,
    Pilgrim edn., London 1965; Vol. II (1840–41), London 1968.
The Speeches of Charles Dickens, ed. K. J. Fielding, London 1960.

BOOKS AND ARTICLES ON DICKENS

Bayley, John. "Oliver Twist: Things as they Really Are", in *Dickens
    and the Twentieth Century*, edd. Gross and Pearson, pp.
    49–64.
Bergonzi, Bernard. *"Nicholas Nickleby"*, in *Dickens and the Twentieth
    Century*, edd. Gross and Pearson, pp. 65–76.
Broderick, James H., and John E. Grant. "The Identity of Edith
    Summerson", in *Modern Philology*, LV (1958), pp. 252–8.
Brown, Ivor. *Dickens in his Time*, Edinburgh (Nelson) 1953.
Browning, Robert. *"Sketches by Boz"*, in *Dickens and the Twentieth
    Century*, edd. Gross and Pearson, pp. 19–34.
Brush, Lillian Hatfield. "A Psychological Study of *Barnaby Rudge"*, in
    The Dickensian, XXXI (1935), pp. 24–30.
Butt, John, and Kathleen Tillotson. *Dickens at Work*, London
    (Methuen) 1957.
Cammaerts, Emile. "Dickens and Balzac", in *Contemporary Review*,
    Mar. 1929, pp. 331–9.
Carey, John. *The Violent Effigy*, London, 1972.
Cecil, Lord David. *Early Victorian Novelists*, London (Constable) 1934.
Chesterton, G. K. *Charles Dickens*, London (Methuen) 1906.
────── . *Appreciation and Criticism of the Works of Charles Dickens*,
    London (Dent) 1911.
────── . *The Victorian Age in Literature*, Home University Library,
    London (Thornton Butterworth) 1913; London (Oxford U.P.)
    1966.
────── . Article "Charles Dickens" in *Encyclopaedia Britannica*,
    Vol. 7, 1970.
Churchill, R. C. "Charles Dickens", in *From Dickens to Hardy*, ed.
    Boris Ford, Harmondsworth 1958.
Cockshut, A. O. J. *The Imagination of Charles Dickens*, London 1961.
────── . *"Edwin Drood:* Early and Late Victorians Reconciled", in
    Dickens and the Twentieth Century, edd. Gross and Pearson,
    pp. 227–38.
Collins, Philip. *Dickens and Crime.* London 1962.
────── . *Dickens and Education*, London 1963.

————— . *"Dombey and Son:* Then and Now", in *The Dickensian,* LXIII (1967), pp. 82—94.

Dabney, Ross H. *Love and Property in the Novels of Dickens,* London 1967.

Davis, Earle, *The Flint and the Flame,* Columbus 1963.

Dickens and the Twentieth Century, edd. John Gross and Gabriel Pearson, London 1962.

Eliot, T. S. "Wilkie Collins and Dickens", in *T. L. S.* (4 Aug. 1927), and *The Dickens Critics,* edd. Ford and Lane, pp. 151—52.

Elton, Oliver. *Dickens and Thackeray,* London. 1924.

Empson, William. "The Symbolism of Dickens", in *Dickens and the Twentieth Century,* edd. Gross and Pearson, pp. 13—15.

Engel, Monroe. *The Maturity of Dickens,* Cambridge (Mass.) 1958.

Fielding, K. J. *Charles Dickens,* Writers and their Work, No. 37, London 1953.

————— .*Charles Dickens, A Critical Introduction* London (Longman) 1960.

Ford, George H. *Dickens and his Readers,* Princeton 1955.

Forster, E. M. *Aspects of the Novel,* London 1927.

Forster, John. *The Life of Charles Dickens,* 3 vols., London 1872—74.

Garis, Robert. *The Dickens Theatre,* Oxford 1965.

Gissing, George. *Charles Dickens,* London 1898.

————— . *The Immortal Dickens,* London 1925.

Goodheart, Eugene. "Dickens's Method of Characterisation", in *The Dickensian,* LIV (1958), pp. 35—7.

Graves, Robert, *The Real David Copperfield,* London 1933.

Greene, Graham. "The Young Dickens", in *The Lost Childhood and Other Essays,* London 1951.

Gross, John. "Dickens: Some Recent Approaches", in *Dickens and the Twentieth Century,* edd. Gross and Pearson, pp. ix—xvi.

————— . *"A Tale of Two Cities",* in *Dickens and the Twentieth Century,* edd. Gross and Pearson, pp. 187—98.

————— . and Gabriel Pearson. See *Dickens and the Twentieth Century.*

Hardy, Barbara. *"Martin Chuzzlewit",* in *Dickens and the Twentieth Century,* edd. Gross and Pearson, pp. 107—20.

————— . *The Art of Charles Dickens,* London, 1970.

Harvey, W. J. "Chance and Design in *Bleak House",* in *Dickens and the Twentieth Century,* edd. Gross and Pearson, pp. 145—58.

Hibbert, Christopher. *The Making of Charles Dickens,* London 1967.

Holloway, John. *"Hard Times:* A History and a Criticism", in *Dickens and the Twentieth Century,* edd. Gross and Pearson, pp. 159—74.

House, Humphry. *The Dickens World,* London 1941.

————— . *All in Due Time,* London 1955.

Huxley, Aldous. "The Vulgarity of Little Nell", in *The Dickens Critics,* edd. Ford and Lane, pp. 153—7.

Jackson, T. A. *Charles Dickens,* London 1937.

James, Henry. *"Our Mutual Friend",* in *The Nation,* I (1865). See *The Dickens Critics,* edd. Ford and Lane, pp. 48—54.

Johnson, Edgar. *Charles Dickens,* 2 vols., London 1953.

Jones, John. *"David Copperfield"*, in *Dickens and the Twentieth Century*, edd. Gross and Pearson, pp. 130—44.

Kettle, Arnold. *An Introduction to the English Novel*, Vol. I, 1951.

———. *"Our Mutual Friend"*, in *Dickens and the Twentieth Century*, edd. Gross and Pearson, pp. 213—25.

Killham, John. "Pickwick: Dickens and the Art of Fiction", in *Dickens and the Twentieth Century*, edd. Gross and Pearson, pp. 35—48.

Lane, Jr., Lauriat. "Mr. Pickwick and *The Dance of Death*", in *Nineteenth Century Fiction*, XIV (1959), pp. 171—2.

———. See also *The Dickens Critics*, edd. Ford and Lane.

Leavis, F. R. *The Great Tradition* 1948.

Leavis, Q. D. *Fiction and the Reading Public* 1932.

Leavis, F. R. and Leavis, Q. D., *Dickens the Novelist*, London, 1970.

Lewes, G. H. "Dickens in Relation to Criticism", in *The Dickens Critics*, edd. Ford and Lane, pp. 54—74.

Lindsay, Jack. *Charles Dickens*, London 1950.

———. "Charles Dickens and Women", in *Twentieth Century*, (1953), pp. 375—86.

———. *"Barnaby Rudge"*, in *Dickens and the Twentieth Century*, edd. Gross and Pearson, pp. 91—106.

Marcus, Steven. *Dickens: From Pickwick to Dombey*, London 1965.

———. *The Other Victorians*, London 1966.

Miller, J. Hillis. *Charles Dickens: The World of his Novels*, Cambridge 1958.

———. Introduction to *Oliver Twist*, New York, 1962.

Monod, Sylvère. *Dickens romancier*, Paris, 1953.

Morse, Robert. *"Our Mutual Friend"*, in *The Dickens Critics*, edd. Ford and Lane, pp. 197—213.

Moynahan, Julian. "Dealings with the Firm of Dombey and Son: Firmness *versus* Wetness", in *Dickens and the Twentieth Century*, edd. Gross and Pearson, pp. 121—32.

———. "The Hero's Guilt", *Essays in Criticism*.

Nisbet, Ada. *Dickens and Ellen Ternan*, London, 1952.

———. "Charles Dickens", in *Victorian Fiction*, ed. Lionel Stevenson, Cambridge 1964.

Orwell, George. *Inside the Whale and other Essays*, London 1940.

Pearson, Gabriel. "Dickens: The Present Position", in *Dickens and the Twentieth Century*, edd. Gross and Pearson, pp. xvii—xxiv.

———. *"The Old Curiosity Shop"*, in *Dickens and the Twentieth Century*, edd. Gross and Pearson, pp. 77—90.

———. See also *Dickens and the Twentieth Century*.

Pearson, Hesketh. *Dickens*, London 1949.

Poe, Edgar Allen. *"The Old Curiosity Shop"*, in *Dickens Critics*, edd. Ford and Lane, pp. 19—24.

Pope-Hennesy, Una. *Charles Dickens* 1945.

Priestley, J. B. *The English Comic Characters*, London 1937.

Pritchett, V. S. *The Living Novel*, London 1946.

———. "The Comic World of Dickens", in *Dickens Critics*, edd. Ford and Lane, pp. 309—24.

Quiller-Couch, A. *Charles Dickens and Other Victorians*, London 1925.
Quirk, Randolph. *Charles Dickens and Appropriate Language*, Durham 1959.
Ricks, Christopher. *"Great Expectations"*, in *Dickens and the Twentieth Century*, edd. Gross and Pearson, pp. 199—212;.
Ruskin, John. "A Note on *Hard Times*", in *The Dickens Critics*, edd. Ford and Lane, pp. 47—8.
Santayana George. "Dickens", in *The Dickens Critics*, edd. Ford and Lane, pp. 135—51.
Shaw, G. B. Introduction to *Hard Times*, London 1912; also in *The Dickens Critics*, edd. Ford and Lane, pp. 123—35.
Stange, G. Robert. "Expectations Well Lost: Dickens's parable for his time", in *The Dickens Critics*, edd. Ford and Lane.
Stoehr, J. Taylor. *Dickens: The Dreamer's Stance*, Cornell, 1964.
Storey, Gladys. *Dickens and Daughter*, London 1939.
Sucksmith, Harvey P. *The Narrative Art of Charles Dickens*, Oxford, 1970.
Swinburne, A. C. *Charles Dickens*, London 1913.
Symons, Julian. *Charles Dickens*, London 1951.
Taine, Hippolyte. *Histoire de la littérature anglaise*, Paris 1863—4.
Tillotson, Kathleen. *Novels of the Eighteen-Forties*, Oxford 1954.
——— . Introduction to *Barnaby Rudge*, London 1954.
——— . See also Butt, John.
Trilling, Lionel. Introduction to *Little Dorrit*, London 1953.
Trollope, Anthony. *An Autobiography*, London 1883.
Van Ghent, Dorothy. "The Dickens World: A View from Todgers's", in *The Dickens Critics*, edd. Ford and Lane, pp. 213—32.
Wain, John. *"Little Dorrit"*, in *Dickens and the Twentieth Century*, edd. Gross and Pearson, pp. 175—86.
Ward, A. W. *Dickens*, London 1882.
Whipple, E. P. *Charles Dickens*, Boston 1912.
Wilson, Angus. "Dickens and the Divided Conscience", in *The Month*, May (1950), pp. 349—60.
——— . "Charles Dickens: A Haunting", in *The Dickens Critics*, edd. Ford and Lane, pp. 374—85.
——— . "The Heroes and Heroines of Dickens", in *Dickens and the Twentieth Century*, edd. Gross and Pearson, pp. 3—12.
Wilson, Edmund. *The Wound and the Bow* (London) 1941.
Woolf, Virginia. *The Moment and other Essays*, London 1947.

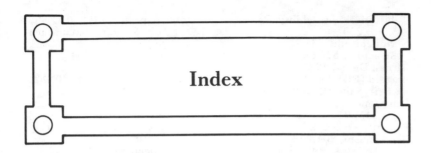

Index

Characters in Dickens's novels are listed individually, followed by the title of the appropriate book. The following abbreviations are used: